L. F.

MARK HOPKINS' LOG
and Other Essays by

LOUIS SHORES

MARK HOPKINS' LOG
and Other Essays by

LOUIS SHORES

Selected by
JOHN DAVID MARSHALL

THE SHOE STRING PRESS, INC.
HAMDEN, CONNECTICUT
1965

Contents

Preface   5

Acknowledgments   7

On Books and Reading

Books: Continuous Communicability [1958]   11
How to Find Time to Read [1952]   13
To Be Truly Informed [1951]   17
Return to Reading [1961]   21

On Librarianship

A Profession of Faith [1958]   31
The Next Generation [1954]   43
The Importance of Library History [1947]   50
A Proposal for the Pyramidal Reorganization
    of the A.L.A. [1938]   55
If I Were a British Librarian [1953]   61
Qualifications of Personnel:
    Training and Certification [1955]   65
Library Literature [1964]   76

On Reference Librarianship

A Frame of Reference [1952]   83
The Practice of Reference [1941]   99
British Reference [1956]   112
The Measure of Reference [1961]   119
Reference Becomes Learning: The Fourth "R" [1957]   128
The Future of Reference in American Society [1957]   138

On Reference Sources

The Half of Knowledge [1957]   147
The Other Half — Where to Find It [1963]   162
Patterns in American Reference Books [1952]   169
Subscription Books and Library Reviews [1948]   185
The Ideal Encyclopedia [1937]   192
Noah Webster's Dictionary [1928]   200
The National Union Catalog of the United States [1952]   203

On Library Education

The Education of an American Librarian [1953]   217
Prologue to a National Plan [1962]   231
Education for Armed Forces Librarianship [1954]   244
Portrait of a Library School:
    Florida State University [1956]   252
What Is *Right* With Library Education [1960]   254
The College of Library Art, 1984 [1964]   258

On the Unity of Library Media

Audio-Visual Dimensions for an Academic Library [1954]   275
Library and AV Center — Combined or Separate? [1958]   283
Enter the Materials Center [1955]   286
Portrait of a Materials Center [1955]   291

On the Library's Role in Education

Mark Hopkins' Log [1951]   301
The School and the Book [1938]   309
Library Logistics in Ideological Warfare [1951]   320
The Essence of Learning [1960]   326
The Library in General Education [1950]   331
The Library Arts College: A Possibility in 1954? [1935]   342
The Undergraduate and His Library [1959]   349
Library-Trained Teachers [1940]   361
Library Logistics in Teacher Education [1951]   368
School Library 21 [1963]   373

Preface

By his teaching, his deanship, his lectures, his Fulbright year in the United Kingdom, his editorship of encyclopedias, his enthusiasm for library history, his devotion to libraries and librarians, books and readers—the world of librarianship is deeply in the debt of Louis Shores. Few other librarians have contributed so much to their profession as has the Dean of the Florida State University Library School.

Library literature, too, owes much to the pen of Louis Shores. A bibliography* of his writings, published by Gamma Chapter of Beta Phi Mu, includes more than a baker's dozen octavos and articles, essays, reviews, numbering well into three figures. There is apparently no end to his contributions to the literature of librarianship, and no one would want it otherwise.

Dean Shores' *Origins of the American College Library, 1638-1800*—based on his doctoral dissertation written at the George Peabody College for Teachers in Nashville, Tennessee—is today acclaimed as one of the pioneer studies in the history of American academic libraries. Long out-of-print and difficult to locate in second-hand bookstores, this study, which was first published in 1934, deserves reprinting; and perhaps one day in the not too distant future it will be. *Basic Reference Sources* (1954)—a considerably revised version of *Basic Reference Books* (1937, 1939)—is widely used as a textbook in library schools, and has been justly described as the Reference Librarian's Bible. Fortunately, a new edition of this work is now in preparation. *Challenges to Librarianship*—a collection of eight essays which he edited in 1953—brought together in a single volume a careful consideration of some of the most important problems confronting the library profession. One reviewer noted that almost every

* *Louis Shores: A Bibliography*, by John David Marshall. "Beta Phi Mu, Gamma Chapter, Florida State University Library School . . . Publication Number One." Tallahassee, Florida: Beta Phi Mu, Gamma Chapter, Florida State University Library School, 1964. 31 pp.

one of the essays published in this volume "condenses what is ordinarily found in a symposium and frequently exceeds in content the findings of an institute." His *Instructional Materials* (1960) has alerted teachers to the wide range of instructional resources available in libraries. As co-founder (with Wayne Shirley) of the American Library Association's American Library History Round Table, Dean Shores serves well the cause of American library history and the writing of it. As Editor-in-Chief of *Collier's Encyclopedia,* he continues to render distinguished service to reference librarianship and to the library profession at large.

For nearly four decades Louis Shores has been writing regularly for educational, library, and literary periodicals. He has contributed to almost every professional journal from the *ALA Bulletin* to the *Wilson Library Bulletin,* and his by-line has also appeared in such magazines as *The Saturday Review, School and Society, Vital Speeches, Coronet, Scholastic,* and *Omnibook.*

Mark Hopkins' Log . . . brings together for the first time in a permanent form a selection of the shorter published writings of Louis Shores. The forty-four articles and essays, addresses and lectures, included in this volume have been selected from some two hundred which appeared between 1928 and 1964 in various journals and anthologies.

The reader of this volume will discover that the essays included not only convey something of the unified diversity that makes up the world of books and libraries, but that they also give him a glimpse of a charming man with wide-ranging and varying interests, deeply devoted to the cause of books and people, libraries, librarians, and librarianship.

The Mark Hopkins of Librarianship speaks in the pages which follow.

JOHN DAVID MARSHALL

University of Georgia
Athens, Georiga
January 7, 1965

Acknowledgments

For giving me permission to compile for publication a selection of his addresses, lectures, articles, and essays, I am grateful to Dean Louis Shores. The preparation of this volume would not have been possible without his encouragement and cooperation. His generous friendship again places me deeply in his debt.

The original publishers, without exception, have been more than gracious in granting the right to reprint the essays included in this volume. I gratefully note here and specifically acknowledge elsewhere their permission to reprint.

I also wish to acknowledge here my debt to Robert G. Clapp, Assistant Dean of the Florida State University Library School, for advice and counsel. He gave "help on certain details which most people don't care about," and for this assistance he has my sincere thanks.

To Mrs. Christine Burroughs, paragon of interlibrary loan librarians, goes a very special thank-you. For their friendly interest in and encouragement of my activities as an anthologist-editor-compiler, I am much obliged to John B. Howell, Jr., David Marshall Stewart, Wayne Shirley, John Clemons, Ray Rowland, George O. Marshall, Jr., and Mrs. Ethel Rose. I too am appreciative of courtesies shown me by William Porter Kellam and Evelyn M. Fritz, Director and Associate Director, respectively, of the University of Georgia Libraries, and of the long sufferance of my landlady, Mrs. Henry West, who has yet for the first time to complain of the noises of my Smith-Corona Portable as I pound on it late into the nights and on weekends. Mrs. Anna Pryor Cobb generously agreed to assist with proofreading, and for this help I am truly grateful.

For graciousness which only considerate and understanding publishers can display, I am grateful to John H. Ottemiller and to his wife, Frances. Their editorial advice and counsel, their continuing interest and support, can never be sufficiently acknowledged.

Lastly, and most of all, I am grateful to my parents for the many opportunities they have given me—and for more too, of course, which can never be put into words.

JDM

On Books and Reading

Books: Continuous Communicability

ON OUR LIVING ROOM MANTEL there is on occasion a photo of the dean (myself) in soldier uniform. When students come to visit they invariably ask "Which war?" in such a way that I am encouraged to say Spanish-American, if not Mexican. But the truth is that although I served in the Second, I can recall the First World War quite well. And of all my recollections of the 1914-1918 struggle none has remained with me so persistently as a certain French general's definition of death.

In war as in probably no other human experience the sudden transformation from the living to the dead ponders the question "What is death?" To this question the French general replied, "Death? Death is sudden incommunicability."

Sudden incommunicability. Somehow that definition of death has remained with me through all these years. Not because it defines death, but because it has given me a definition of life. For if death is sudden incommunicability, then life must be communicability. And this definition of life all at once gives meaning to the past, present, and future of the book.

To begin with, I understand the term book in the same generic sense as does the former president of the American Library Association. To me, as to Ralph Shaw, the book comprehends all the media of communicability through which mankind gives evidence of life. The term book includes hard covers and soft covers, periodicals and pamphlets, pictures and maps, films and filmstrips, tape and disc recordings, broadcasts, and telecasts, and perhaps two score or more classes of formats. In terms of this definition I confidently answer the question "What is the future of the book?" with all the assurance of the French general. Why, the future of the book is the same as the future of life. As long as the book lives there

Reprinted from *The Saturday Review*, 41: 26, March 22, 1958, by permission of the publisher.

is communicability; there is life. Whenever the book ends we will have sudden incommunicability; we will have death.

The implications of this bit of personal-professional philosophy extend beyond the sort of Maginot Line some publishers, booksellers, librarians, and authors have been attempting to excavate ever since another Frenchman, Maurice Duhamel, in 1938 doomed the book. To paraphrase a contemporary of Duhamel's who may already have begun to collect his perspective from history, there is nothing to fear but fear. The book is in no greater danger than life itself.

Whatever this new "Battle of the Books" may be, its elements are very little different from its Swiftian precursor. In the Lilliputian essayist's day the threat to the book appeared to come from quality and quantity. About the former Swift wrote sardonically, "It is with libraries as with other cemeteries . . . that a certain spirit hovers over the monument till the body is corrupted, and turns to dust . . . which to some may happen in a few days. . . ." The future of such books is short, and rightly so, but hardly representative of the book as a whole. The book of quality has indubitably proved it can survive with life itself.

As for quantity, the doomsday prediction is almost as old as printing itself. Barely a century after the invention, Martin Luther wrote "The multitude of books is a great evil." Yet for four centuries since, book production has increased in almost geometric ratio. Concern, therefore, about either quantity or quality as a threat to the book has proved to be thus far no more than a concern.

Nor is the imagined threat from technology any more potent. From the standpoint of information or research Ralph Shaw has proved statistically that gadgets are too stupid to be able to store, retrieve, or disseminate knowledge as nimbly as the printed book. What is more, as automation releases semi-skilled humans from assembly-line drudgery, higher and higher IQ's such as are attained from reading books are needed to run automation. And as for recreation, David Mearns has put it deftly: "Can you imagine any one curling up in bed with a microfilm?"

Finally, the debate over audio-visual materials is occasioned by the failure of some of us to recall our own professional history. Librarianship has never been and is not now basically a profession

of formats. We have always prided ourselves on our mission of con-
servation and dissemination of the world's best ideas. In various
ages we have carried on our work with clay tablet, with papyrus
roll, with illuminated manuscript, with printed book, with pressed
disc, with celluloid film. Each new format has been resisted by some
fine old bibliophile. Listen to this from Vespassiano's life of the
illustrious fifteenth-century Italian Duke Frederigo of Urbino:

"In his library all the books are superlatively good, and written
with the pen, and had there been one printed volume it would have
been ashamed in such company." Of which of us librarians shall it
be written some centuries hence that we were ashamed to have good
books in the library unless they were printed?

Books are books in whatever quantity or quality, in whatever
order or format. Individually they are symbols of individual consciousness. Collectively in libraries they represent what humanity to
this point has been able to comprehend of that mysterious universal
consciousness.

As long as there is life man will try very hard to communicate
with man, and even harder to communicate with God. This continuous communicability inherent in human life insures the future of
the book.

How to Find Time to Read

IF YOU ARE AN AVERAGE READER you can read an average book at
the rate of 300 words a minute. You cannot maintain that average,
however, unless you read regularly every day. Nor can you attain
that speed with hard books in science, mathematics, agriculture,
business, or any subject that is new or unfamiliar to you. The

Reprinted from *The Wonderful World of Books*, edited by Alfred Stefferud,
Copyright © 1952, by Alfred Stefferud, published in a trade edition by Hough-
ton Mifflin Co. and in a paper bound edition by The New American Library of
World Literature, Inc., by permission of The New American Library of World
Literature, Inc.

chances are you will never attempt that speed with poetry or want to race through some passages in fiction over which you wish to linger. But for most novels, biographies, and books about travel, hobbies or personal interests, if you are an average reader you should have no trouble at all absorbing meaning and pleasure out of 300 printed words every 60 seconds.

Statistics are not always practicable, but consider these: If the average reader can read 300 words a minute of average reading, then in 15 minutes he can read 4,500 words. Multiplied by 7, the days of the week, the product is 31,500. Another multiplication by 4, the weeks of the month, makes 126,000. And final multiplication by 12, the months of the year, results in a grand total of 1,512,000 words. That is the total number of words of average reading an average reader can do in just 15 minutes a day for one year.

Books vary in length from 60,000 to 100,000 words. The average is about 75,000 words. In one year of average reading by an average reader for 15 minutes a day, 20 books will be read. That's a lot of books. It is 4 times the number of books read by public-library borrowers in America. And yet it is easily possible.

One of the greatest of all modern physicians was Sir William Osler. He taught at The Johns Hopkins Medical School. He finished his teaching days at McGill University. Many of the outstanding physicians today were his students. Nearly all of the practicing doctors of today were brought up on his medical textbooks. Among his many remarkable contributions to medicine are his unpublished notes on how people die.

His greatness is attributed by his biographers and critics not alone to his profound medical knowledge and insight but to his broad general education, for he was a very cultured man. He was interested in what men have done and thought throughout the ages. And he knew that the only way to find out what the best experiences of the race had been was to read what people had written. But Osler's problem was the same as everyone else's, only more so. He was a busy physician, a teacher of physicians, and a medical-research specialist. There was no time in a 24-hour day that did not rightly belong to one of these three occupations, except the few hours for sleep, meals, and bodily functions.

Osler arrived at his solution early. He would read the last 15 minutes before he went to sleep. If bedtime was set for 11:00 p.m., he read from 11:00 to 11:15. If research kept him up to 2:00 a.m., he read from 2:00 to 2:15. Over a very long lifetime, Osler never broke the rule once he had established it. We have evidence that after a while he simply could not fall asleep until he had done his 15 minutes of reading.

In his lifetime, Osler read a significant library of books. Just do a mental calculation for half a century of 15-minute reading periods daily and see how many books you get. Consider what a range of interests and variety of subjects are possible in one lifetime. Osler read widely outside of his medical specialty. Indeed, he developed from this 15-minute reading habit an avocational specialty to balance his vocational specialization. Among scholars in English literature, Osler is known as an authority on Sir Thomas Browne, seventeenth century English prose master, and Osler's library on Sir Thomas is considered one of the best anywhere. A great many more things could be said about Osler's contribution to medical research, to the reform of medical teaching, to the introduction of modern clinical methods. But the important point for us here is that he answered supremely well for himself the question all of us who live a busy life must answer: How can I find time to read?

The answer may not be the last 15 minutes before I go to sleep. It may be 15 minutes a day at some other time. In the busiest of calendars there is probably more than one 15-minute period tucked away somewhere still unassigned. I've seen some curious solutions to the problem of finding time for reading.

During army days in the last year of the war I discovered a Pfc. in my squadron who seemed unusually well-read. I found in his 201 file a remarkable civilian and military biography. His four years of service included two overseas, all meritorious but without heroics. Had all of his recommendations for promotion gone through he would have had not only his commission, but probably the rank of captain. But here he was, still a private first-class — because, despite the military emphasis on education, efficiency, loyalty, and all other criteria for determining promotion, accident plays a most important part. Every time this Pfc. had been recommended for promotion,

except once, he had been transferred, or come up against table of
organization limitations, or a new change in regulations, or a superior officer who had filled out the forms incorrectly or forgotten
them in his third right-hand drawer. And so he had remained a Pfc.,
and had taken his reward in reading. The amount he did in the
army was prodigious.

I was curious about his method. And one day, before I asked
him, I found a partial answer. Every day the enlisted men put in
an hour of drill and formations. During that time at least one fairly
long period of rest was called. Imagine my surprise on my first
visit to the drill field when, at the command "rest!" I saw one man
in the whole long line pull out a paper pocket book and begin to
read, standing up.

When I talked with him, I found that from boyhood he had developed the habit of carrying a little book in his pocket from which he
read every minute he was not doing something else. He found a book
especially useful and relaxing during the periods of waiting which
all of us experience daily — waiting for meals, buses, doctors, hair
cuts, telephone calls, dates, performances to begin, or something to
happen. There were his 15 minutes a day, or more. There were his
20 books a year — 1,000 in a lifetime.

No universal formula can be prescribed. Each of us must find
our own 15-minute period each day. It is better if it is regular.
Then all additional spare minutes are so many bonuses. And, believe
me, the opportunity for reading-bonuses are many and unexpected.
Last night an uninvited guest turned up to make five for bridge.
I had the kind of paper book at hand to make being the fifth at
bridge a joy.

The only requirement is the will to read. With it you can find the
15 minutes no matter how busy the day. And you must have the
book at hand. Not even seconds of your 15 minutes must be wasted
starting to read. Set that book out in advance. Put it into your pocket
when you dress. Put another book beside your bed. Place one in your
bathroom. Keep one near your dining table.

You can't escape reading 15 minutes a day, and that means you
will read half a book a week, 2 books a month, 20 a year, and 1,000
or more in a reading lifetime. It's an easy way to become well read.

To Be Truly Informed

WHEN THE BOOK AGENT on your front porch displays his variegated prospectuses of a new wonder book that will answer all of the family's questions at the painless cost of a dollar down and a dollar a week, what do you do?

Do you shout a suspicion-roused "no" and slam the door? Or do you invite him in and end up by signing a contract which you may have increasing reason to regret?

Somewhere between these extremes there is a reasonable consumer approach. Despite the occasional falsification and misrepresentation experienced by householders with book agents, in an increasing majority of cases the door-to-door book salesman represents old and established publishing firms whose products in many instances are as vital to the home as refrigerators and dishpans. These firms are known as subscription book publishers and they specialize in the production of reference books for the home, business, and the library.

Subscription book publishers sell directly to the consumer through their agents who call on you at your home. These publishers sell reference books, including Bibles, encyclopedias, dictionaries, atlases, collections of children's literature, various handbooks, and manuals dealing with household and vocational problems. Often a subscription book publisher will team up with a tradebook publisher to produce a good reference book that will be sold in the bookstore, through the mails, and in the individual home.

What the consumer needs to know is how can he tell when the book agent on his doorstep has a good product and is representing a reputable publisher. That question is important because questionable products sponsored by illegitimate firms are still being peddled house-to-house and many a householder has lived to regret an ill-considered commitment.

Reprinted from *The Saturday Review*, 34: 34-35, February 3, 1951, by permission of the publisher.

If there is a professionally trained librarian in your community you should seek advice from him. But first be sure you are consulting a trained librarian and not the clerk who stamps the books you borrow from your public library. The librarian, if he doesn't know the publisher or product, will consult certain sources.

If the reference book has not been reviewed by *Subscription Books Bulletin*, for instance, for some reason the librarian will undertake to evaluate the work himself, using criteria that he learned in library school, which can be found in a volume such as this writer's "Basic Reference Books." These criteria include scope, authority, arrangement, treatment, format, and special features. Under authority, for example, the reputation and previous publications of the publisher come in for scrutiny.

After the close of World War II six of the strongest subscription book publishers organized themselves as a Reference Division of the American Institute of Textbook Publishers. These six publishers and their principal encyclopedias are: Encyclopaedia Britannica, Inc., Chicago — Encyclopaedia Britannica; P. F. Collier and Sons, Inc., New York — Collier's Encyclopedia; F. E. Compton and Co., Chicago — Compton's Pictured Encyclopedia; Grolier Society, New York — Encyclopedia Americana; Field Enterprises, Inc., Chicago — World Book Encyclopedia; and United Educators, Chicago — American Educator.

Each of these publishers also has issued other works, and any book bearing the imprint of any of these firms is at least worthy of the householder's consideration. This group of publishers, the Federal Trade Commission, and the Subscription Books Committee of the American Library Association have been actively developing a code of fair practices for the protection of the book consumer.

From these subscription book publishers as well as from trade and textbook publishers come reference books essential in every American home.

What then is the essential American Home Reference Library? The actual titles will probably not be the same for any two households. But there are certain classes of reference books that are almost indispensable. I suggest that the following fifteen classes would form an adequate basic collection for most American families:

(1)
THE BIBLE
There are many versions and editions. Selection will be based on church membership and the advice of your pastor.

(2)
ADULT ENCYCLOPEDIA
Leading American examples are "Americana," "Britannica," "Collier's," for multi-volume sets: "Columbia," "Lincoln Library of Essential Information," for one-volume works.

(3)
CHILDREN'S AND YOUNG PEOPLE'S ENCYCLOPEDIA
Leading American examples are "American Educator," "Britannica Junior," "Compton's Pictured," "World Book." One not arranged alphabetically is "Book of Knowledge."

(4)
ADULT DICTIONARY
Leading American unabridged examples are "Webster's New International," "Funk and Wagnalls New Standard"; leading American abridged (over 100,000 words) are "American College," "Funk and Wagnalls College Standard," "Webster's New Collegiate," "Winston's."

(5)
CHILDREN'S AND YOUNG PEOPLE'S DICTIONARY
For high school age: "Thorndike-Century Senior" or "Webster Students"; intermediate grades: "Thorndike-Century Junior" or "Webster Elementary"; very young children: "Golden" or "Rainbow."

(6)
FIRST AID
Standard is the "American Red Cross Manual," although there are others.

(7)
INFANT CARE
The U.S. Government Printing Office has delivered over six million copies at twenty-five cents each of its publications under that title.

(8)

HOUSEHOLD

For repairs, improvement, decorations around the house there are many manuals. One of the best is "Woman's Home Companion Household Book."

(9)

COOKBOOK

Leading American examples include "Boston Cooking School," Givens' "Encyclopedia of Cooking," "Settlement Cook Book," and "Woman's Home Companion Cook Book."

(10)

ETIQUETTE

Emily Post is almost a synonym, but there are an increasing number of other good books and one or two especially for teen-agers.

(11)

GARDEN

Numerous good ones are available. Some examples are E. L. Seymour's "New Garden Encyclopedia," Norman Taylor's "Encyclopedia of Gardening," John Wister's "Woman's Home Companion Garden Book."

(12)

ATLAS

Leading American examples are "Rand McNally Cosmopolitan," "Hammond Library World," "Hammond Complete World"; the leading British example is "Bartholomew Advanced Atlas of Modern Geography."

(13)

YEARBOOK

To keep up with the world during the past year any one of these yearbooks will prove highly informative and entertaining: "Americana Annual," "Britannica Book of the Year," "Collier's Yearbook," "New International Yearbook."

(14)

ALMANAC

For quick facts and statistics to settle that family argument: "Information Please Almanac" or "World Almanac."

(15)

NEWSPAPERS AND MAGAZINES

Every American household already subscribes to several but a balanced diet provides at least one good daily newspaper, and one weekly and one monthly magazine of interest to every member of the family, which may include a news, book review, literary, pictorial, woman's, man's, child's and hobby interest magazine as required.

With these fifteen reference basics regularly represented and kept up to date in the American home we can count on one more bulwark in our way of life — a truly informed people.

Return to Reading

WITHIN RECENT MONTHS both my professional and my personal life have been invaded by a single, persistent, and almost haunting theme. The only comparable experience I can recall is at times when a bit of melody from a great symphony or a passage from the Bible kept repeating itself inside of me. In just that way this theme is coming to the surface of my consciousness every time I think about Khrushchev and the cold war, or about libraries and their destiny in this world. Since these two subjects involve nearly all of my waking hours, you can understand how impelling this theme, "Return to Reading," has become in my life.

From the *Saturday Review* for March 22, 1958, I repeat the first three paragraphs of my article "Continuous Communicability" which the editors made the editorial for the first National Library Week:

"On our living room mantel there is on occasion a photo of the dean (myself) in soldier uniform. When students come

Reprinted from *The Church Library*, 2: 5-9, January-March, 1961, by permission of the publisher, The Sunday School Board of the Southern Baptist Convention, Nashville, Tennessee.

to visit they invariably ask 'Which war?' in such a way that
I am encouraged to say Spanish-American, if not Mexican.
But the truth is that although I served in the Second, I can
recall the First World War quite well. And of all my recollections of the 1914-1918 struggle none has remained with me
so persistently as a certain French general's definition of
death.

"In war as in probably no other human experience the
sudden transformation from the living to the dead ponders
the question 'What is death?' To this question the French
general replied, 'Death? Death is sudden incommunicability.'

"Sudden incommunicability. Somehow that definition of
death has remained with me through all these years. Not
because it defines death, but because it has given me a definition of life. For if death is sudden incommunicability, then
life must be communicability. And this definition of life all
at once gives meaning to the past, present, and future of
the book."[1]

If we look at communicability in America today, we see some
startling evidences of national life. There is on the one hand a production phenomenon such as the world and certainly no other nation
today has achieved. And there is on the other hand such a degree
of incommunicability among our people as to suggest that most
of us are dying or even very near death.

Look at the statistics. In late, round figures nearly ten billion
dollars annually is being spent by the American people on the great
media of communication. About two billions of this total goes to
the two principal viewing facilities, namely TV and the movies. The
figure of some 50,000,000 TV sets in American homes receiving
programs from nearly 700 commercial stations appears to be stabi-
lized. Although theater attendance is declining, nearly 18,000 movie
houses attract 45,000,000 customers weekly; customers apparently
are willing to pay a star actor half a million a month while com-
pensating a good teacher of their children less than half a thousand.

[1] Louis Shores, "Continuous Communicability," *Saturday Review* (March 22,
1958).

Nearly another billion dollars annually goes to the basic listening media — radio and recordings. An all-time high of over 150,000,000 radio sets receive programs from 4,000 AM and FM stations. High-fidelity and stereophonic enthusiasts have pushed annual disc and tape recording sales to nearly a half billion dollars. Perhaps some consolation should be found in the fact that Van Cliburn's first commercial recording, a performance of the Tschaikowsky B-flat minor *Piano Concerto*, sold last year 300,000 copies in the first six weeks; true, not quite as good as the one million advance orders averaged for each of nineteen Elvis Presley records.

Hopefully, more money was still being spent on reading than on listening or viewing. The latest figures indicate a revenue well over six billion dollars for books, magazines, and newspapers. As might be expected newspapers got over four-and-a-half billions, magazines three-quarters billion, and books just under a billion. Combined daily and Sunday circulation figures provide a daily average of over 50,000,000. In any one month more than 180,000,000 magazines are bought by the American people.

As for books, the symbol of reading, publishers in America issue about 13,000 titles in one year. The last full year's sales showed over 800,000,000 copies of these books sold for a gross of $919,-000,000. Paper bounds, of course, lead with nearly a quarter of a million copies distributed through newsstands and book stores. Juveniles and textbooks follow. Adult trade books totaled only 32,000,000 copies and brought $67,000,000 gross. A surprising volume of 58,000,000 encyclopedias grossing $223,000,000 is a hopeful sign.

On the surface, communicability seems high enough in our nation. The production figures are impressive and the most media, with the possible exception of movies, have shown increases. One might glibly assume all is well with books and reading in America.

But according to a recent Gallup Poll, 61 percent of all Americans do not read a single book during any one year, save possibly here and there in the Bible. This is particularly dismaying when we consider that half of all our adults live within a mile of a free public library, and only about a fifth of them ever go inside a library building. It is almost frightening in the face of steadily increasing leisure time. All of us who work for pay can attest that the work week has been steadily reduced from sixty to forty hours and in some instances even to thirty-six or thirty-four hours. The galaxy of labor-saving gadgets that have inundated our homes through the modern miracle of "nothing down and low-low payments" has released countless other previously committed hours. Add to all this the scientifically admitted lengthened life span and we all have the right to say, "surely we now read more."

Actually, reading has increased but not as much as other uses of leisure time. Without considering time spent on bridge, clubs, spectator sports, golf, socializing, and other togetherness activities, here are some estimates of attention to communicability in the American home. Watching television, for example, per home, per day in these United States of ours is calculated at six hours. Listening to radio in the average day in our households throughout the land takes two hours. On the average, individual Americans put in a half hour a day in the movies, although this takes usually a chunk of about three hours at a time once or twice a week. The mode in America is also about a half hour a day with the newspaper, mostly comics, sports and woman's page, and another half hour with the magazine picked up with the groceries at the supermarket, or reading one of the other mass media such as the *Reader's Digest, Life, Saturday Evening Post,* or *Better Homes and Gardens.* If statistics mean anything, and they usually mean less than they tell, Americans listen to recordings on the average of about half hour a day. You and I wish we could visualize rapt attention to a Beethoven symphony, but we fear it is fidgeted wiggling to a pea-green, seasick, adenoidal torment.

What about book reading? There is no published time average that I could discover. But I made a quick calculation. Even counting the paperbacks on the newsstands, those that display a girl in a dress that wouldn't choke her, as well as paper bound books of merit, American consumption annually comes to about four books a year. Assuming that 60,000 words per book would be a fair average and that the desirable reading speed of 300 words a minute would have to be reduced to 200, our nation's mode of book reading is per person 1,200 minutes a year. Put this up against the other time allocations per day per medium and we have

television	6 hours
radio	2 hours
movie	$\frac{1}{2}$ hour
newspaper	$\frac{1}{2}$ hour
magazine	$\frac{1}{2}$ hour
records	$\frac{1}{2}$ hour
book	5 minutes

In the words of one of our columnists we Americans can say for our homes this is "My Day": sleep eight hours; work six hours; communicate ten hours. Assuming that the sleep and work periods are now irreducible, what about the daily ten? Is our use of these vital hours, individually and nationally, conducive to the high destiny to which we are dedicated?

One answer to that question can be found in the relative restlessness and frequent unhappiness in which our nation finds itself from time to time. At the moment, Russia, fall-out, inflation, teen-age delinquency, and an extraordinary epidemic of adult mental illness, possibly in that order, are causing us the most national discomfort. To every one of these ailments we have applied the utmost of our material resources. The Communists have frightened us into spending over forty billions annually for defense. Much of that money has gone into hydrogen bomb tests, the current cause of the strontium-90 jitters. We suspect that giving our high school youngsters their own automobiles, unlimited spending money, and assurance that working to earn any of it is beneath their dignity may contribute something to the irresponsibility that permeates a generation fully capable of improving the imperfect world we are leaving them. And as for the mentally ill among us, the statistics on state institution increases are common knowledge.

This must give us pause to ponder. As the wealthiest nation in the world and the kindest and most generous we have not achieved that peace of mind for which we apparently hunger. If we admit it to ourselves, we are aware of a lack of inner calm. For a few minutes each Sunday morning most of us grasp at a fleeting vision of something beautifully out of this world. Knowing no better we seek to buy it the rest of the week by storing up one treasure after another. Or we attempt to escape into a video world as ephemeral as the one it images.

What is the answer? I have found it in a return to reading. Without competing in any way with the evangelist whose work for God is so mightily needed, but rather to reinforce it, I plead for a reading revival. I plead for reading, not alone because of books and libraries, but as a way to that inner calm so necessary to national health. The very act of reading calls for some quiet and repose — necessary preludes to thought. I call for upping the national daily average of book reading from the present five minutes to at least fifteen. I urge us all to begin an unbroken habit of opening a good book at least once each day and reading it quietly, peacefully, and with concentration for no less than a quarter of an hour at a time. As a librarian with four decades of dedication to my profession, I promise the nation a revelation in reducing jitters and calming nerves. But I promise much more. Out of such a national reading habit I foresee the development of a national mind with a much higher IQ than we can now collectively claim. Out of such a high IQ many solutions, not now foreseeable, may come. We may prove to be more than a match for Soviet Sputniks without falling back on the now unsportsmanlike excuse that Russians are using German scientists. This high national IQ may teach us how to control fallout, or better yet show us a way to a weapon without the hydrogen bomb's boomerang qualities.

It is even possible that somewhere in all this reading someone will come up with a way for individual enterprise, that magnificent economic concept that enables man increasingly to develop the world's resources, to control the spiral of prices and wages. How important this is we can understand every time a Russian propagandist says they will not have to go to war to conquer us. Inflation will do the job for them.

To the frantic parents and teachers of high school youngsters there may be support for a reading revival. Every study of children's reading indicates a fall off in adolescent years. Increased physical growth and activity during this age should be and can be acknowledged in many different ways without eliminating periods of thought, quiet, and reading. Discipline through books and increased responsibility for earning a living can go hand in hand toward building a better next generation.

After World War II, bibliotherapy came into its own. The University of Richmond Medical School, as well as many hospitals, has done much to help the mentally sick through guided reading. How important this library contribution can be to the health of the nation is underlined by increasing evidence that a considerable portion of even our physical ailments are caused by mental disturbances. One recent medical article, for example, attributes a high percentage of skin diseases to mental causes. With bibliotherapy now an established fact it is evident what reading has to contribute to the last of the five great concerns of our nation today.

As librarians, the challenge and obligation forced upon us by these five great national concerns are inescapable. If we ever permitted ourselves the luxury of routine performance on our jobs, which any of us will doubt, certainly we cannot now. We cannot because we must surely know that any of the material solutions mankind has tried in the past have failed. We cannot, because we know only too well how unconvinced most of the people are that libraries have within them the human resources to prevent world catastrophe.

Our national mentality must be so fortified that it can withstand these perennial enemy thrusts at our national composure that result in waves of "scapegoatism" and that create inferiority complexes and attitudes of defeatism among us. We must prevent these popular outbursts against our science, our education, our Government because we are not first in every competition. We must, somehow restore our sense of balance and perspective.

This then is the strategic situation in World War III. We are maintaining parity and probably superiority in physical resources. But we are losing the war on the psychological front. We are losing it at home because mental health is declining, because our youth is degenerating, because our economy is floundering. And we are losing it abroad because the Communists are communicating more effectively to the more unfortunate peoples of the world. The tragedy is that the other way of life means the subjugation of the individual's freedom and dignity and creativity.

We must shift the emphasis in both our defense and our offense. Our mental resources must come in for a greater share of attention. This can be accomplished only by strengthening our national mentality. One of the greatest sources of mental power in the United States is our libraries. In them is everything great and good man has ever thought or done. Our people need to be armed with the good deeds and great thoughts of all times — the eternal verities. With these, psychosis, degeneracy, and inflation, at home, can be overcome. From these good deeds and great thoughts will come the power to cope with fallout and to prevail against communism.

Lest I leave the wrong impression, I hasten to add that this return to reading must not be just to any reading at all. It must be to good reading. There is even now too much bad reading, reading of the obscene and reading of the subversive. Better no reading at all than the indiscriminate time wasting that goes on too often.

Many read without purpose, without a guiding light, but reading for reading's sake is obviously not the intent of a return to reading. Today the world is beset by all kinds of purposes — purposes so compelling that unless they are fulfilled, and soon, this world without end will end for us.

The return to reading seeks to balance action with meditation, activity with thought, materialism with spirituality. Only in such a balance is there any future for all of us.

On Librarianship

A Profession of Faith

"LIBRARIANSHIP is one of the few callings in the world for which it is still possible to feel unqualified admiration and respect."

So wrote Jan Struther in her delightful book, *A Pocketful of Pebbles,* in 1946.

"Almost every other profession," she continued, "has been more or less debunked, either by theorists or by the merciless cold daylight of human events. Lawyers, scientists, bankers, brokers, politicians — we may not actually question their integrity, but it is possible in our blacker moments to make out a pretty serious case against their usefuless."

Flattering as this comparison is to us and grateful as we are to the author of these words we must nevertheless face up to the fact that librarianship is not attracting young people these days in numbers sufficient to supply demand.

At last count there were some 15,000 library jobs begging for candidates. These jobs were of all kinds. Many of them were, of course, beginning positions at extremely modest salaries. But there were also a considerable number at a salary significantly beyond the national average family income.

Yet virtually every library school reported its latest graduates as well as its older alumni nearly all placed. What was worse a backlog of unfilled positions punctuated by employers' distressed pleas jammed placement officers' job files.

The jobs were of all kinds. There were the endless requests,

"A Profession of Faith: First Mary C. Richardson Lecture" (Geneseo, New York: State University Teachers College, 1958) is reprinted by permission of the Division of Library Education, State University College, Geneseo, New York. The lecture was delivered on March 27, 1958.

written almost in desperation by employers, for catalogers. At this writing any feeling of rejection those who catalog might previously have felt should be entirely dispelled. For the cataloger today is in the position of virtually writing her own professional ticket on the employment market.

Not far behind is the demand for childrens' and school librarians. It is easy to explain the shortage here. Nearly every one of the 48 state departments of education has moved to enforce school library standards, and prominent in these standards is the requirement of professionally trained library teachers. Furthermore, elementary schools are demanding librarians as never before. Two Florida cities alone are opening 70 new elementary schools in the next two years that need librarians. There is hardly a state today that could not employ in its schools twice the number of librarians graduated in that state each year.

To illustrate how acute the school library shortage is nationally it is significant to note the comparative demand as among school teaching areas. Each year there is published what is known as the Index of Teacher Demand. This is a ratio between the demand and supply of teachers by areas. Until recently the kind of teacher with the index of highest demand was the one who taught in the elementary grades. Now the area with the index of highest demand appears to be school librarianship.

Similarly, in the special field, an extraordinary demand for librarians has been created since World War II by government and industry. The armed forces alone have attracted a considerable number of library school graduates to positions of importance both here and abroad. So, too, has the State Department for its information centers. Various other government agencies like the Departments of Health, Education and Welfare; Agriculture; Interior; and Labor; and independent establishments like the Atomic Energy Commission, Veterans' Administration and units too numerous to enumerate, have crowded civil service lists with vacancies.

Industry, too, stimulated by defense production has become increasingly aware of the librarian's potential for employee welfare and research. This has resulted in the creation of positions never conceived before. In my area recently one chemical plant anxious to employ a man librarian with science and foreign language background offered one of our students, still three months off from graduation, a position at a beginning salary of $6,000. Another recent male graduate is heading an aircraft industry's library at a salary close to $10,000.

It will be seen from this that the number of library opportunities during the last few years has been increasing in almost geometric proportions. Salaries have become so advantageous that a year ago *U. S. News and World Report* indicated that lawyers and librarians would receive the highest beginning salaries of all June graduates.

But while this phenomenal increase in opportunities has been developing the number of professional librarians has hardly increased in arithmetic ratio. The one professional truth we all seem to accept is the fact that there are not enough qualified librarians, and the shortages are apparently increasing rather than declining. What is the solution?

Obviously, we all say, the answer is accelerated recruitment. But recruitment has been going on almost continuously. An ALA national committee on recruitment supported by state efforts has worked hard at the task of luring young people into librarianship. Almost as industrious in their efforts have been the individual library schools.

We ourselves at Florida State have just completed what we tabbed our R100 project, a planned effort during the past year to interest 100 young men and women of promise in librarianship as a career. Our State Library Association aroused as never before by the shortage has made recruitment its single objective for the year. Yet despite all of these thoughtful and sincere efforts the shortages remain. Indeed they may even be greater than before.

I put these two phenomena side by side. An eminent author describes our profession as "one of the few callings in the world for which it is possible to feel unqualified admiration and respect." Our young people prefer to flock to the professions that have been in the words of this author "more or less debunked." What is the explanation?

The explanation, I am convinced, can be discovered in a comparison of these two appraisals. This profession of ours — what is

it really? What do we who practice it believe librarianship to be?
And what estimate of us have they who are not in our work?

As a part of the *Public Library Inquiry* Alice Bryan interpreted
revealingly many of the features of our professional portrait as it
hangs in the gallery of occupations. For example, as a composite,
stereotype, she writes:

> Librarians are usually pictured as inhibited old maids, zeal-
> ously guarding their precious books against mutilation, loss,
> and over-long use, while enforcing a tomb-like silence within
> the sacred precincts of the reading room.

If that is the picture of the librarian that young people have
then we haven't much further to look for our recruitment failures.
But is it?

Let's really examine this stereotype of us. It is true we are in
the United States a profession for women. Despite the increased
male ratio in our accredited library school enrollments, women outnumber men about four to one in American library positions. Dr.
Bryan reported that 92% of all public librarians were women.
However, this preponderance of women is not universally true of
our profession. In most countries the ratio is the other way. In the
United Kingdom, for example, over 90% of the librarians are men.
Even in the United States the majority of top administrative positions
are held by men. There is no reason, therefore, why librarianship
should be considered a feminine profession.

There is even less cause for the insinuation that librarianship
is effeminate. The profession's masculinity is attested by Dr. Bryan's
application of the Gamin factor "M" to a sampling of her respond-
ents. This factor tests the personality of men for masculinity and
of women for femininity. The men average 6 on a 10-point scale.
We all know men librarians who are good athletes, extroverts, leaders of men. Robert Downs has named a good football team filled
with capable grid heroes drawn from our profession. Furthermore,
occupational aptitude tests taken by our men librarians show promise for business, law, engineering, architecture and other professions.
Under the circumstances it is not accurate to stereotype the profession as feminine and its male members as effeminate.

We come next to the "old maid" part of the picture. It is true that many centuries ago Sir Thomas Bodley, the Elizabethan bibliophile who restored the Bodleian Library to Oxford, declared that a librarian should not be "encumbered with marriage." But that admonition has hardly been followed by the profession at any time. Today, more than two-thirds of the men in the profession are married and more than one-fourth of the women combine marriage with their library career. This does not take into account the large number of women who have married out of the profession. Furthermore, the divorce rate among librarians is far below the average for the nation. It is obvious that the implication of celibacy, forced or preferred, in the stereotype of the profession is not supported by facts.

Dr. Bryan in discussing the factor of the marriageability of librarians reveals some interesting asides. All the evidence shows as much femininity among the women librarians as among women in almost any career group. On the Gamin test, for example, where the low score reveals femininity the sampling of women librarians showed a score of 3. In response to a query, 64% of the unmarried women librarians indicated they would like to marry and 39% indicated they would like to give up their profession and devote their full time to homemaking. These, I submit, are evidences that women in librarianship are as feminine as women in any other career group.

Interestingly enough Dr. Bryan reveals that "professional men seem partial to librarians as spouses," and adds "to a much greater extent than are the professional women." This may be due, as she points out, to the fact that professional men receive more help from their mates than do the professional women. But as a man I prefer to attribute the fact to the presence of so many beautiful, charming, inspiring and intelligent ladies in our profession. At any rate, Sir Thomas Bodley has been ignored by us. We are most certainly not a celibate profession.

A third insinuation implicit in the stereotype is that we are a housekeeping profession, concerned more with the care-taking and handling of books than with the books themselves. Unfortunately, we have at times tended to give that impression to young people as well as to others outside the profession. Every school teacher who wants to transfer to librarianship looks upon the course in catalog-

ing and classification as the secret handclasp into our professional
fraternity. Too many high school youngsters carry with them the
impression that charging and shelving books with meticulous precision is the life work of the librarian.

But this attention to order and organization need not be against
the profession. On the contrary, with a combination of perspective
and humor we might conceivably heighten the admiration of the
lay public. It can be pointed out, for example, that sorting out and
selecting from some fifty million titles the particular one a reader
wants is a bit of art and science that borders at times on the miracu-
lous. You recall the late Dr. Wilberforce Eames' report on his experience with the curator of a Treasure Room when he tried to discover
what was the system of arrangement of the books. The curator
replied, "We use the chronological system, except when we don't
want to." And of course the exceptions made it almost impossible
to follow the rule.

It is to the credit of librarianship that when the records of civilization became so numerous that their location became ever more
uncertain the profession produced several systems of classification.
In my opinion the contribution of Melvil Dewey is in the same relation to Bibliography and Epistemology as the contribution of Carl
von Linne, the Swedish naturalist, is to Botany and Zoology. Charge
it to my professional bias when I say that the decimal device of
the DC shows at least as much creative genius as the binomial feature of the Linnaean classification.

Or take another phase of the housekeeping aspect-acquisition.
Several years ago I sat down in one of our university cafeterias
beside a young man who was eating alone. In the opening moments
of our conversation I discovered he was a candidate for the bachelor's degree in our School of Business, come commencement six
weeks hence. I discovered also that his aim was to become a buyer
in a department store, but that there was a shortage of jobs and
a surplus of applicants.

I asked, "Do you really want to be a buyer?" He again assured
me enthusiastically.

"Is there any special sort of merchandise you want to buy?"

"Oh, almost anything a department store sells and that I know something about."

I then asked, "Do you know how much money the average American library spends for books each year?" He didn't and so I told him. "Say," he said, "that's big business." I agreed. "And I suppose books are merchandise, too?" I nodded. "And I'll bet there are wholesalers and discounts and you have to know the customers you are buying for?" The boy was racing ahead of me. "And you say there is a shortage of librarians?" I could confirm that because I had more requests for acquisition librarians than I could fill. "I never thought there was any place in library work for a business major."

This story can be shortened for the point. That boy went to library school and is now succeeding as an acquisition librarian. I was impressed by the fact that we were not translating our opportunities into the language of the laymen. I was convinced that our young people with the right orientation could begin to look up at our organization instead of down on our housekeeping.

But what troubles me even more than the insinuations of effeminacy, celibacy and drudgery in the stereotype of our profession is the charge of pseudo-scholarship. It is my constant hope that many a bookish boy or girl without serious introversion complexes will choose our profession as their life work. But it is my frequent fear that not only scholars in other fields, but in our own, will so belittle our efforts as to leave a distinct distrust of librarianship as a scholarly pursuit.

Many of us, I know, will recall Mary Wright Plummer's authentication of Mark Pattison's gibe at the profession in his biography of Isaac Casauban, the classical scholar who was made librarian to Henry IV of France. Wrote Pattison (the English scholar of the 19th century) of Casauban the librarian:

> The use which he made of the library was one which no librarian ought to make — it was to read the books . . . he did nothing for arranging or cataloguing. . . .

And he concluded, "The librarian who reads is lost."

Unfortunately, this flippant and satirical line is found as often in the writings of librarians themselves as in the works of their critics. Sprinkled through out professional literature are quoted satires purporting to prove an allergy on the part of American libarians to either the physical or the spiritual book, or to both. Edward Young back in 1728 expressed the contempt of the scholar for the superficial librarian in this couplet:

> Unlearned men, of books assume the care,
> As eunuchs are the guardians of the fair

The attempt to identify the profession as a whole with the allergies of a few is to me quite unfair. It is my belief, based on four decades of association with librarians, that overwhelmingly most of them were attracted to their profession by a heartfelt love for books and a desire to share their pleasure in these great creations with their fellow men. Agreed that many demands of modern life make inroads into reading time. Agreed further that all librarians do not have equal interests of appreciation in relation to either format or content. It is, nevertheless, not demonstrable that librarians in the majority, or even in a significant minority, have little interest in books.

There is within all of us the instinct of the collector. Who among us does not like the touch of vellum, or the sight of illumination? Some of us are stirred further. We recognize that just as script and print were preceded by clay tablet and papyrus, manuscript and book may well be followed by recording and film. Our propensity to collect embraces an even wider range of formats — hard and soft covers, hand-written and typed manuscripts, flat pictures and hard objects, celluloid reels and pressed disks. The urge to gather all of these varied formats of the basic book proves the librarian to be the true friend of books.

Even more unfair are the underestimations of librarianship's relations to research and creation. Not many years ago, a chemistry professor, who was not only a campus colleague but who had become a close personal friend, anxious to help me build enrollment for a new library school said generously, "We have several students who can't quite make the grade as research chemists, but I believe they would make good librarians." And then he added, "There is a great need in all our important researches for someone to check our references for us and locate our journals."

I searched my heart carefully to be sure that there was present at least as much humility as I believe the scientist should have to deserve scholarly recognition. As a reference librarian I have treasured the memory of bibliographic errands run for researchers, some famous and others not so worthy. There has been no greater pleasure than performing routine locations of materials for teachers and students. I have always considered it part of my professional dedication to give help to anyone engaged in any sort of investigation, whether or not it measured up to the loftiest definition of research.

But at the same time I have never doubted for a moment that there are among us librarians individuals with research capabilities as great as those found among members of almost any profession or learned field. Historical evidence exists for that. Our own first president of the American Library Association, Justin Winsor, was an historian of considerable stature.

As for the so-called scientific method, librarians have been nothing loathe. When its impact dramatically touched the social studies, librarianship under the leadership of its Graduate Library School in the University of Chicago, adopted the method, and with consummate skill applied it to the problems of library service. In the three decades since, librarianship has produced a body of research literature which if no better is certainly no worse than the average contribution made by the natural or social sciences. And the prospect is that when man in a new renaissance rediscovers the limitations of this approach to reality, librarianship may well be in the vanguard of the neo-humanism.

Stereotypes. Effeminacy, celibacy, drudgery, and pseudo-scholarship, these are some of the distortions that go into our professional stereotype. But stereotypes are not confined to librarianship. Every occupation has a stereotype. So does every race, religion, nationality, political party, and so does every one of us as an individual.

Usually stereotypes are distortions. All of us here are certain the stereotype of librarianship I quoted to you is distorted. But the fact remains that such a picture exists, and exists all too often in the minds of those young people we want to recruit to our work. What can we do about it?

I am convinced we can do something both as a profession and as individuals.

As a profession we must move toward greater unity. I am aware of most of the causes of schism. I am only too conscious of the forces that drive us toward more and more specialized organizations. Within every state association several types of libraries are represented. Each of these types of libraries meet separately to concentrate on problems peculiar to that type of library. This is as it should be. School librarians need to meet to discuss the problems peculiar to schools. So do public, college, and special librarians. The need for specialization cannot be overlooked. But the hazard of over specialization needs some attention, too. When separate organizations tend to encourage isolation, suspicion and antagonism the threat to unity is far reaching.

The importance of professional unity for recruitment cannot be exaggerated. We are still a small profession in numbers when compared to such larger groups as physicians, lawyers, teachers, bankers. When we tend to break down into even smaller professional autonomies we confront the youngsters with bewildering beginning decisions and later personal tragedies.

Let me be specific. There are many librarians who believe the professional education of a school librarian should be quite different from that provided for a public or college librarian. In order to comply with this professional dictum the library schools are forced early to guide students into a specialized program, sometimes so specialized that public library certification agencies cannot accept such preparation.

Let me describe a case any library school head will duplicate. A young woman who was certain her field of interest was elementary school library work enrolled in a school library program. Following counsel she puts blinkers on and limits her study to library service in schools. Since she was especially interested in the intermediate grades she learned to resent the time wasted on book selection for grades 7-12. Once graduated and state-certificated she hopefully went on her way to her first school library job. A year later she met a young man who was working on his doctorate, in Washington, D.C. They were married. To supplement the meager stipend from his graduate fellowship, she accepts the most lucrative opportunity available as cataloger in the Library of Congress. When she discovers her ineptness she writes bitterly, as a loyal alumna, to the library school for not guiding her elementary school interests more broadly.

The other side is equally disconcerting. We have the young men with the research bug and excellent supporting background in science and languages. They resent angrily the suggestion that part of their studies should deal with the selection of popular adult literature and consider intolerable any introduction to what they call "Kidlit." And yet one of these young men has recently had the manuscript for a children's book accepted, which he dedicated to our Kidlit course, and the other, who reads seven foreign languages and is within dissertation distance of his Ph.D. asked me the other day if any public library children's department would be willing to consider his application.

As a profession we need unity. We are all librarians. Certainly we have our specialties, and those specialties, have even further specialization. But there are still enough things in common among school librarians and university librarians for them to be part of an overall profession.

When I was president of the Florida Library Association I built our convention around the theme "We are all librarians." At one of the general sessions we had in succession a school, public, college, and special library leader tell the entire association in what way his interests were different, and in what way similar to the concerns of librarians of other types of libraries. Everyone agreed it was an exciting professional meeting.

So I make my first appeal for unity of our profession. Such unity manifested through a single, overall articulate library association, locally, in a state, or region, or nation can do much to replace the distortions of a stereotype with the fidelity of a portrait.

I make my second appeal to us as individual librarians. We still suffer from an inferiority complex. Dr. Bryan reports:

> As compared with the average male university student the typical male librarian is rather submissive to social situations. . . .

I take that to mean that in adult life we are still diffident about classing our contribution to society with that of the teacher, lawyer, engineer or physician. In the academic family on the campus we are still unwilling to see ourselves as any more than accessories in the business of higher education and research. This the younger generation senses and interprets as a professional inferiority complex.

So I say to you the stereotype is untrue. The portrait of a librarian by Jan Struther which I read to you at the beginning is very much nearer to the truth.

I believe that the events of this century are inevitably thrusting our profession into a position of strategic significance for the future of mankind. During the remainder of this century our world will make historic decisions. I cannot feel, despite our present adoration of nuclear energy, that the decisive force will be there. Rather I believe a spiritual renaissance will save the day for us.

That renaissance will come out of the vast collection of ideas contained in the libraries of the world. As the preservers and disseminators of these ideas librarians become at once the leaders of this renaissance, and the profession of librarianship becomes an occupation of destiny.

It is probably the anticipation of this role yet to come that led Jan Struther to write in 1946:

> Librarianship is one of the few callings in the world for which it is still possible to feel unqualified admiration and respect.

And that is the feeling any thinking person has today as he looks at a true likeness of the librarian in a good portrait.

The Next Generation

WHATEVER LIBRARIANSHIP HAS BEEN IN THE PAST, it is becoming strangely different in the present. The next generation of librarians is already beginning to experience an education in library school so divergent as to become almost unrecognizable to the practicing members who prepared for their profession before the last world war. If the lady, old or young, vigorously stamping the book behind the desk, ever really did symbolize the American version of the bibliothecal science, she is certainly fading fast from the changing occupational concept of those who work for pay in libraries.

There are many forces, of course, shaping this new look in librarianship. Others may attach more importance to other influences. So there may be no doubt about the choice in this paper; five movements are identified as the revolutionary ones that at mid-century are recasting a profession with a new vitality. Described by single terms, these five developments are, not necessarily in order of importance, 1) audio-visual media; 2) microtexts; 3) science researches; 4) censorship; 5) psychological warfare.

The difficulty the educational world had in defining the forerunner "visual education" still haunts the term that succeeded it. In their article for the *Encyclopedia of Educational Research* (p. 1323) Edgar Dale and Charles F. Hoban, Jr. write "The term 'visual education,' while psychologically a misnomer, is used in the meaning of the integration of sense experiences on the basis of *visual* materials."

The same can be said for audio-visual education. As a matter of fact, integration of sense experiences on the basis of a great variety of materials is becoming increasingly the essential ingredient of all modern education. Because no fewer than forty categories of

Reprinted from the November, 1954, issue of *Education*, by permission of The Bobbs-Merrill Co., Inc., Indianapolis, Indiana.

instructional materials have been identified in the schools of America. These materials range all the way from textbook to 16 mm. sound film, through such classes of instructional media as children's books, reference books, magazines and newspapers, flat pictures, maps and globes, museum objects, film strips, slides, phono-recordings, television, and the school journey.

All of these media are the means by which great and good ideas are communicated between teachers and pupils. They are also the agents of exchange in ideas among all the people of the world. Taken together, they are the record of civilization, and the library cannot escape the responsibility of its mission to preserve and disseminate the total record of mankind. Looked at that way, there is substance to the slogan for libraries Edgar Dale has proposed: "Your Library Has the Best Ideas in the World." (Dale, Edgar, "The Challenge of Audio-Visual Media," in Shores, Louis, *Challenges to Librarianship*, Tallahassee, Florida State University, p. 104).

"Not By Books Alone" is the title of the Rochester Public Library film, and that title describes all librarianship as it is increasingly being conceived. The change means that in place of book courses in our library education, there must come now materials courses. Instead of the conventional introduction to book selection, there is now developing a basic Library Materials study. This is not the old book selection course with an afterthought unit on "non-book" materials, but a balanced materials course in the whole range of media through which mankind communicates. And what is occurring in the scope and sequence of the old book selection course is also developing in the rest of the professional core. Administration, cataloging and classification, reference, bibliography, and all of the other courses are taking increasing cognizance of ideas in non-book form.

Inevitably, if the records of mankind increase in geometric ratio libraries must grow accordingly. The vision of a Yale University Library in the year 2038 with approximately 200,000,000 volumes occupying 6,000 miles of shelving and requiring 750,000 catalog drawers that must occupy no less than eight acres of floor space is enough to cause one long professional nightmare. The partial answer of librarianship is in microtexts.

Microtexts are photographed reductions of original texts to fractions of the original format size. The oldest and most common microtext is microfilm, which comes in reel form and which was introduced nearly fifty years ago. Another transparent type of microtext is the so-called *microfiche*, used extensively in European continental libraries. Two opaque microtexts — the microcard, three inches by five inches, and the microprint, six inches by nine inches — are growing in popularity. These four types of microtexts are pointing the way to the solution of the problem of library growth.

But the microtexts are doing something even more revolutionary. Among research libraries, concerned with the preservation of all the records of mankind, the professional principle generally accepted is one of concentration. This is based on the assumption that since all libraries cannot contain everything, it is necessary for a few large libraries to divide among themselves the responsibility for major concentrations. This principle pervades the so-called Farmington Plan, for example, in which certain research libraries assume the responsibility for concentrating large collections of designated foreign materials. This principle is behind the union catalog idea, the cooperative bibliographic center, and indeed a whole series of steps taken professionally to accomplish what is called bibliographic control.

Now the appearance of the microtext in ever increasing volume, and the threat of a third world war so destructive that a significant portion of mankind's records might be permanently destroyed, have combined to force the rethinking of the concentration concept. Indeed, today librarianship is face to face with the same sort of revolution as confronted the military profession in the Second World War.

In the first disastrous Philippine campaign of 1942, General Douglas MacArthur, a product of ground force education, insisted upon the concentration of our supply of flying fortress bombers as security against possible sabotage. The air force strongly urged the dispersal of these bombers as a defence against enemy air attack. MacArthur's concentration principle prevailed, and the Japanese air force came over the Island and destroyed our air power in one attack.

This lesson of war may have been learned by librarianship. But a considerable period of reorientation is still ahead. By means of microtexts, it should be possible to disperse the more rare and expensive records of mankind to hundreds if not thousands of libraries. Such dispersal might change considerably the concept of the function of research libraries.

Library education cannot escape the responsibility for pointing out to present and future classes the implication of microtexts, not only as a solution to the taxing problem of library growth, but also as a means of forestalling any fatal concentration of library resources. The library schools, indeed, must assume serious responsibility for preparing a generation of librarians to deal with what might well be the most calamitous of holocausts for the records of civilization.

In 1952 it had been estimated that not fewer than "a million useful scientific articles are published yearly in some 50,000 scientific journals. . . ." What science needed was the dissemination of these researches to the points of related investigation. An added urgency to this requirement was given by the hovering third world war and the consequent armament race between east and west. How then can librarianship unlock for science the door to this cascade of investigation?

Both bibliographically and technically, librarians everywhere are grappling with the problems of bibliographic organization. Union catalogs, cooperative reference, indexing, and abstracting are manifestations of the vast bibliographic effort that emanates from conferences and institutes. Microtexts and other reproducing devices all the way to television and facsimile for speedy transmission are evidences of technological thinking.

Library education can do no less than acquaint the next generation with these efforts. Even as recently as a decade ago union catalogs, cooperative reference, abstracting, and microtexts occupied a minor position in the library school curriculum. Television and facsimile are barely mentioned now. To the library school student of today these matters must be presented, not alone for their present worth, but as a stimulus to the young librarian to go further.

Particularly as librarianship must serve science increasingly, a reorientation of pre-professional education emphasis must be considered. Predominantly, the librarians of previous generations have brought humanities and social sciences majors to their library school admissions. The first president of the American Library Association was a historian. Concentrations in English language and literature, in sociology, in history, and indeed in every field outside of the natural sciences, has characterized the education of the librarian in the past. The demands of the time, regardless of the philosopher's concern about the overemphasis, cry for the science-conscious librarian. Such consciousness involves attention to the seven desiderata Charles Harvey Brown has so adequately listed. (Brown, C. H., "Librarianship and the Sciences," in Shores, Louis, *Challenges to Librarianship*, 1953, p. 89-90.)

An indication of library school awareness of the need is found in the general education emphasis on the natural sciences, now part of the pre-professional requirement. Encouragement to library school applicants to submit science specializations is another evidence. And in the library school curriculum the presence of a separate science bibliography course, frequently followed by concentrated seminars in specific phases of a science, promise that the next generation of librarians will be more like the profession Dr. Brown and others want for our research libraries.

Whether we like it or not, censorship has affected professional practice and principles during the last few years to a greater extent than ever before. We have had to rethink some of our sacred selection tenets. The Library Bill of Rights, though a noble document, perplexes the old as well as the young practitioner when he attempts to apply its statements to the local conditions of his library. "Freedom to read," in the abstract, seems incontrovertible in the general session of an A.L.A. convention. But in the intimacy of the classroom, or in the closed board room of a trustee meeting besieged by crusading camera men and flaming reporters, the black and white become a muddy gray.

The case for the other side, championed by Senator McCarthy, might appear particularly vulnerable to the majority of the profession. But the position of some thoughtful library leaders, that censorship to a degree and of a kind is inherent in the very professional process of selection, whether that selection is based on financial limitations or some selecting committee's tenets on art, is less easy to shrug off. The Associated Press feature writer, Irene Corbally Kuhn, in her article "Who are the Censors?" (*American Legion Magazine*, 57:14 ff., July, 1954), unfavorable as it is to the liberal side of issues, puts her finger on the danger of a liberal censorship.

Whichever of the two major censorship problems confronting librarians today — communism and obscenity — are analyzed in the current literary or other art outputs, one cannot escape the conclusion that the unconventional is favored. The appeal of socio-economic fiction and non-fiction that expose meticulously squalor and mayhem in various segments of our way of life is undeniably tidal. Nor can the best sellerdom of novels done in the "astringent" vocabulary of Partridge, whether such solecisms are "necessary to the development of characters" or not, be written off as the choice of the vulgar masses. On the contrary, the writer of elegant phantasy begins with a handicap, not only before the eyes of the publisher's recently emancipated first reader, but when passed in review before the seasoned critics who man our journals of sophistication. How long could a voice cry in this wilderness that James Jones' opus is adolescent mediocrity and the Oscar awards to the Hollywood version further proof of the degeneration of critic America?

Confronted on the one hand by a professional document that advocates both sides of a debatable issue and on the other hand by a professional tradition of liberalism, the librarian of this generation is hard put to it not to neglect the orthodox. Perhaps this is as it should be. The librarian must ever be mindful of his dissemination mission as it affects new ideas. Preservation of the old, the other half of the librarian's *raison d'etre*, has always come more easily to the profession. Only in this preference the librarian should be made aware of degrees of censorship and informed that censorship, itself, as it has come to be understood in our American society, is also an issue with at least two sides.

This professional library education is doing, I am convinced, even more fully than librarianship itself. Look at almost any syllabi or reading lists of American library schools, and you will be struck with the conscientious attention this subject now gets. And if you could be present in the class discussions, the lounge gossip, the club meetings of our library school students, you would be impressed by the seriousness of the young generation's ponderings.

Which leads to World War III. Let us hope it will never develop into the major physical combat of its two predecessors, but become eventually, of necessity if not of choice, a world war of ideas. Such a struggle is now going on everywhere, on both sides of the Iron Curtain. One has only to visit our U.S. State Department Information Centers to sense the elements of psychological warfare.

Well, if libraries have the world's greatest ideas, and ideas are the principal ammunition of the war, librarians become at once the principal components of the world's psychological armies. This writer has many times before hailed his profession as an occupation of destiny. Nearly three decades of participation might conceivably contribute to bias on that point, but not to the extent of expressing impatience with any colleague who offered as refutation the fact that librarianship had provided no complete panacea for the world's ills. There is no thought that librarians alone should manage the world's future, despite a belief that many other occupations have done and could do worse; but there is the firm conviction that the next generation's sights should be raised.

The profession of librarianship, in its modest whisperings and tiptoe promotions, has too long underrated its comparative contribution. It has been wont to look upon the callings of medicine, law, engineering, business, and indeed almost anything, it seemed at times, as more challenging, glamorous, important, than its own, meagre little tasks. Let librarianship never forget its essential tolerance, graciousness, universality, love-for-fellow-man. But let those who practice hold their heads high and tell themselves the objective truth. Preparation for library leadership is as difficult, deep, fundamental, daring as education for any life occupation. In its practice is a process so vital to life that within it may be found the solution to the riddle of the universe even before it is discovered in the physical or biological sciences, or even in philosophy, art, or religion. The limitations of this paper prevent the exploration of this idea further than to reiterate that the world's greatest ideas are in libraries, and that librarians are not only the ideas' custodians, but also their disseminators, and increasingly their discoverers.

All this, library education must convey to the newest professional novitiate. A feeling of importance, so vital to effort and happiness in any work, is no less fundamental in the education of a librarian. The growing attention to "esprit de corps" within the profession is noticeable not alone in the "Principles" courses offered in library schools, but in a majority of units that comprise the whole professional curriculum.

Well, there they are. Five movements that are transforming librarianship and library education. A new generation, facing the most formidable future yet, inherits many handicaps bequeathed by human and therefore erring parents. But the new generation has also from those who preceded it the embryo of a new idea and the beginnings, crude as they are, of new equipment. Call it faith and nothing more, but faith born out of two decades of preparing young people for our calling: I believe the next generation will advance the Kingdom through our profession as never before.

The Importance of Library History

AFTER THREE SCORE YEARS AND TEN, our national professional association, on petition by fifty of its members, has activated a round table for the study of library history.

That the American Library Association should have waited so long may be considered surprising or not, depending upon the individual's professional priorities. True, the first president of the A.L.A.,

Reprinted from *An American Library History Reader*, edited by John David Marshall, Copyright, 1960, The Shoe String Press, Inc., Hamden, Connecticut, by permission of The Shoe String Press, Inc. The essay here reprinted is a paper read before the first meeting of the American Library History Round Table at the June, 1947, Conference of the American Library Association in San Francisco, California.

Justin Winsor, was himself a distinguished historian. True, also, is the fact that during the last seventy years many scholars of history have served with distinction as librarians. Officially, too, our association has cooperated with the American Historical Association in efforts of mutual interest, not the least of which has been the *Guide to Historical Literature*.[1] And such basic history reference works as Larned,[2] (also a librarian), Ploetz' *Epitome, Chronicles of America, Pageant of America,* and the Cambridge histories, to cite only a few, have through the years had enthusiastic library support.

Despite this natural affinity between historians and librarians the first seven decades of our professional organization's existence have not produced much library history. An evidence of the paucity of library history research can be found in Lawrence S. Thompson's "Translator's Preface" to Albert Predeek, *A History of Libraries in Great Britain and North America*.[3]

> "The first and only study of British and American libraries from the Renaissance to the beginning of World War II has been contributed . . . by Dr. Albert Predeek, director of the library of the Technische Hochschule, in Berlin-Charlottenburg, which was bombed and burned in November, 1943."[4]

Predeek himself writes, "There is no general description and history of British librarianship," in his "Notes" to *Great Britain from 1850 to the Present*,[5] and he adds in his notes on the United States of America, "In spite of extraordinarily large number of monographic studies there are very few comprehensive works."[6]

These observations are supported by the 460 items of bibliography which reveal many studies, essays, surveys, and other pieces of phases of administration, technical processes, selection, finance, statistics, but relatively few that can be described as library history, *per se.*

Justification for this neglect can be found in the parallel of our nation's history. Driven to pragmatism by the severities of fashioning a living out of a wilderness, our forefathers struggled with economics long before they undertook esthetics. Likewise, spurred by

[1] For notes, see page 55.

the desire to extend library service to all of the people, our library
pioneers devoted themselves to the bread and butter problems of
finance and buildings, circulation and technical processes, organization and administration. There was simply no time for the luxury
of history.

This necessity can be understood. But when the bug of research
bit the profession in the early thirties the continued neglect of history was more difficult to understand. James Westfall Thompson, a
historian, did considerable with medieval libraries. But even the
Graduate Library School at the University of Chicago in its early
days considered library history with apology as an area of research.
As I wrote in my own doctoral dissertation, ". . . libraries so careful in the preservation of all other materials only too frequently
have failed to organize and preserve their own records."[7]

The tragedy of this neglect and apology for library history is
emphasized in any consideration of the meaning of history itself.
If we accept both the broad definition of history as the story of man's
past and the specific charge to preserve the records of civilization,
then the negligence of librarianship approaches a professional mis-
demeanor. How can we assume responsibility for the dissemination
of these records and at the same time suppress through procrastina-
tion an important segment of them? If institutions constitute a significant phase of historical study, then which single institutional type
can have greater importance to the story of man's past than the
repositories of the record?

Imbued with the conviction of the importance of library history,
Dean Wayne Shirley of the Pratt Institute Library School and the
writer began at the very first post-war A.L.A. in Buffalo to plan for
a unit in our professional association. We were encouraged by Carl
Milam, Executive Secretary, Orwin Rush, first Executve Secretary of
the Association of College and Reference Libraries, Stanley L. Par-
gellis of the Newberry Library, and many other librarians with an
interest in the history of their profession.

This first meeting of the American Library History Round Table
is, therefore, in itself of historical importance. It begins what I
hope will be an official recognition by the A.L.A. of the importance

of library history. It inaugurates, also, what I believe will be systematic attention hereafter to the chronicling of our professional
achievement as manifested in the ever increasing dissemination of
good ideas through libraries. As a result of these meetings we should
guarantee the publication of at least two or three solid historical
essays each year.

It is difficult to predict what special interests will develop as a
result of these Round Table meetings. The opportunities are almost
without limit. Perhaps as good a place to begin is with our own
libraries. If no systematic collecting of memorabilia has been undertaken in the past, it would be well to go back to our own shops and
begin now gathering and organizing.

You know better than I what resources are available. Legal
documents for most libraries' origins exist. The charter, if there
is one, provides a starting point. Annual reports of the librarian
and public library board or college library faculty committee minutes are rich in primary materials. Nor should the library's records
be overlooked. The accession book, before it is offered sacrificially
to the Great God Efficiency, should be exploited creatively for the
story of a library's book selection. Mines of information are often
hidden in circulation statistics pre-empted for budget promotion.
Among the borrowers' cards, if they have been retained for any time,
are the elements for mixing and compounding materials into chronicles of unexpected portent. For I dare say that much innovation
today is a repetition of yesterday's costly professional mistakes.
Hidden in the books, themselves, are often forgotten inscriptions
and dedications to the library, to say nothing of annotations van-
dalizing public property. In short, the true library historian will
overlook nothing in the library or the community that might even
remotely contribute to the story of an institution of historical significance.

After our own library, there are our associations, local, state,
and regional, principally. How many city and county library associations have chronicled their story? Not many, I fear. Even more
astonishing is how few state library association histories are noted
in our bibliographies. Can it be that our library schools have con-

sidered the subject beneath master essay, leave alone doctoral dissertation? Then there are the regional organizations. We in the South have two. The Southeastern is a confederation of the libraries of nine states, and the Southwestern of six. Both the Pacific Northwest and New England have distinguished regional library associations. If their histories have been published, I confess I have discovered no entry in the bibliographies I have consulted.

I look at our great national association and wonder at the neglected opportunities. The Association of College and Reference Libraries and its predecessor, the College and Reference Division, have a history almost as old as that of the A.L.A. itself. Without listing them here, there are other units of the A.L.A. so rich in incident as revealed by the *Proceedings* that I marvel the officers have not established historical projects before this. There are, in addition, other national library associations like S.L.A. and associated organizations like the school library groups in education associations, and bibliographical and publishing agencies with library implications that would fill a section of good research studies. And I haven't even touched on government bureaus, federal and state, concerned with libraries.

What about the librarians? Biography is no inconsiderable auxiliary of history. It requires no oracular powers to foresee revival after revival of interest in American library pioneers. The spectacular notables like Melvil Dewey, Charles Amni Cutter, John Cotton Dana, William Frederick Poole, and others will hardly escape repeated attention here. It is even probable that their private lives exposed in these meetings will result in "standing room only" signs, after a while. But much more important is the possibility that library history will discover the unsung greats among our predecessors and contemporaries, too, the tiptoeingest whisperers among our colleagues whose talents are sometimes overlooked by nominating committees. Library history can thus restore perspective and grant some token of belated recognition to those who deserved more in their professional lifetime.

The importance of history to civilization has been recognized philosophically, scientifically, spiritually for lo these many centuries.

It is inconceivable that librarianship concerned with the records of civilization can continue to relegate its own chronicle to insignificance. The birth of the American Library History Round Table attests to the growing importance of library history.

[1] Ed. by George Matthew Dutcher, *et al;* prepared by the Committee of Bibliography of the American Historical Association in cooperation with the American Library Association, 1931.
[2] *History for Ready Reference,* Springfield, Massachusetts, 12v.
[3] Chicago, American Library Association, 1947. p. v.
[4] *Ibid.,* p. v.
[5] *Ibid.,* p. 132.
[6] *Ibid.,* p. 149.
[7] Shores, Louis. *Origins of the American College Library.* New York, Barnes & Noble, 1935. p. ix.

A Proposal for the Pyramidal Reorganization of the A.L.A.

IN SPITE OF ITS VAST POTENTIALITIES for professional advancement, there is increasing evidence that the influence of our national organization is waning in certain quarters. Instead of a single, strong, consolidated association to represent librarianship in the society of professions, we now have many weak, and frequently duplicating, library groups. Instead of a unified campaign against the social problem of library inaccessibility, we now have several independent and frequently competing movements. Instead of a nationally planned attack on the question of source materials, there are now independent and unaffiliated drives from different organizations. As a result, efforts at spreading library service are being dissipated and rendered comparatively ineffectual.

Reprinted from *ALA Bulletin,* 32: 1013-1018, December, 1938, by permission of the publisher.

There are now, in addition to the American Library Association, five affiliated and seven non-affiliated national library organizations. Within the A.L.A. itself, there are 75 committees and boards (not counting subcommittees), 12 sections, and 15 round table groups![1] This says nothing at all about the regional, state, and local library organizations, sometimes affiliated and sometimes not, which demand the interest of most of the same librarians. And this, further, says nothing at all of the school library sections of state teacher associations which increasingly rank first in interest with the majority of school and teacher-librarians, a vast horde of library workers who in many instances are not even touched by the A.L.A.

From the standpoint of the individual librarian, this multiplicity of professional organizations presents problems so complex that it is no wonder more library workers are outside the A.L.A. than in. There is, for example, the problem of time. If conferences, institutes, and meetings continue to pile up as they have, it is probable that the librarian who attends all the meetings he thinks he should in the interest of his own and his library's advancement will have no time to spend at home. Further, it is certain that the variety and multiplicity of his professional dues, from fifty cents to five dollars, will mount to a total so large that eventually they will constitute a major item in his budget.

There is unmistakable evidence that coordination of the various sections, committees, and boards has not been entirely achieved. Sections continue to duplicate each other or to work in related spheres without correlation or cooperation. Who can deny, for example, that the Board of Education for Librarianship, the Association of American Library Schools, and the Professional Training Section have much in common, or that the Association of Research Libraries, University Libraries Subsection, Committee on Archives and Libraries, and the Committee on Public Documents work in the same or closely related fields? Yet in each group there is either an affiliated or non-affiliated national organization, a board or committee, and a section, which works independently and sometimes competitively.

Somewhat perturbed by these and other problems, various individuals, members, and committees have begun casting about for

[1]For notes, see page 61.

solutions. Some of these solutions have appeared in the A.L.A. *Bulletin* with proposals for reclassification of membership. A third Activities Committee, under the chairmanship of Charles H. Brown, was appointed, and on May 13, 1938, that committee issued a tentative statement[2] covering eight points, that expressed well what undoubtedly a large portion of the membership has been thinking.

Just how these eight points are to be realized, the third Activities Committee has wisely refrained from stating for the present. It has, instead, invited suggestions, plans, differences of opinion, and even 100 per cent indorsement of the *status quo*. The following pyramidal plan aims to remedy most of the weaknesses enumerated. To be sure, it may present others as, or more, serious, but it is believed such weaknesses are related to detail and not to principle. Modifications would, of course, be gladly accepted.

The principal features of the pyramidal reorganization may be summarized as follows:

1. All library organizations, affiliated and non-affiliated, in the United States and Canada are to be drawn into a national organization which shall consist of:

    a. Nine national divisions — 5 by type of library and 4 by kind of work.

    b. Seven regional organizations — 6 in the United States and 1 in Canada, these in turn to be subdivided into 48 state and 9 provincial organizations.

2. At the top of the pyramid are an executive board, a council, and general committees.

3. The 9 national divisions are, 5 by library type: public library; college, university, and research libraries; school libraries; special libraries; library training institutions; 4 by library work: acquisitions, preparations, circulation, reference.

4. Each of these 9 national divisions shall include an executive committee, an advisory board, departments, and committees as needed.

5. The function of the executive committee is policy forming; the function of the advisory board, research.

6. Regional organizations for the northeast, southeast, southwest, west, northwest, and central sections of the United States and for Canada shall be modeled on the plan of the national organization.

7. Each regional organization shall have one representative on the national executive committee and proportional representation in the Council based on membership.

8. Dues will be paid once each year and apportioned, one-half to national, one-quarter to regional, one-quarter to divisional organizations. Amount of dues will be based on class of membership (see classification proposed by Membership Committee).[3] Each member upon payment of dues will be entitled to membership in national, regional, and two divisional organizations (one by work and one by library).

A member may pay only national dues and sacrifice regional membership but he cannot become a member of a state or regional chapter without first paying national dues. It is suggested that full membership dues for one year be $6, and that associate, student, and institutional memberships be adjusted to this base. Thus the national would receive $3; each division, designated by member, $.75; the regional, $1.50, a portion of which might be allocated to constituent state or local organizations.

Based on the affiliated and non-affiliated organizations, sections, groups, committees, and the interests they represent,[4] the following outline of the pyramidal reorganization is submitted:

I. NATIONAL ORGANIZATION

A. — Executive Board
President, president-elect, retiring president, second vice president, treasurer, 9 divisional chairmen, 7 regional representatives.

B. — Council
Executive Board, ex-presidents of the Association, 25 members elected at large, one representative from each division, chairman of each general standing committee, chairman of each regional and state association.

C. — Committees
(Present ones fitted into scheme; it is expected some will be eliminated by coordination.)

A.L.A. Activities
Annuities and Pensions
Awards
Bogle Memorial
Chapters and Divisions
Code of Ethics
Committee Appointments
Committee on Committees
Constitution and By-Laws
Council Program
Editorial
Elections
Federal Relations
Federal Relations to Libraries
Finance
Fire Insurance
International Relations

Latin America, Library Cooperation
  with
Legislation
Library Administration
Library Architecture and Building
  Planning
Library Equipment and Appliances
Library Extension Board
Library Radio Broadcasting
Library Revenues
Library Terminology
Membership
National Library Planning
National Parks, Libraries for
Nominating
Program
Program for A.L.A.
Publicity
Resolutions
Salaries, Staff, and Tenure
Special Membership
Travel
Uniform Statistical Report Forms

D. — *The Five Divisions by Library Type*
  1. DIVISION OF PUBLIC LIBRARIES
     a. *Executive Committee*
        Chairman, elected by members
        of division; secretary, ap-
        pointed by chairman; chair-
        man of each department;
        three members chosen at
        large by members of divi-
        sion.
     b. *Advisory Board on Public Libraries*
        Chairman, appointed by exec-
        utive committee; secretary,
        recommended by executive
        committee to executive
        board, as member of head-
        quarters staff; specialist on
        public libraries.
     c. *Departments*
        County and regional libraries
        Large city libraries
        Medium city libraries
        Small city libraries
        Trustees
        Staff organizations
     d. *Committees*
        Adult Education
        Adult Reading

Work with the Blind
Work with the Foreign Born
  2. DIVISION OF COLLEGE, UNIVER-
     SITY, AND RESEARCH LIBRARIES
     a. *Executive Committee*
        (See D1)
     b. *Advisory Board on College Libraries*
        (See D1)
        Secretary on college libraries
        on headquarters staff.
     c. *Departments*
        University libraries
        Research libraries
        College libraries
        Teacher-training libraries
        Junior college libraries
     d. *Committees*
        Archives and Libraries
        Resources of American
          Libraries
        Joint Committees with Asso-
          ciation of American Univer-
          sities, Association of Amer-
          ican Colleges, American
          Council on Education, etc.
  3. DIVISION OF SCHOOL LIBRARIES
     a. *Executive Committee*
        (See D1)
     b. *Advisory Board on School Libraries*
        (See D1)
        Secretary of school libraries
        on headquarters staff.
     c. *Departments*
        Elementary school libraries
        Junior high school libraries
        Senior high school libraries
        Public library work with chil-
          dren
        Board of education and teach-
          ers' libraries
     d. *Committees*
        Library Service to Children
          and Young People
        N.E.A. and A.L.A. Joint Com-
          mittee
        N.E.A. and A.L.A. Joint Com-
          mittee on Recreational
          Reading List
        Parent Education
        State Education Associations
          and A.L.A.

4. DIVISION OF SPECIAL CLASSES
OF LIBRARIES
  a. *Executive Committee*
     (See D1)
  b. *Advisory Board*
     (See D1)
     Secretary of special classes of
     libraries on headquarters
     staff.
  c. *Departments*
     Agricultural libraries
     Business and technology
     libraries
     Engineering libraries
     Law libraries
     Medical libraries
     Music libraries
  d. *Committees*
     A.L.A. and A.A.L.L.
     A.L.A. and A.M.A.
     Hospital Libraries
     Institution Libraries
     Nursing School Library
     Oberly Memorial Award
5. DIVISION OF LIBRARY TRAINING
  a. *Executive Committee*
     (See D1)
  b. *Advisory Board (B.E.L.)*
     (See D1)
  c. *Departments*
     Professional training
     Accredited library school
     faculties (A.A.L.S.)
     Short courses
  d. *Committees*
     Fellowships and Scholarships
     Special Projects
     Joint committees with each of
     other four divisions

*E.—The Four Divisions by Library
Function*
  1. DIVISION OF ACQUISITIONS
    a. *Executive Committee*
       (See D1)
    b. *Advisory Committee*
       (See D1)
    c. *Departments*
       Order and book selection
       Periodicals
       Religious books
    d. *Committees*
       Book Buying
       Periodicals

Reprints and Inexpensive
Editions
Joint Committee with Booksellers and Publishers
Importations
2. DIVISION OF PREPARATIONS
  a. *Executive Committee*
     (See D1)
  b. *Advisory Committee*
     (See D1)
  c. *Departments*
     Cataloging
     Classification
     Binding
  d. *Committees*
     A.L.A. Catalog Code Revision
     Bookbinding
     Cataloging and Classification
     Cooperative Cataloging
     Library Binding Institute and
     A.L.A. Joint Committee
3. DIVISION OF CIRCULATION
  a. *Executive Committee*
     (See D1)
  b. *Advisory Board*
     (See D1)
  c. *Departments*
     Lending
     Readers advisers
  d. *Committees*
     Forms
     Statistics
4. DIVISION OF REFERENCE AND
BIBLIOGRAPHY
  a. *Executive Committee*
     (See D1)
  b. *Advisory Board*
     (See D1)
  c. *Departments*
     Art reference
     Bibliography
     Microphotography
     Public Documents
  d. *Committees*
     Bibliography
     Photographic Reproduction of
     Library Materials
     Public Documents
     Subscription Books
     Union List of Serials
     Union Catalog of Latin
     American Books
     Visual Methods

This proposed reorganization will promote unity and integration. It would, of course, be possible to organize a federation of library associations which would be an organization in name only. Effective action and the avoidance of duplication cannot be obtained nearly as well through a loosely knit federation of library associations as through a closely knit organization.

[1] Based on the A.L.A. *Handbook*, 1937.
[2] "Aims of the Third Activities Committee," A.L.A. *Bulletin*, 32: 679-80, October, 1938.
[3] A.L.A. *Bulletin*, 32: 245-56, April, 1938.
[4] A.L.A. *Handbook*, 1937.

If I Were a British Librarian

I SHOULD LUNCH AT CHAUCER HOUSE as frequently as possible. For there one feels the world professional pulse as nowhere else. Hardly a day passes by that a librarian from America or India or Africa or Scandinavia or Australia does not drop in to join British librarians and Library Association staff members for lunch and conversation.

The topics range from the "Rabelaisian to the Ranganathian" as Mr. Welsford has so aptly observed. On any day one can hear the theory of classification debated profoundly by W. Berwick Sayers, James Stewart, Jack Wells of B.R.B., who by the way is doing more to develop D.C. day by day than almost any librarian in the world, and Bernard Palmer, that ardent disciple of Colon classification, who with Wells has given the profession one of the most thoughtful little books on classification. One can also keep up with his fellow librarians the world over — because librarians, like other people, like to talk, and out of the talk comes continuous revision of our professional directory.

Reprinted from *ALA Bulletin*, 47: 14 ff., January, 1953, by permission of the publisher.

But is it not alone for these memorable daily luncheons that I believe I should keep close to Chaucer House. It is because there the Library Association has through the years developed a professional center where one can come again and again to renew his faith in his life work. There one can have access to one of the great libraries on librarianship, served by one of our top reference librarians — Henrik Jones, the Deputy Executive Secretary of the Library Association. To me, Henrik Jones is the perfect reference librarian. Daily he is in the position that Oscar, the famous Waldorf Chef was once when he cooked for the chef's convention. Henrik Jones' L.A. Library is a clearing house for the reference libraries and information services of the United Kingdom. He takes the "hard nuts to crack" and with almost uncanny regularity turns up with the answer. Yet he is so self-effacing that he always insists that the Library get the credit with its patron — not he.

So, as a British Librarian, I'd be sure that I was a good L.A. member, first. I'd try to pass the challenging series of professional examinations — entrance, registration, and final — and treasure that F.L.A. (Fellow in the Library Association) when I earned it, as few other things I own or covet.

Nor would I want much changed in the present professional education of British Librarians. In the past there have been three roads to professional library competence — experience, academic specialization, and professional library education. Extremely competent librarians have been developed by traveling only one of these paths. But increasingly, full professional preparation calls for all three — library experience, academic specialization and library school. British professional preparation is tending to recognize all three.

College graduates are exempt from the first of the three professional examinations. A significant portion of the L.A. examinations now involve academic qualification. It is my opinion that the current L.A. examination tests approximately what is suggested by our A.L.A. 1951 standards for library schools.

I should be very proud of British library achievement. No nation in the world has better public library coverage. In the United Kingdom over 99% of the people have access to free library service. What is more, a public library card holder in one city has the same privilege in most of the other cities of the United Kingdom. (I do hope some day we will come to that in the United States, so that if I am a registered borrower in the Oakland, California, Public Library and happen to be visiting in Newark, New Jersey, I can use my Oakland card in Newark.)

And I should be equally proud of the great advances in cooperative research library service. To stimulate still further development, I should work for closer integration of the efforts of the L.A. with those of ASLIB and the D.S.I.R. It would be my professional desire to bring the good men together regardless of which one of the three paths to professional competence they have traveled. It is a fact that in Britain, as in the United States, there are highly qualified academic librarians without professional library training. There are also very competent librarians without either academic or professional education. Librarians in these two classes who have already established themselves in the profession should probably not be asked to take the same examination as those just beginning library work. If their professional fellowship could be earned in a more distinctive way it would do much to unify the library profession.

In the family of professions, librarianship is not numerically large. If we tend to break up into even smaller organizations every time a group of us differs with the over-all association, we render inarticulate even the small voice we have in society. I should, therefore, as a British librarian, work for the strengthening of one professional library association to represent all librarians. And within that one association I should do all I could to see to it that every phase of librarianship and every point of view have adequate means of expression, either through sub-organization or through written and spoken media of communication.

One of the most difficult decisions for me would be choosing a place to live and work. I am in love with so many places and people in England that almost anywhere in a library in the British Isles would be challenging and satisfying. Some of my favorite places are Derbyshire, Bristol, Manchester, Glasgow, Edinburgh, Belfast, Dublin (Eire), Cardiff, Birmingham, Leeds, Sheffield. But these are only some of the fine libraries I saw.

I have never liked large cities to live in. There is only one excep-

tion, and that is London. It is the most satisfying city in the world
I know. For me London is far superior to Paris or New York.
London has at once charm, tradition, culture, and above all that
self-discipline that marks a superior civilization.

My favorite university is Cambridge. But I hasten to add I
should be very happy in Oxford and in the "red brick" universities
I visited. Nor shall I ever forget the people who administer the university libraries. Among them are some of our finest scholars and
keenest professional thinkers.

So you see why the decision would be so difficult. If I had not
visited so many places it would be easier. I could then be in the
position of my British counterpart, who having never visited Florida,
would like to settle in California, and who having yet to look forward
to experiencing the vigor and imagination of professional library
development in the South can decide to choose his professional staff
from the East and Midwest. Unlike Mr. Collison*, I had the advantage of a smaller area to visit and the disadvantage of having to
choose among many places and libraries, all of superior quality. I
should, therefore, be quite content in almost any locality in Britain
where a real professional library challenge existed.

Finally, if I were a British librarian I should temper our national
trait of modesty sufficiently to inform American librarians what we
are thinking and doing professionally. I believe British librarians are
better informed on American librarianship than American librarians
are on British librarianship. My nine months proved an eye-opener.
In the areas of classification, cooperation, union catalog, documentation, library education, citizens advisory service, rural and urban
public library service, and special library development, British librarianship compares very favorably with American librarianship.

The two associations — L.A. and A.L.A. — have grown up and
worked together for nearly three quarters of a century now. Together
they have demonstrated effectively the potential strength of an English-speaking union in one area. As part of my professional mission
as a British librarian I should work sincerely for deeper understanding among all of the English speaking peoples as a prelude to even-
tual world-wide fellowship.

* "If I Were An American Librarian," *ALA Bulletin*, 47: 15 ff., January, 1953

I cannot close this piece without a heartfelt thanks to the Fulbright Commission and to all the other agencies which make these exchanges possible. When the final chapter on World War III is written, I have no doubt that the exchange of librarians, scholars, and others will have been evaluated by historians as among the most effective weapons against world catastrophe.

Qualifications of Personnel:
Training and Certification

UNIVERSALLY, ASSOCIATIONS define their membership by qualifications. Library associations are no exceptions. The constitution of virtually every professional organization studied by this writer supports this fact. The section or paragraph on objectives is almost always followed by one on "who may join." Inevitably the association must establish classes of membership and the qualifications for each.

Even the 1853 Librarians' Conference in New York City planned to qualify its members almost as soon as it set up its objectives. On the very first day of the meeting a resolution to Congress was under way asking that Charles Coffin Jewett, then librarian of the Smithsonian Institution, be authorized to prepare a library manual with which better to qualify the membership. Similarly, after Justin Winsor and his six colleagues received the American Library Association charter from the Commonwealth of Massachusetts on December 10, 1879, it was followed shortly by a bylaw authorizing the Executive Board to appoint a committee of eight on library training. Again, Roy Stokes has described elsewhere in this issue how the Royal Charter and Bye-Laws of the Library Association contains two

Reprinted from *Library Trends*, 3: 269-278, January, 1955, by permission of the publisher.

specific commitments on qualifications: "To promote whatever may tend to the improvement of the position and the qualifications of Librarians" and "To hold examinations in Librarianship and to issue Certificates of efficiency."[1]

If there is agreement among associations that promoting qualifications of personnel is a major professional objective, there is also some disagreement among national library organizations as to the medium through which the association can best influence better qualifications among its members. Stated simply and with all the cautions that should accompany simplification, national library associations can be divided today into two camps on this issue of improving qualifications. In one the national library associations stress certification of individuals, in the other the national associations favor accreditation of institutions. Although most national library associations exert influence on both certification and training of its members, it is safe to say that in those nations where the national association administers a national examining agency there is relatively less control of training agencies. Conversely, where professional opinion is opposed to a national professional examination, the association tends to exert greater influence on the training agencies.[2]

For the sake of contrast some of the activities in the areas of personnel qualification by the Library Association of the United Kingdom and by the American Library Association are compared. These two national associations, more than perhaps any two others, illustrate the positions of each camp. They are the two oldest professional library organizations in the world. For three-quarters of a century they have rather consistently indicated the direction in which they think a library association can best influence the development of personnel qualifications.

Almost from the start the A.L.A. evidenced a greater interest in training than in certification. Within seven years of its organization and hardly four years after the receipt of its charter, the blueprint for the first professional library school in the world was on its conference table. As a matter of fact, in the very year A.L.A. was chartered Melvil Dewey[3] wrote, "we need a training school for preparation for the special work. The village school mistress is provided with normal schools by the hundred, where the best methods of teaching are taught. Physicians, lawyers, preachers, yes even our cooks have special schools for special training. But the librarian, whose profession has been so much exalted, must learn his trade by his own experiments and experience." The plan for a library school was accepted by Columbia College at a full meeting of its trustees in 1884, and on January 5, 1887, the School of Library Economy was officially opened.

In 1890 the first standing committee on training for librarianship was established by the A.L.A.[4] Two years later the second library school, that at Pratt Institute in Brooklyn, opened its doors. Drexel Institute in Philadelphia followed in 1892 and Armour Institute in Chicago in 1893. By 1917, the year of American entry into World War I, no fewer than fourteen full-fledged library schools had been activated and an Association of American Library Schools organized. Meanwhile Mary Wright Plummer for the A.L.A. Committee on Training for Librarianship had issued a comprehensive report in 1903.[5] Then in 1909 the A.L.A. created a Professional Training Section for its membership providing a forum to support committee action.

Quite different from this early, continued, and distinguished effort to improve qualifications of library personnel through training is the more deliberate and casual professional interest in certification. One searches the literature in vain for an impassioned appeal for certification like Melvil Dewey's for a library school, or for an exhaustive report on national certification comparable to Mary Wright Plummer's tremendous job on training. Not until 1916, the year before the end of this early pre-World War I period, did the A.L.A. Council appoint a Committee on Standardization of Libraries and Certification of Librarians. After three years more the outlines of a national certification system were presented at the Asbury Park Conference in 1919, informally approved, and referred to the Council. Two years later the Committee on National Certification and Training submitted a suggested plan of certification. Still nothing significant happened. By 1923, the year of the Williamson Report, the total result of all efforts toward certification were laws in two states, Wisconsin and New York, requiring some form of certificate for persons employed in public libraries. Four other states, California, Iowa, Minnesota, and South Dakota, had adopted some scheme of voluntary certification.[6]

In Britain the story of the Library Association's first fifty years was almost exactly the opposite. The Royal Charter itself authorized the association to proceed to certification by holding national examinations in librarianship. In July 1885 the Library Association held its first examination in accordance with a syllabus it had previously prepared. Three candidates presented themselves then, and every chartered librarian since has had to pass the national examinations in order to be certified as professional librarians.

On the other hand, not until 1919, with the beginning of the University of London School of Librarianship, could Britain be said to have established a library school. Provisions for library training had been made long before, of course. At the fifteenth annual meeting of the Library Association, J. J. Ogle of the Bootle Public Library read a paper on a "Summer School of Library Science," and in the summer of 1893 such a school was held. Subsequently the association's Summer School Committee changed its name to Education Committee, and a program of training library assistants began in 1898. But that program was quite different from the one fostered through the library schools by the A.L.A.

In 1902 the Library Association began a period of co-operation with the London School of Economics where courses were offered in bibliography, classification, cataloging, library law, and library economy. This arrangement, though it failed to create a complete library school, nevertheless provided instruction in an academic center for librarians in the London metropolitan area. But it still left library assistants in the rest of the United Kingdom without adequate opportunity to prepare for the national examination. Consequently in 1904 the Library Association launched its correspondence program and called upon certain provincial colleges to offer lectures on library economy and bibliography. Several agencies responded, notably Manchester School of Technology, John Rylands Library (also in Manchester), the University of Leeds, and Armstrong College, Newcastle. All of this instruction had a single purpose: to enable the students to pass the national examination.

Inevitably these early emphases—on certification in Britain and on training in the United States—continued. That is not to say the Library Association has been disinterested in training agencies nor that the A.L.A. has ignored certification. It is to say that the trends in both countries as described in the following paragraphs establish clearly the fact that in the United Kingdom training exists almost exclusively for the purpose of preparing candidates to pass the national certification examination; in the United States certification or evidence of professional competence is dependent upon graduation from an accredited training agency.

After World War I the Library Association steadily encouraged creation of more training opportunities for those who desired to pass the national examination for certification. Nevertheless, all of the efforts pointed in a direction quite different from that taken by its American counterpart. With one possible exception not a single British library school can be said to be accredited today by the national library association in the way American library schools are accredited by the A.L.A. The possible exception is the University of London School of Librarianship. To the extent that its graduates are exempt from the registration examination, (the examination which leads to an associateship in the Library Association) the London school is comparable to an accredited American library school in its relationship to the national association. But to the extent that its graduates, after graduation from the library school, must take the final examination to be admitted to full fellowship in the association, the London school is unlike American accredited library schools.

The other nine British library schools have no accreditation from the Library Association in the American sense. Their college graduates, like the graduates of any college, are exempt from the first or entrance examination. But they must take both the registration examination for the associateship, and when the times comes, the final examination for the fellowship to be certificated. The Library Association, however, does list these nine schools in its *Yearbook* along with the University of London, under "Facilities for Study and Training for the Examinations" as "Schools of Library Training."[7]

In addition the Library Association lists correspondence courses conducted under the auspices of the Association of Assistant Librar-

ians, part-time courses offered by various schools and colleges to
prepare for various aspects of the examination, summer schools,
and occasional courses. Above all, the Library Association prepares
and publishes a detailed syllabus on which the examination is based,
a very full bibliography, and the most recent examination itself.
There can be no question that the Library Association devotes a
considerable portion of its resources to training, but it is also evident
that the direction of its efforts is quite different from that taken by
the A.L.A.

That difference can be further shown by reviewing the greater
emphasis placed by the A.L.A. and its members on training during
the period since World War I. At the Asbury Park Conference in
1919 C. C. Williamson, then with the Rockefeller Foundation, recommended to the association that they create a board with a permanent
staff headed by a competent expert as executive to (1) formulate a
standard scheme of grading library positions; (2) decide minimum
qualification of training and experience for each grade and issue
certificates to all applicants who qualify; and (3) examine and
approve schools that meet standards and give graduates of such
schools, automatically, certificates of appropriate grade.[8] In successive
steps the association appointed a Committee on National Certification
and Library Training in 1920; a Temporary Library Training Board
in 1923; and a permanent Board of Education for Librarianship in
1924 of which Adam Strohm of the Detroit Public Library became
the first chairman. It is worth noting that even though Williamson
placed great stress on certification, and the first of the three groups
appointed by the association named certification first in its title, the
permanent board that resulted, nevertheless, had only education in
its name.

The famed Williamson Report, itself, made much of certification.[9]
One of its major recommendations was for a national examining
board with responsibilities not only for the quality of library
training but for the qualifications of individual librarians. The fact
that the institutional accreditation recommendation alone has been
adopted in the two decades since would seem to indicate the
American climate for national examination is much less favorable
than that in Britain.

During the period of transition from the old fifth year Bachelor of Science degree programs to the present Master's degree programs there was a slight flurry in behalf of national examinations. Mary D. Herrick made a strong appeal for such an examination in 1950,[10] but a questionnaire survey[11] seemed to indicate lukewarm interest if not genuine professional allergy toward the idea.

In summary, the British professional position on the qualifications of personnel, as reflected by the action of the national library association, has been to establish qualifications through a national examination administered by the Library Association and to encourage the development of training opportunities to prepare candidates for this examination. The American position has been to accredit the training agencies through careful supervision, evaluation, and inspection and then to accept the graduates of these institutions as automatically certificated.

The reason for the comparative neglect of certification by the A.L.A. is not difficult to understand. Britain is a small compact geographical unity; the United States comprise forty-eight autonomous units, jealous of their individual certification authority. Recent resistance to federal concentration of powers probably has not helped any national certification movement. The range of library development in the various sections of the country and the diversity of problems found in the different states complicate an over-all plan of national certification.[12]

Nevertheless, considerable A.L.A. effort has gone into various aspects of certification and standardization. Following the appointment by the A.L.A. Council in 1916 of a committee on Standardization of Libraries and Certification of Librarians, considerable professional discussion of certification ensued. Although a potent opposition expressed the belief that national certification would stifle librarians of the "original, genius" type, the association nevertheless proceeded to study positions and personnel through several committees and boards. One of these committees sponsored a survey of all library activities in the United States which resulted in significant pictures of library personnel.[13]

The A.L.A. Board of Salaries, Staff, and Tenure, and its co-operating committees have probably advanced the United States

farthest along the road of certification. From its activities several
important publications have resulted. The first of these was the
so-called Telford Report of 1927, *Proposed Classification and Compensation Plan for Libraries.*[14] Developed in co-operation with the
Bureau of Personnel Administration of the Institute for Government
Research, the report represented the findings of numerous job
analyses of library positions. For the first time the duties of various
library positions were described and the qualifications necessary to
perform those duties stated. For the first time, also, library positions
were graded. Here was a truly solid foundation for national certification if the nation of librarians had a notion to permit anything
of that sort.

The Telford Report was followed in 1929 with a separate report
for budgets, classification, and compensation for university and
college libraries, which superseded that part of the original report.[15]
These reports were monumental. They affected certification in states
and municipalities subsequently. Because of these reports the various
regions of the nation moved toward standardization of position
specifications in libraries. Revisions of these reports followed with
the publication of budgets, compensation, and classification plans
for municipal libraries in 1939,[16] and for institutions of higher
education in 1943,[17] the latter a joint project with the Association
of College and Reference Libraries. Taken together, these reports of
the Board on Salaries, Staff and Tenure, the work of various state
and municipal civil service groups, and the interest of the Board of
Education for Librarianship, as well as individual librarians, represent a considerable associational effort in behalf of certification.
The fact remains, despite the current action of the Council, that as a
nation the United States is still far from any general professional
acceptance of national certification by government or by association.

Agreeing that some greater measure of uniformity in assuring a
minimum standard of professional competence is needed in the
United States if librarianship is to take its place among the strong
professions, what can be done? In this writer's opinion a national
plan of examination and certification such as the British have,
although it has many advantages, would have little chance of professional acceptance here. Both the medical and law precedents are for

state rather than federal control. The accredited library schools feel very strongly that they are more competent to examine their own graduates. There is, besides, the American educational objection to making the end-all of the learning process a final examination.

In view of these considerations it appears to the writer that national certification in the United States of professional librarians must come not through federal government action but through increased professional influence on training agencies and on state certification agencies. This influence should follow American historic lines rather than the British direction. But this influence should also become more positive at certain points in both the training and certification areas.

In the training area, the new standards of 1951 [18] are a significant and forward step in the direction of establishing a professional minimum for the qualifications of personnel. These standards are daily consolidating the position of librarianship in the graduate faculties of American universities. It is these standards which have restored a measure of that uniformity which is essential to the unity of any profession or of any academic discipline. Through these standards the drift and chaos which followed World War II were halted and replaced by direction and order. But the 1951 Standards and the interpretative manual that accompanies them provide a guide for only one segment of the profession, albeit a very important segment.

What is needed now is some direction below and above. Despite the desirability of a five-college-years basic program, the need and the necessity for something less still exists. Community libraries everywhere, urban as well as rural, could use a four-year graduate for a variety of reasons related to supply, salary, and the actual requirements of the positions involved. Indeed, there is considerable evidence that many of these libraries could do well with some junior college graduates. Further, begining teachers in the nations' school systems need not have more than four years of college. For these and other reasons, there is an urgent need to plan two- and four-year programs with junior colleges, teachers' colleges, and other institutions of higher education offering courses in librarianship that are not part of accredited five-year programs. That considerable work has already been done in this area is abundantly evident in such publications as *Standards for Library Science Programs in Teacher Education Institutions* [19] and in other efforts to arrive at a common pre-core in short courses.

Many of the leaders in the profession are not graduates of accredited library schools. Through experience, academic specialization, and self-study these librarians have arrived at a high stage of professional competence. Neither in Britain nor in the United States is there a method by which these librarians may be certificated except through the regular channels. In Britain it means passing of the national examination; in the United States professional acceptance comes through graduation from an accredited library school. Although eventually one or both of these should be the only gateway to certification, the time does not appear to be here for librarianship to turn its back upon either academic competence or leadership in closely related fields.

In consequence it might be desirable for the A.L.A. to establish a type of advanced seminar-examination certification. Admission to this type of examination might be based on such prerequisites as a number of years of highly successful library experience, an outstanding contribution to librarianship, a distinguished academic record in one of the university disciplines, or creative work in one of the peripheral areas like publishing, archives, museum curatorship, bibliography, and documentation. The examination itself might take the form of a major essay in the examinee's specialty followed by an oral defense before his peers.

For all others who wish to enter the profession and cannot through an accredited library school, the A.L.A. might well administer jointly with the library schools a set of national examinations. These examinations and the syllabi accompanying them would serve to standardize the work of the many short course programs offered. Certificates to fit the various levels of examination would be of inestimable help to state certification agencies and to civil service commissions.[20]

A library association's responsibility for the qualifications of personnel is inescapable. Whether the association can be most effective by regulating training agencies more or by administering certification through examination is debatable. The American and British associations exemplify each emphasis. It is probable that the qualifications of personnel can be best influenced by equal attention to training and certification.

[1] Library Association. *Year Book 1951*. London, The Association, 1951, pp. xxiv-xxv.
[2] Shores, Louis: Education of an American Librarian. *Library Association Record*, 55:33-39, Feb 1953.
[3] Dewey, Melvil: Apprenticeship of Librarians. *Library Journal*, 4: 147, May 1879.
[4] American Library Association. Committee on Library Training: Reports. *In Papers and Proceedings of the Twelfth General Meeting of the American Library Association . . . 1890*, p. 91.
[5] American Library Association. Committee on Library Training: Report of the Committee. . . . *In Papers and Proceedings of the Twenty-fifth General Meeting of the American Library Association . . . 1903*, pp. 83-101.
[6] Tai, Tse-Chien: *Professional Education of Librarianship*. New York, H. W. Wilson, 1925, pp. 129-130.
[7] Library Association, *op. cit., pp.* 24-28.
[8] Williamson, C. C.: Some Present Day Aspects of Library Training. *A.L.A. Bulletin*, 13:120-126, July 1919.
[9] Williamson, C. C.: *Training for Library Service: a Report Prepared for the Carnegie Corporation of New York*. New York, 1923.
[10] Herrick, Mary D.: A National Examination? *Library Journal*, 75: 132, Feb. 1950.
[11] Kavanaugh, Irene M., and Wescott, Elizabeth C.: A National Examination as a Basis for Library Certification. *Library Quarterly*, 21: 198-205, July 1951.
[12] Linschied, C. H.: Certification Today. *Library Journal*, 77: 1451-1455, Sept. 15, 1952.
[13] American Library Association: *Administrative Works of Public Libraries and of College and University Libraries*. (A survey of Libraries in the United States, Vol. 1) Chicago, The Association, 1926, pp. 87-126.
[14] Bureau of Public Personnel Administration: *Proposed Classification and Compensation Plans for Library Positions*. Washington, D.C., The Bureau, 1927.
[15] American Library Association. Committee on the Classification of Library Personnel: *Budgets, Classification and Compensation Plans for University and College Libraries*. Chicago, The Association, 1929.
[16] American Library Association. Board on Salaries, Staff and Tenure: *Classification and Pay Plans for Municipal Public Libraries*. (Mimeographed) Chicago, The Association, 1939.
[17] American Library Association. Board on Salaries, Staff, and Tenure: *Classification and Pay Plans for Libraries in Institutions of Higher Education*. (Mimeographed) Chicago, The Association, 1943. 3v.
[18] American Library Association. Board of Education for Librarianship: *Standards for Accreditation of Library Schools*. Chicago, The Association, July 13, 1951.
[19] American Library Association. Board of Education for Librarianship: *Standards for Library Science Programs in Teacher Education Institutions*. Chicago, The Association.
[20] American Library Association. Board on Personnel Administration: *Civil Service and Libraries*. Chicago, The Association, 1947.

Library Literature

IN THE MOOD of this seventh decade of our century I am compelled to begin apologetically: if our professional writings can be called "literature" they must certainly be exposed as inferior.

Orally and in writing we have been confronted by the charge that too many librarians want their name in print. They have nothing to say and they say it badly. And the inevitable conclusion is that we are an accessory profession with an unsubstantive, ancillary discipline. Possibly so.

There are several ways to test this contention. One way is comparatively. I assume that the alleged low level of the literature of librarianship has been determined not only by comparison with the world's great classics in imaginative writing but with the landmarks in the subject disciplines and the applied professions.

A librarian has probably never written anything approaching *Hamlet* or the *Iliad,* or *Paradise Lost* or *Tom Jones.* Even if Thales and the Grimm brothers are identified also as librarians it behooves us, in support of the thesis "librarians can't write," to look the other way when writers are cited who have at various times associated themselves professionally with libraries. It is undoubtedly true that no professional librarian *per se* and certainly no graduate of an accredited library school has yet earned the right to be ranked with the giants of creative literature.

Comparatively, however, how many doctors, lawyers, engineers or other professionals among contemporaries are placed with the current darlings of realism by sophisticated literary critics? A case in point is Doctor Archibald Joseph Cronin, British physician, whose library-approved novels like *The Citadel* and *The Keys of the Kingdom* earned him the reputation that one critic summed up as that of "the pale but legitimate inheritor of the Victorian storytellers. . . ." Although no careful analysis has been made of current literary figures who might even remotely be identified as librarians, it would not be hazardous to assume that our profession would be represented by imaginative creations comparable in esthetic position to that of Cronin and other doctors and lawyers who have turned to fiction or drama as either a sideline or another career.

If librarianship like other professions has contributed no big name to the contemporary "true to life" cult it has at least produced a wholesome and creative school of literary criticism. With the tip-toe, whispering diffidence of our bookmanship we have never openly recognized that our selection criteria could stand up against the standards of the critics who write for our sophisticated reviews. Indeed there have been apologists among us who have retreated in embarrassment at the discovery that previous editions of selection aids like the *Fiction Catalog* recommended unfavorable title ratios for paired authors like William Faulkner and Bess Streeter Aldrich.

As a member of the A.L.A. Intellectual Freedom Committee (for six years) I could not escape recurring reflections over our censorship offensive. So very often we were in the position of defending someone's *freedom to read* the ugly, the partially true. Our intellectual diet seemed unbalanced by any accompanying *responsibility to read*. On the firing line of literary evaluation the reverse of our professional contention that "censorship is negative, selection positive" was frequently demonstrated.

I recall, among many incidents, tracking down an allegation that a book reporting an illicit affair between a white doctor and a Negro women patient that ended in the former's murder had been suppressed in Florida libraries. When it turned out that the publisher had refused to sell the book in Florida and that despite this self-imposed censorship copies had been obtained through devious means by Florida librarians and placed on the open shelves as an evidence of our professional bill of rights, I felt little exaltation. By our solid selection criteria, and in the estimation of literary critics, this was an incredibly poor book. Yet the full force of our intellectual freedom effort went to encourage diverting public reading time from something better to this.

But the principal dissatisfaction with librarians' writing appears to be with our professional books and articles. It is possible that a considerable bulk of the current content of our library journals is not earth-shaking, not likely to expose any significant horizons nor even to restate with any new insight the obvious. Perhaps we like to read what we know or to be told how to proceed with minutiae. But are we more pedestrian than other professions, other disciplines?

From time to time we librarians browse and even concentrate in other subject literatures. Ever since my introduction by Miss Ulrich, as a member of the New York Public Library periodical room staff, to time and responsibility for reading in other places, other fields, I have been painfully aware of the morass of mediocrity in journal writing generally. With or without the background can you imagine a scientist or layman curling up in bed with a juicy red apple to read the amplification of a typical *Chem Abstract* contribution? Nor have I been able to discover among the examples of good writing gathered for college and school English anthologies many models drawn from current social science journals.

So there remains the final indictment of librarian writings: too little research. Ever since my own indoctrination as a student, beginning with the second year after the opening of Chicago's Graduate Library School, I have "identified" problems as passionately as the next librarian. And almost as vindictively I have declared "research is needed." Following which, I have relaxed as the nodding heads who heard me confirmed that I had established myself a member of the holy order of scientific investigation.

Possibly librarianship was a little late in the academic world to adopt the scientific method. But under GLS leadership our profession proceeded like good disciples to produce in three decades a sizeable (in proportion to our members) body of research literature. In recent years, even as remorse overcame snobbishness, I have been startled at the results when I asked my students in a "Literature of Librarianship" course to separate in the current output the "research" from the "non-research" (the sheep from the goats).

The professional status symbol in library science is now so absolute that a library school student will not even try a sonnet without keeping one eye cocked on the standard course in methods of investigation.

I try to make a case for the position that our library literature is vastly inferior to that of other disciplines, other professions. Perhaps that will be proved by the scientific method, by a correlation coefficient, by some variation of the Gallup poll. But I will be unconvinced as long as I have on my library shelves John David Marshall's three gracious anthologies of library literature.[1] Among the inclusions are some that will meet the most exacting measures of research advocates.

Yet the hope for our library literature is that we have not abandoned the other, the non-research. The Rhodes scholar, poet, novelist Edward Weismiller has written recently ". . . the civilization Western man has known is dying of facts . . . we must go back to asking ourselves useless questions . . . who am I? why am I alive?"[2] For these questions the so-called substantive disciplines have no inclination. Each department of the academic curriculum is apparently bent on proving to God that the key to the kingdom is either chemistry, or anatomy, economics or some other specialization steeped in scientific research.

Possibly because librarianship serves all of the segments of knowledge equally and impartially it holds within its compass the only true approach to reality. Perhaps it is this lack of recognition of potential, this parrot-imitation of the parts by the whole that accounts for the biggest part of any deficiency in our library literature.

In any case one cannot read at least some of the essays that comprise our professional output without thanking God for librarians who deliberately chose in a world of specialisms to devote themselves to a study of the sum total.

---

[1] *Books, Libraries, Librarians, contributions to library literature; Of, By, and For Librarians, further contributions to library literature; An American Library History Reader, contributions to library literature.* Hamden, Connecticut, The Shoe String Press, Inc., 1955, 1960, 1961.
[2] "Fact and Fancy." *Atlantic Monthly,* Oct. 1963, p. 93-95.

On Reference Librarianship

A Frame of Reference: The 1952 Library Association Annual Lecture

I

IN LESS THAN SIX WEEKS my Fulbright term here will be over. The past seven months have been among the happiest of my life. I shall never forget your hospitality, your cordiality, your friendship. You have been good to us. Sincerely I say "Thank you," and may these exchanges flourish so that more of you will present us with an opportunity to reciprocate over there.

The purpose of the Fulbright exchange is to promote better mutual understanding between the United Kingdom and the United States. This year there are some sixty seniors in the professor category, and 170 juniors in the post-graduate student class, representing nearly every academic discipline and professional service, here from America to learn. In the United States there is a comparable British group. The exchange is a true one in every way. Each group is expected to live like the host people. We receive our income in pounds sterling; your group is receiving its money in American dollars. We have a ration book and are on the national health panel. In only one respect is there a greater limitation imposed on us than on you: no £25 travel allowance for the continent.

Two of us are librarians. Miss Helen Mahar of New York State is here to study library service to children; my major interest is reference. In the course of my study I have learned many things— some professional and some otherwise. This annual lecture, therefore, provides me with an opportunity to recite to you some of the library and other lessons I have learned during this session.

To begin with I have learned something about a way of life which

Reprinted from *Proceedings, Papers and Summaries of Discussion at the Bournemouth Conference, 1952*, by permission of the Library Association. (Louis Shores is the *first* librarian and the *first* American to be invited to give the Library Association's Annual Lecture. —JDM)

I have previously admired from afar— from India and in books.
That something is the graciousness, maturity, and self-discipline
that adds up in my appraisal book to the highest civilization history
has yet recorded.

I have learned also a great deal about professional relationships.
In Chaucer House it has been my good fortune to meet many of your
library leaders and to witness first-hand a demonstration of co-operative effort. In that connection your label "working party" is so
much more meaningful than our "committee." I am impressed with
the business-like manner in which you proceed with your agenda;
with the grace and elegance of your conferences. But above all I
have glowed in the warm fellowship of Chaucer House.

I wonder if you know what your Chaucer House means to
librarians all over the world. Before I experienced it myself I heard
American, Canadian, Australian, and Indian librarians speak of
Chaucer House much as the Mohammedan speaks of Mecca. This
was subsequently confirmed on the continent of Europe. Out of these
comments grew the conviction that the supreme debt a librarian
owed to his profession was to visit Chaucer House before he died.

There is no doubt that Chaucer House has become the symbol of
world librarianship. Great movements stem from the intangibles of
personal relationships. At Chaucer House I have experienced something akin to a professional rebirth. It is difficult to put into words
just what has caused that, but perhaps I can re-create some of the
memories that will give me nostalgia for the rest of my life.

What is Chaucer House? For me it is your Executive Secretary
graciously presiding at the noon-day meal to which librarians from
all over Britain and the world come daily to promote librarianship.
It is Henrik Jones, patient, kindly and considerate to every one,
amazing me constantly with his rich reference service to the profession. It is the informal discussions of librarians, the triangular
debates among Mr. Stewart, Mr. Palmer, and Mr. Wells ranging
in scope, as Mr. Welsford once observed, from the Ranganathian
to the Rabelaisian. It is Manchester in the person of Mr. Charles
Nowell and others, discussing life, letters and Londoners, and
protesting that the postal address of Manchester City Library is not
Salford 2. It is Mr. Berwick Sayers, Mr. Irwin, Mr. Hill, Mr.

Munford, Mr. Oldman, Mr. Francis and very many others who from time to time join the "regulars" and contribute to the table-talk that is at one moment profound and at the next "folksy." It is the good cheer of the staff Christmas party with your President and his charming wife, the youngest and happiest of all. It is morning coffee and afternoon tea, a custom I shall most certainly introduce at home.

And it is the more serious and formal functions: the meetings of Council, a lesson in parliamentary procedure as well as in professional thinking. It is the notable recognition to the Duke of Edinburgh for his service as President of the Library Association, with cheering University of London students outside the Council Chamber. It is an informal luncheon for the Librarian of Congress, infinite in its contribution to mutual understanding. It is all these things we cannot measure in pounds and shillings that we charge to public relations. But to me it is the very body and soul of librarianship.

I hope we can acquire more of this spirit of librarianship in America. I hope you will never let it get away from you under the guise of economy of time and money. May Chaucer House continue ever as a beacon light for all of us who devote our lives to library service everywhere in the world.

II

I am conscious of the deep honour implied in the privilege of delivering the Library Association's Annual Lecture. What makes me especially humble on this occasion is the realization that this is your 75th birthday, an anniversary our American Library Association observed last year. As I approached my effort I prayed for only one achievement, that I might be another link in the bond that has tied librarians together across a wide ocean, individually, through their libraries, and through the two national associations.

With this in mind I have turned back the pages of our proceedings and journals in both associations. In this bit of investigation I have been aided by Henrik Jones at Chaucer House and by Dave Clift, the Executive Secretary of the A.L.A., and his associate, Miss Anita Hostetter.

To the first A.L.A. conference held in Philadelphia, October 1876, Mr. James Yates, librarian of the Free Public Library of Leeds, came as a delegate and was elected a vice-president of the meeting. Last October I bade *bon voyage* to Mr. F. G. B. Hutchings, the present librarian of Leeds, as he flew to Philadelphia for our 75th anniversary. To my amazement, the American librarian assigned to meet him at the New York airport was my regular room-mate at A.L.A. conferences, Wayne Shirley, who immediately wrote me, and I quote with no intention to disturb his modesty, "If Mr. Hutchings is representative of British librarians there is no doubt that the calibre of their professional people is higher than ours."

In September 1877, twenty-one American librarians attended the organization and first meeting of the Library Association of the United Kingdom. John Winter Jones, then chief librarian of the British Museum, in his presidential inaugural address graciously gave credit to American librarians for the idea of holding a conference. But a greater debt to the Library Association was acknowledged for the A.L.A. by George B. Utley in his book *Fifty years of the American Library Association* when he wrote, "One of the pleasantest and most gratifying features of its (the A.L.A.'s) half-century of activity is the close and cordial relationship which American librarians have had throughout the years with their fellow workers in the British Isles, which has resulted not only in many warm personal friendships but also in a number of important co-operative international enterprises."

To enumerate all of our associations would consume most of this Annual Lecture; but since this is a birthday party, I should like to mention a few, if you will forgive me for any unintentional omissions.

In 1913, at Kaaterskill, N.Y. (before my professional time I willingly admit) Mr. L. Stanley Jast addressed a general session of the A.L.A. on *Present conditions and tendencies of library work in Great Britain*. Then, coming down to my professional life (although I was not in attendance at that particular conference) Henry Guppy addressed a general session of the A.L.A.'s 50th anniversary conference in Atlantic City on *The Power of personality*. Other delegates at that conference were R. Farquharson Sharp, Walter Powell,

Septimus Pitt, and Ernest A. Savage. Delegates nominated by the
Carnegie United Kingdom Trust included Miss A. S. Cooke, Charles
Nowell, Richard Wright, F. J. Peplow, R. J. Gourley, The Earl of
Elgin, and Thomas Gorrie.

In 1932 at New Orleans, Lt.-Col. John Malcolm Mitchell, your
president that year, addressed our general session on *The Library
movement in Great Britain* and spoke informally at the Adult Education Round Table. The following year Arundell Esdaile came to
Chicago to address our general session on *The Social responsibility
of the modern library* and our periodicals section on *Periodicals
in Great Britain*. Also at that session were John D. Cowley, who
spoke to our County Libraries Section, and Angus Fletcher, director
of the British Library of Information in New York.

In 1934 at Montreal, your distinguished delegation to the A.L.A.
Conference included H. Idris Bell, R. J. Gordon, Edgar Osborne,
James Ross, R. D. Hilton Smith, P. S. J. Welsford and John A.
Wilks. The A.L.A. conference in New York in 1937 was honoured
by the presence of Henry A. Sharp, and the meeting in Boston of
1941 welcomed Herbert Maurice Cashmore who addressed our gen-
eral session on the subject of *British library service in war time*.
When the A.L.A. resumed its annual conferences in Buffalo after
the war in 1946, Edward Sydney, addressed a general session on
Libraries in a new world. It was a pleasure to have Mr. J. H. P.
Pafford, Goldsmiths' Librarian, University of London, present at
our 1947 San Francisco meeting.

In addition to these contributions to our annual conferences we
have been favoured by out-of-conference visits by British librarians.
The visit of Sir John Forsdyke and Dr. Henry Thomas of the British
Museum early in 1945 and the lectures at library schools by Lionel
McColvin of Westminster, as well as his visits to our libraries, are all
vividly remembered.

Your President, himself, has told me that the greatest compliment
he received in America was from a truck driver in Kansas City who
said to him: "For a foreigner you've certainly learned to speak
English very rapidly."

I shall not undertake to name all of the American librarians who

have visited here. Perhaps this short recollection will be representative. R. R. Bowker, publisher of the *Library Journal,* attended the
Cambridge meeting in 1882. The first president of the A.L.A. and
one of our most distinguished U.S. historians, Justin Winsor, was
present at your Reading meeting. When the L.A. sponsored the first
International Conference of Librarians in 1897 in London, we sent
94 American librarians. To Glasgow in 1907 we sent one of our
most distinguished cataloguers, J. M. C. Hanson, and to the Jubilee
in 1927 at Edinburgh there went no less than 82 American librarians, among whom were six former A.L.A. presidents, and the
Executive Secretary, designated as official delegates. One result of
this conference was the organization of the International Library
and Bibliographical Committee.

Since the war, the visitors have included Luther Evans, Ralph
Ulveling, A. M. Lydenburg, Charles David, Flora Ludington, Milton
Lord, Ralph Munn and many others. But it should not be assumed
that the visitors to each country have been confined to those who
had already reached some degree of eminence.

Actually some 40 to 50 librarians in earlier stages of their careers
have travelled in each direction in the post-war period alone.

Among the joint projects of our two Associations these have
certainly had lasting benefits: *Poole's index to periodical literature*
covering the period from 1802-81; the 1908 *Cataloguing rules for
author and title entries,* compiled by committees of the two
associations.

During World War II, the two associations worked side by side.
In 1942 the Library Association invited American and Canadian
librarians serving in the armed forces to make themselves known to
British librarians and to the Association Headquarters. The A.L.A.
sponsored British Book Week, 24th-30th October, 1943, and the following year the A.L.A. Council approved distribution to Amercian
librarians of a booklist interpreting Britain. The list, recommended
jointly by the British Council, National Book Council, and Library
Association, was published in 1946 by the A.L.A. under the title
British civilization and institutions.

This is by no means a complete catalogue of our co-operative
efforts. It is sufficient to show, however, that we are not strangers

to each other, and that perhaps librarians are in the vanguard of promoting understanding among the English-speaking peoples of the world.

III

For your fifth Annual Lecture you have asked me to address you on the subject of my major interest. Because I was curious about these annual lectures I investigated their origin and history. Mr. J. D. Stewart in a letter to your Council in April, 1946, suggested the inauguration of a series "similar to those delivered as memorials to some societies such as the Royal Society, Royal College of Surgeons." I have noted with interest, although you may receive this information with alarm, that these lectures have steadily increased in length. The first Annual Lecture in 1948 contained 2,240 words; the second 3,584; the third 4,480; and the fourth just over 5,000. You may be relieved to know that the fifth will reverse the trend.

IV

In physics, the term *frame of reference* is defined as "an arbitrary set of axes . . . with reference to which physical laws are formulated."[1] The thesis of this lecture is that the present, ideological conflict between east and west is presenting librarianship with a set of axes which calls for an augmented concept of the library's information function. Under this new concept Reference is tending to be redefined as the *promotion of free inquiry*.

Now the implications of such a definition can be important not only for reference service and librarianship but for the whole trend of the conflict that now confronts mankind. We of the Western World hold free inquiry to be one cornerstone of our way of life. Inherent in our concept of progress is the belief that uncensored and unrestrained investigation leads inevitably to truth. The Reference Service of any library is the critical point at which this concept is likely to be tested. Through their information facilities libraries of the world may win the decisive battle for the freedoms we claim as our heritage.

[1] For notes, see page 98.

The obstacles to free inquiry are both material and spiritual. In all of our English-speaking nations, despite the greatest wealth in the world, there are not sufficient pounds and dollars to provide the necessary library facilities. Nor has the science of librarianship reached the level of adequacy demanded by the accelerated complexity of human existence. Even more serious than either of these two material limitations is the restriction imposed by the fear and threat of ideological warfare. Because of the intense conflict between at least two of man's theories of life, free inquiry faces a menace of censorship more subtle than any comparable obstacle that has ever been placed against the human mind in its search for the truth.

Free inquiry is handicapped no little by material limitation. In the U.S. there are still some 50 million people without free access to reference materials. My own state of Florida, glamorous with the ultimate in amusements, denies free public library service to 99 per cent of its rural folk by providing not a single county library in all of its 67 counties. This is not said boastfully but with some effort to temper the overseas belief that America and money are synonymous terms.

By comparison the picture in the United Kingdom is much better. If the statistics I have are up-to-date, your county libraries serve about 19 million people; and there is not a single county in all of the United Kingdom without some free library facilities.[2] Proximity to other centres and growing generosity in accepting library tickets from any public library are increasing the availability of information to all of the people. Despite your admirable progress, however, I have no doubt that the Library Association here would agree with the A.L.A. there that the professional objective of providing the best books for the greatest number at the least cost is still short of attainment.

Free inquiry depends first of all, therefore, upon the availability of library materials. Unavailability of even a single medium of communication needed by any inquirer is an obstacle to free inquiry imposed by the limitation of material resources. These media of communication comprise all of the records of man: not only books, but films and recordings, picture and museum objects and the whole gamut of what we nowadays call audio-visual materials. The first requirement of free inquiry, therefore, is the existence within a reasonable distance of all the records of mankind. This condition you in the United Kingdom have approached more clearly than we in the United States.

The second condition for free inquiry, or adequate reference, is accessibility. Toward the perfection of this feature, librarianship strives unceasingly and with increasing awareness of complexities. Reference and bibliography together have sought to establish such control over the increasing flow of records as to create instant access to materials and information.

But to date, the race between dissemination and production has been lost by library science to the social and natural sciences. For all of our significant technical strides in cataloguing and classification, in indexing and abstracting, in all of the devices that lead to what we now call bibliographic control, we have not succeeded in disseminating information rapidly enough for the needs of either research or education.

V

Reference responsibility to research is particularly critical today. It has been estimated "that about a million useful scientific articles are published yearly in some 50,000 scientific journals and yet about half of these are never indexed or abstracted anywhere. To all intents and purposes half a million articles are lost and the research might just as well not have been done. . . ."

Even if most of these articles are abstracted *eventually*, the fact remains that the object of "lessening the time interval between a discovery in the laboratory and its application in production" [3] has been seriously thwarted. This fact can be critical in the national drive to increase production. It may well be disastrous in the international armament race. Here is a real research challenge to reference: to find some way greatly to accelerate the rate of disseminating information to the points of imperative need.

It is not a challenge to be met by scattered individualized information services. It requires a bold type of co-operative reference effort. The genesis of that effort is already evident in several significant co-operative ventures.

In this newer capacity reference adds to its present functions—
answering questions, compiling bibliographies, organizing and
administering reference collections—such activities as abstracting,
indexing, and even investigating in subject fields. In this process
reference may yet lead to new responsibilities which in turn will
change the position of the reference librarian from his present
status of *aid* to *full partner* in research. This becomes particularly
the case where the librarian in the special library has double preparation in both the subject and the professional field.

Without this double preparation the whole mission of reference
aid to research is defeated. The subject specialist without professional library preparation retards dissemination through inept
handling of sources. The librarian without subject background delays
production through inadequate understanding of the problems.
Intelligence suggests there is no either-or; it must be both. The
question as to which is more important or should come first seems
irrelevant. Trends in university and professional library education
indicate clearly a new generation of reference workers prepared
concurrently in professional and subject matter. Such preparation is
manifest in the Library Association examinations.[4]

Out of such preparation really significant reference performance
is proceeding. One manifestation is the union catalogue, an idea in
which British librarianship has pioneered. The whole concept of the
National Central Library plan transcends our own union catalogue
developments. As William Warner Bishop conceded [5] the advantage
of your N.C.L. union catalogue over our L.C. union catalogue lies in
the fact that yours is truly national and ours is not. Behind your
N.C.L. union catalogue is the support of the London Boroughs'
co-operative buying and subject specialization programmes as well
as the union efforts of the other regions. In this N.C.L. enterprise is
the germ of a reference potential for research such as has only begun
to be utilized.

Another significant reference service is the *British National
Bibliography*. Reference appreciation for the weekly and cumulated
comprehensive and descriptive lists of British publications is enthusiastic on both sides of the Atlantic. But what is sometimes
overlooked is the tremendous classification service offered by the

B.N.B. Since classification is the key to research reference, and since Decimal Classification has at least the advantages of universality and mnemonics over all other schemes, the activation of an agency which currently augments the code for classifiers is a boon to reference of inestimable value.

A third significant factor is the co-operative efforts of the special technical libraries and information bureaux. In this movement Aslib and the D.S.I.R. have displayed creative leadership. The *Report on technical information services*[6] presents evidence of an advanced type of reference thinking in the area of applied scientific research. Aslib is contributing strategically also with a co-operative reference service especially for small industry. It is, besides, undertaking some needed indexing of university theses and unpublished translations in the Commonwealth, micro-filming of war-time enemy technical journals, and orientating of professionally untrained information officers. Its four periodical publications promote the development of reference technique.

In all of this co-operative reference effort, however, no one factor is as important as personnel. The Library Association, through its single function of examining and chartering librarians, has introduced into reference service individuals of such professional calibre as to provide capable allies for the subject specialists in their mutual effort to extend the frontiers of knowledge. Through these individuals and with the co-operative support of the Association's membership, union catalogues, indexing, abstracting, bibliograhpic, and documentary reproduction projects have been consumated.

But of especial portent for the future of reference is the work of two Library Association bodies. One of these, the Reference and Special Libraries Section, has already in its first year of existence contributed to professional education, and to acquisition and organization of reference sources. The other, the Working Party on Library and Information Services, has presented an interim report on co-operative acquisition and dissemination that may well be a milestone for research everywhere.[7] Under this scheme it is aimed to assist scientific, technical and humanistic research and development by making available to all who require them any and all library materials. To accomplish this task of providing complete coverage,

a plan for division of specializations among regional reference and
national special libraries to support the British Museum and the
National Libraries of Scotland and Wales is full of possibilities. The
plan is a logical development of the regional co-operation already in
practice, and it offers a basis for a clearing house of abstracting,
indexing, bibliographic, and photo-reproduction services.

Micro-reproduction is certainly revolutionizing the reference
process. As micro-texts become the medium for an ever greater
portion of our research literature, the time may soon come when
all libraries will acquire complete collections of everything their
patrons need. This should not be discounted as a possibility in speeding up reference aid to research, and Fremont Rider's thoughtful
little book[8] is commended for re-reading in this connection.

And since this is an age of speculation, one other technical
development seems promising for reference. During World War II
the air forces depended upon a television-like device called *facsimile*
for instant transmission of weather maps, and other visual materials.
Perhaps it is not beyond the limits of the probable to describe a
network of reference agencies in libraries transmitting instantly over
facsimile facilities the latest laboratory discovery for application to
production, thus virtually eliminating the delay interval between
discovery and application.

VI

Informational service to education, largely the responsibility of
public libraries for the out-of-school population and of college and
school libraries for the in-school students, is basic to the whole process of free inquiry. By means of lists, reading guidance and answers
to inquiries, we have contributed significantly to keeping the people
informed. I have in a recent article in the *Saturday Review*[9] indicated
by broad categories what the American people wanted to investigate
during 1951 in eight of our leading public libraries. The variety of
the people's inquiries, the emphasis on such major public issues as
Korea, the United Nations, graft and corruption in politics, taxes and
prices, as well as on such curiosities as five-letter words for crossword puzzles and "how to cook a raccoon" show that no limitations
were placed on free inquiry by our American reference departments.

Judging by my examination of questions asked in more than a score of British public libraries I have visited thus far, I should say, if anything, you are even more liberal in your acceptance of inquiries from the public. I am particularly struck by the fact that in so many localities the public library is accepted as the official information agency and indeed the public librarian himself is designated by the government as the Public Information Officer.

If I cite an individual public library it is by no means my intention to imply that the service is unique or even best performed there. It so happens that I first met the confidential citizen's advisory service in the Luton Public Library. There I found not only a separate room—separate from the general reference service— but strategically located so as to be both accessible from the side street and detached from public interruptions. There I found a most advanced type of reference service dealing with many of the confidential and personal problems that some of our professional literature insists is not the province of reference.

Since I use no names I hope I break no confidences by reading from my notes some of the questions handled in that reference service:

1. Where can I get my deaf aid repaired?
2. Can landlady turn out daughter if mother dies?
3. How can I get a housekeeper's job?
4. Where is there a home for an old man?
5. Some one to do contract ploughing.

You may side with what has been called the close constructionist theory of reference work which holds "that the prime duty of a library is not to find answers but to organize its material effectively and teach patrons to help themselves."[10] If you do, then perhaps this citizen's advisory service which you pioneered during World War II will not appeal to you.

Or you may care to re-read W. S. Learned's words in the *American public library and the diffusion of knowledge:*[11]

"Strong tendencies now apparent in many progressive cities indicate the ultimate development in most communities of an institution where a great range of useful information available in print may be secured authoritatively and quickly.

It will be a center as familiar to every inhabitant as the local post office and as inevitably patronized. It will constitute the central intelligence service of the town. . . .

"The conspicuous and indispensable feature of such an institution . . . is a well-specialized service. . . . The purpose . . . is first to overcome the reluctance people have to seeking information. . . . This is a task for an expert possessing personal tact, intellectual sympathies and appreciation, a thorough knowledge of a certain field of material. . . ."

In that case you will see in this citizen's advisory service, stimulated by World War II, the embryo of a great offensive weapon for World War III, whether that war simmers warm as now or boils hot later.

Make no mistake. The Russians are already in possession of this weapon. They have given a dangerous twist to the library's function of reference. With a skill that is more commendable than its purpose, Russian reference service in unbelievable strength is disseminating, before as well as behind the iron curtain, "loaded" information. It is informing the people in such a way that the west must look evil and the east good. To Russian librarianship, reference has become not the process of free inquiry but the medium of indoctrination. And because there are no compunctions there about how much the reference worker shall do for the inquirer, a thorough job of disseminating communist doctrine is under way all over the world.

Not so in our libraries. Despite the tendency of our slightly left-of-centre press, both here and in America, to publicize the isolated cases of library censorship and to ignore the overwhelming library commitment to free inquiry through its "Bill of Rights," our libraries in the English-speaking world are providing information on both sides of debatable issues. I have yet to discover a single public or college library in the United States or in the United Kingdom that does not have at least one copy of Karl Marx's *Das Kapital*. There is besides, a considerable collection of communistic and Soviet literature available to patrons in these libraries. No effort is made in our reference departments, to my knowledge, to prevent free inquiry into the Soviet way of life. Do the libraries of the U.S.S.R. reciprocate on the American and British way of life? As Soviet propaganda intensifies everywhere, pressure may increase in our communities to "load" information on our side. I have faith in our commitment to free inquiry. I believe we will continue through our reference agencies to make available all of the information because that has been our ultimate strength in these world conflicts.

The menace to free inquiry is more in the tendency of our people to read, or listen to, or look at media of communication that favour one side, exclusively. Since the beginning of my residence here last September I have sought to read Tory and Labour publications equally. I take no sides in the domestic issues. I merely note the fact that, even in the short term of my residence, I can tell before reading its articles what position the *New Statesman* will take on an international issue involving the U.S.S.R. and the U.S.A. I dare say I can make a similar prediction on the *Spectator* or the *Economist*. We can, of course, match that type of editorializing in the United States. Just as some of your periodicals fear Britain may become the 49th state, our Chicago *Tribune* and other isolationist publications have long contended the United States is already only another British colony.

The point is that in our way of life there is always an opposition. Your organic law and ours, which we inherited from you, guarantee the rights of an opposition press. That is our strength.

The danger to that strength is as much within as without. There is a tendency among us to read and view and listen to only that which supports our position. We tend to subscribe to the *New Statesman* and to read the newspapers and books that support that position, exclusively; or to read the *Spectator* and everything on that side. In either case we grow increasingly intolerant of the opposition and approach a mental stage that is alarmingly totalitarian.

From the standpoint of free inquiry, our press and other media of communication need augmentation. National intelligence requires clearing houses of information for all of the people. Such clearing houses must do more than merely subscribe to both the *New Statesman* and the *Spectator*. These clearing houses must somehow provide an information service that will foster free inquiry on public issues. Reference must therefore envisage more than passive reception of enquiries; it must anticipate questions the people will ask about all sorts of issues. It must be as purposeful in balancing the inquirer's investigations as the totalitarian reference service is in unbalancing them.

That I consider the high educational mission of our free public library. It must not only provide an opportunity for the perpetual reader of the *New Statesman* to read the *Economist* and *vice versa*, but it must somehow stimulate a desire upon the part of all our people to understand both sides of public issues. It must support the schools and colleges in developing a national mind that will understand life is not a series of blacks and whites, but greys, and that calamities occur at least as often from human inadequacies as from human villainies. That kind of national mind the British people have, in my opinion, to a greater degree than any peoples I know on this earth. And I attribute that largely to the longest unbroken tradition of free inquiry history has yet recorded.

In the midst of man's mightiest conflict, at the height of his greatest moral struggle, when he appears nearest to materialistic commitment, I have every hope he will turn from force to truth for his decision. The way to truth is free inquiry. Over that way the free public library through its reference service stands guard. It is my deepest professional hope that you and I and our colleagues all over the world will rise to the keenest challenge and opportunity ever presented to a single occupation, and help save mankind from disaster by keeping the roads of free inquiry open all over the world.

---

[1] *Webster's New International Dictionary*, 1946, p. 1001.
[2] Munford, W. A. *Penny Rate.* 1951. p. 121.
[3] Report on technical information services. *Journal of Documentation.* June, 1951. vol. 7, p. 95 (92-112).
[4] *Students' Handbook.* 1952.
[5] Bishop, W. W. Union catalogs. *Library Quarterly*, 1937. vol. 7, p. 36-49.
[6] *Op. cit.*
[7] *The Co-operative Provision of Books, Periodicals and Related Material.* Library Association, 1949, 5 p.
[8] Rider, Fremont. *The Scholar and the Future of the Research Library.* New York, Hadham Press, 1944, 236 p.
[9] "What Americans Wanted to Know in 1951," 9th February, 1952. vol. 35, p. 36-39.
[10] Wyer J. I. *Reference Work*, A.L.A., 1930, p. 6-8.
[11] Harcourt, 1924, p. 12-14.

The Practice of Reference

EVERY FRIDAY NIGHT over a coast-to-coast hookup a popular radio program exploits America's fundamental reference interest. The success of "Information Please" indicates the importance of questions and answers to our people and suggests the potential power of reference work once it is harnessed to the nation's needs and interests. Nothing short of an insatiable curiosity on an infinite number of subjects can account for the growing number of quiz programs and the consistent demand for such services as the Frederick Haskin Bureau disseminates through our daily newspapers.

That this national delight in questions and answers, the backbone of all reference and research, has been stimulated by world developments and by an increasing sociological interest at home seems certain. At the bottom of this national curiosity about things is concern about our society and where we are headed in this mighty world revolution now under way. Social surveys, educational investigations, governmental hearings all involve the marshaling of facts before an objective judgment can be rendered. It is only natural therefore that this constant search for information should influence the less serious pursuits of our leisure and result in radio quiz programs, movie contests, and newspaper crossword puzzles all of which demand exacting reference service. And when to all this is added the grave business of war with its army of research workers needed to track down facts for defense, the responsibility of our reference calling appalls us.

There can be no question that the changes in our educational system, our social order, our civilization are steadily thrusting the reference worker into the class of most highly demanded and skilled workers. The only question is whether we who practice the craft of

Reprinted from *College and Research Libraries*, 3: 9-17, December, 1941, by permission of the publisher.

reference are ready for the new demands to be made of us. For us the time has come to decide whether we will take our place among the skilled technicians now keenly sought by our government as well as by private agencies, or whether we will see a new army of workers developed outside of our library profession.

Reference work as we have heretofore conceived it has probably most succinctly been defined by Richardson (26)* as "the finding of books and the finding of facts." But even Richardson saw the broad responsibilities which this simple statement implied — mastery of sources, understanding of people for whom information from these sources was to be interpreted, and ability to teach others to help themselves. To him reference work was something very much like good teaching, only definitely superior. He saw in reference the foundation of good research. And so the reference librarian to him in those days was a cross between a good reseach worker and a good teacher, a cross which is most often sought for in school and college faculties today.

Strangely enough, ever since Richardson's formulation of reference philosophy, American college and school teaching has been approaching his ideal of good reference service. Gradually we have seen conventional classrooms give way to a sort of glorified reference procedure variously called honors reading, autonomous courses, independent study with the teacher steadily forced to take on the skills of the reference librarian. In 1934 I described what I then discerned as such a development, and several colleges, notably St. John's at Annapolis, have all but become "Library Arts Colleges."

What is more, certain advanced experiments have already been described in our professional and in educational literature which show clearly how close to good reference work the newest education is becoming. One institution is contemplating release of its instructors from part of their teaching duties so that they may give reference service in the library.

Now if educators on their side have been approaching the reference concept in their teaching procedures, what have we as reference librarians been doing? For the most part I believe we have been

---

* Numbers in parenthesis refer to libraries and readings at the end of the article.

concentrating on the refinement of our techniques. I think many of us have been doing so with an awareness of the changing educational demands and our own probable new role. But I believe for the most part we have been more concerned with the means than with the possible new ends of reference work.

Partly to check this assumption and partly to discover some of the more promising aspects of reference practice in American libraries today, Sarah H. Griffiths, chairman of the Reference Section, and I addressed a joint informal letter to a selected group of reference librarians in college and public libraries, in which we asked for "detailed description of projects or policies which contribute to efficient reference service." And we added, "Of necessity this request is somewhat general because we do not wish in any way to shut out devices, techniques, or procedures that might appear to be too small or unrelated. We wish to emphasize that anything done in your reference department, large or small, that you think other reference workers would like to know about should be included and described in your own way.

"As specific as we can be, we would like to have from you:

1. A detailed description of a favorite project that has stood the test of time and has been refined until it is in good order, or
2. A policy that tends to strengthen the department and to bind the staff into a unit."

Of course we realized that this was not one of those scientific inquisitions for which research in the social sciences has become justly famous, and in which you mark one thing with an "X," a second thing with a check, and a third thing with a zero, and come out with a formula answer that delights the investigator and flabbergasts the practitioner. But we did realize also that in the present under-developed stage of reference literature any attempt to formalize answers in advance would defeat our purpose to obtain statements of reference practice as the reference practitioner of today would describe these practices.

Although the twenty-two libraries that replied (seventeen public, five university) do not represent a large number, they do cover a wide enough range in size and geographical location to provide a sample. And as a result of this preliminary query it is now possible to construct a more precise instrument for investigating reference practice in the majority of American libraries.

The nature of this instrument is suggested by the various aspects of current reference practice into which the descriptions of projects and statements of policies included in the twenty-two letters can be organized. Its three main divisions would deal with,

I. Sources, their acquisition, organization, and interpretation
II. Personnel, its in-training and in-service preparation
III. Services, including fact finding, research, instructional, and publicity

The first observation is the ever-widening concept of what a reference source is. Time was when the four thousand titles in Mudge or the smaller collection in Kroger were looked upon as the legitimate tools of those real reference craftsmen who always found their answers. To the public, "reference" has always meant something that could not be taken out of the library. More usually we have recognized certain types of sources—dictionaries, encyclopedias, yearbooks, handbooks, directories, atlases, serials, indexes, and bibliographies—as pure reference books. Today even this concept has been broadened to include a great variety of ephemeral and serial printed matter, and the more revolutionary audio-visual aids, from pictures and museum objects to films and radio recordings.

But as in the past, certain classes of reference sources are receiving particular attention because of their frequent and characteristic use for answering questions. Chief among these collections of sources are the so-called "quick reference" tools usually placed behind the reference desk or in proximity to the information booth. These consist of yearbooks, directories, statistical and financial services, civil service manuals, receipt books, and of course, a copy of the *World Almanac*. Generally they are marked with a special symbol, red dot (8), blue star (22), red star, and may include genealogy and annuals. Current issues of the periodical indexes and especially heavily-used tools like Thomas' *Register* may be placed very near the desk (13).

Public libraries and especially technology departments cite national defense demands as especially responsible for renewed emphasis on trade catalog collections (6). As many as eighteen thousand trade catalogs are reported (7) and several carefully worked out systems for making them speedily available are described. These include Princeton filing (1) or shelving in specially built bookcases with narrow upright shelves, and detailed indexing by firm and subject, either separately in the reference department, or in the main catalog (1).

As in the past, city and telephone directories are useful reference sources. From 200 to 250 of each can be found in most public libraries (16) and they are kept up to date either by the local telephone company (6) or through exchange with other libraries (15).

Among the other common types of reference materials that have become "favorite projects" through careful organization are pictures (11), clippings (13), college catalogs (8), museum objects especially related to local history (1), maps (12), a reference document depository (6), and a film of the local newspaper files (8). One library boasts of twenty-nine thousand separate pictures subject-cataloged, and a collection of museum objects that includes hoop skirts and spinning wheels (11).

In the organization of these materials for reference, considerable ingenuity is evidenced. Most commonly this creative ability finds expression in numerous and varied homemade indexes for which a strong local need is felt. Representative are indexes to periodicals not indexed by Wilson (8), to the location of periodicals in the *Union List of Serials* (9), local events, clubs, facts, educational opportunities, newspapers (8), quotations not covered by standard reference tools (14), bibliographies on useful subjects (13), reference materials in nonreference sources (19) (21), features in local newspapers (16), costumes (8), Edgar A. Guest (8).

Some of these indexes are so ingenious in detail that some description is here warranted. A useful index file (13) has been made up of stray, curious, frequently sought, miscellaneous, and otherwise promising facts. A "Local Book of Current Information" (16) features among other things the salaries of city, county, and local, state and Federal government officials, members of various boards of trust, local budgets, and so forth. In the same library local newspaper features such as columns, commentaries, and even cartoons are indexed with date and paper indicated. An index to advertising pictures by subject as well as an index to other pictures by artist, nationality, title, and subject is notable. A systematic check of all local and state societies yields an up-to-date directory of officers, purposes, addresses nowhere else available (17).

Several libraries supplement printed sources such as the *Book Review Digest*, the *Bibliographic Index* (3) (21). Serials of local interest, unindexed books, and facts later than those found in the current *World Almanac* are indexed, and in the last two, placed in the books themselves (11). Likewise state documents are indexed for local references (15) and in the same library a glossary index by subject is maintained. By means of this latter index definitions of rare terms in obscure books and monographs are rescued from oblivion. A similar indexing enterprise undertakes to reveal obscure names of persons and places from out-of-the-way directories.

Other unusual indexing projects include that of "California Mineralogists' Reports Arranged by Name of Mine, District, County, Mineral" (6); secondhand catalogs which are clipped for local imprint items to answer questions about the value of patrons' attic discoveries (10); and city ordinances, another variation on the local indexing theme.

One of the most widely encouraged indexing projects is that to local educational opportunities (1). Two copies of each school catalog are received, one for clipping and pasting on the index card and the other for filing. Thus at a glance one can tell in how many places courses on a certain subject are offered.

Biographical indexing is quite common in spite of the two current biographical services now available, thanks to the recommendation of this Reference Section. For the most part these indexes emphasize individuals "not so great" or local in reputation. One library adds death dates with rather gruesome regularity to its various "who's who's" (10). Another library (17) questionnaired its own local authors and prepared a who's who pamphlet for general distribution.

Two university libraries report significant indexes to reference materials in nonreference sources. One of these indexing projects (19) is confined chiefly to periodicals and does a splendid job of discovering directories, glossaries, statistics frequently lost in bound volumes of journals.

The other project (21) is called a "Classed Catalog of Reference Materials" and is really an index to reference materials in all non-reference sources. It brings to light bibliographies in current serials, for instance, lists of theses, items in various monograph series and in stack materials. Catalog-approved analytic form is used for this indexing which thus becomes a sort of supplement to the *Bibliographic Index*.

In summary, reference librarians are continuing to make a major contribution to the selection and organization of reference sources that cannot but aid materially all of those agencies and individuals now hotly engaged in the pursuit of stray facts and serious investigations.

First among the policies that tend to strengthen the department and bind the staff in a unit are frequent round tables on new reference materials (3) and on questions and problems that have arisen in the daily tasks. Strong participation by staff members in the formulation of procedures and the planning of organization is noted. Unanswered or difficult to answer questions are discussed by the staff.

But most significant in the twenty-two letters is the trend in the direction of subject specialization. The anomaly of a walking encyclopedia equally equipped to aid research in all fields appears to be on the way out even in medium-sized public libraries. Departmentalizing and assigning of individual staff members for reference duty to the departments related to the individual's equipment (3) are accepted policy in public libraries. And in university libraries the tendency is to organize reference service by curriculum and research fields (22).

Strongly stressed by several reference librarians is the need for closer cooperation with the catalog department. Too often in the opinion of one (2) the reference librarian is inadequately trained in cataloging. "My experience has been that too many library school graduates think they want to do reference work and too few have sufficient background, the ability to organize material, or sufficient knowledge of cataloging . . . many of them can search out information, but few of them seem able to make records that others can use. Somewhere along the line the library schools (familiar professional goats) have failed to impress their graduates with the importance of the fundamentals of cataloging and many files are suffering from this defect."

Somewhat to offset this defect this correspondent continues, "we are trying here to have frequent short staff meetings of all those who do reference work . . . our plan is to pool information, to call attention to obscure sources, to examine all new books, both reference and circulation, to keep a record of questions not answered satisfactorily, and to post frequently on the staff bulletin board new subjects added to the catalog and to the vertical file."

Another reference head requires all of her staff members to divide their time equally between the two departments (20). As she puts it, "a knowledge of the catalog is extremely valuable to readers. A knowledge of the point of view of readers seeking information is also of value to the catalogers in their work." Since an important segment of reference work in this library concerns itself with information about books, this cataloging-reference work combination provides the reference worker with good in-service bibliographic training.

Although the increasing emphasis on bibliographic training and subject background suggests increasing awareness of the reference worker's research responsibilities no corresponding intimations of impending greater teaching responsibilities is evidenced. True, university libraries are continuing variations of their freshman courses and some advanced bibliographic units for graduate students and teachers, but neither university nor public reference workers have yet succeeded in crossing the bridge that separates reference service from classroom teaching. The nearest thing to it reported is a high school cooperation plan (4).

What then are the services that American reference librarians are performing? Aside from the time devoted to the organization of materials and personnel for these services, answering questions and promoting use constitute the principal functions. Fact finding, research, instruction, and publicity are the big four in the reference librarian's daily calendar of duties.

Fact finding questions are usually defined as those that can be answered quickly by one specific fact, such as the population of a city, the name of a place, the birth date of a person, etc. In some libraries these "short order" reference questions are handled mostly in the circulation department (11) and turned over to the reference department only if they require more than ten minutes search.

If questions are not immediately answerable most reference procedures call for recording of the question on a form slip with the reader's name and the time wanted. Answers are promised later and if the patron has a phone he is called (13). While the question is in the process of being answered it is kept in a visible file (11) or in a card quick-reference file (8). As soon as the answer is found the reader is notified and the record filed for future reference if the question is one which suggests future value (16). One reference librarian has even suggested that these cards containing answers be filed in the main catalog under subject (25).

If the assistant of whom the question was asked is unable to find the answer, he cites the sources consulted, initials the card, and hands it to the head of the department who then either assigns it to other assistants in succession until the answer is found or undertakes it himself. Failure to discover a satisfactory answer leads to appeals for outside help from authorities locally by telephone and out of town by mail (8). Continued failure results in submission to the fugitives department of the *Wilson Library Bulletin*.

A somewhat different procedure is followed with research questions. The distinction between reference and research is probably not clear-cut, although there is a vague feeling that the former is popular and the latter scholarly. From the standpoint of the reference worker, research questions are the type that cannot be answered with a simple fact. They involve an unlimited amount of material and time and are never liquidated although they may be satisfactorily disposed of for the purposes of the inquirer.

Various policies and procedures have been formulated by refer-

ence departments. A psychologically simple and direct policy has
been adopted by one department (14), "Get something into the
inquirer's hands at once . . . even if it does not contain the full
answer. This serves to occupy him and take him away from the
information desk to a chair, giving the librarian a chance to collect
pertinent data for him and to take care of other patrons."

Another department (10) has worked out an ingenious device
for informing the reader who constantly leaves his seat, when his
material is ready. "Cards fastened with Scotch tape to the upright
section of a metal book end" advise the reader to inquire at the
information desk for the answer to his reference question.

As for the actual searching techniques involved in locating
answers and materials no department seems to have developed any
such step by step routine as Carter Alexander has suggested (23).
Possibly this is considered too elementary for a library school
graduate who is at least expected to know basic reference materials
well enough to relate sources to questions instantly. Two basic
principles, however, well stated by Bagley (24) are generally
accepted as necessary in handling reference questions: (a) Work
from the simple to the complex, searching first in the more obvious,
popular sources and last in the specialized out-of-the-way tools, and
(b) Proceed from the broad to the specific, beginning with the general background tool rather than with the detailed monograph.

In the course of answering questions some instruction in the use
of the catalog and periodical indexes is generally given, but as one
public library put it "no systematic instruction is given . . . students
are encouraged to do their own research" (13).

Two instructional projects, however, are particularly worthy of
note. One is a systematic cooperative scheme developed with the high
school (4). The chief features are a schedule worked out with the
teachers to prevent overcrowding of the public library reading room,
cooperation in working out assignments, and staggered use of
various reference materials. To accomplish this the reference
librarian visits the high school daily to secure and discuss assignments and to provide teachers with lists of reserves and other related
materials. The last three or four years of current magazines are kept

in the reference room and other adjustments in the organization of the collection are made as dictated by the seasonal demands.

The other project is a library instructional program carried on for the nurses in the hospitals of the city (16). With some variation this program has been offered to other groups.

One other project which provides educational cooperation although it is not direct instruction is service to teachers and others carrying graduate work and writing a thesis or dissertation (1). From the time the candidate's thesis subject is known, the library files a card and begins to accumulate citations to all materials in the library bearing on the problem. These materials are gathered and placed at the candidate's desk upon request, where they remain until the degree has been awarded.

The most popular methods of acquainting readers with available reference services and materials is through the media of exhibits, newspapers, organizations, and reports.

Significant exhibits in the fine and practical arts do much to call attention to reference services. Tying up displays of paintings, sculpture, handicrafts, pottery, and so forth, with reference materials and with local individuals and groups is one publicity job undertaken by a reference department (1). In the same library industrial exhibits featuring products by local firms and displays of trade catalogs constitute another regular reference responsibility. Garden and travel exhibits in the spring (8) and window sill displays of reference tools helpful in various contests (8) are other projects.

A number of libraries edit for the local newspaper weekly "Information Please" departments. The column "Library Patrons Want to Know" is prepared from recorded interesting, unusual, or popular questions asked in the reference department (6). Occasionally some questions are made up to call attention to new reference tools recently acquired.

Most of the reference departments work very closely with organizations (17). Talks to clubs, and letters and telephone calls for business people are frequent (8). Advice to clubs in selecting topics for study, to home and business people for developing a home library, and to every one on where to buy and sell old and rare titles is almost routine (14). One suburban library specializes in telephone reference service (5) and another (1) keeps a daily record of telephone calls, and publicizes them.

In addition to some statistics on the number of questions answered, most reference departments are now including sample questions and some descriptive notes on the nature of various investigations. One library (1) culls from the daily records of questions asked, representative ones which can be grouped around an alphabetic list of topics, such as addresses, animal life, architecture, dwelling places.

The practice of reference in American libraries is on the threshold of something new and big. Librarians, educators, and research workers are all groping for some new understanding of the interrelations of their respective jobs. Increasingly, teachers are replacing conventional classroom recitations with reference procedures, and research workers are endeavoring to master reference techniques and materials, while the reference librarian struggles to extend his usefulness to both.

To date the reference librarian's efforts have seemed to focus on further refining his organizational skills and enlarging his knowledge of materials rather than on integrating his services with social needs. He has seemed to be less concerned with initiating services to society than with improving time-worn services previously established. As a result, others less well prepared technically have exploited the newer demands of social and educational surveys, teaching, defense, and even popular curiosity.

The real challenge confronting the reference worker is in the unconventional demand from schools, from industry, from government that has not yet been formulated or verbalized into a recognizable reference question. The real question confronting our professional group is this, "Have we the imagination and the courage to initiate an information service that will speed up emergency research? Can we bridge the gap between formal classroom and informal library with an instructional service that will improve the learning process? Will we accept the responsibility of satisfying popular curiosity entertainingly?"

Paraphrasing the "jingo" British policy, "We have the sources, we have the personnel, and we have the services too." There is no question we can undertake the broader practice of reference if we will.

LIBRARIES AND READINGS CITED

Cooperating Libraries—Public
1. Bridgeport, Conn. (Sarah H. Griffiths, reference librarian)
2. Council Bluffs, Iowa (Eva T. Canon, librarian)
3. Detroit (Mabel L. Conat, reference librarian)
4. Haverhill, Mass. (Louise D. Crowell)
5. Highland Park, Ill. (Mary A. Egan, librarian)
6. Long Beach, Cal. (E. H. Davis, reference librarian)
7. Los Angeles (Althea Warren, librarian)
8. Louisville (Edna J. Grauman, reference librarian)
9. New York (Ralph H. Carruthers, in charge photographic service)
10. Pittsburgh (Alice Thurston McGirr, reference librarian)
11. Pomona, Cal. (Sarah M. Jacobus, librarian)
12. St. Paul, James Jerome Hill Reference Library (Helen K. Starr, librarian)
13. St. Paul Public (Irene Knapton, in charge industrial arts room)
14. Seattle (Doris L. Mitchell, reference assistant)
15. Des Moines, Ia. (Lucille Stull, reference assistant)
16. Rochester, N.Y. (Gladys E. Love, reference librarian)
17. Denver (Doris Wells, reference librarian)

Cooperating Libraries—University
18. Indiana (Estella Wolf, reference librarian)
19. Wisconsin (Louis Kaplan, reference librarian)
20. Yale (Anne S. Pratt, reference librarian)
21. Joint University Libraries (Frances Cheney, reference librarian)
22. Teachers College, Columbia University (Clara Esther Derring, reference librarian)

Cited Readings
23. Alexander, Carter, "Technique of Library Searching." *Special Libraries* 27: 230-38, Sept. 1936.
24. Bagley, W. A. *Facts and How to Find Them.* Pitman, 1937.
25. Betten, F. S. "Catalog Is to Serve the Patron." *Catholic Library World* 8:1, Sept. 15, 1936.
26. Richardson, E. C. *The Reference Department.* American Library Association, 1911.

British Reference: "The process of free inquiry necessary to education and research"

AMERICAN LIBRARIANSHIP has generally defined reference as the library's information service. Our literature has discussed and developed this definition with particular attention to how much aid should be given to the reader. Dr. Wyer has classified our American reference philosophies as "conservative," "moderate" or "liberal," ranging our professional beliefs from doing nothing for the reader that he can do for himself to doing as much as possible for him. It may surprise you to learn that conservative Britain, by our definition, favors a liberal reference philosophy.

Evidence can be found both in research and in educational libraries that British reference librarians are performing all of the duties listed in the ALA Classification and Pay Plans for institutions of higher education in the first instance, and for municipal libraries in the second. But what is stimulating is the something extra they have added to our concept of reference. In the case of research references they seem to be a mile or two farther along the road to bibliographic organization. In the case of educational reference, they seem to have nearly attained William S. Learned's ideal intelligence centers. The result is that the British are pushing our concept of reference toward a redefinition.

Behind the effort to redefine there is an urgency not yet felt over here. It arises from the almost continuous state of war in which Europe has found itself and the necessity imposed on Britain by its proximity to the continental conflict. Into this continuous alert the British Nation has poured every resource at its disposal, including libraries. And under the lash of first fascism and then communism, British librarianship has developed a brand of reference that promises startling directions.

Reprinted from *ALA Bulletin*, 50: 288-291, May, 1956, by permission of the publisher.

These directions are both educational and research. Together, these two branches of reference services, one predominantly contributing to the information of the people, and the other toward the advancement of knowledge and invention, provide an invulnerable defense against subversive forces. And, in the races with first, the fascist nations, and now with the communist world the reference service of British libraries has steadily been redefined as the *process of free inquiry necessary to education and research.*

As I visited British libraries I saw many instances of reference activity that parallel our own. In the public libraries where the mission is predominantly educational, I saw the information function performed about the way it is here. The reference room contained basic American as well as British reference sources, but with the addition of a collection that duplicated often referred-to stack books. This proved very helpful in the case of certain standard and much circulated works which could thus always be consulted in the library.

A ready reference collection consisting of directories, handbooks and other fact-finding sources is found close to the entrance to the reference room. Inquiry logs are maintained and at the end of the day the chief reference librarian or the assistant chief reviews all of the questions referred.

To supplement printed sources British reference libraries carry on extensive local and cooperative indexing projects. The most common of these are, of course, related to the needs of local industry and community enterprise. Since airplanes and tobacco are principal industries in Bristol, for example, the public library there indexes systematically a great many serials and separates relating to these two subjects.

Thus far I have described services that are not startlingly different from ours. Perhaps the descriptions that follow are typical of your library but I am certain they are not common in the reference service of our public libraries.

There are two reference services found in the British municipal public libraries that push the liberal interpretation of reference to the limit. One of these is the so-called Civic Information Service. In many, if not most, British communities the public librarian is the official information officer for the community, and the public library is the information center. The reference aim of U.K. libraries is to get people to realize that the library is the community agency for information on any subject. I overheard two women on a bus in Sheffield. Said one women to the other, "You go to the public library; they'll tell you what you want to know."

In the shadows of the restful York Cathedral, a renovated 12th century cathedral house just outside the main entrance to the York Public Library serves as the civic information center. It is operated by the public library and performs the double function of informing the residents and guiding the tourists. In the course of a day the library staff there will help organize conducted tours, answer fact-finding questions and refer to the main building inquiries requiring extended search.

Amidst the bustle of the striving industrial life in not too distant Sheffield the public library there operates an extensive civic information service. It consists of three parts: (1) information to residents; (2) information to inquirers outside the city, and (3) the Personal Inquiry Service. Among other things the public library's information service publishes for the city the *Civic Record*. It maintains a great variety of local indexes, guides and directories. In the heart of the downtown section it provides street, bus and building location expertly. Sheffield citizens, in an endless stream, pour into the Civic Information Service of the Public Library located on the ground floor of the building. Truly here the public library has become the intelligence center for a community. For folks outside the city, C.I.S. provides a mail order information service. In anticipation of inquiries about industrial, recreational, cultural opportunities in Sheffield the library staff has prepared numerous pamphlets for distribution.

But most startling is the Personal Inquiry Service, the second of the two unusual reference functions found in British public libraries. Developed during the blitz, when homeless, stunned citizens separated from their loved ones by the devastation of bombing needed aid desperately, P.I.S. in British public libraries after the war has continued to provide an intimate, confidential information service to citizens.

P.I.S. does no social work itself, but it puts people in contact with the right social welfare agencies. Usually, P.I.S. is placed in the library in such a way that it is easily accessible from the street yet isolated from the rest of the library. The library assistants are selected not only for their reference equipment but for that personal quality which encourages troubled people to confide. All requests are confidential and protected.

The Personal Inquiry Service in Sheffield and in Luton are among the best. In the latter city I had access to the inquiry file. There were queries affecting health, employment, marriage, divorce. But these were not general questions such as are asked in our reference departments. They were specific: "My husband has gone off with another woman, what shall I do?" "Can the landlord make us move while we are waiting for the settlement of an estate?" "I need a lawyer and can't afford to pay for such services." The impression I had as I visited these Personal Inquiry Services was that here is an advanced type of reference concept—one that you will find described as a sort of professional utopia in Learned's *American Public Library and the Diffusion of Knowledge.*

Many other aspects of British reference library service are impressive. The fact that reading guidance is an integral part of reference in so many places is revealing. For example, Ilford's outstanding reference service can be said to be built around the Readers Advisory Service. When a new borrower registers there he feels almost as though he has just been honored by being elected to an honorary society. A member of the reference staff gives him a personal orientation taking him on a tour of the library. On his registry blank he is invited to indicate his special interests and thereafter the reference department keeps him informed of new books and reading matter in his interest field. Should he subsequently take a book in an additional area, that subject is noted on his registry and thereafter he receives also information about new material in that field.

These are by no means all of the devices and innovations I saw in British public libraries, but these are enough samples to indicate that reference is mobilized for community service in such a way as to suggest awareness of the world conflict.

Nor are the individual libraries alone in this struggle. Compactness of geography assists in an advanced development of inter-library cooperation. The 28 London boroughs, each a city of considerable size, have a union catalogue, and an accession agreement which allocates among them subject and fiction specializations and a most generous exchange of borrowers' privileges. Indeed, it is almost generally true that a borrower's card from any public library in the United Kingdom will be honored in any other library. (Wouldn't it be wonderful if, say a Jacksonville, Florida, Public Library card could be used in the Los Angeles, California, Public Library?)

What is true of the London boroughs is true of the rest of Britain, which is divided into library regions. Each of these regions has a union catalog of the libraries in that region with a liberal inter-library loan and reference service. Materials too rare to be loaned are photo-reproduced, copied or abstracted by the regional clearing house, financed by the libraries of the region.

At the apex of this cooperative lending and reference service is the National Central Library, located in London, next door to Chaucer House, the Headquarters of the Library Association. There are to be found all of the regional union catalogs on sheafs. These sheaf catalogs are binders of carbon sheets sent in by the various regional union libraries continuously. Contrary to my first impression, these sheafs are fully as easy to use as the card catalog and more convenient to maintain.

I rode the mobile units of two rural counties — Miss F. E. Cook's Lancashire and Mr. Osborne's Derbyshire. In both I took copious notes for use in developing our Florida extension program. Here I want to report some rural reference I thought was good.

In Lancashire, the mobile unit brings into central reference, subject requests by rural readers. These requests specify no title nor provide the reference worker with the type of specificity that can be determined through cross examination. The reference librarian has to reason and often decide what is on the inquirer's mind since he cannot in many instances reach him even by phone. For example, on the day I was in Preston, headquarters for the central Lancashire library, I traced an inquiry about North Rhodesia. Since there was no more on the query slip the reference librarian was hard put to determine whether the inquirer's interest was in colonization, travel, history, culture or any one of a dozen phases of the subject. By consulting the borrower's card for the inquirer the reference librarian discovered major interest in native dances. The material the reference librarian sent out on the mobile unit exactly answered the patron's question when it turned out later that the specific request was for a description of a Mat used for tap dancing in North Rhodesia.

At Preston three sections of the library are concerned with rural reference. The Reference section handles all non-fiction except 500's and 600's and handles all inquires brought in by the mobile unit from rural areas. The Technology Section handles the 500's and 600's and deals with most of the inquiries that come from industry and agriculture. Then, there is a Request Section which undertakes all bibliographic and readers advisory questions.

Gathering these observations together the impelling impression is that public libraries in Britain cooperatively have accomplished almost 100% opportunity for the people to be well-informed. Libraries have achieved this remarkable service first through a high degree of cooperation of its regional and central library, second through its personalized citizen information service, third through its extension of reference to its rural areas, and fourth through an unlimited opportunity for free inquiry on any subject by all of the people. Reference service in Britain, therefore, can be said to be supporting education to the extent of consciously stimulating free inquiry.

The overwhelming impression about reference service to research in Britain is one of urgency. As if the Russians were breathing on their necks, British industry races with a competitor it does not underestimate. For if there is going to be a war Britain wants to have the advantage of radar discoveries such as she had over Germany in World War II. And British scientists and technologists have already given notice with their jets that they will have leadership in at least one phase of warfare.

Under the stimulation of such agencies as D.S.I.R. (Department for Scientific and Industrial Research) British librarians and information officers are almost continuously abstracting research wherever it is reported, and disseminating it to the point in Britain where comparable investigation is under way. This process underscored at least three reference concepts that we in America have not come fully to accept or universally to provide.

The first of these concepts recognizes that in research the inquiry may and should originate with the librarian about as often as with the investigator. Thus I discovered in Britain that the reference librarian (usually a subject specialist) was asking the question today that the investigator himself was not ready to ask until tomorrow. Often by that time the librarian had also the answer.

The second of these concepts is the urge and necessity felt by the reference librarian to develop his own sources continuously and cooperatively. Abstracting responsibilities are divided among the various research libraries and the resulting abstracts reproduced on uniform sheafs for exchange.

A third concept is equal attention to customer organization. By means of continuous, cooperative abstracting, bibliographic organization is strengthened. But by means of continuous records of investigations under way in various parts of the United Kingdom, customer organization is effective to the extent that abstracts related to a particular investigation are rushed there immediately. In this connection, teletype, radio teletype and even facsimile are being employed.

The effect of these three concepts on British reference is the steady construction of a vast network of information services for research.

These are enough illustrations of British thought and effort in reference and other aspects of librarianship to suggest closer study of their professional literature by us. It behooves us not to underestimate any of their investigations simply because so many of them fail to pay tribute to the so-called "scientific method." What we must understand is that this "method" is well known to them, and that they are concerned about our heavy reliance on quantitative measures. They recognize what their great physicist, Sir James Jeans, once wrote: "The universe looks more like a great thought than a great machine."

The Measure of Reference

CALL IT a professional illusion. The fact remains there have always been a few reference librarians who have believed their service is measurable. Cannons' *Bibliography of Library Economy* records the efforts of the past—valiant though futile. And *Library Literature,* as well as *Library Science Abstracts,* reports scientific, statistical, philosophical, historical struggles with the problem of evaluating reference as it is found in academic, public, school, and special libraries.

On the one hand, administrators insist on performance figures; and on the other, reference librarians respond with statistics that are at best invalid or unreliable. It is not that the reference worker is less intent on evaluating his own work than is his employer. It is rather that the reference librarian understands how variable and intangible are the reference service elements.

When the Detroit Public Library reported for 1959/60[1] its central library had answered 798,000 reference questions and all Detroit agencies had handled 2,115,657 questions, what did it mean? Well, based on the city's 1960 population (1,670,144) this could be considerably better than A.L.A's post-war standard of ½ to 1 question per capita.

But is it really? Would the Detroit definition of an "informational question" exactly describe the concept of a reference question expressed so aptly by the distinguished emeritus reference librarian of Baltimore's Enoch Pratt Free Library? "Headwork, not leg work" characterizes the professional reference question, Miss Mary Barton once said in a letter to Joseph Wheeler. Yet we know that some

[1] For notes, see pages 127-128.

Reprinted from *The Southeastern Librarian,* 11: 297-302, Winter, 1961, by permission of the publisher.

libraries record every "contact" between patron and attendant
while other reference departments are selective either by choice or
by the compulsion of overwork.[2]

If that much variation can be found among public libraries
what other variations in question-counting exist in libraries o.
higher educational institutions? In school libraries? In specia
libraries? Just what is a reference question, and does each reference
question count equally as one? Does a nod in the direction of the
card catalog count more than the failure to locate an obscure incu-
nabulum, though the latter requires ever so much more time and
educated effort than the former? These are some of the doubts that
beset the reference librarian as he submits to his director's demand
for some kind of count to put into that all important annual report

And as if the perplexity over the reference question and how to
count it were not enough, what about those other services performed
by the reference department of any library? As often as not the
reference librarian is the designated staff member to offer instruction
In academic libraries he does it informally during freshman orientation, and countless times throughout the college year — every
time a student wants help on the use of the card catalog, the *Readers*
Guide, or the *Stateman's Yearbook*, or when a faculty member
doesn't know about the *Union Lists of Serials* as an aid to locating
the nearest library with that missing journal volume. Formally, the
reference librarian most frequently gives the freshman course on the
use of the library, or the library unit in the English class.

In public libraries the reference librarian informally instructs the
public in library use, and frequently lectures to community groups
on how to get the most out of its public library.

All that has been said for academic libraries can be said for
school libraries and much that is done in academic and public
libraries occurs in special libraries. Well, how do you measure this
instruction, formal and informal, and how much does it count in
comparison with answering reference questions?

Nor do these two major functions — information and instruction — encompass all of the reference activities. There are, for
example, the numerous bibliographies compiled by reference

librarians in all types of libraries. The end products may be short lists of six entries on a popular subject or an intrinsic literature searching project for an original bit of investigation. How do you measure these reference efforts and equate them with those that go into answering questions and teaching library use?

Reference is a variegated aspect of librarianship and as such it often performs critically in organization and administration, in resources and technical processes, in circulation and dissemination, in program planning and public relations. A reference division has personnel, quarters, and equipment, and some administrative effort must go into such things, for example, as staff scheduling and materials housing. There is the exacting responsibility for selection, not alone for so-called "R" books, but often for pictures and pamphlet files, for audio-visual media, for microtexts, for documents, and realia, and maps and globes. And when it comes to negotiating inter-library loans or accomplishing microfilming or photocopying, the reference librarian more often than not is the responsible officer. Well, how do you measure these things so that the administrator can make a case for a bigger budget next year? Even more important, how do we reference librarians evaluate these things for ourselves so as to know how effective we are?

Late last year the Reference Services Division of the A.L.A. activated a Committee on Reference Standards and Statistics.[3] In her charge to the Committee, President Frances N. Cheney, who had already directed a vast, pioneering survey of public library reference, asked that statistics be added to the standards responsibility because they "could not very well be separated." How statesmanlike this decision was can be underlined by examining the U. S. Office of Education's statistics for various type libraries.

The Committee's first meeting last A.L.A. "Mid-winter," though largely devoted to explanation, produced, nevertheless, a significant redefinition of Reference. Not that the term had lacked attention in our professional literature, but rather that the variations in scope had often been startling.

For example, as early as 1930, Wyer[4] had cited the "conservative," "moderate," and "liberal" schools of Reference thought, and our professional dictionary had discreetly chosen: "That phase of library work which is directly concerned with assistance to readers in securing information and in using the resources of the library in study and research."[5]

None of these, however, encompassed post-war trends in "information retrieval"; nor the British vanguard of "confidential enquiry"; nor what Dr. Wheeler has called "library-initiated reference"; nor research in which the reference librarian is an equal member, if not the innovator, in an investigating team; nor the "promotion of free inquiry" in a world at cold war.[6]

In consequence, the Committee under the leadership of Samuel Rothstein and Henry Dubester developed this statement.[7]

1. Reference services in a library should be recognized as a central responsibility of library administration, specifically organized to ensure the optimum use of the library's collections.

2. The distinguishing feature of reference services is in its relationship to the library's patrons. These services are of two essential types — direct and indirect.

3. Direct reference service consists of personal assistance provided to library patrons in pursuit of information. Direct reference service may take many forms, each of which may consist of a number of activities, of which only the most frequent and representative are cited below:

   (a) *Instruction* in the use of the library and in the use of items in the library's collections. This service may range from demonstration of how to fill out a call slip to explanation of the use of catalogs, bibliographies, and reference works, to assistance in interpreting the contents of materials in the library's collections. The central feature of this instruction, irrespective of its level or its intensity, is to provide guidance and direction in the pursuit of information, rather than providing the information itself.

   (b) *Information Service.* This service may range from answering an apparently simple question through recourse to an obvious reference source, to supplying information based on search in the collections of the library, combining competence in bibliothecal techniques with competence in the subject of inquiry. The character and extent of library information service will vary with the kind of library, with the patron the library is designed to serve, and with the skill, competence, and professional training of the reference librarian providing the information service. Characteristic functions of information service are finding specific data or facts, interpreting the material or information found, translating, abstracting, literature searching, and others. The central feature of information service, irrespective of its level or its intensity, is to provde an end product in terms of information sought by the library's patron.

4. Indirect reference service comprises the preparation and development of catalogs, bibliographies, and all other reference aids which help in providing access to the library's collections and which extend the library's services through cooperation with other, or larger, or more specialized libraries. This recognizes the significant role of the technical or processing services of the library as indispensable to the reference function.

General Note: No outline of the reference function in libraries can truly correspond to the realities of day-to-day work with the library's public. The level, character, and variety of reference service that has been traditionally offered by libraries is a product of many factors, including the size of the library, its physical and fiscal resources, as well as its philosophy of service. The foregoing outline offers a concept of reference service which is broader in scope than many libraries can achieve. It recognizes, however, that the reference functions, as described, are in fact provided by libraries large and small, without necessarily being recognized as such. Effective understanding of the nature and the role of reference service in libraries should lead to more efficient and effective development of such service and of administrative recognition of its central role in the overall mission of the library.

From this preliminary definition the Committee has next turned its attention to the activities of Reference. What constitutes the reference function in every library type? What does the reference librarian actually do? An effort to categorize the various reference activities has resulted in a highly preliminary checklist, far from appealing to the Committee. But for what it is worth here is the checklist:

ACTIVITY

I. *Reference Assistance*
    1. Fact questions — In library
    2. Fact questions — On phone
    3. Fact questions — By mail
    4. Searching
    5. Reading Guidance

II. *Research Assistance*
    1. Information Retrieving

2. Abstracting
3. Translating
4. Literature Searching
5. Literature Summarizing
6. Material Interpreting
III. *Instruction*
  1. Informal — Card Catalog
  2. Informal — Library Collection
  3. Formal — Class Unit
  4. Formal — Group
  5. Formal — Course
  6. Writing Handbooks, Bulletin to Aid Library Use
IV. *Program Planning*
  1. Group Meeting
  2. Discussion Group
  3. Reading Club
  4. Film Forum
  5. Record Club
  6. TV and Radio
V. *Bibliography Compiling*
  1. For Groups
  2. For Individuals
  3. For General Distribution
  4. To Support Classroom Instruction
  5. To Support Research
VI. *Selection*
  1. "R" Materials
  2. Books, Pamphlets, Documents
  3. Pictures

4. Films, Filmstrips, Slides
5. Microforms
6. Disk and Tape Recordings (Sound)
7. Other Materials (Realia, Maps, etc.)
VII. *Reference Organization*
  1. Ordering Books, Documents, Pamphlets
  2. Bindery Preparation
  3. Weeding Files, Books
  4. Clipping Newspapers, Magazines
  5. Indexing Local Materials
  6. Microfilming and Photocopying
  7. Negotiating Inter-Library Loans
  8. Organizing Genealogical Sources
  9. Supervising and Training Personnel
  10. Acquiring and Arranging Equipment
  11. Posting Signs, Printing Directions.
  12. Writing Copy for Newspapers, and Public Relations
  13. Community Resources Liaison
  14. Preparing Statistics, Records, Reports

Several directions now confront the Committee. Refinement of the preliminary checklist by reference librarians in all types of libraries is necessary if a useful instrument is to result. Committee members have already indicated inherent weaknesses in the preliminary checklist. The smaller library which has no separate reference department[8] may engage in many of these activities but not necessarily as part of the reference function. Nevertheless, an analysis of the reference jobs is preliminary to a more detailed study.

What is then proposed is to select representative libraries of each type distinguished for their reference service, and to "case-study" them. If these libraries are truly the best examples of effective reference service, what makes them excellent? How can their excellence be measured objectively?

Which brings us back to the main Committee assignment. How shall we measure reference? What can we count to give us a quantitative appraisal of reference?

Looking at current common methods of measuring reference service in American libraries, "perhaps the most common is the keeping of a running tally of questions asked."[9]

If some of these methods are looked at hard there is both cause for dismay and hope. Certainly the time factor is not reliable. Competence of the staff, richness of the collection, and any number of other factors accent the variables. Classification of questions by type, or by inquirer, or by sources consulted, or by purpose, all present formidable obstacles both as to validity and reliability.

There is some professional difference on the value of recording all questions. Miss Hutchins feels that "a file of all questions asked does not contribute greatly to an evaluation of the service."[10] But the late Bob Christ of Duke University contended that a full record of questions and citations revealed collection weaknesses and deficiencies in staff training and supervision.[11]

The case for studying the inquirer is put forcefully by Haygood,[12] who points out the effect of showing how many students, housewives, manual workers, etc., use the service.

Considerably more attention has been given to classifying questions by types. This, Sally Poundstone[13] has suggested, is imperative if reference librarians are not to be accused of inflating their statistics by lumping their directional and locational queries with requests for assistance of a more challenging nature. Studies of classifications of questions by type are summarized in *Basic Reference Sources*.[14]

In some ways British librarianship is further along in its efforts to measure reference. It was my good fortune recently to have the opportunity to sit in committee meeting in Chaucer House with the Library Association's counterpart of our A.L.A. Committee.[15] From the considerations during the morning session it was quite apparent that our colleagues across the Atlantic were contending with the same dilemmas. Behind them was a literature as considerable as ours, frequently proposing about the same solutions. For example,

Barlow[16] in 1938 introduced the time element into recording and measuring reference. He suggested four categories: (1) requests for specific sources; (2) queries answered quickly (fact-finding); (3) queries taking 5-15 minutes; and (4) queries taking over 15 minutes.

Carnell[17] weighed the reader/material count, the former to be an attendance tabulation aided by the turnstile, and the latter, presumably, to involve a checking record. But she rejected the plan because of the bad psychological effect it would have on both the patron and the staff.

A rather ingenious idea was described by Lamble[18] who proposed "Reader-Hours" as a unit of measure. It involved, however, the complex and time-taking account of every reader from the time he entered until he left the reference department.

With these and other efforts at their disposal the Library Association Committee has thus far turned to the tangible measures of reference service first. Already the first result has appeared in print as a measure of the reference collection.[19] A second step appears to be a study of reference personnel. Two-fold is the approach here: practice and training. A national survey of reference library staffs through questionnaires is underway. In connection with the North Western Polytechnic School a pilot four-weeks reference course based on practice is to be offered. Mr. Toase of the Committee has been named to supervise it. It is hoped that similar courses will be offered in other regions of the United Kingdom.[20]

Considering the deliberations of the British Committee on Reference Standards against the beginnings made by our American committee one possibility appears to be to concentrate on the "indirect reference service" as more reliably measurable. Recalling the first A.C.R.L. Committee on Classification and Pay Plans of which I was chairman, the most creative idea was Fremont Rider's "Service Unit." Something like this in the form of a "Reference Service Unit" (RSU) has recently challenged me. The RSU might just possibly be useful both for the direct and indirect services.

For example, direct reference service consisting of personal assistance to library patrons might well be measured in terms of both the educational level of the patron and the type of question. Both of them might be based on the class of reference library and the predominant character of its patrons. Weighing of these might require the advice of an expert statistician. Success, however, might for the first time provide a common unit of measure for all reference services in every type of library. Certainly, this approach for the indirect reference is already supported by the early A.C.R.L. score card and by the more recent British committee's work with reference stock.

The quest for a better measure of reference continues and the Committee earnestly seeks suggestions from their reference colleagues everywhere.

[1] Detroit. Public Library. *Annual Report,* 1959/60.

[2] Margaret Hutchins in *Introduction to Reference Work* (Chicago, A.L.A., 1944), p. 10, defines a reference question as "a request for information of a definite nature which the inquirer expects to find in printed material and their like, or for a certain work or works not located in the library."

[3] The members of the committee are:

HENRY J. DUBESTER, Chief, General Reference and Bibliography Division, Library of Congress.

NEAL R. HARLOW, Dean, Rutgers University Graduate School of Library Service.

CHARLES HIGGINS, Assistant Librarian, State Library, Lansing, Michigan.

BLANCHE JANECEK, Librarian, High School Library, Laboratory School, University of Chicago.

SAMUEL ROTHSTEIN, Director, School of Librarianship, University of British Columbia.

ROSE VAINSTEIN, Special Librarian, Services Branch, U.S. Office of Education.

MILDRED VANNORSDALL, Adult Services Supervisor, Lane Public Library, Hamilton.

LOUIS SHORES, Dean, Library School, Florida State University, Chairman.

[4] Wyer, James Ingersoll. *Reference Work; A Textbook for Students of Library Work and Librarians.* Chicago, A.L.A., 1930, Chapter 1.

[5] American Library Association. Editorial Committee. Subcommittee on Library Terminology. *A.L.A. Glossary of Library Terms.* Chicago, A.L.A., 1943, p. 113.

[6] Shores, Louis. "A Frame of Reference," *Library Journal,* 78: 88-93, January 15, 1953.

[7] This statement includes Dr. Rothstein's amendments which arrived too late for inclusion in *RQ* version, July, 1961.

[8] Of 1,167 libraries studied in the Public Library Reference Survey, one-half did not have a full-time person assigned to reference; nearly 100% of school libraries are in this same position. With increasing dispersal of the reference function, large libraries tend to complicate activity categorization.

[9] Rogers, Rutherford D. "Measurement and Evaluation," *Library Trends,* 3: 177-187, October, 1954.

[10] Hutchins, *op. cit.,* p. 199.

[11] Christ, Robert W. "Recording Reference Service," *College and Research Libraries,* 8: 23-27, January, 1947.

[12] Haygood, William Converse. *Who Uses the Public Library? A Survey of the Patrons of the Circulation and Reference Departments of the New York Public Library.* Chicago, University of Chicago Press, 1938, p. 4.

[13] Poundstone, Sally. "What Records Do You Keep on Reference Work?" *Library Journal,* 82: 2750-3, November 1, 1957.

[14] Shores, Louis. *Basic Reference Sources; An Introduction to Materials and Methods,* Chicago, A.L.A., 1954, pp. 5-8.

[15] Mr. E. Hargreaves of the Birmingham Public Library is chairman. Other members include Dr. A. J. Walford, editor of *Guide to Reference Materials,* and C. A. Toase, associated on the *Guide.*

[16] Barlow, S. H. "A Suggestion for Estimating the Use of the Reference Library," *Library World,* 41: 29-30, August-September, 1938.

[17] Carnell, Edith Jessie. *Library Administration,* London, Grafton, 1947, pp. 132-134.

[18] Lamble, J. Hoskin. "Statistical Representation of Reference Library Use." *Library Association Record,* 4th series 18: 291-292, September, 1951.

[19] Library Association. Reference, Special and Information Section. *Reference Library Stocks: an Enquiry into Reference Book Provision in the Rate-supported Libraries of England and Wales.* London, Library Association, 1960.

[20] Minutes of a meeting of the Reference Library Sub-Committee . . . held at Chaucer House Friday, 24th March, 1961.

Reference Becomes Learning: The Fourth "R"

TO BEGIN WITH, I assume we are all concerned with education. Some of us have dedicated ourselves to the development of the very young, in elementary schools and in public library children's departments. Others of us serve adolescents in high schools and in young people's divisions of community libraries. Still others of us are responsible to older readers — to college students and to men and women in all walks of life. Essentially we who are assembled here today are concerned that all of these segments of our nation shall read much and well, to the end that we shall have a national

Reprinted from *Bulletin of School Service, College of Education, University of Kentucky,* 30: 12-19, March, 1958, by permission of the publisher. This essay also appeared in the April, 1958, issue of the *Kentucky Library Association Bulletin* and is reprinted by permission of the President of the Kentucky Library Association. The essay was originally given as an address to Kentucky librarians at a meeting sponsored by the Department of Library Science of the University of Kentucky and held in conjunction with the annual Educational Conference, October 26, 1957.

mind competent to cope first with the extraordinary world problems ahead and second with the new challenge of the universe waiting for us out there in space.

This intense interest we have in education does not by any means make us averse to research. On the contrary it is this very interest in educating all of the people that we believe will create an adequate climate for investigation. What we are saying is what the late Justice Oliver Wendell Holmes once said so well. "We need education in the obvious more than investigation in the obscure."

At this stage in our dedication to nuclear research and even to outer space it is entirely possible that the so-called scientific method has strangled our creativity and blinded us to a better approach, one which would lead us away from our present concern with sensory appearances and toward an extrasensory discovery of reality. Without education, without an opportunity for those who follow to test their own potentials for leadership we must inevitably face another dark age of stagnation. Our interest in education is therefore as important to research as it is to the institutions charged with the responsibility of improving our national mind.

Unfortunately we live in a cycle of educational skepticism. The entire nation has been aroused over Johnny's inability to read and to think in a way that augurs not well for the schools. For the very critics of our American education indulge themselves in the same kind of superficialities they accuse the schools of countenancing. Universally, the criticisms begin, "What's wrong with our schools?" — reversing immediately the natural sides of a debate by making of the negative the affirmative. It is here contended that at least as effective a critique of American education can be started by asking the question, "What is right with our schools?"

One answer to that question is the growing emphasis on libraries. Increasing recognition of the fact that education is essentially communication, and that effective learning is dependent upon good communication between teacher and pupil is certainly correct. Implementation of this concept with growing support for libraries of all kinds is one tangible evidence of what is right with education.

Last summer Congress made a start toward extending public library service to all of the people by authorizing appropriations of up to seven million dollars a year for five years to be matched by the states in an effort to provide books and other materials for people in rural America. Our colleges and universities continue to double their collections at the rate of at least once every sixteen years. Libraries once limited almost entirely to the better secondary schools are now penetrating all high schools and an increasing number of elementary schools.

Having indicated something that is not only right but better than ever before in our American education, it is proper to ask what improvement is possible? Certainly considerable. Let the day never come when we will rest and say our education is perfect.

Obviously we are not yet financing our libraries adequately. Inevitably history will decide whether the way we apportion our national wealth today between missiles and books is right or even smart. Elsewhere I have expressed the opinion that World War III, already upon us, will be very much less a physical than a psychological conflict. To the side able to disseminate the best ideas will undoubtedly go victory. In such a struggle it seems almost like a dissipation of our resources to expend so much on military and so little on mental and spiritual preparation. To paraphrase the appraisal of the French Maginot line, never has a nation been prepared so adequately for World War III with the weapons of World War II as is the United States today. May the future historian not call us to account for failing to prepare our people adequately in the great struggle for men's minds.

But just as obviously, we are even yet not utilizing fully the support that is being given to education. In the first place, it is doubtful that libraries are receiving an adequate portion of the education dollar. Considering the potential of books and other media of communication in the learning process, it must be evident that a dollar per pupil for printed materials and half that amount for so-called audio- visual media (to which the better schools aspire) is hardly a standard, these inflationary days, reckoned to assure the younger generation access to the world's best ideas in their most palatable formats.

So that the entire appraisal of American education today will not be reduced to dollars and cents, however, it is well to look at what we are doing with what we have. Are we making full use of our library resources? Is the skill we as librarians and teachers mastered in library schools and teachers colleges being translated into effective school learning? Do the educational principles we accepted in the halls of ivy result in successful applications for that modern version of the little red school house or in the libraries of town and gown?

A caustic negative to all of these questions can be expected from those who find everything wrong with today's three R's. In support of the contention that the nation's schools have generally deteriorated, high school graduates' answers on various cultural tests administered as a prerequisite to college admission are cited. Some of these answers are almost unbelievable if not ludicrous. They have in other years furnished amusement as "Boners." At least two little volumes collected for Viking Press and illustrated by the ever rollicking Dr. Seuss will continue to comfort those who see nothing right with American education.

"Sir Walter Raleigh," wrote one high school senior, "was the undertaker of the Jamestown Colony," and another pupil identified the Puritans as the people who "found an insane asylum in the wilds of America." As for the Bible, it was invented by Gutenberg and written by King James I. Mount Everest is located in Europe although only recently joined to the Alps. And geometry is the science of bisexing angels. These and other bits of misinformation written by pupils in desperation, while treated humorously are too often taken as index of the uneducated state of our school population.

If such stray bits of history and science and literature are really to be considered as evidence of our faulty education then more attention to locating facts and authenticating them must be given in our schools. Our concern must be, however, not alone with facts but knowing how to find them. "The half of knowledge" goes the famous slogan over the arches of many of our libraries, "is knowing where to find it." More strongly than ever the more solid appraisals of learning take into account the learner's ability to locate information. If it is to be so then the craft of the librarian comes ever more sharply into educational focus. For, what are we saying but redefining education as reference?

In its simplest terms reference may be defined as the process of locating information. From his earliest years in school the child is involved in the same fundamental process, striving in response to sensory stimuli and some yet undefined extrasensory impulse to allay an insatiable curiosity. Learning and reference can be seen at once, therefore, to be made of the same elemental stuff.

This being true we find in our hands the potential for real learning. We understand all at once that the whole process of learning in and out of classrooms is a sort of variegated reference procedure. If we look real hard at how we are teaching and learning today we must come to the conclusion that education is better today than yesterday in the R of reference, a fundamental at least as important as the other three, since it is conceded by most educators to constitute at least the half of learning. At least we have more books and other library materials in our schools, communities and colleges than we had a half century ago during the golden age of hard learning. Whether we are yet using them adequately is another matter. The chances are we could extend the skills of reference to more teachers and pupils.

Take the matter of word meaning. There is no aspect of learning more essential. It is the bedrock of two of the other R's — reading and writing. Its teaching is basically a matter of reference. Its successful learning is dependent upon dictionary tool use. Without adequate dictionary mastery there can be only the kind of inability at reading Johnny is accused of these days.

This does not happen very often now. But in Tennessee many years ago an English teacher asked her class to go to the library and look up a word in the "big" dictionary. All of her pupils were equally industrious and copied only the first meaning given by the "big" dictionary. Yet approximately half of the class was right and half wrong. How did that happen? It happened because there were actually two "big" dictionaries in the library. To all outward apparances they looked monstrously alike and equally dirty. But they were not the same. One of the two "big" dictionaries always gives the earliest meaning of a word first, and consequently the children who consulted this "big" dictionary copied a meaning that was popular in Chaucer's time but hardly understood today. The other children consulted the dictionary which gave the commonest meaning first. Such failure to distinguish between "big" dictionaries is much less in evidence now and further proof that we are improving in the fundamental R of reference.

Or take another instance of information seeking. Because I cite experiences in Tennessee I am sure you will understand that I am merely drawing from the scene where I spent most of my professional life rather than reflecting on the educational development of that fine neighboring state. A high school history teacher wrote in to protest the absence of any information on "phalanx" in the *Encyclopaedia Britannica*. Unwilling to believe that this was so, we consulted the index and found numerous references to parts of articles in which the term "phalanx" was adequately treated. When the citations were sent on, the teacher embarrassedly admitted she had consulted only the "P" volume of the set. Such failures to recognize the large subject pattern of an encyclopedia like the *Britannica* which treats no fewer than 500,000 subjects in its 50,000 separate articles is now less frequent. We have steadily strengthened the fundamental R of reference in our teaching and learning.

But considerable still remains to be done. The full potential of the R book is only beginning to be realized. There is a reluctance on the part of the teacher to use the reference book as fully as she uses the textbook. Part of the reluctance stems from warnings librarians and reviewers have offered about sets. And some of this stigma has carried over even to such sets as good encyclopedias.

Because I have devoted so much of my life to editing and advising I probably am a bit more enthusiastic about this class of reference book. I have participated in the development of at least three of the good school and one or two of the major adult sets. As some of you know, I have been since the war an associate editor of a new encyclopedia whose name I refrain from mentioning now because as a member of the Lions' Club I might well be fined by the tail twister for advertising. Because of this experience and because of my own learning and teaching experiments with encyclopedias I should like to share with you some of the educational possibilities of this class of reference books.

The most obvious use for the encyclopedia is ready reference.

Numerous and ingenious devices for quick fact finding have been developed including the famous *Compton* fact-index which identifies as it locates, and the *World Book's* classified reading guide which synthesizes the many short related articles into a unified whole. Attention to index and cross reference use in the encyclopedia will contribute to improved reading and writing skill as well as to a store of ready knowledge.

But there are even more important possibilities in an encyclopedia. As early as my own high school days I discovered for myself the power of the overview device. When I elected to take the separate course in economics offered during my senior year by the youngest and prettiest teacher in the school I was determined to do well. Before the semester opened I went to the library and read the *Britannica* article on economics. It gave me a wonderful introduction to what was a new subject for me then. I found that I could anticipate each topic as the teacher approached it and this anticipation fired me to learn and to challenge her approach and treatment. Such anticipation and challenge by the pupil inevitably resulted in what Kayserling calls creative understanding. I believe I earned my A motivated not entirely by my "crush" for the teacher. For subsequently throughout my college and graduate school career I followed the same procedure arming myself for each new course with an overview of the subject found in a good encyclopedia. It has been exceedingly gratifying to me to see teachers using this device with their pupils as they start a new unit.

Although it is true many sets offer much less value than an equal amount of money could buy in separate good books, I am afraid that is not so in the case of encyclopedias. Consider the fact that the good encyclopedia spends upward of one million dollars to produce its work. Much of the money goes to pay authorities who are world famous in every subject field. But the good encyclopedia does not stop there. It employs an editorial staff of writers and curriculum experts to review and test every one of the great authorities' contributions.

In this connection I recall two incidents that illustrate the care with which encyclopedias are prepared. The editors of one of them invited an outstanding authority to do an article on a subject in his field. What he submitted was the last word in authority and would have passed muster before a jury of his most critical peers. But it could never have been read with any understanding by children. To remedy this the article was rewritten and shown to the authority. His reaction was explosive. What followed were a number of re-writings both by him and the editors, and on the fourteenth all were satisfied that the article was authoritative and readable. Very few separate books can afford to devote that much time of so many people to a single segment of a work.

The other incident almost resulted in a suit. Another encyclo-pedia invited a certain scientist to do an article on a very difficult and deep subject. One very gloomy Monday morning his manu-script arrived in the mail room of the publishing company. The boy in the mail room sorting the incoming material aimed the scien-tist's contribution for the encyclopedia's mail bag but missed and actually put it in with unsolicited manuscripts for another publica-tion. As a result, the famous scientist received his manuscript back with only a little yellow slip which read, you know how, if you have ever been rejected in this way, "We regret we cannot use your manscript at this time," with the usual routine pat on the back, "but keep trying young fellow; you may make it some day." The indignation of the famous man almost melted the long dis-ance wires. But it helped the encyclopedia obtain an article that was as readable as it was scholarly.

Consider also the amount of thought and finance that go into art work in the good encyclopedia. I recall the year I taught in a New York City upper east side junior high school, when I dropped out of Columbia graduate school to retrieve my finances. Most of the children had never been outside the city. When I asked them how large is a cow, some of them showed with their little fingers a size equal to the picture of a contented animal on the outside label of a condensed milk can. To be sure, that was the only cow they had ever seen.

The relative size of animals concerned the editors of *Compton's*. Children had been told that a giraffe's neck was long, but not how long in relation to the height of a dog's or a mouse's or an elephant's. Ideally if we had been able to get all of the important animals of the world to pose for our camera in their respective abodes we would have accomplished all that we hoped for in establishing relative animal size. That hope, however, stimulated us to achieve the same objective. We arranged with the Firld Museum to line up stuffed animals for a panoramic shot.

I have cited the encyclopedia at such length only because it is considered the backbone of good reference. The implication is obvious. Since reference is an essential R in learning it is important that our school libraries be stocked with many good reference books. It is even more important that our teachers and pupils learn to use reference tools ever more effectively.

Advocates of motion picture use in the classroom (I am one of these advocates) have devoted themselves to promoting good utilization. With each film there is usually provided a teaching guide, and teachers are encouraged to preview the film before teaching with it. Carefully worked out procedures for exploiting the motion picture in the classroom abound in audio-visual professional literature.

We have made a start in helping the teacher use reference books in teaching, but I believe only a start. Guides on encyclopedia use produced by publishers are available and librarians would do well to order a supply of these for teachers and pupils. But even more is needed if the power of the R book is to be brought into learning. Taking a cue from the motion picture enthusiasts, we could do with a bit more of teacher previewing of reference materials. And our teacher education, now at last aroused that its interns shall learn how to thread projectors, might well allocate some teacher education time to a more careful study of basic reference tools.

As we appraise critically the education of our next generation it is inevitable that we should look hardest at what is happening to the three R's. They are still important and they must not be neglected. But they are no more important than the fourth R, the reference R. Because as our knowledge increases in almost geometric proportions with each year it becomes impossible and really undesirable that all of us should know everything. What we really hope education will do for the next generation is to prepare them to be able to find out about anything. In terms of this objective Reference becomes learning. Reference is indeed the very essence of learning.

There is still another reason why reference becomes all important. The generation to succeed us faces two of the greatest challenges ever to confront mankind. One of these is of this world. In the next few years mankind will have to choose between two historic ways. The choice will be right only if mankind is sufficiently informed. There is no heavier responsibility on the schools today than to teach children how to find the truth. That is why reference becomes the most important of all the R's.

But a more exciting challenge awaits us "out of this world." At the moment, our space efforts are concentrated on rockets and the means of physical survival out there. Back of the necessary know-how is basic preparation in reference. The scientists and the technologists are even now relying on the skills of reference to locate the needed facts.

Here is a closing surmise. As education and research both increase their reliance on the fourth R, the method of reference, science will gain an ever greater tolerance for the social sciences, for the humanities, and for the introspective soul-searching that has always been assigned to religion. Out of that tolerance may yet come a far more startling approach than even the scientific method has been able to produce.

May all of us, teachers and librarians, rededicate ourselves to the fourth R so that our children and children's children will come ever closer to the kingdom.

The Future of Reference in American Society

THIS IS BOTH THE FAVORED and the unfavored role on this program.

Since it deals in futures for American society and for our reference craft, there is no obligation to document out of the past, or even to study the present. What is required is an oracle, or a bit of precognition, or a thorough grounding in extrasensory perception. With a free rein to one's imagination one can write his own professional "1984" and defy anyone to disprove the prognostications. That much is a favor.

But on the unfavored side there is the Welsh proverb:

"To deal in prophesies is to deal in lies."

And I cannot forget what James Russell Lowell wrote in those ingenuous *Bigelow Papers*:

"Don't never prophesy — onless ye know."

The one who essays a prediction on the part our profession may play in the years to come, cannot help but repeat Shakespeare's words:

"We know what we are, but know not what we may be."

Weighing the favors against the handicaps, there is still something within us that is tempted by the challenge. After all, as Walt Whitman pointed out once:

"The future is no more uncertain than the present."

Reprinted from *Wilson Library Bulletin*, 32: 286-288, December, 1957, by permission of the publisher, The H. W. Wilson Company, New York City. The essay here reprinted is a paper given at the meeting of the Reference Services Division during the 1957 Conference of the American Library Association in Kansas City, Missouri.

And like Thomas Jefferson:

> "I like the dreams of the future better than the history of the past."

So here goes. It will not be without effort. I have never appreciated more the words of A. C. Bradley in his *Lectures on Poetry:*

> "Research, though toilsome, is easy; imagination, though delightful, is difficult."

To begin with, then, let me make a dire prediction of war. That may be the essential element in American society from now until or beyond Orwell's title year. If "The best of prophets of the future is the past" as Lord Byron wrote, then we have only to look back to VJ day. Since that time the conflict between East and West has been almost continuous.

But far more significant than manifestations of physical combat has been the undeniable global conflict of ideologies. In the dozen years since the close of World War II, the battle over men's minds has accelerated noticeably. So intense has become the American effort to defend and extend our way of life both at home and abroad that the very fiber of our society has experienced a tightening if not a strengthening. Out of psychological warfare, for example, has developed the support for such overseas weapons as cultural and educational exchanges, information agencies, and voices of America. Out of this type of combat has come a new understanding of the military term "survival" and the hazard of brainwashings.

And at home new standards have been unfurled to rally the legions of intellectual freedom and control. The Fifth Amendment has assumed new proportions, and even intellectually restrained men have volunteered to witness against their erstwhile colleagues and peers. It is a day of book-burning alarms and vindictive vigilances by conservative and liberal, each convinced that the other is the censor. And it is a day of preserving a vision we call the American Way, which our profession through libraries has tried to materialize into a Heritage of America program.

If after all of these evidences there are still some lingering doubts about the warlike nature of the American society in which we live, look around at the economic and social conflicts — between capital and labor, between white and black, between poverty and wealth. Only an ostrich could fail to see war in these contrasts. Certainly the immediate future of American society inherits the elements of present conflict.

What then can be the future of reference in such an American society? I ask myself this question and come back with an answer that is both startling and convincing. The role of reference is one of destiny. We may well have within our profession of librarianship, and particularly in that aspect of it we call reference, the grail for our American society. If I appraise the nature of this global conflict in which we now are engaged, the decision will come without the weapons on which we are staking our fiscal resources now.

Just before World War II, a military genius commented on the Maginot Line, "France is perfectly prepared to fight World War II with the weapons of World War I." I am frightened by the chance the United States may be appraised by the historians of tomorrow as the nation perfectly prepared to fight World War III with the weapons of World War II.

We are today pouring countless sums of money into physical weapons. Those who direct the defense of this country are risking our all on such physical tools as nuclear bombs and guided missiles. Yet even now there are signs that these destructive weapons will never be used. Already arctic and antarctic zones of inspection are being talked. Neither side sees the force in such instruments necessary to conquer the other side.

What the thoughtful are anticipating more clearly each day is the importance of public opinion. Since VJ day what victories have been won by either side have been ideological. Force has steadily succumbed to ideas. This was true in Egypt where vastly superior British-French forces had to abandon their invasion. It was previously true in Israel, in Thailand, in India, and on a score or more fronts where differences have kindled to red or white heat. In each case a world opinion has settled the issue.

Here then is the force of greatest potential in World War III — a world idea of the true and the beautiful. The elements of such a world idea are the accumulated wisdom of the ages plus the discoveries and revelations yet to come. Libraries always have contained the world's best ideas. Librarianship has continuously increased its concern with the dissemination of these ideas. And it has assigned the major responsibility for this mission to that branch of librarianship we call reference.

Against the background of an American society destined to be at war during the immediate future, I make my first and most fundamental prediction for the future of reference. In terms of James Ingersoll Wyer's range of definitions for conservative, moderate, and liberal reference, the redefinition of reference now under way cannot be termed less than radical. I attempted to state this new definition of reference for the British Library Association's seventy-fifth anniversary meeting in Bournemouth, after observing for a whole year the way their libraries were pushing our frontiers, as "the process of free inquiry necessary to education and research."

The radical feature of this redefinition of reference is primarily in the concept shift from referendum to initiative. Reference in all three of Dr. Wyer's definitions is intrinsically passive. Regardless of the amount of help offered the reader none of it is initiated by the librarian. In educational reference the librarian waits until the question or assignment is brought to the desk. In research reference the subject specialist first indicates what assistance he wants. The reference librarian is never more than an aid who located the desired materials or information. Haughtily, the specialist has often, with our concurrence, segregated the menial handwork of reference from the privileged occupation of research.

Even now in our libraries this radical redefinition of reference is in evidence. One of the most effective teaching jobs is being done in our schools and colleges, in our communities and research agencies by the reference librarian. On the research front reference librarians subject-equipped are assuming full partnership in investigation and frequently now making the decisive discovery. It is therefore not difficult to make the next predictions.

First of all reference method is likely during the next few years to succumb to automation. The scientific method, so-called, committed inextricably to a sensory approach to reality is likely to sway scholar and layman alike for a number of years yet to come. The fascination in push-button living will inevitably overcome the gadgeteers among us and we will have a spell of mechanized reference. This may enlist the best electronic sorters we can invent. I have already seen a demonstration of things to come. In our military a request for a picture of a Russian woman washing her clothes in the Volga was filled by pushing a series of buttons on a huge robot that then popped up like a toaster a mounted 35mm positive with all of the requirements.

Our hard-won interlibrary loan code is even now being threatened by antiquity. A wonderful little machine, used by the Air Force weather service, called facsimile now transmits electronically hundreds of miles away any page of text, map, picture, or other representation.

But wonderful as technology is, it will not take too many years to rediscover its limitations. No statistical proof is necessary to demonstrate that gadgets are too stupid to be able to store, retrieve, or disseminate knowledge as nimbly as the human mind requires it. What is more, as automation releases semi-skilled humans from assembly line drudgery, higher and higher reference IQ's will be needed to direct automation. Inevitably reliance on the human mind and soul will return. The age of science will give way to a neo-humanistic era.

Out of this new humanism may come reference method even more startling than the push-button. What this new direction may be is probably being heralded in the parapsychology laboratories of Duke University and an increasing number of universities. With mounting evidence that extrasensory phenomena are real, possibly nearer reality than our sensory science findings, reference may well enlist telepathy, precognition, and even psychokinesis.

Lest these terms remain as just so many words let me illustrate. One of Upton Sinclair's less known novels is one called the *Overman*. In it the hero is shipwrecked on an island where the inhabitants communicate not through language but directly by means of thought wave. Consequently when the hero regains consciousness and discovers a beautiful girl hovering over him he produces on her face without a single word a crimson blush. Now consider for a moment what that would mean to the frustrated cross-examining reference librarian who complains that the reader would rather die than tell you precisely what information he wants. That telepathy and precognition are undeveloped gifts within all of us is now a reasonable certainty. Whether our minds can move physical objects is still to be determined by the series of investigations now under way. Nevertheless, I predict reference method in our future American society will rely more on extrasensory talents within the librarians than on sensory equipment without.

These two developments, a redefinition of reference as the process of free inquiry and the increasing use of extrasensory method, will have a decisive effect on the course of World War III. In the struggle between East and West for men's minds victory will inevitably come to the side with the world idea nearest to perfect beauty and truth. To discover, extend, and disseminate the various aspects of this idea libraries all over the world will be engaged. Reference as the process of free inquiry will be the very essence of this effort.

I predict therefore that in the very next few years the reference librarian will emerge as the most strategic professional in our entire family of world occupations. The demands on him from research and education will exceed anything we now know. Increasingly he will become, as he already officially is in many British communities, the information officer. Great decisions of state and faith will be based on the expert and facile findings of the skilled reference librarian. Courts will wait in hushed anticipation of the expert testimony of the reference expert. A strengthened United Nations will base its adjudication between nations on the investigations of reference librarians. And all over the world people will contribute to that world opinion that will win battles and World War III largely on the information reference workers bring them out of the great libraries.

We face a great professional responsibility in the American society of the future. In the hands of the incompetent and the unscrupulous this reference power can become a force for evil. It could be used to enslave the people and produce Orwell's *1984*. But in the hands of the profession I know this reference power will have the power for good that has always motivated librarianship. Under the redefinition of reference the process of free inquiry will go forward toward truth and beauty.

The challenge of the future to us as reference librarians is awesome. But I have faith that our colleagues of this generation and of the next are equal to it and that our destiny is to help bring the kingdom to this world.

On Reference Sources

The Half of Knowledge

OF ALL THE VARIOUS DICTIONARY DEFINITIONS of scholarship I have encountered this is the one that appeals most to me. It says simply that scholarship is "The sum of the mental attainment of a scholar."

Over the front entrance of our former university library building, these words, often ascribed to that prolific versifier "Anon.," are still visible:

"The Half of Knowledge is knowing where to find it."

Alongside this aphorism must go the other one, credited by Boswell to Samuel Johnson:

Knowledge is of two kinds. We know a subject ourselves
Or we know where we can find information on it.

The two halves of the sum of the mental attainments of the scholar, therefore, appear to be *what* and *where*.

As a librarian who has tried faithfully to serve all of the disciplines impartially despite his own humanistic leanings, I have often marvelled at the overwhelming academic emphasis on the *what* and on the comparative neglect of the *where*. It has too often seemed to me that our higher education concerned itself disproportionately with one half of the sum at the risk of providing the student with a total that added up to less than the whole.

Somewhat to restore the balance I should like to share with you some of my experiences in a neglected half of scholarship. I should like to address myself to that part of the sum which enables the true scholar to find information on his subject. All of the records of mankind are, of course, the sources for all we know. But among the millions of tables, papyri, hard and soft covers, serials, celluloid,

Reprinted from *Phi Kappa Phi Journal*, 37: 11-23, Winter, 1959, by permission of the publisher. The essay here reprinted is the text of an address presented on Scholarship Day to the Berea College Chapter of Phi Kappa Phi on May 23, 1957.

films and filmstrips, tape and disc recordings, and other classes of media of communication that must comprise the mythical, universal bibliography, now hopelessly scattered, a comparatively small group of sources hold the key to all man's knowledge.

These sources are known as reference books. They comprise a unique and neglected literature. English departments in our colleges and universities feature courses devoted to various literary forms, such as the novel, poetry, drama, essays, the oration, letters. But to my knowledge there is not a single course devoted to the literature of reference, outside of professional library schools. Yet the literature of reference constitutes the essence of that other half of knowledge, the *where*.

A reference book can be defined simply as any book used for specific information. In a sense every book can be used as a reference book. A Shakespearean play consulted for the identification of certain lines, or a popular novel referred to for identification of a character becomes temporarily a reference book. But some books are almost always used only to refer to; they are never meant to be read through from cover to cover.

Imagine curling up in bed to read *Webster's New International Dictionary* through from page 1 through page 3,214. It simply is not done. Only Pierre Van Paasen to my knowledge has ever claimed to have read a reference book completely, and what a reference book. In *Days of Our Years* he writes that he read through the *Encyclopaedia Britannica.* (Let's hope not including Volume 24, because that is largely an index of some 500,000 entries.)

What distinguishes a reference book from all other kinds of books is the fact that it is not meant to be read from cover to cover, but to be used for specific information. In most libraries the reference book is further identified by the letter "R" before the classification number. Reference books, as a rule, do not circulate for home use, though there have been some recent relaxations.

It is estimated there are in all languages some 10,000 reference titles in the world. Most of these are listed in such retrospective bibliographies as Winchell's *Guide to Reference Books.* I have included a representative review of some 500 titles in my book, *Basic*

Reference Sources. About 300 new and revised reference books are issued each year. These are reviewed in many journals, but nowhere more critically than in the American Library Association's *Subscription Books Bulletin.*

Taken together, these 10,000 titles constitute not only the "where" but the gist of the "what" half of scholarship.

There are many kinds of reference books. Each class has its peculiar potential for locating information. In terms of scholarship needs we can begin with the quest for definition. Problems of terminology confront every investigation at the outset. The obvious type of reference tool is the dictionary. It is so obvious that even in our secondary schools we sometimes overlook the elements of dictionary use.

I ask your indulgence in a parable. In a certain high school English class the teacher asked the pupils to look up the meaning of a word in the "big" dictionary. On the assumption that every member of the class was equally diligent and copied only the first definition, a surprising result followed. When the students handed in their written definitions, half of the class were right, and half wrong. How did that happen? Simply because the ambiguous reference to the "big" dictionary did not distinguish between the two American unabridged works whose outward appearance is monstrously similar, but whose inner organization is sometimes frustratingly different. In the case of the pupils who consulted the first definition given in *Webster's New International Dictionary* the meaning was that current in Chaucer's time, since that dictionary gives its definitions in chronological order, the oldest meaning first. The pupils who consulted *Funk and Wagnalls New Standard* met first of all the meaning common today.

Definitions are only one aspect of dictionary use. Vocabulary scope can be even more critical. It does the scientist no favor to recommend that fine unabridged *Webster's New International Dictionary* if he is seeking an authoritative definition of "radar" because even at this late date the term is not in its alphabetical place. Nor is a colloquialist helped by consulting the incomparable *Oxford English Dictionary* for a four-letter word that recurs generously in a recent Pulitzer Prize novel. Stangely enough, however, if you will read conservative *Webster's* fourth definition of the word "It" (I-T) you will find a shocking recognition of the popular appreciation of feminine pulchritude, because *It* is also defined as "personal charm and magnetism."

To use a dictionary intelligently the true scholar must know the limitations of the various works he consults. For all English dictionaries suffer from some form of abridgement. The earliest English dictionaries like Robert Cawdrey's *Table Alphabetical* of 1604, or the work of John Milton's nephew, Edward Phillips, completed in 1658, were limited to "hard" words because it was assumed every one knew the meanings of the easy ones.

We know that the great dictionary of Samuel Johnson was limited in a number of ways. In imitation of the Latin European dictionaries of the eighteenth century Dr. Johnson limited the vocabulary to the words he considered proper. This censorship was not all bad. The national academies of France, Italy, and Spain were really concerned with codifying, so to speak, their respective national languages. Since England had no comparable national academy, its scholars naturally turned to its one-man learned society. Samuel Johnson's own cocksureness that he alone could do what had taken the efforts of so many in the other nations is described in this bit of dialogue from Boswell's *Journal:*

> Dr. Adams: "But sir, how can you do this in three years? The French Academy which consists of forty members took forty years to complete their dictionary."
> Dr. Johnson: "I have no doubt I can do it in three years . . . three to 1600 so is the proportion of an Englishman to a Frenchman."

Actually the dictionary required about eleven years. The plan addressed to Philip Dormer, Earl of Chesterfield, was published in 1747, and the dictionary itself in 1755. It represents even today an almost unbelievable achievement for one man. But the *Dictionary* can hardly be called unabridged. Its limitations are reflected not only in its vocabulary, but often in its definitions which frequently distort through complexity, bias, or feigned modesty.

For example, Johnson defines:

> NETWORK, as anything reticulated or decussated
> at equal distances with interstices beyond the
> intersections.

During the period when Johnson hoped for a pension and was frequently disappointed he wrote this definition of that word.

> PENSION, pay given to a state hireling for treason
> against his country.

Johnson's contempt for the Scottish people, often alluded to by Boswell, found its outlet in this definition:

> OATS, a grain which in England is generally given
> to horses, but in Scotland supports the people.

To this a Scot wit retorted, "England is known for its horses and Scotland for its people."

Samuel Johnson's definition of a lexicographer and consequently of himself was modest enough: "A writer of dictionaries; a harmless drudge."

Nor was the first great American dictionary which followed early in the last century unabridged. Noah Webster studied diligently the work of his predecessors and produced in 1828 *An American Dictionary of the English Language* which contained 70,000 words —12,000 more than in Johnson's dictionary. But despite this increase and attention to Americanisms the Webster dictionary was not unabridged. Its dominant note was still the critical one expressed by his national predecessors—the scholars must tell the people what words they may use.

The big change came to English lexicography in 1857 when Dean Trench read his paper of protest before the London Philological Society, "Some Deficiencies in Existing English Dictionaries." The keynote was expressed in these words: A dictionary is "an inventory of the language. It is no task of the maker to select the good words of the language. . . . He is an historian not a critic."

Although this idea had never been expressed so forcefully before, it had actually begun to take shape in the work of the Grimm brothers in Germany. Early in the nineteenth century they had set out to discover and record the language of the people. As sometimes happens, the world will probably remember the Grimms longer for their by-product, the famous folk tales they picked up in the process of listening for the words of the people, such as the one re-immortalized by Walt Disney as "SW and the 7 D's" (Snow White and the Seven Dwarfs). But the fact remains their end product was a German language dictionary that recorded faithfully all the words used by the people. The first volume of the Grimms' *Deutsche Worterbuch* appeared in 1854.

Three years later Dean Trench launched our greatest English language dictionary. Some 1300 scholars on both sides of the Atlantic were enlisted to assemble some 5,000,000 quotations from 5,000 writers—quotations that would illustrate every shade of meaning for every word in our language. The task took seventy years and resulted in the OED, the *Oxford English Dictionary*, which you can examine with wonder and fascination on your own college library shelves.

But despite its monumental proportions the OED is not complete. A very large fraction of the people's vocabulary had to be omitted. The obscene words of pornographic literature were deliberately excluded. These terms, in case you are interested, or because you are involved in a critical study of the contemporary novel of so-called realism, can be found in at least two special dictionaries. One of these is a British work by Eric Partridge, titled *Dictionary of Slang and Unconventional English*, from the preface of which I cannot resist quoting the author's purpose:

> I have given them all. (My rule, in the matter of unpleasant terms, has been to deal with them briefly, and as astringently, as aseptically as was consistent with clarity and adequacy; in a few instances I had to force myself to overcome an instinctive repugnance; for these I ask the indulgence of my readers.)

The other is an American work by L. V. Berrey and Melvin Van den Bark called *American Thesaurus of Slang*. It is not arranged alphabetically, although it does have an alphabetic index.

Concurrent with this progress toward scientific unabridgement in our English language dictionaries, there is a contemporary effort toward objective abridgement. Today, there are several classes of abridged dictionaries graded to age levels and requirements. There is, for example, the so-called college or adult abridged dictionary with a vocabulary of up to 150,000 words available at prices ranging from five to ten dollars. This is the type of dictionary most of us can afford for our own personal use and includes such examples as Webster's *New Collegiate,* Funk and Wagnalls' *College Standard,* the *American College Dictionary.* It was the last which rode the commercial wave of popularity with tooth paste and chewing gum by advertising in big green letters "this dictionary, also contains chlorophyl."

There are school dictionaries with further abridgements up to 80,000 words and down to 30,000 words. Examples of these are the Thorndike-Barnhart series and the Webster-American Book Company titles. There are also fascinating primary or picture dictionaries for very young children with as few as 300 words. All of these classes of dictionaries base their vocabulary selection not on the will of one authority but rather upon a scientific principle, the so-called Thorndike frequency technique devised by the American psychologist. Statistically, the literature for a particular grade level is analyzed, and words arranged in the order of their frequency. Consequently, a dictionary limited to 30,000 words presumably includes the 30,000 that appear most frequently in the writings most read by the group for whom the dictionary is intended.

Besides definition and vocabulary scope, spelling and pronunciation are important considerations in the selection and use of a dictionary for locating terminology information. We all know that the British spell such words as *labor,* l-a-b-o-u-r, and take that into account when we are using a dictionary published in England. But we are all troubled by the spelling variations found in American dictionaries depending upon the degree of simplification accepted. "Thru" is rapidly being accepted, but probably "bot" is not. And certainly the advocacy by the late Melvil Dewey, author of the Decimal Classification and earliest secretary of the Simplified Spelling movement, of "ar" and "hav" without the end "e" in either case has had no noticeable acceptance.

Pronunciation variations are also stimulated by our British colleagues. In our editorial office we were for many months disturbed by a London associate who was forever calling for the "clark." His patience tried, the clerk one day expostulated, "Don't call me clark; the correct pronunciation is 'cloyk.' "

There you have it. The differences in pronunciation are not only between London and New York, but among New York and Boston, Chicago and Charleston. Hollywood apparently requires all of its starlets to say "ither." But which pronunciation would you say most dictionaries favor—"ither" or "eether"? Regardless of the answer itself, the most important part of our learning is to know where to find out, and to recall that at least one of our unabridged dictionaries gives in tabular form the preferences of leading dictionaries on controversial pronunciations.

Almost as frequently as we need to know *where* to locate information on terms we need to be able to find out about people. In our reference literature there is a rich collection of biographical sources. To handle these tools adequately it is necessary to divide all persons into the living and the dead, and into notables and specialists.

For the dead notables there are monumental national biographies.

Britain points proudly to its DNB, a seventy volume, plus, set of nearly 30,000 biographies of individuals "Of British or Irish race who have achieved any reasonable measure of distinction in any walk of life. . . ."

The DNB's distinguished editor, Sir Sidney Lee, commenting on the problem of selecting names for the *Dictionary of National Biography*, wrote in the preface:

> Actions, however beneficent or honourable, which are accomplished or are capable of accomplishment by many thousands of persons are actions of mediocrity, and lack the dimension which justifies the biographer's notice. The fact that a man is a devoted husband and father, an efficient school master, an exemplary parish priest, gives him in itself no claim to biographical commemoration.

In the DNB the longest single article, some forty-nine pages, is devoted to Shakespeare. The Duke of Wellington gets thirty-four pages; Francis Bacon and Oliver Cromwell thirty-two pages each; and Queen Elizabeth I, twenty-eight pages.

Our American counterpart, the *Dictionary of American Biography*, is the result of the combined effort of the American Council of Learned Societies and the late publisher of the New York *Times*,

Adolph S. Ochs, who underwrote the undertaking with a $500,000 donation. In the selection of the names for inclusion, three criteria were established: (1) no living persons were to be included; (2) no persons who had not lived in the territory now known as the United States; (3) no British officer serving in America after the Colonies had declared their independence. Within these limitations persons elected for inclusion in the DAB were "Those who had made some significant contribution to American life in its manifold aspects." The application of these principles resulted inevitably in some curious inclusions. For example, a column and a half is devoted to Lydia E. Pinkham.

But if selection of dead notables is difficult, consider the choice of living ones. Every civilized nation has its "who's who" type of reference book. France calls it *Qui Etes Vous?* and Germany *Wer Ists.* In England it is just plain *Who's Who,* published every year. And in the United States it is *Who's Who in America* issued every two years. The last volume, that for the biennium 1954-55, lists about 50,000 notable Americans out of about 160,000,000 people. This represents roughly about 1 in 32,000. How are they selected?

Two bases are indicated by the publishers: (1) *official position,* such as President of the United States, governor of a state, president of a college, etc.; (2) *creation,* including writing, composing, painting, inventing, investigating, discovering, etc. A few foreigners are included solely because of their identification with American life. Otherwise, it can be stated the publishers conscientiously apply their criteria to all nominees.

Other sources for information about persons are directories of specialists. An outstanding example is the three-volume *American Men of Science* devoted to physical, biological, and social scientists. Another is the *Directory of American Scholars,* largely concerned with men of letters who have distinguished themselves in the humanities. A third is the selected biographical directory known as *Leaders in Education.* Among these biographical directories, plus a few more like *Current Biography,* which features people in the news, the universal *Webster's Biographical Dictionary,* regional collections, and the unique *Who Knows--and What,* are the answers to where to find out about notable persons.

After persons, there are places. We are more one world conscious than ever. The airplane and radio made us so. But even more, the 12,000,000 GI parents of World War II, and police actions since, have produced a young generation conscious of places never mentioned in geography books — places like Karachi and Accra, Ascension and Natal, Belam and Maiduguri, Myikitina and the Hump, Taiwan and Teheran, where people they love won critical battles and where transcontinental airlines today refuel for round the world hops.

Sources for these places are of several kinds. There are verbal tools like gazetteers, primarily dictionaries which identify in alphabetic order the rivers, lakes, mountains, cities, and other geographical features of the world. *Webster's Geographical Dictionary* and the *Columbia Lippincott Gazetteer* are representative. Then there are the guide books for the traveller concerned with the cultural sights and the hot spots for after midnight entertainment. The name Baedeker has for nearly a century been the guide to Europe for American tourists.

But much more effective has been the atlas. Ever since the sixteenth century geographer, Gerhardus Mercator, or his son brought together in one volume a collection of maps under a cover which portrayed the mythological giant bearing the burden of the world on his broad shoulder, this major class of reference books has had a prominent rack in our libraries. There are many notable examples. In America our leading cartographic publishers produce good, if not artistic, atlases. Rand McNally, which this year celebrated its centennial, features the *Cosmopolitan* for home and library, and the large *Commercial* for library, industry, and business. Hammond, Cram, and others offer a variety of map collections at different prices and sizes. All of these atlases at long last have become cognizant of our one-world geography. All have paid particular attention to such regions as the Pacific, Arctica and Antarctica, the Persian Gulf Area, the GI points of concentration, and a USSR that can be seen in its total stretch from Brest-Litovsk to Vladivostock without keeping one finger on the map of Europe while looking at the map of Asia.

The problem that still confronts the American atlas user is whether to consult a superior foreign collection of maps which neglects comparatively important places in the United States, or a domestic atlas with fewer good maps and more emphasis on home towns. The new *Times Survey Atlas*, of which three volumes have appeared, reveals cartographic excellence and gives promise of remedying the relative neglect of our country that has characterized foreign atlases in the past.

Terms, persons, places are three of the *whats* along the road to scholarship for which the scholar must know the *wheres*. Without a knowledge of dictionaries, biographical and geographical sources, the other half of knowledge is harder to come by. The same might be said for the sources of trends, statistics, allusions, formulae, documents, how-to-do, and countless other problems that confront the investigator. A startling recognition of this neglected phase of our scholarship is evident in the sudden and insatiable demand for librarians, bibliographers, documentalists, abstracters, and indexers in industry, government, and agencies of research. The *where* of knowledge finds support in the increasing attention on our college campuses to courses dealing with the sources and method of scholarly investigation. In these attentions to the *wheres* of knowledge the accent on reference tools is marked. And of all types of reference books there is one that crystallizes the half of knowledge that deals with the *where* more dramatically than any other.

Since the beginning of scholarship, scholars have at various times undertaken to organize all that man knows of significance in one master work. The complete works of Plato or Aristotle constituted such a circle of knowledge for ancient times. Pliny's *Natural History* of the first century has often been cited as the earliest encyclopedia. Although not a naturalist, Pliny meticulously analyzed some 2,000 ancient books by 100 different authors to compile a classified collection of some 20,000 facts. There were many other notable attempts to provide a single "where" for all the "what" of scholarship down through the Middle Ages and up to modern times: the Dominican monk Vincent of Beauvais compiled an encyclopedia in 1260 under three major heads — history, science and morals; the African Capella produced an allegorical work on the seven liberal arts in verse; the English printer Caxton published the first encyclopedia in our language in 1460; Ringelberg of Basel is presumed in 1541 to have created the first work that used the term encyclopedia; Cornelli in Italy is generally credited with the first alphabetical set; and in France, a series of famous encyclopedia efforts by Voltaire, Pierre Bayle, and Louis Moreri finally culminated in the great eighteenth century French Encyclopédie, product of Diderot, Voltaire, Rousseau, Montesquieu, Turgot, and a galaxy of scholars. Whether this work was one of the major causes of the French Revolution, or whether Madame Pompadour rescued the set from oblivion by her curiosity about the origin of rouge, is of less importance for our purpose than the fact that such a great coterie of scholars was impelled to summarize the significant knowledge of mankind through cooperative effort.

Within a few years the great English effort began. The first edition of the *Encyclopaedia Britannica* appeared serially starting in 1768. For nearly two centuries now scholars from all over the world have contributed their collective knowledge to this enterprise which has come to symbolize encyclopedia for the English-speaking people. Though largely American financed since Sears Roebuck first gained control, the *Britannica* continues today through the affiliation with the University of Chicago to summarize man's significant knowledge.

Other great encyclopedic works have since arisen to provide competition. The *Americana,* for example, in its thirty volumes, has for well over a hundred years espoused an American emphasis. More recently *Collier's Encyclopedia,* with which I have had the opportunity to serve as advisory editor since its beginning in 1946, has sought to introduce additional principles as a basis for summarizing man's knowledge. All of these sets, plus other American and foreign works, and encyclopedias especially created for children and young people, are to be found in our homes and on the shelves of American libraries. Their adequate use and understanding are a basic aspect of the *where* as well as the *what* of knowledge.

Consider this matter of selecting the significant knowledge. There are now so many facts in the world that to include them all would take no fewer than the 50 million books it is estimated the world has produced. How to select and compress into some 20 volumes this plethora of learning is enough to confound the profoundest of learned men. Earlier it was easier when the scholar dictator merely said this is the important knowledge because I say so. The predatory rights of my subjects and of my favorite colleagues are of prime significance. All other fields constitute trade education or the elbowings of the nouveau riche.

A reflection of this philosophy made itself evident not only in the content of encyclopedias but also in the curricula of higher educations. The seven liberal arts of the medieval universities included Latin, rhetoric and grammar, logic, arithmetic, geometry, astronomy, music. It did not include chemistry or physics or biology or botany; it did not even include history, much less political science or economics. Shockingly there was no literature, or art, or philosophy. And when these subjects did appear for the first time no doubt they were accorded the same "trade school" tolerance they were in turn to give sociology and psychology, and later, education and home economics, and even later, such subjects as hotel and restaurant management and baking science. It was to be expected, therefore, that the same scholars who determined the content of the university curriculum would also decide on the scope of the encyclopedia.

But the man on the street had yet to be heard. The number of angels who could dance on the point of a pin concerned him less than the number of bricks it would take to build a good house. Encyclopedia editors began to study people's interests and allocate space to subjects accordingly. The long articles on monism versus dualism gave way to consumer education and the space formerly devoted to Thomas Becket went to Thomas A. Edison. The shift of emphasis was from the scholar's circle of knowledge to the layman's popular interest.

The encyclopedia today is truly a summary of the knowledge most significant to modern man. It is accessibly arranged. In its best form the encyclopedia is a crystallization of man's finest efforts to balance the *where* and *what* of knowledge into a sum that will most nearly represent scholarship. That the effort is not easy I can assure you firsthand.

It was my good fortune at the close of World War II to be invited to serve as a member of the charter board of editors commissioned to create an entirely new encyclopedia of some fifteen million words, one on which the publishers were prepared to spend upward of two million dollars. On a bright spring morning in 1946 I entered the editorial offices of Crowell-Collier and began to consider with my six colleagues, drawn from six other campuses, this simple task of presenting all the knowledge significant to the English-speaking people in language they could understand, so organized that any fragment of it would be instantly located. Once found it would have to be absolutely authoritative, unbiased, artistically illustrated, and meticulously documented, and presented in such sequence that the uninitiated might self-educate.

This is no time to sketch an encyclopedia editor's nightmares. But perhaps there is just enough time to clinch a definition of scholarship by a few references. As a first step we seven finally accepted 78 departments of knowledge. My Princeton colleague agreed most reluctantly to such "trade school" areas as "Home Economics," and "Sports and Games." But in the end he compromised in return for several departments in his one area of linguistics. How much this phase of encyclopedia building reminded me of my part in the university sub-committee on overlapping of the curriculum committee. Then followed the allocation of wordage, dividing up the 15 million for which the publisher would pay among the departments, and the appointment of the department editors. For the entire first year while I was commuting back and forth between New York and Tallahassee every two weeks we compiled lists of topics entitled to separate articles. It was heavy work, and there was much deliberation and evaluation of academic disciplines. At times the tensions between the natural and the social sciences became great over wordage allotments, but not as great as that between the chemists and the physicists. Always the result was what results are among true scholars — increasing appreciation and respect for colleagues' disciplines. And inevitably there are pranks even among scholars.

I recall one time when we reached the letter "P" that the subject prostitution appeared with no departmental assignment. To my surprise it turned up the next day in the sheaf of assignments for the editor of the department of sports and games.

Once the department editors had agreed on the topics and the wordage the next step was to invite authoritative contributors. All of us reviewed nominees critically, both from the standpoint of their knowledge and their ability to write for laymen. It is not always true that he who knows his subject can teach it. The late Orientalist Dr. Breasted once wrote a very scholarly article on Egyptology for a children's encyclopedia with which I was then associated. No child could possibly have understood it. Before authority and editor could finally agree on both content and form exactly fourteen versions were prepared.

Among the contributors invited to write a major science article for *Collier's Encyclopedia* was a very famous California Tech scientist. When he sent in his manuscript, it arrived in the large mail room of Crowell-Collier along with hundreds of other manuscripts, most of them unsolicited ones which used to come in daily for magazines like *Collier's, Woman's Home Companion,* and *American* which were then published by the firm as well as the encyclopedia. I imagine what happened was that the mail boy in sorting the mail aimed the Cal Tech scientist's manuscript for the encyclopedia bag but missed; instead, the envelope dropped into the *Collier's Magazine* bag. In that office the manuscript became not the prize we were anticipating, but just another unsolicited one.

On a Monday morning the long distance call from California fairly sizzled. Never before had this world famous scientist had a manuscript returned. But to add insult to injury there was not even a letter from us. There was only a little yellow printed slip which merely said, "We regret we cannot use this manuscript at this time," plus a little pat on the back which said, "Keep trying young fellow. You may make the grade some day."

Meticulously we had to watch for propaganda. Bias creeps in even where an author has a reputation. We were actually asked to see to it that our account of the Civil War was impartially written from the Southern point of view. Articles dealing with the Reformation were read by Catholic and Protestant scholars. The subjects of communism, political parties, and the New Deal were scrutinized by protagonists and antagonists alike. If a single article could not satisfy, two articles representing conflicting views were included.

Many problems confronted the editors during the decade of construction. In the end 20 volumes appeared. There was no feeling of perfection among any of us who have labored with this work. We have never ceased our effort to present continuously a balanced summary of the *what* and *where* of all we know. Through a process encyclopedists call continuous revision we read regularly assigned parts of the set for corrections and up dating.

I commend any good encyclopedia to you as a synthesis of scholarship. It represents that balance between the *where* and the *what* that defines our objective. In an encyclopedia all scholarship has joined to create that unity which is the essence of all learning.

On this scholarship day may I join you in praying for the fulfillment of Phi Kappa Phi's motto:

"The love of learning rules the world."

The Other Half — Where to Find it

STILL DISTINGUISHABLE OVER THE ARCHWAY of our former university library are the oft-quoted words of that prolific writer Anon:

"The half of knowledge is knowing where to find it."

After more than three decades as teacher and librarian, mostly in higher education, there are extended moments of concern over the continued neglect of knowing where.

The essence of this half of knowledge is a rich literature of reference, some 10,000 books in all languages, of which a select, basic few titles deserve early mastery.[1] Despite some brave attempts

[1] For notes, see pages 168-169.

with "library use" instruction in elementary and secondary schools, and orientation units or library courses for college freshmen, there are still distressing signs that our undergraduates do not know where to find it. Indeed, in even some of our better graduate schools, doctoral candidates can be found wasting research hours unaware of such basic finders as *Facts on File* or *Keesing's,* or the annual (for over a century) *Statesman's Yearbook* or (for over two centuries) *Annual Register.*

Perhaps this is so because too many of our teachers of grade through graduate students do not know their reference books too confidently. Predominantly our teacher education has tended toward the pragmatic belief that materials are learned best in relation to something else—to method, to subject, to curriculum, to the child, to psychology of learning. Unquestionably there is some value to incidental learning. But somewhere, some time, also, teachers need to study materials *per se,* the whole range of school formats from textbook through teaching machine, the strengths and weaknesses of each type of educational medium for a particular learning circumstance.

Among all of the hundred or more different types of instructional materials now found in our nation's schools and colleges, none deserves more careful attention than the "R" book. Its potential for "the other half" hasn't even begun to be tapped by teachers and students.[2] Primarily, this is so because only a very few of the books that stand on the reference shelves in our libraries are known and used in classroom learning.

Reference books are unique literature. They are not intended to be read through from cover to cover. Because they are used to refer to for information, the better examples of R books have format designs and arrangement patterns not usually found in reading books.

Modern reference books, for example, give attention to such visuals as the transparency overlay, to color, to three-dimensional map, to pictograph, chart, table, diorama. So that information may be more readily available, reference book editors have done very much more with index variations and with such devices as fact boxes, page makeup, bleed photos, caption-legend extensions of illustrations than is found in most books.

In other respects than arrangement and format, the R book leads the parade of instructional materials. No regular textbook, or for that matter, no educational motion picture or even ETV program can afford the all-star cast of editors, world scholars, artists, cartographers, production experts that team to produce today's good encyclopedias, unabridged dictionaries, or distinguished atlases.

Evidence of inadequate acquaintance with reference books is illustrated in dictionary use. Frequently teachers will ask pupils to look up a word in the "big" dictionary, as if there were only one. In most libraries the two most frequently consulted dictionaries look almost alike. But there are fundamental differences between *Webster's Third New International*[3] and *Funk and Wagnalls New Standard*.[4] In the matter of definition alone the former gives the oldest meaning first, and the latter the commonest, regardless of whether that meaning is historically the oldest or the newest.

Nor are these two the only "big" dictionaries of the English language. No college student should let his freshman year advance very far before he begins to consult the "O.E.D." The great *Oxford English Dictionary*,[5] now available to libraries in a $300 set of 13 volumes, remains unconsulted for too many hours of each college day simply because neither instructor nor student is aware of its treasures.

How many times, for instance, has a stray quotation been futilely sought in a quotations book like Bartlett or Hoyt and pursued no further because the searcher was unaware that O.E.D. includes nearly two million quotations to illustrate word meanings. These excerpts were culled from some five million extracts by 1300 scholars of English language and literature. Because each quotation appears under the word it illustrates, finding a quotation in O.E.D. is almost easier than finding it in Bartlett or Hoyt.

But O.E.D. provides much more than quotations. Detailed etymology, scientific pronunciation, meticulous definition that traces meaning changes through the centuries, and spelling variations are only a few of the resources that O.E.D. offers the dictionary user.

Almost as important as the big dictionary in the library is the abridgement chosen for one's personal use. Based on the vocabulary size classification I have offered in *Instructional Materials*, most college teachers and students will make their choice among college abridged dictionaries. The college abridged dictionary contains from 100,000 to 150,000 entries, selected usually on the basis of frequency of word occurrence in adult literature. Although this means an inclusion of less than one third of the words found in the unabridged works, the bulk of the omissions will be obsolete or rarely used terms. And the differential in price (under $10 versus over $40) will justify reference to the library's larger work when occasion demands.

There are at least a half dozen good college dictionaries available at prices under $6. *Webster's Seventh New Collegiate*,[6] although based on the controversial unabridged "Third," is somewhat more conservative in its choice of vocabulary, capitalization, and identification of persons and places. Its 130,000 entries include some 20,000 new words, about 5,000 persons, and 10,000 places. It has, besides, retained that identifying feature, the rhyming dictionary section.

This year, rival Funk and Wagnalls has released its new competitor for the *Webster Collegiate*. With over 150,000 entries, the *Standard College Dictionary*[7] provides in its single alphabetic sequence one of the largest vocabularies found in any desk dictionary. Most striking is the page makeup with its wide columns, appealing type and illustrations.

A sturdy competitor of both these "old line" efforts is the *American College Dictionary*[8] with about 132,000 entries. It follows the Funk and Wagnalls pattern of including persons and places in the same alphabetic sequence. For the latter, about 300 spot black and white maps give meaning to geographical references. There is also another Webster,[9] not published by Merriam but by the World Publishing Company of Cleveland. Its 142,000 entries provide rather clear and simple definitions.

The good encyclopedia properly used is the backbone of good learning. It is a summary of the knowledge most significant to mankind. In the preliminary pages of any major set are listed authorities to conjure with. Ingenious devices to accelerate finding, from whole-letter volume guides to fact-indexes, are monuments to that other half of knowledge.

Time out has to be taken to study the encyclopedia as an educational medium, however. Unless some attention is given to such intricacies as specific versus broad subject article pattern, to classified versus alphabetic arrangement, to scattered map versus concentrated atlas features, to indexing variations, to bibliographic placement and purpose, tragic abuses will follow.

There is a grim irony in the prohibitions on encyclopedia use imposed by some teachers and principals. Because so many of our youngsters indulge in copying, usually the early part of an encyclopedia article, their instructors blame not their own faulty instruction but the encyclopedia. It is precisely like throwing the baby out with the bath.

But there was the good student who never began a college course in September without getting an overview of the subject from a good encyclopedia. It stirred him to anticipate the teacher's unfolding of the content; to nod his head in approval when the teacher's sequence and treatment approximated that of the outstanding authority who had written the encyclopedia article; to debate the issue silently or in essay when the classroom trend was contrary to the position of the encyclopedist. In some pedagogical books this is also a manifestation of learning.

And there was the good student who skillfully searched index and cross references in the encyclopedia for interrelationships, for perspective on topics often related in the classroom only to the discipline represented by the course. The encyclopedia, he discovered, was interdisciplinary, an approach to knowledge by some of the world's greatest minds working together to fit the subject segments into the cosmic circle.

English language encyclopedias today can be broadly classified by level and scope, and perhaps by cost. The big three — *Britannica*,[10] *Americana*,[11] *Collier's*[12] (in order of earliest publication date) — are all adult, comprehensive, world-wide in perspective.

All three have upward of 20 million words and cost in excess of $300. Authorities from the great universities of the world and from many government, industrial, and other agencies are responsible for the text. An editorial staff of over a hundred, in each case, con-

tinuously edits and updates the content. Illustration augments text
with a skill and artistry unmatched anywhere in the universe of
educational media. A map program for a major encyclopedia rarely
costs less than a half million dollars. When birds and fish, costumes
and vegetation are presented, usually in color, distinguished subject
specialists team with renowned artists to create reproductions meticulously accurate and stirringly informing.

Somewhat less comprehensive and costly are the adult, popular
encyclopedias represented by the British *Chambers's*[13] and the
U.S. *American Peoples*.[14] The former contains some 15 million
words and the latter about nine million.

Encyclopedias especially correlated with elementary and secondary curricula have introduced significant innovations such as the
whole-letter volume guide, a high ratio of illustration to text, readability, and attention to classroom needs. Leading examples of the
alphabetically arranged school encyclopedias are *Compton's*,[15]
World Book,[16] *Britannica Junior*,[17] *American Educator*[18] (again in
order of earliest publication date, counting predecessors). Among
the classified school encyclopedias *Book of Knowledge*[19] and *Our
Wonderful World*[20] are leading examples.

There are some scholars who would contend that only European,
non-English language encyclopedias are worthy of study. Certainly
the college student who reads Spanish should acquaint himself with
"Espasa," French with the latest *Larousse*, (and only out of historical curiosity with Diderot's biased opus, and for comparison with
the more deft American handling of the classified arrangement, the
contemporary *Encyclopedie Francaise*), German with *Der Grosse
Brockhaus* (pioneer in the specific subject pattern), Italian with
Enciclopedia Italiana (for its striking photogravure plates) and
Russian with the *Bol'shaya Sovetskaya Entsiklopediya* (for its contemporary espousal of the Diderot "ax-grinding" encyclopedism).

Perhaps the dictionary and encyclopedia, because they encompass the scope and arrangement of nearly every one of the other
dozen types of reference books, suggest something about lost learning opportunities. We have, at Florida State University, both a
freshman course on library use in learning and a graduate course

on library use in research. In both courses there is an opportunity
to browse in the reference collection and discover where to find it
for every course on the current schedule, for every investigation on
the academic horizon.

Even those who know the major encyclopedias seldom use their
yearbooks for contemporary happenings. There was the history student with short notice assignment for an authoritative summary of
the situation in the USSR today. In his library course his future was
saved by five reference titles that somehow had not become a part
of his four years of higher education: *Britannica Book of the Year*
which gave him the area, population, capitals, etc., of the 15 repub-
lics; *Statesman's Yearbook,* centenary edition, where an elusive
aspect, religion, was objectively treated, and a compact bibliography
included; *Annual Register,* the 204th annual volume, which covered
the key political and diplomatic events; the U. S. *Facts on File* and
the British *Keesing's,* which week by week summarize and cumulate
the happenings in that country.

Perhaps this, at least, demonstrates some attention to the other
half.

---

[1] Shores, Louis. *Basic Reference Sources* (Chicago: American Library Association, 1954), p. 17-21.
[2] Shores, Louis. *Instrumental Materials* (New York: Ronald, 1960), p. 63-98.
[3] Webster's Third New International Dictionary of the English Language,
Unabridged (Springfield, Mass.: G. & C. Merriam, 1961).
[4] Funk & Wagnalls New Standard Dictionary of the English Language (New
York: Wilfred Funk, 1961).
[5] The Oxford English Dictionary (Oxford: Clarendon Press, 1888-1933).
[6] Webster's Seventh New Collegiate Dictionary (Springfield, Mass.: G. & C.
Merriam, 1963).
[7] Funk & Wagnalls Standard College Dictionary (New York: Wilfred Funk,
1963; text ed., New York: Harcourt, Brace, 1963).
[8] American College Dictionary (New York: Random House, 1961).
[9] Webster's New World Dictionary of the American Language (Cleveland:
World Publishing Co., 1962).
[10] Encyclopaedia Britannica (Chicago: Encyclopaedia Britannica, Inc., 1963),
24 V.
[11] Encyclopedia Americana (Washington, D.C.: Americana Corporation, 1963),
30 V.
[12] Collier's Encyclopedia (New York: Crowell-Collier Publishing Co., 1963),
24 V.
[13] Chambers's Encyclopaedia (London: Newnes, 1955), 15 V.
[14] American Peoples Encyclopedia (New York: Grolier, 1963), 20 V.
[15] Compton's Pictured Encyclopedia (Chicago: F. E. Compton & Company,
1963), 15 V.

16 World Book Encyclopedia (Chicago: Field Enterprises, Inc., 1963), 20 V.
17 Britannica Junior (Chicago: Encyclopaedia Britannica, Inc., 1963), 15 V.
18 American Educator Encyclopedia (Lake Bluff, Ill.: United Educators, Inc., 1963), 10 or 14 V.
19 Book of Knowledge (New York: Grolier, Inc., 1963), 20 V.
20 Our Wonderful World (New York: Grolier, 1963), 18 V.

Patterns in American Reference Books

THE WORLD'S REFERENCE BOOKS now comprise a literature so extensive that it is no longer possible to compile an inclusive bibliography. There are, for example, some 5,500 titles in Miss Winchell's admirable 7th edition of the *Guide to reference books* just issued by the American Library Association. Miss Winchell does not claim that all of the world's reference books have been included. Because, beside the chance that a truly good reference title may have escaped even the thorough and careful workmanship that Miss Winchell's book exemplifies, there is the fact that many books not called reference books have high reference potential.

Even more important is the rate at which new reference books are appearing. The third annual reference book round-up which appeared in the 9th February *Saturday Review* listed nearly 150 titles, mostly American, the harvest of a single year. *Publishers' Weekly*, likewise, in its annual issue devoted to reference books uncovered a number of other titles. With all this it becomes evident that the quantity of reference titles is now so great that no one practising reference librarian can be expected to know them all by name, leave alone by scope and arrangement for job mastery. And as for the library school student, the list is already so long for examination cramming that he must face with dread each new title.

It becomes increasingly important, therefore, both from the standpoint of the veteran and the tyro that fewer titles and better principles be the guideposts of reference literature orientation. To

Reprinted from *The Library Association Record*, 54: 284-291, September, 1952, by permission of the publisher.

that end I have endeavoured to even a greater extent than in the two
previous editions to devote myself in the third edition of *Basic reference books* to criteria and production, with a limited number of
specific titles for illustration.

Reference book appraisal. Reference books may be defined as
books published primarily for consultation rather than for continuous reading. In a liberal sense any book may become a reference
book if it is referred to for a specific bit of information. A Shakespeare play consulted for the exact wording of a specific line
becomes for that purpose a reference book, even though it was meant
for continuous reading. On the other hand the *Encyclopaedia Britannica* is not meant to be read through continuously from the first
to the last volumes, although Pierre Van Paasen claimed to have
done so. We can only hope that he found all of the 24th volume
readable!

In the United States today reference books are issued by three
kinds of publishers. Trade publishers like Macmillan, Scribner and
Harper, who have given us such reference classics as the *Encyclopedia of the social sciences*, the *Dictionary of American biography*,
and the *Dictionary of classical antiquities*, distribute their publications through the book store. Textbook publishers like the American
Book Company, and Scott, Foresman, and Winston, whose recent
contributions to the school dictionary field have notable lexico-
graphic significance, depend largely on school systems' adoptions
for their distribution.

A third large class of publishers known as subscription book
publishers specialize largely in reference books. Their method of
distribution is direct — publisher to consumer through a representative who calls at the individual home. In 1946, six of the largest
American subscription book publishers organized themselves into a
branch of the American Textbook Publishers' Institute. These six
and their principal reference works are:

Encyclopaedia Brittanica, inc., *Encyclopaedia Britannica*
F. E. Compton and Company, *Compton's pictured encyclopedia*
P. F. Collier & Sons, *Collier's encyclopedia*
Grolier Society, *Encyclopedia Americana*
Field Enterprises, inc., *World Book Encyclopedia*
United Educators, inc., *American educator.*

Appraisal criteria. In the evaluation of reference books, authority is a primary criterion. If the publisher's integrity is impeccable, a reasonably authoritative reference work may be expected. Inevitably such a publisher will select competent editors and contributors. Such a staff should produce an objective compilation of information accessibly arranged. If to the seasoned scholarship that has always characterized reputable reference works there is added what has more recently engaged the attention of publishers — a readable style, popular subjects, plentiful, applicable and attractive illustrations, adequate indexing, and bibliographies keyed to the resources available to the public — libraries will indeed be helped along the way of informing the people.

Unfortunately not all reference books measure up to standards. From earlier days we have numerous inferior reference titles still being peddled door-to-door in America. And we have some not so good that are on our library shelves. But we have more means than ever through which the alert reference librarian can detect inferiorities.

Among the sources for appraising reference books, the new 7th edition of the *Guide to reference books* must come first. Inclusion alone commends consideration; the annotations aid in selection. Then there is the *Subscription Books Bulletin,* a quarterly issued by the American Library Association which reviews new reference books courageously. Each review closes with the brave words, "Recommended" or "Not recommended," and publishers have learned to respect these opinions of the committee. Other current sources are the *Saturday Review,* probably the nearest thing to *The Times Literary Supplement* on our side of the Atlantic, sections in the *Wilson Library Bulletin* and in the *Library Journal.*

In the end, the reference librarian must make his own recommendation. Cumulated judgments over the years will show in his reference book stock. And, significantly enough, any number of professional visitors will form their opinion of the library bookstock as a whole largely on the quality of the reference collection. Indeed, I have found in over thirty years of library visitation that there is a very high correlation between the quality of the reference collection and that of the bookstock as a whole.

What, then, constitutes a basic reference collection? In the three editions of *Basic reference books* I have tried to arrive at a professional answer, not merely in terms of titles, but in such matters as types and patterns, criteria and principles. It is of these patterns and principles that I shall speak, using the list of 100 American basic reference books, appended, merely to illustrate the points.

As you will note, I have grouped the general basic reference books in thirteen classes. The special reference books concerned with special subjects comprise another large division of *Basic reference books* that I shall not consider in this paper. This, fortunately, makes it unnecessary for me to evaluate either *Kempe* or the *World list*, even though both are in *Basic reference books*.

Dictionaries. Of the thirteen groups of reference books none has received more attention recently by American publishers than English language dictionaries. For the purpose of study I have classified these books by vocabulary size. The largest or unabridged dictionary is planned to be inclusive and to contain upward of 400,000 entries. Of these, the oldest and most recently revised is *Webster's New international*[1] with over 600,000 entries. It still gives the oldest meaning of a word first, divides its page so as to provide a separate alphabetic sequence for obsolete and less used words, and separates persons and places in two appendix lists. On all of these features, as well as on some others, its chief competitor *Funk & Wagnalls New standard* differs. The commonest meaning of a word, whether its earliest or latest, is given first. In this principle, *Funk & Wagnalls* breaks not only with *Webster*, but with *O.E.D.* and with most of the great unabridged works.

From a reference standpoint the dictionary pattern achieves its form through these important features: vocabulary size, definition, alphabetic arrangement, spelling and pronunciation preference. To a lexicographer much more is important in dictionary making, but on the reference firing line these are the critical points more often than any other. Vocabulary size will certainly influence the reference librarian's choice of a dictionary for an obsolete, obscure, specialized or recent term. From this standpoint, only the *O.E.D.* and the two American unabridged dictionaries will qualify.

[1]For notes, see pages 182-185.

The major difference in definition sequence has already been pointed out. In an American secondary school an English teacher once assigned a class of pupils to consult the "big" dictionary for the meaning of a word. I am sorry to report that not all of our secondary school students are imbued with the zeal for research and therefore most of them copied the first definition. You can readily understand that the youngsters did not distinguish between the two over-size volumes and that about half of these unambitious came back with a meaning that was current in Chaucer's time!

But true English meanings, themselves, have been tampered with by Americans. Take the two-letter word "it." Some years ago we had the Hollywood phenomenon of a shapely actress named Clara Bow. Now who are lexicographers to resist popular interest, especially since Dean Trench's famous pronouncement before the London Philological Society that the people make language and the dictionary-maker to be truly scientific must accurately record what the people say? Accordingly, if you will look in the latest edition of *Webster's New international dictionary* you will find that the fourth definition of the word "it" is "personal charm and magnetism." Although this definition does not quite convey the picture of Clara Bow in a bathing suit, it is a reasonable concession to science!

Separation of personal and place names from each other and from all other words will not seem strange to you who have worked with the *O.E.D.* which omits proper nouns and adjectives almost entirely. But in reference work there are some who contend for the single alphabet of common and proper nouns as well as all other words. In response to that reference need, Funk & Wagnalls has produced the *New standard*[2] arrangement.

Our American dictionaries favour different spellings and pronunciations — not only different from British but often different from American sectional custom. It goes without saying that we favour *labor*. But other simplifications range all the way from Melvil Dewey's curiosities of the editions before the present 15th to a diffident *thru* in *Webster's*, and a determined "bot" in *Funk & Wagnalls*.

Complementary to the unabridged dictionary are various abridgements. By vocabulary size they range from the largest abridgement like your *Shorter Oxford* and our *New century*[3] down to the picture primary of which we have recently had almost an epidemic. The largest abridged omits only the obsolete words and, with its vocabulary of over 200,000 words, easily meets most reference demands in terminology.

A very popular type of abridgement is our so-called "college abridged" dictionary with a vocabulary of just over 100,000 words. Our leading examples are the *American college*[4] and *Webster's New collegiate*,[5] although there are at least three more good examples. In this dictionary class some interesting selection techniques are being employed to determine just what words shall be included. The approach is functional and statistical — an American research fetish. With variation in detail, the general idea is to count the frequency with which words appear in the literature the people read, and create a ranked list. The 100,000 words in the English language most frequently used in print and speech are then included in the dictionary.

This principle was first used in connection with the school dictionaries, of which the *Thorndike-Century junior*[7] was something of a pioneer. In 1933, the American psychologist, Edward Lee Thorndike, published the results of his word frequency research in literature for children. The result was a series of school dictionaries in which dictionary and textbook publishers formed an alliance. Such an alliance is that between Century and Scott, Foresman, the textbook publisher, in the production of the *Thorndike-Century*[6] series. A rival alliance is that between the G. & C. Merriam Company, publishers of the Webster dictionaries, and the American Book Company, textbook publishers.

Of great interest to school and children's librarians is the new picture primary dictionary. Actually these belong in the genealogy of the old "A is for apple" alphabet books. The new picture dictionary, of which the *Rainbow*[8] is a good example, rarely includes over 1,800 words. In place of definitions the child is given either a bright, coloured picture, or a sentence. The picture dictionary is intended for children from 4 to 7 years old and aims to develop the dictionary habit early by teaching the alphabetic arrangement of words.

Reference has much need for supplementary dictionaries to relieve the strain on the unabridged works and to amplify aspects of language. Principally, questions deal with usage, synonyms and shades of meaning, abbreviations, slang, dialect, pronunciation and other details. Titles 9-15 give one American example for each.

Encyclopedias. Of all classes of books none is more symbolic of reference than the encyclopedia. It is the tool we use first most often, if we accept such statistical studies as have been made. Yet it is probable that we have less professional agreement on what an encyclopedia should be than we have on almost any other kind of book.

To begin with, we are sharply divided on the concept of scope. From Aristotle's time, at least, the circle of knowledge described by the scholar has been the accepted scope of an encyclopedic work. But if one will trace the evolution of the encyclopedia he will find that certainly by Diderot's time a proletarian bias was beginning to stretch that circle. Toward the end of the 19th century it was openly argued that an encyclopedia should be a layman's tool, since the scholar should consult original specialized researches rather than a general work in which his specialty is only a minor topic. This argument became a trend. It is no secret that scholars lament the passing of the 9th edition of the *Britannica.*

But with that lament not all reference librarians will agree, nor will even all of our scholars. H. G. Wells wrote a brilliant section on the place of encyclopedias in modern civilization in his *Wealth, work and happiness of mankind,* in which his major tenet was that the encyclopedia should interpret scholarship to the layman. If I understand this concept of an encyclopedia rightly, it means (1) information of greatest interest for the layman, and (2) presented through a medium best understood by the layman.

Encyclopedia appraisal will undoubtedly be influenced by the appraiser's concept of an encyclopedia. If he believes in the traditional "circle of knowledge" scope, then he will find the trend toward popularization disappointing. On the other hand, if he believes content and presentation should be aimed at the layman, he will be impatient about a lengthy article on "monism and dualism" and the complete disdain of a subject like "jitterbugging," to cite extremes for contrast.

These conflicts will explain certain restrained reviews of the new *Chambers' encyclopedia* by some librarians, and most enthusiastic ones by others. In terms of the traditional concept of an encyclopedia, *Chambers'* is an intelligent and compact achievement. Judged by the advocates of a popular medium, the selection of subjects, the space allocations and the illustrations are inadequate.

Strangely enough it was the *Chambers' encyclopedia* edition of 1878-80 which was the basis for the American encyclopedia which led the way in the newer concept. In 1886 the first edition of the *International encyclopedia*, which had acquired American reprint rights to *Alden's Library of universal knowledge* as well as to articles in *Chambers'*, appeared. Subsequently this became the *New international* which deliberately set out to discover what information the common man sought most and then proceeded to employ journalists to rewrite scholars' contributions so that the writing would be readable.

Even more than the *New international*, the American school encyclopedias carried the concept forward when both *Compton's*[21] and the *World book*[22] employed educators as an advisory board to select subjects and make space allocations on the basis of children's curricular and extra-curricular needs and interests. Illustration in quantity keyed to the text gave a tremendous dramatic quality to learning. For a new understanding of encyclopedias I commend a careful study of these two sets.

In the adult field, realization of this newer concept has come more slowly, but its influence grows steadily more apparent in both the *Britannica*[17] and the *Americana*.[16] It has come more strikingly in the new *Collier's encyclopedia*, with its colourful format and its deliberate selection of subjects. A library advisory committee, of which I was fortunate to be the full-time member, agreed to build a new encyclopedia from the ground up entirely on the new concept. We weighed the appraisal hazard with no little concern, especially since the publisher was prepared to invest generously. We were certain that inevitably library reviewers would count the number of subjects in traditional sets not found in this newer set. Despite that, we voted to do what we thought we should to build an encyclopedia for the people of today.

I was personally responsible for the definition of an encyclopedia we adopted: "A summary of the information significant to the English reading peoples of the world in a medium universally understood." To arrive at content and space allocation, we canvassed periodicals and newspapers for two decades. Our assumption was that the large circulation publications could not remain in business unless they chose subjects that interested people most.

The result is not as different as one might suppose. Basic knowledge is in *Collier's*, authoritatively done by experts whose reputations are less behind than before them; but so, also, are the more common everyday interests. Both types of information have been presented in text and illustration as appealingly as possible. There are over 100 pages on all phases of aeronautics in the first volume alone. The article on the ballet has been cited again and again for its effective combination of word and picture. A new global geography is in the specially designed maps where, among other things, the U.S.S.R. appears undivided by continents. Contributors' bibliographies were extracted from the author's articles and given to a staff of librarian-bibliographers for critical evaluation in terms of (1) providing a stepping stone from the article to further information, (2) availability in book stores and libraries, (3) bibliographic accuracy. Wherever necessary the librarians, who included subject specialists, augmented the lists and then combined them into an integrated, eclectic bibliography.

This detail about *Collier's encyclopedia* is not intended as a promotion. It is given to illustrate an instance of librarian-publisher co-operative exploration to build a better reference book. Inevitably, the final product will not please all members of our profession. It represents only one of several good approaches to the building of an encyclopedia.[19, 20]

Yearbooks. Not the least of the problems that contribute to the insomnia of encyclopedia editors is keeping the set up-to-date. Today a publisher completes a set at a cost of a million pounds. Tomorrow some new discovery of science renders a significant portion of the encyclopedia obsolete. To cope with this calamity, editors have developed at least three devices. One of these is the quarterly supplement which has the disadvantage of providing the user with an

increasing number of alphabets to consult. Another plan is so-called
"continuous revision" under which the publisher issues a revised
printing each year with approximately 10 per cent of the content
changed. Since the average consumer cannot afford a new set every
year, there are financial disadvantages. A third device is the so-called
"insert" used by *Nelson's Loose-leaf encyclopedia* and by many
special sets in the subject fields of law and medicine. The chief disadvantage is the expense of the loose-leaf binder and the procrasti-
nation of the owner in replacing the old pages with the new.

The most popular device is a fourth plan of issuing a yearbook.
Of these annual encyclopedias the *Britannica book of the year*[24] is
probably the most successful, although most of the standard sets
now issue reasonably useful yearbooks.[23, 25]

Independent of encyclopedias, but supplementing them nevertheless, are the almanacs of the Whitaker type. Our two leading
examples are the nearly century-old newspaper, *World almanac*,[27]
and the very young radio-inspired *Information please almanac*.[26]
With these two should go a somewhat different annual, the *American
yearbook*,[28] which authoritatively with the co-operation of the
learned societies summarized developments in each of the subjects
and major human activities. When all of these are added to two
more British annuals—*Statesman's yearbook* and *Annual register*—
a reference library is equipped to answer a very large number of
the reference questions asked daily in our libraries.

Persons, places and agencies. A considerable volume of reference
business concerns quick facts about persons, places and agencies.
These are directory-type questions and here American reference
book publishers have contributed richly.

Biographical sources can be classified by the three broad classes
of people they list: (1) notables, (2) specialists, (3) commoners.
(I could not use the last category in America and therefore at the
suggestion of one of the critics of my manuscript I renamed it
"We the people.") Directories of notables are further subdivided
by life and death. Our great reference book for the latter is the
Dictionary of American biography[31] modelled after your *D.N.B.*;
our best known continuation for the former is *Who's who in*

America,[32] which is patterned after your *Who's who*. We have, besides, at least two biographical sources whose scope transcends the time and place of our own nation. One of these, *Webster's Biographical dictionary*,[29] is a universal collection of notables alphabetically arranged; the other (by means of tables) indicates contemporaries in all areas of human endeavour from ancient to present times.[30]

But our most recent biographical reference efforts have been in the field of specialists. World War II created an extraordinary demand for "know-how" and out of that need was born a unique reference tool, first suggested by the editors of the *Saturday Review*. The reference book has the distinctive title, *Who knows—and what*.[35] It is divided into two parts—knowers and subjects. If one wants to know who is a specialist on antiques, bees, cauliflower, or xenias, yoghurt, zebras, he has only to look up the subject and be referred to a number of authorities. Inevitably the first edition was criticized for omissions and some faulty selections. But since the publishers also publish our half-century old *Who's who in America*, conscientious and progressive improvement may be expected. Other specialist directories of note are the three published by the Science Press in Lancaster, Pa., one for educationists,[36] another for scientists,[37] and a third, somewhat out of date but in the process of revision—the *Directory of American scholars*, limited to specialists in the humanities and social sciences.

Geographical sources. Reference requirements have created three basic patterns for geography sources. The atlas confronts American librarians with a dilemma. British cartography is still superior to ours but the British atlas naturally gives much more emphasis on British places and much less on American places than our reference requires. Our leading American atlas publishers are Rand McNally and Hammond. The *Cosmopolitan atlas*[40] was developed in connection with the maps for *Collier's encyclopedia* and introduced several innovations including a single map to represent all of the U.S.S.R., both in Europe and in Asia.

The gazetteer, frequently a feature of the atlas, appears also as a separate alphabetic place locator in such a title as *Webster's*.[38] For descriptions of the out-of-way places and for travel data, the guide book, made famous by the Baedeker name, is indispensable. In America, the Roosevelt administration, among other things, enlisted unemployed, starving writers during the depression to create a guide book series[39] that to this day is the best key to places in the 48 states. There is one book for each state and additional volumes besides for highways, rivers, and other natural features. *U.S. number one*, a title which refers to the Atlantic coastal highway from Maine through Florida, a distance of about 2,000 miles, describes everything of interest along that route.

Directories. Information queries about agencies are almost as frequent as those about persons and places. Educational institutions, scientific societies and business firms and products probably lead in these inquiries. Assistance is indicated in titles 42-45. A note about the last should cite the section on trade names which locates the manufacturer of products like Kleenex and Kardex.

Handbooks and manuals. I have distinguished the handbook, a compilation of facts, from the manual, a guide on how-to-do, make or perform. Both types of reference tools are essential for quick reference. In the former group are tools dealing with curiosities,[40] statistics,[47] documents,[48] parliamentary procedure,[49] allusions,[50, 52] quotations[51] and calendar.[52] In the latter I include cookery books,[54] household,[55, 57] and gardening manuals,[56] health,[58, 59] etiquette,[60] and correspondence aids.[61]

Serials and sources. Ayer's Directory[63] is more than a list of American newspapers and periodicals with circulation figures. It is really a good place directory for very small places in the U.S. Ulrich's list, because of its frequent revision, provides an excellent checklist by subjects of the world's periodicals. Although not revised as frequently as necessary, the *Union list* provides an invaluable guide to U.S. library serial holdings.

Titles 66 to 75 represent a personal selection of U.S. newspapers and periodicals that represent daily newspaper,[66, 67] weekly news service,[68] comparable to *Keesing's*, weekly news magazine (and if you prefer *Time* you have popular support), commentary,[70] illustrated,[71] quality,[72] review,[73] sophisticate[74] and digest[75] magazines.

Indexes and bibliographies. An *Index to indexes*, by subject and form,[76] is the unique contribution of one of our American reference librarians. Our two most used indexes to books are one for adults[77] and one for children.[78] The former is a continuation issued semi-annually with frequent cumulation. The latter has undergone periodic revision and tends to cover the whole school range of reading materials.

Our bibliographic tools divide broadly into two classes: eclectic and comprehensive. *Bookman's manual*,[84] although intended for booksellers, has always proved the best book selection text in my classes. Through different procedures the A.L.A. *Booklist*[85] and the *Wilson Book Review Digest*[86] undertake each year to select for evaluation the most significant books of the year. The former selects some 1,200 of the 10,000 titles published each year on the recommendation of a professional committee. The latter indexes about 80 book review periodicals indicating whether reviewers were favourable or unfavourable by means of a plus or minus symbol.

Other eclectic tools undertake to list basic books for school,[87, 88] public,[89] college and special libraries.

Comprehensive bibliographies are, of course, represented by *P.W.*[90] and *C.B.I.*[91] We have added to our *P.T.L.A.*,[92] an annual collection of U.S. publishers' catalogues, an index by author and subject. Our quarterly *Bibliographic index*[93] is an alphabetic bibliography of bibliographies that can be used as a current continuation of Besterman's retrospective list.

Audio-visual sources. In American libraries increasing reference use of films, filmstrips and recordings is a decided trend. The *Wilson Educational film guide*[94] and *Filmstrip guide*[95] are basic currents, and Falconer[96] is the retrospective list for the latter. Many books are devoted to recordings but the Gramophone Shop's *Encyclopedia*[97] is still most useful. In our Library School at Florida State University we developed a guide to A.V. sources[98] that provides an overview for the uninitiated.

U.S. government publications. Lastly, for our federal U.S. government publications the *Monthly catalog*[100] is now the only current source to use. For a guide to the production, distribution, and organization of the publications of what I understand is now the largest publisher in the world—Government Printing Office Washington, D.C.—I commend the latest edition of Miss Boyd's book.[99]

Conclusion. This omnibus review of an even 100 reference books published in the U.S. was intended less as an annotated bibliography than as a list of illustrations of patterns and trends in American reference book production. It is my opinion that unless these thirteen types are adequately represented by both British and American titles of excellence, any reference collection in public, university and special libraries on both sides of the Atlantic will fall short in meeting patrons' inquiries. It is therefore suggested that, over and above any specialized selection of reference sources the individual library may make, systematic development of the basic general reference collection is essential to adequate information service.

AMERICAN BASIC REFERENCE BOOKS
I. DICTIONARIES

A. — *Unabridged*
1. Webster's New International Dictionary. 2nd ed. Merriam, 1950.
2. Funk & Wagnalls New Standard Dictionary. Funk & Wagnalls, 1950.

B. — *Abridged*
3. New Century Dictionary. Appleton, 1948.
4. American College Dictionary. Random, 1948.
5. Webster's New Collegiate Dictionary. 2nd ed. Merriam, 1949.
6. Thorndike — Century Senior Dictionary. Scott, Foresman, 1950.
7. Thorndike — Century Junior Dictionary. Scott, Foresman, 1942.

8. Rainbow Dictionary. World Publishing Co., 1947.

C. — *Supplementary*
9. Perrin. Writer's Guide and Index to English. 1951.
10. Webster's Dictionary of Synonyms. Merriam, 1942.
11. Shankle (G. E.). Current Abbreviations. Wilson, 1945.
12. Berrey (L. V.) and Van den Bark (M.). American Thesaurus of Slang. Crowell, 1947.
13. Wentworth (H.). American Dialect Dictionary. Crowell, 1944.
14. Mathews. Dictionary of Americanisms. 1951.
15. Kenyon (J. S.) and Knott (T. A.). Pronouncing Dictionary of American English. 2nd ed. Merriam, 1949.

II. ENCYCLOPEDIAS

16. Encyclopedia Americana. Ency. Amer., 1951. 30v.
17. Encyclopaedia Britannica. 14th ed. Ency. Brit., 1950. 24v.
18. Collier's Encyclopedia. Collier, 1949-50. v. 1-17 (in progress).
19. Columbia Encyclopedia. 2nd ed. Columbia U.P., 1950.

20. Lincoln Library of Essential Information. 16th ed. Frontier Press, 1946.
21. Compton's Pictured Encyclopedia. Compton, 1950. 15v.
22. World Book Encyclopedia. Quarrie, 1949. 19v.

III. YEARBOOKS

23. Americana Annual, 1923-. Ency. Amer., 1923-.
24. Britannica Book of the Year, 1938-. Ency. Brit., 1938-.
25. Collier's Yearbook, 1939-. Collier, 1939-.
26. Information Please Almanac, 1947-. Farrar, 1947-.
27. World Almanac and Book of Facts, 1868-. World-Telegram, 1868-.
28. American Yearbook, 1910-19, 1925-. Nelson, 1929-.

IV. BIOGRAPHICAL SOURCES

29. Webster's Biographical Dictionary. Merriam, 1943.
30. DeFord (M. A.). Who Was When? Wilson, 1941.
31. Dictionary of American Biography. Scribner, 1928-37. 20v. and index. Supp. 1944.
32. Who's Who in America. Marquis, 1899-.
33. Current Biography, 1940-. Wilson, 1940-.
34. Biographical Index of American Artists. Williams & Wilkins, 1930.
35. Who Knows — And What. Marquis, 1949-.
36. Cattell (J.) and Ross (E. E.). Leaders in Education. Science Press, 1948.
37. Cattell (J.). American Men of Science. Science Press, 1949.

V. GEOGRAPHICAL SOURCES

38. Webster's Geographical Dictionary. Merriam, 1949.
39. American Guide Series. Various publishers, 1937-49.
40. Rand McNally Cosmopolitan World Atlas. Rand McNally, 1950.
41. Hammond New World Atlas. Garden City, 1947.

VI. DIRECTORIES

42. National Research Council Handbook of Scientific and Technical Societies and Institutions of the U.S. and Canada. 5th ed. Bull. of Nat. Res. Council, 1948.
43. U.S. Office of Education Directory, 1912-. Govt. Prt. Office, 1912-.
44. American Council on Education. American Universities and Colleges. 5th ed. Amer. Council on Educ., 1948.
45. Thomas' Register of American Manufacturers. Thomas, 1905-.

VII. HANDBOOKS

46. Kane. Famous First Facts. 1950.
47. U.S. Statistical Abstract.
48. Commager (H. S.). Documents of American History. 5th ed. Appleton, 1949.
49. Robert. Rules of Order. 1951.
50. Benet (W. R.). Reader's Encyclopedia. Crowell, 1948.
51. Stevenson (B. E.). Home Book of Quotations. 5th ed., rev. Dodd, 1947.
52. Douglas (G. W.). American Book of Days. Wilson, 1948.
53. Langer (W. L.). Encyclopedia of World History. Rev. ed. Houghton, 1948.

VIII. Manuals

54. Woman's Home Companion Cook Book. 1950.
55. Woman's Home Companion Household Book. Collier, 1950.
56. Seymour (E. L. D.). New Garden Encyclopedia. Rev. ed. Wise, 1946.
57. Hiscox (G. D.). Henley's 20th Century Book of Formulas. Rev. and enl. ed. Henley, 1947.

58. American Red Cross. First Aid Textbook. 1949.
59. Pomeranz and Koll. The Family Physician. 1951.
60. Post (E.). Etiquette. 1950.
61. Taintor and Monro. Secretary's Handbook. 1949.
62. Kingery. How To Do It Books. 1950.

IX. Serials and Sources

63. Ayer's Directory of Newspapers and Periodicals. Ayer, 1880-.
64. Ulrich's Periodicals Directory. 5th ed. Bowker, 1947.
65. Union List of Serials in Libraries of the U.S. and Canada. 2nd ed. Wilson, 1943. Supp. 1945.
66. N.Y. Times.

67. Christian Science Monitor.
68. Facts on File.
69. Newsweek.
70. Collier's or Saturday Evening Post.
71. Life or Look.
72. Atlantic or Harper's.
73. Saturday Review of Literature
74. New Yorker.
75. Reader's Digest.

X. Indexes

76. Ireland (N. O.) An Index to Indexes. Faxon, 1942. 3v.
77. Essay And General Literature Index, 1900-. Wilson, 1934-.
78. Rue (E.). Subject Index to Books for Primary Grades. A.L.A., 1943.
78. Rue (E.). Subject Index To Books for Intermediate Grades 2nd ed. A.L.A., 1950.
79. Poole's Index To Periodical

Literature, 1802-. Houghton 1891-.
80. Reader's Guide To Periodical Literature, 1900-. Wilson, 1905-
81. International Index To Periodicals, 1907-. Wilson, 1916-
82. Vertical File Service Catalog 1932-. Wilson, 1935-.
83. N.Y. Times Index, Vol. 1- 1913-. N.Y. Times, 1913-.

XI. Bibliographies

84. Graham (B.). Bookman's Manual. 6th ed. rev. and enl. Bowker, 1948.
85. The Booklist, 1905-. A.L.A., 1905-.
86. Book Review Digest, 1905-Wilson, 1905-.
87. Children's Catalog. 7th ed. rev. Wilson, 1946. Supps. 1948, 1949, 1950.
88. Standard Catalog for High School Libraries. 5th ed. Wilson, 1950.

89. Standard Catalog for Public Libraries, 1950 ed. Wilson 1950.
90. Publishers' Weekly.
91. Cumulative Book Index and U.S. Catalog, Wilson, 1898.
92. Publishers' Trade List Annual, 1873-. Pub. Weekly 1873-.
93. Bibliographic Index. 1937-. Wilson, 1938-.

XII. AUDIO-VISUAL SOURCES

94. Educational Film Guide, 1936. Wilson, 1936-.
95. Filmstrip Guide, 1948-. Wilson, 1948-.
96. Falconer (V. M.). Filmstrips: A Descriptive Index and User's Guide. McGraw Hill, 1948.
97. Gramophone Shop Encyclopedia of Recorded Music. 3rd ed. rev. and enl. Crown Pub., 1948.
98. Florida State University. The Audio-Visual Way. 1948.

XIII. U.S. GOVERNMENT PUBLICATIONS

99. Boyd (A. M.). U.S. Government Publications. 3rd ed. rev. Wilson, 1949.
100. U.S. Government Publications Monthly Catalog, 1895-. Govt. Prt. Off., 1895-.

Subscription Books and Library Reviews

SUBSCRIPTION BOOKS have been defined as books sold directly by the publisher to the consumer.[1] In the early twenties publishers of such books, through house-to-house sales by agents, sold numerous sets under innumerable titles. Many were standard reference works approved both for library and home use. Many more were antiquated and nearly worthless, misrepresented to the unwary consumer by various and ingenious devices.

Repeated instances of misrepresentation, high-pressure methods, and overcharging resulted in a cooperative effort on the part of librarians to educate and to protect the book consumer. In Massachusetts the state library association began the publication of a bulletin in which every set that came to its attention was reviewed. The Pacific Northwest Library Association also reviewed these sets for its region in a *Subscription Books Bulletin*. As the subscription books business spread and the number of firms and titles multiplied, librarians petitioned their national professional organization to study the problem with a view to protecting the consumer.

[1] For notes, see page 191.

Reprinted from *A.L.A. Bulletin*, 42: 606-609, December, 1948, by permission of the publisher.

In 1926, therefore, the American Library Association appointed a committee to "consider what the A.L.A. might do with regard to subscription books." Under the chairmanship of Julia Ideson, then librarian of the Houston Public Library, a detailed study was made.

Briefly, the committee recommended that the A.L.A. begin at once to evaluate continuously all known subscription publications, that it disseminate these evaluations to librarians, and that it encourage librarians to share this information with educators and householders in their communities. To implement these recommendations, the committee urged the A.L.A. to take over at once the P.N.L.A. *Subscription Books Bulletin,* and "to work with subscription book publishers for the purification of their business from within." It even hinted at the possibility of a study comparable to the one for correspondence schools sponsored by the Carnegie Corporation of New York. The committee closed its report with these words:

"Your committee believes that the question of the subscription book is one that cannot longer be ignored by the American Library Association and recommends that it be taken up as soon as possible; this in carrying out the Association's avowed purpose of the best reading for the greatest number."[2]

As a result of these recommendations, the American Library Association appointed the first Subscription Books Committee with May Wood Wigginton, Denver Public Library, as chairman. The first issue of the *Subscription Books Bulletin* appeared in January 1930. It contained a statement of aim.[3] As the committee saw its mission, there was "need for a central advisory service on encyclopedias, subscription sets, and various allied compends. . . ."

To librarians the committee promised aid in the "best investment of their limited funds." Through librarians the committee hoped to be able to serve and protect householders and educators. Nor was the legitimate publisher to be neglected. Wrote the committee, "If publishers will allow our final aim to be the lucid defining of a good subscription work and will avail themselves of this honest criticism to bring their sets to a higher level of excellence, we shall all be happily served in turn."

The legitimate publisher was quick to avail himself of this criticism. Even in 1924, before the Subscription Books Committee came into being, a group of some thirty-one subscription book publishers had met with John F. Nugent, of the Federal Trade Commission in Washington, to consider trade practices. Out of this conference had come fourteen resolutions condemning virtually every one of the malpractices opposed by librarians and educators.

When, therefore, the first issue of the *Subscription Books Bulletin* set forth nine "cooperative measures which publishers might take to eliminate those things which educators and the general public might properly criticize . . . ,"[4] the librarians were merely restating what the legitimate publishers had already resolved should be remedied.

Both codes covered such practices as editor deception, omission of previous copyright dates, leather substitutes, misleading titles, raised prices, free sets and expensive supplementary services, club or society memberships, agent proselyting, premiums, the use of independent agents for dirty work, testimonials, and the adoption of names very similar to reputable ones for the sole purpose of misleading the consumer.

Because the nine cooperative measures have always served as the foundation for reviews published in the *Subscription Books Bulletin*, they are here briefly summarized.

1. EDITORS AND CONTRIBUTORS. Don't list a contributor as an editor. Either have articles signed or indicate the extent of the contribution each individual has made.

2. TITLE. Don't choose a title that tends to confuse and to suggest undue prestige.

3. PUBLISHER. Indicate clearly the real publisher and don't permit the distributor to put his imprint on the work.

4. EDITION. Don't call a supplement, or a new printing with a few plate changes a new edition. Always give the genealogy of the set, indicating on the title page all previous titles and the extent of the revision.

5. DATE. Give all copyright dates on the verso of the title page.

6. CONTENTS. Librarians consider a comprehensive index, good

bibliographies, clear maps, and helpful illustrations important. "Before spending thousands of dollars on reference sets for the use of libraries, go to libraries and find out what is needed there."

7. BINDING. If several bindings are available, inform the customer before he purchases the most expensive.

8. SELLING METHODS. These practices are bad: Don't sell the same set at various prices. Don't threaten a price advance in the near future. Don't claim the price is below when it isn't. Don't offer a free set and an expensive service. And especially, when you are selling a librarian, show the whole set or a whole volume. Don't show what the publisher calls a "pross" and the librarian calls a "mongrel."

9. ADVERTISING. Represent the publication truly.

The publication of the first *Subscription Books Bulletin* in January 1930 was a history-making venture for the American Library Association. For the first time one of its publications was to list and review "not recommended" publications. Inevitably, this would be unpopular with some publishers and not easy on library reviewers. There would be pressures, borderline cases, occasional inconsistencies and differences of opinions among the experts. It was felt that the headaches might have their compensations if, as a result of these reviews, the book consumer was educated and the legitimate publisher aided in his war on the illegitimate.

As a final precaution, the committee boxed an italicized statement which it has carried in each issue since, and which an occasional reader has overlooked. Permission to quote a review in full is granted only to the publisher of the work reviewed. Permission to quote a review in part must be obtained from the A.L.A. No pronouncement is to be considered the official view of the A.LA..

In the eighteen years that have elapsed between Miss Wigginton's first year as chairman and Joseph W. Rogers' current chairreputation for fairness. Despite changing personnel there has been manship, the Subscription Books Committee has built an enviable an amazing consistency in the criteria applied.

There can be no doubt in the minds of librarians or publishers as to the power of an *S.B.B.* rating. The original Subscription Books Committee has had its highest hope realized. Today the *S.B.B.* has become a potent influence for good. It is making the book consumer conscious of values as never before. It is teaching schoolmen and schoolwomen what to look for in a set. It has helped the librarian to spend better the limited community funds at his disposal.

Has it helped the subscription book publisher? To answer this question objectively, every encyclopedia review in *S.B.B.* from January 1930 to date was carefully reviewed several times. In all, over fifty different encyclopedia titles have been the subject of some ninety-two reviews. Over one-third of these reviews concluded with the dread words, "Not recommended." Another third carried a recommendation with limitations. In every case reviewers have stood by the basic standards set forth both in the librarians' nine "cooperative measures" and in the subscription publishers' fourteen "resolutions."

In order to reduce these ninety-two reviews to a tangible guide for publishers and editors of encyclopedias, a checklist of "do's" and "don't's" has been developed and summarized in the recent proceedings issue of the *A.L.A. Bulletin.*[5]

Among librarians there are many debatable issues regarding subscription books. There is no unanimity on the question of short versus long topics. It is not certain that a signed article is necessarily better than an unsigned one. In many cases the article that is the work of collaboration between scholars and rewriters is better. There are also differences of opinion on format. Some favor the two-column page over the three-column, and continuous paging for the whole set. Paper stock is another controversial subject. Some libraries do not want a heavy book and yet are reluctant to see half-tone illustrations, which require heavier paper, omitted or even inserted at some distance from the related text.

These debatable issues offer an opportunity for publishers and librarians to work together toward solutions. They provide the individual publisher that enterprise opportunity which is the heart of our competitive system and the essence of our progress.

At various times the subscription book publishers have undertaken cooperatively to improve the quality of their products and the distribution methods employed. After the Trade Practices Conference in 1924 and the S.B.C. suggestion of cooperative measures, a joint meeting of librarians and publishers was held in New Haven in 1931. Some fifteen publishers, under the sponsorship of the Subscription Book Publishers of the National Association of Book Publishers, participated. The stated purpose of the meeting was to formulate a code of practice for the publication and sale of subscription books. That purpose was only partially fulfilled in thirteen of twenty-five articles of faith originally proposed; the other twelve were held in abeyance.

Two years later the code was published under eighteen headings. These covered every one of the points made previously by publishers and librarians. When the N.R.A. came along, these eighteen principles were codified into twenty-four rules of trade practice, which lasted barely a year until they were invalidated by the Supreme Court. Later, in 1938, the Supreme Court upheld a Federal Trade Commission decision which was based on one of the fair trade practices.

Not discouraged, the F.T.C. and the subscription publishers tried again in 1940. A preliminary conference was held in New York, and at a subsequent hearing in Washington, a set of "Twenty-one Trade Practice Rules for the Subscription and Mail Order Book Publishing Industry" was developed. Then came the war and the interruption of everything.

There is no better tribute to the continued desire of both publishers and librarians to work together for the improvement of subscription books than the fact that at the very first postwar A.L.A. Conference in Buffalo, both groups met under the sponsorship of the Subscription Books Committee. There have been several meetings since, and the subscription book publishers have moved to organize again in the interest of better book business for all.

What then of the future? The strong-arm sales method of the early twenties seems generally unpopular with both reputable publishers and librarians, in spite of the fact that there have been some recent eruptions. Illegitimate publishers are in for a rougher time if reputable publishers and librarians continue to cooperate. Just how these groups can work together more effectively is certainly worthy of some consideration.

There are those who believe that the time has now arrived when the reputable subscription publisher should share in the educational and evaluative functions carried on by librarians through the Subscription Books Committee. Others believe the librarians should continue to edit the *Subscription Books Bulletin* independently of the publishers. If this seems advisable there is nothing to prevent the subscription publishers from establishing their own journal devoted to the advancement of the industry and the improvement of subscription books. It is certainly true that the trade publisher has problems and interests quite different.

From every standpoint the future of the subscription book seems more promising than ever. Like the librarian, the subscription publisher is in a position to contribute significantly to the information of the American people. The potential market is unlimited. With the aid of librarians the subscription publishers can surpass all previous sales volume by cooperating to remove consumer suspicion of the book agent and by providing the best possible conditions for competition. As Americans we know the best games are played when competition is under the same rules. A code of rules developed and enforced by the industry cooperatively will insure the freest and fairest conditions for competition.

Of one thing subscription publishers may be assured—librarians are sympathetic and will do everything possible to help the legitimate subscription publisher in his worthy enterprise.

[1] Kerr, Grace. "Subscription Books," *Library Journal*, 54: 9-13, January 1, 1929.
[2] *A.L.A. Bulletin*, 23: 142-43, June, 1929.
[3] *Subscription Books Bulletin*, 1: 1, January, 1930.
[4] *Ibid.*, p. 2-4.
[5] *A.L.A. Bulletin*, 42: P88-89, September 15, 1948.

The Ideal Encyclopedia

ALONG WITH THE BIBLE and the dictionary the encyclopedia is the most essential part of a library. Housewives may harden themselves against the agent at the door nine times out of ten, but the tenth time they will finally concede the possibility that something in that ten-volume compendium will improve Mary's home work. Librarians may preach against sets for small libraries, but in the last analysis they will recognize in encyclopedias the backbone of all reference work. Weekly literary reviewers may develop a knack for writing detective stories by running down errors in the newest edition of the encyclopedia, but in the end they will refer to it constantly in the preparation of that weekly page. In short, if there is one book which is universally knocked and needed it is the encyclopedia. But to date the knocks have not resulted in the formation of very clear needs.

Survey the opinions of encyclopedia users today and you will find the great mass inarticulate on the qualities desirable in a household set. There is a general feeling that somehow the encyclopedia lends intelligence, refinement, and alertness to the family but that feeling rarely translates itself into home use. For that reason, no doubt, so many more spurious sets seem to be sold in the American home than works of merit. Nor is this condition confined to the home. For years an army of tramp book-leggers has marched from schoolhouse to schoolhouse depositing worthless sets for which they have received testimonial letters and a subscription to ten years of "service" paid for in advance.

To remedy this situation, three classes of critics have worked diligently. Foremost among them have been librarians who have offered free advice based on accepted book selection principles. In 1930, the American Library Association launched *Subscription Books Bulletin*, which thru its appraisals has carried the name of

Reprinted from *Wilson Bulletin for Librarians*, 11: 678-681 ff., June, 1937, by permission of the publisher, The H. W. Wilson Company, New York City.

the A.L.A. to many a rural school principal and teacher who had
never heard of the Association before. To S.B.B. much credit is due
for courageous exposés of worthless publications. It is hoped, however, that the Subscription Books Committee will not permit its
reviews of standard works to deteriorate into lists of petty date and
spelling errors, but that rather it will formulate from time to time
positive principles to which librarians can subscribe, and by which
reputable publishers can be guided. Such articles as that by Mr.
Ward on Children's Encyclopedias might more frequently find their
way into the *Bulletin*.

Nearly as articulate as librarians have been literary reviewers,
but not nearly so constructive. The reviewer, much more of a detective than the librarian, only too frequently concerns himself with
ferreting out misspelled names, incorrect dates, "slips that pass in
the type," and other minutiae reckoned to enhance the reviewer's
reputation for scholarship. Whether the reviewer admits it or not the
model for this type of appraisal was fashioned long ago by Voltaire
in his *Philosophical Dictionary* and brought to a high state of perfection by Willard Huntington Wright in his *Misinforming a Nation*.
What the literary reviewer contributes positively is largely traditional. To him an encyclopedia only too frequently is or should be
the complete circle of knowledge for a graduate of the mediaeval
university. Only too often the reviewer has looked upon the encyclopedia as a scholar's rather than as a layman's aid.

To a very large extent publishers have been influenced by this
conception. Reluctantly they have popularized and simplified material and adapted their methods of selection. But in the last analysis
the publisher has been forced to be practical. Cost of production
and possibilities of distribution have forced him to consider the
average rather than the exceptional consumer. As a result, the publisher has had to begin by asking himself first, what can the average
purchaser afford to pay for my product. The answer to that question
has determined very largely what the publisher could do in terms of
authority, scope, arrangement, format, and special features. Within
the limits of his budget, the reputable publisher has set up standards
and endeavored to give the utmost in value. Regardless of the shady
ventures exposed again and again, there has always been as there is

today a solid core of the subscription trade interested in improving the quality of their product. These publishers, years ago, undertook to set up standards and regulate the practices within the trade thru their own organization and with the help of the Federal Trade Commission. But the reputable publisher's plight has not been a happy one. He has been between two fires constantly. On the one side there has been the intense competition of the shady publisher and on the other side the withering criticism of writers and librarians, which criticism frequently has had so little constructive to offer.

To a lesser extent this has been true of the librarian's efforts. No doubt many a librarian-reviewer has dogged patiently one fact after another thru the pages of a standard work hoping for a reward in the form of some item of misinformation, but such negatives have been compensated for by the formulation of certain standards. These standards have been presented in a variety of sources in different forms and been accepted more or less in the book selection divisions of librarianship. But these standards have been repeated in library schools so uncritically of late that time has come for a re-evaluation of the criteria themselves.

Perhaps the most often quoted standards are the three cardinal principles offered by Miss Mudge in her *Guide to Reference Books*,[1] and the thirteen tests on these three points. The principles recognize authority, bibliographies, and arrangement as of paramount importance, and suggest a systematic check of publisher, copyright date, editor, general appearance, preface, balance, bias, revision, authority, illustrations, bibliographies, arrangement, and special features. Almost as frequently cited is the bibliographer's approach indicated in Dr. Wyer's[2] scheme which examines in sequence literary, bibliographic, and typographic features. Under the first head come such points as accuracy, up-to-dateness, contributors' authority, style, balance, bias, history of the work, viewpoints. The bibliographic features are in succession, arrangement, alphabeting, bibliographies, date, cross references, maps, illustrations, supplements. Under typographic features, paper, type, binding, press-work, page make-up, and number of volumes are included.

[1] For notes, see page 200.

Several other sets of criteria for encyclopedia evaluation have been developed. For example, an excellent outline is included in Miss Adelene Pratt's little book, *Encyclopedias; How to Use and Evaluate Them*, written especially for *Compton's*. A comparison of these and other plans is included in the reference text book by the writer published by the A.L.A.[3] For the present discussion it is sufficient to indicate that librarians' criteria classify under five general heads: Authority, Scope, Arrangement, Up-to-Dateness, Format.

1. Authority in an Encyclopedia

Librarians' pronouncements on *authority* have only too frequently centered around the point of signed articles. Admittedly the signature of notable writers added considerable responsibility to the material in an article at a time when the encyclopedia was primarily a scholar's tool, but the importance of the signature has been minimized today if not absolutely vitiated by the practice of having an authority sign his name to an article which he did not write but is willing to approve. There will be many librarians agreeable to sacrificing the autograph under such questionable conditions. Further, it may be seriously questioned whether an encyclopedia is not squandering its resources purchasing big names when the same amount of money will buy a greater quantity of reliable material adequately interpreted for popular consumption. It was the *New International Encyclopedia,* an old favorite among librarians, which was one of the first with courage enough to throw overboard the autograph standard as hollow and meaningless. The *New International* found the combination of authority and readability more desirable than a union of detail and dullness. In this criterion therefore one cannot help feeling that publishers have been slightly misled into expenditures not warranted by the returns.

2. Scope of an Encyclopedia

At the key to the whole situation is the matter of *scope*. Fundamental to the conception of an ideal encyclopedia is the question, for whom? The encyclopedia has evolved most gradually from the status of a scholar's tool to the position of a household utensil. One

can no longer look upon the encyclopedia in a democracy as the
complete circle of knowledge for the medieval scholar. Rather, there
is decided evidence that the encyclopedia must serve the masses here
and now—that the materials which make up the set must be concerned with those things vital to the every day life of the man on
the street. If this be the case, what snobbery is it to bewail the
loss of detail in an encyclopedia. Indeed, it is sheer redundancy to
provide the scholar with such a general tool. For him there are
already so many sources which begin where his background leaves
off. But for the layman there are only too few materials on his
reading level. To this writer, therefore, the *Britannica's* Fourteenth
Edition was a most enlightened forward step which we hope will be
only the first in developing a ready reference work for the layman.

The next steps are already being taken by the school encyclopedia
and they are in the direction of scientific selection. The school
encyclopedias have determined their scope by the demands of the
school curriculum. The adult encyclopedia would do well to select
its content on the basis of adult interests today, apportioning space
accordingly. If 100,000 people turn out for a sporting event regularly, no modern encyclopedia can afford to ignore sports and their
part in American life.

3. Arrangement of an Encyclopedia

When it comes to *arrangement* there is a striking divergence of
opinion among librarians. Today one finds two well-defined arrangement patterns among encyclopedias. The one favored by *Britannica*
and *Compton's* tends to provide longer articles embracing a great
number of related topics. Such an arrangement calls for an index to
point out the many smaller topics included in the large subject
article. The other pattern, favored by the *Americana, New International,* and *World Book,* tends to provide a short article for nearly
every topic, and numerous "see" or "dummy" references for the
remaining topics. On the comparative value of these two schemes,
publishers have been much confused by librarians. For example, as a
professional group we have preached the index habit and have had
index instruction written into school courses of study almost from

the kindergarten up. Yet, Miss Wigginton has found the other arrangement more popular among American adult readers.[4]

Somewhat interested in the problem, the writer has compared the facility with which both schemes are used by high school and college students. The studies thus far are inconclusive. There does not seem to be a whole lot of time saved either way. For example, on a hundred questions chosen from a list asked in a high school library the index was found to be on an average one-eighth of a minute faster per question, when the users were instructed in both the index and cross reference devices. When I asked high school students to express a preference the class voted for the index pointing out that when in the case of the cross reference arrangement it was necessary to look in two places, no reference was given to specific pages. In other words, though the single alphabet appears to be a time-saver generally, it is a time-loser on such a case as the following, quoted from a standard work:

LONG, HUEY P.
see
UNITED STATES

in which it is necessary to peruse a long article in order to find the specific topic dealt with in a few lines. Physical difficulties of folioing prevent page citation such as is possible with an index.

4. Up-to-Dateness and the Encyclopedia

We librarians have a way of saying that yearbooks keep an encyclopedia *up-to-date*. Strictly speaking the best the yearbook can do is keep the encyclopedia-user up-to-date. As for the encyclopedia itself, it suffers the pathetic fate of going irretrievably out of date the moment it is off the press. The only possible exception is the loose-leaf insertion encyclopedia like *Nelson's* in which every old page is theoretically replaced by a new one as soon as the old material is out-dated. Encyclopedias with loose-leaf supplements go out of date as surely as those with yearbook, magazine or other supplements. As yet the problem of up-to-dateness is unsolved. The methods now employed are (1) yearbooks (*Americana, New Inter-*

national, World Book) ; (2) periodicals (*Britannica*) ; (3) loose-leaf supplements (mostly questionable sets) ; (4) loose-leaf inser-tions (*Nelson's* and law and medical reference sets) ; (5) yearly revisions (*Compton's, World Book*). Of these, loose-leaf insertions are still the best if encyclopedia owners will make insertions punc-tually.

5. Format of the Encyclopedia

The school encyclopedias have led the way in *format*. Illustra-tions will continue to increase in importance. These illustrations already dramatic to an extent never dreamed of when the first static cuts found their way into staid circles of knowledge can be expected to comprise an even larger portion of the text. There will be arrange-ment improvements with a device which will incorporate the best features of index and cross-reference, perhaps taking a cue from legal reference books and numbering topics instead of pages.

The Ideal

H. G. Wells, who has devoted a section of the chapter "How mankind is taught and civilized" to the role of an encyclopedia in a progressive civilization conceives the ideal as

"a general summary of thought and knowledge which will serve as the basis for common understandings between specialists and for the ideology of education, and so become a guiding centre for the intellectual activities of mankind."[5]

Such an encyclopedia, Mr. Wells believes, must be endowed and perhaps sponsored by a great university or by the League of Nations. He suggests that the alphabetic arrangement of the whole work be abandoned, and that we return to a classified arrangement of material into twelve broad fields, to be followed with a dictionary index. On this last, Mr. Wells is positive: "Good indexing is abso-lutely essential to an efficient encyclopedia."

In summary, certain encyclopedia trends stand out:

1. As concerns *authority,* responsibility for articles is being divided between specialists who know the subject and inter-preters who can translate this knowledge into non-technical language for the layman, thus practically destroying the importance of signed articles as a criterion for evaluating encyclopedias.

2. *Scope* will be increasingly determined by scientific investigations of the reading interests of groups for whom the encyclopedia is intended.

3. *Arrangement:* There is a growing realization that omission of an index may mean shorter articles, repetition of information, an increased number of "see" references, and complicated devices to reestablish broad relationships.

4. *Up-to-Dateness:* The loose-leaf *insertion* is still the most promising device if users will cooperate.

5. *Format* will change in the direction already taken by the school encyclopedias.

It follows therefore that the ideal encyclopedia is not at present for sale on the open market. There are, however, several splendid sets available, and on the basis of criteria established this article ventures to make some evaluations. It suggests,

I. For School Libraries: Buy school encyclopedias *first*, certain standard lists to the contrary notwithstanding. This applies from elementary school thru junior college for the following reasons:

(1) *Authority* in school sets like *Compton's* and *World Book* is excellent. Readability is distinctly superior, as are general attractiveness manifested in page make-up, illustrations, style, legends and captions.

(2) *Scope:* Selection of materials is based on scientific study of curriculum as well as of young people's extra-curricular interests.

(3) *Arrangement: Compton's* and *World Book* represent the two different arrangement patterns at their best. Altho *Compton's* index is less extensive, its form and placement are better than *Britannica's*. Likewise *World Book* has succeeded in improving the "see reference" device by a series of related topics at the ends of articles.

(4) *Up-to-Dateness:* Because of frequent revision at least once a year, the school encyclopedia no matter when purchased will never be more than a few months old.

(5) *Economy:* The school encyclopedia can be purchased for considerably less. As soon as funds permit, *Americana* and *Britannica* should be added.

II. For Public Libraries: *Americana, Britannica, Compton's,* and *World Book.*
III. For Senior Colleges, University and Research Libraries: *Americana* and *Britannica.*

[1] 1936, pp. 39-40.
[2] *Reference Work,* 1930, pp. 20-21.
[3] Shores, Louis. *Basic Reference Books,* A.L.A., 1937, Chapter 3.
[4] *Horn Book,* March, 1935. vol. 11, p. 93.
[5] *Work, Wealth and Happiness of Mankind.* 1931. vol. 2, p. 840.

Noah Webster's Dictionary

"DISTRICT OF CONNECTICUT, SS. Be it remembered, That on the fourteenth day of April, 1828 . . . Noah Webster of the said district hath deposited in this office the title of a book, the right whereof he claims as author, to wit: *An American Dictionary of the English Language,* by Noah Webster, LL.D., in two volumes." So, the fly-leaf of the first edition, published exactly one hundred years ago, announced the completion of that work which has become the household authority of the English language.

Only an uncommon man could have produced a book so comprehensive and at the same time so influential. Noah Webster was born in Hartford, Connecticut, in 1758. He was graduated from Yale about the time of the outbreak of the Revolution. A fervent patriot, he joined the militia and served under his father as a captain. After the cause of independence had been practically established, he turned to the fields of human endeavor where he could be of greatest service to the new country. For the next few years, he taught school in Hartford, studied law, edited several newspapers and returned again to his work of education.

Now that the country was independent, Webster saw, more than anyone else, that a tremendous amount of education would be necessary to maintain this independence. He started a school of his own at Goshen, New York, and there in 1783, he published his spelling book, which for over a century did more to reduce illiteracy in this country than any other single agency. How influential *Webster's Spelling Book* really was, can be ascertained by the fact that in 1889, an annual sale of over a million and a half copies was recorded. In all, over sixty-two million of these little literacy courses had been distributed to build up a reading populace. And then, as though not yet satisfied with this service for Americanism, Webster set to work upon a key which should unlock a free and independent American language and literature.

It was not that Noah Webster was laboring under an "anti-British" complex (though that complex would have been more excusable in Revolutionary Boston than in twentieth-century Chicago), for he was too much of a scholar. It was rather that Webster foresaw a sectional estrangement because of colloquialisms that distances would imprison in each locality. As Webster, himself, put it in the introduction to his first edition, "It is not only important but . . . necessary that the people of this country should have an American dictionary". . . for, "Language is the expression of ideas, and if the people of one country cannot preserve an identity of ideas, they cannot retain an identity of language."

Nevertheless, Webster did not shut his eyes to what had been done before, merely because it had been done by Britishers. Instead, he voyaged across the ocean at a time when seafaring was as much a risk as transatlantic flying is today, and visited the repositories of lexicography in England. He looked back to the first attempts at collecting the words of the English language into convenient form and he found that not till 1616, the year of Shakespeare's death, had there been anything like an English dictionary. He saw this first example of English lexicography which John Bullokar, its compiler, called *The English Expositor*, and was impressed with its crudity. Webster saw, too, those later examples, like Henry Cockeram's *English Dictionarie* and Thomas Blount's *Glossagraphia,* and he was not impressed at all. But when he came to Nathaniel Bailey's *Universal and Etymological English Dictionary* and saw there an honest attempt to include all the words in the language and at the same time to trace their derivation and indicate their pronunciation, his scholarly faculties were all attention.

Finally, when he re-examined Dr. Samuel Johnson's famous dictionary he realized why it was this standard work's influence persisted even in America. What mattered it that Dr. Johnson occasionally permitted his prejudice to influence his definitions, as for example when he defined "oats" as "a food for horses and Scotchmen." Ostensibly, it was then the best dictionary in any language. It contained a number of innovations in lexicography, among which the use of quotations to illustrate meanings was outstanding. And it marked an epoch in the development of the English language by determining the form, meaning and use of English words.

No wonder, then, that Webster limited himself at first to merely correcting and revising the best English dictionary in existence to meet the needs of his own people. But after he had completed the first two letters of the alphabet, he gave that plan up and set to work in scholarly earnest. He realized that science and new discoveries had originated so many new words that anything short of a new work would be inexcusable. Therefore, he spent the next ten years studying the origin of words in twenty languages. From this study he prepared a synopsis of comparative words having the same radical letters, and thus he was able to trace their sources.

The synopsis was the basis of his dictionary. He corrected what he had written of the dictionary and then completed the remainder. By 1828, his work was done and there stood a collection of 70,000 words, 12,000 more than the American edition of Todd's Johnson Dictionary. Of this first edition, 2,500 copies were offered for sale in America and 3,000 in England.

After the death of Noah Webster in 1843, his work was carried on by scholars. A new edition was issued by his son-in-law, Professor Chauncey A. Goodrich and the original two volumes were brought into one. In 1864, the "Unabridged" appeared for the first time with an increased vocabulary of 114,000 words. Then, in 1890, Webster's work ceased to be purely American. *Webster's Interna-*

tional Dictionary "Marked the fact that the work of Webster . . . had won wide recognition in Great Britain and its colonies . . . and had become a standard authority throughout the English-speaking world."

The National Union Catalog of the United States

BIBLIOGRAPHIC ORGANIZATION in the United States today is looking more than ever to the Library of Congress in Washington. A fortunate phenomenon for American librarianship is the willingness of the National Library to perform services for all of the nation's libraries and to work with them in national planning. You, of course, know what a boon to our catalogues the printing and distribution of cards has been. You know also the L.C. classification, a scheme increasingly being adopted by scholarly libraries everywhere. More recently you have had experience with the Library of Congress author and subject catalogues appearing in printed book and serial form. These services as well as many others add up to a bibliographic direction that is steadily guiding American libraries to better control of the research resources of the nation.

Of all these national services by the Library of Congress none is more challenging to scholarship and librarianship than those that come under the head of "union catalogs" in the annual reports of the Librarian of Congress. This is so because implicit in the union catalogue definition is co-operative effort on the part of libraries and scholars. Inevitably such co-operation stimulates thinking and planning together. And out of that comes not only bigger and better union catalogues but, what is more important, bibliographic planning on a truly universal scale.

Reprinted from *The Library Association Record*, 55: 178-182, June, 1953, by permission of the publisher. The essay here reprinted is a paper read at a seminar series on U.S. libraries and librarianship, held in Rome, Florence, and Naples, March-April, 1952. The citations in parentheses refer to the list of references at the end of the essay.

Although this discussion is concerned largely with the National Union Catalog of printed books, it is necessary to understand that even its 13 million cards may be eventually the smaller part of a total project which now envisages listing and locating virtually all of the records of civilization whether in book, serial or audio-visual form. It is therefore desirable at the outset to identify what are likely to be the three major divisions of the ultimate universal catalogue:

(1) The National Union Catalog of printed books, plus the auxiliary catalogues, the catalogue cards from foreign sources, the *American imprints inventory*, the *Central Catalog of Slavic translations and abstracts* and probably the *Index to special collections*.

(2) The Union Catalog of Serials, which at present consists of nothing more definite than the *Checklist of certain periodicals*.

(3) The National Register of Special Materials, still very largely in the planning stage.

The National Union Catalog yesterday. As early as 1900, Herbert Putnam, then Librarian of Congress, anticipated the value a national finding list of books would have for scholarship, and authorized the exchange of Library of Congress printed catalogue cards for cards printed by other United States libraries (10). This was the beginning of the union catalogue idea and the subsequent annual reports provide a stimulating story of the development of a plan for bibliographic organization.

The life of the National Union Catalog divides into four periods. From the origin of the project through 1926 the union catalogue developed into a collection of nearly two million cards (8). The majority of these cards came from the Library of Congress, but a considerable number came also from the other great co-operating libraries. Four libraries were in the original group: New York and Boston Public Libraries, Harvard College, and the John Crerar scientific and technical library of Chicago. Shortly after, a second group, as they began to print catalogue cards, joined the project: the Newberry special library in the humanities, and the Universities of Chicago and of Illinois. A third group joined in 1902 when the Library of Congress began adding cards which were printed for other governmental libraries.

The 1914-18 war emphasized the necessity for bibliographic organization and indicated the incompleteness of the union catalogue effort to date. In 1926 it was estimated that there were about 8 million titles in American libraries with potential value to research (8). This meant that the National Union Catalog was barely 25 per cent effective and that at least six million more entries were needed.

Through a Rockefeller grant of $250,000 by John D. Rockefeller, Jr., accelerated development was made possible. "Project B," begun on 31st August, 1927, and completed 1st September, 1932, when the grant expired, added 6,344,356 cards to the union catalogue. But it did much more. It placed the union catalogue in a position of importance both in the Library of Congress and among the libraries of the nation. Above all it laid the foundation for a plan of operation and organization. Into the project were brought the interest and support of the library profession, the A.L.A. Council having sponsored the request to Mr. Rockefeller. And to the direction of the work came the best bibliographic talent. Dr. E. C. Richardson was appointed consultant on administration. Ernest Kletsch became the first administrator, and W. D. Johnston as director of special collections succeeded, before his death in 1928, in creating the nucleus for the *Index to special collections*. During this period, 116 printed library catalogues were incorporated in the union catalogue and a more thorough job was done on the libraries of Harvard and Princeton (8).

The close of Project B launched the third period in the life of the union catalogue and the union catalogue division. Kletsch was appointed director and served in that position until 1937 when he was succeeded by the present director, G. A. Schwegmann, Jr. What characterized this period was a return to austerity. The $18,000 appropriated for the year 1933 was a difficult reduction after five annual $50,000 budgets. Nevertheless, for this whole depression and war period to 1st July, 1943, a budget average of $25,000 a year was attained.

Another 3,355,941 cards were added, bringing the total number to 11,700,197. More important was the steadily widening library representation. Brown University, Arnold Arboretum and Kress Library were some of the notable collections included. But of especial importance was the tapping of an important union catalogue in Philadelphia. Also history-making was the exploitation of *New York Public Library Bulletin* lists and the Historical Records Surveys imprints project (8).

On 1st July, 1943, the fourth period opened with an appropriation of $51,700. We were at war and the need for "know-how" was urgent. More than ever, research was demanding bibliographic organization that would reduce the interval between discovery and application. Feverishly and in many government agencies intelligence wrestled with the basic reference problem of locating information quickly.

In its own way the National Union Catalog made a contribution. Three significant projects contributed another 1½ million cards to the central clearing house. About 300,000 cards were typed from microfilms made of various federal libraries in 1937 in the District of Columbia. Another 900,000 cards resulted from cards for L.C. added entries for personal and corporate names, and a final 384,192 cards came from the selected checking of the Cleveland and Philadelphia union catalogues. Other resources tapped during this period were Yale, the union catalogues of North Carolina and of Southeastern Michigan. Late in 1944 the Union Catalog Division was made responsible for the *American imprints inventory*.

On 5th March, 1948, the name National Union Catalog became official. Since then, two assignments have especially emphasized the fact that the scope of the National Union Catalog is to be broadened greatly. On 5th July, 1949, the Microfilming Clearing House was established as a central information point on microfilming projects and plans. Last 19th November an assistant chief to plan and create national registers for non-book library materials was appointed. Presumably his responsibility will cover not only historical MSS. and other special collections, but maps, films, pictures, recordings and various forms of records.

The National Union Catalog today. From the current reports of the Librarian of Congress (10c) a concept can be gained of the scope of the book, serial and non-book union catalogues. Of these, the National Union Catalog, which records primarily the location of printed research materials in the libraries of North America, now consists of a main catalogue and a supplement, the latter not readily accessible to users, largely because of the filing stages in which it is. "This supplementary catalog," notes the report, "has been growing at an alarming rate during the past few years, despite all efforts to reduce it, and the goal of maintaining currency in filing operations seems almost impossible of achievement with the present staff."

In addition to the main and supplementary catalogue there are four auxiliary catalogues totalling, as of the current report, 367,612 cards, distributed among the following union catalogues (10c):

Slavic	....	248,278
Hebraic	....	61,665
Japanese	....	46,780
Chinese	....	10,889

All of these catalogues are filed separately in their respective language divisions.

Of the other auxiliary catalogues relating to printed books, the *American imprints inventory* is notable. This project was started in June, 1937, as a phase of the Historical Records Survey, itself a part of the depression-inspired W.P.A. Its purpose was to attempt to record every American imprint, state by state, from the beginning of printing to 1876, the date when the *American catalog* began. (For a few western states the date was extended to 1890.) The end products anticipated for the Library of Congress were: (a) a union catalogue of title slips representing holdings of American libraries of books, pamphlets, and broadsides printed in the U.S., for that period; (b) checklists drawn from this material covering publications of one state or city within certain periods. A master file of 14 million type slips, representing approximately 1,300,000 separate titles, was reduced to 7 million. To date about sixty regional and state checklists have appeared and about forty-five more are in preparation.

Also worth noting is the *Index to special collections*. This consists of two card indexes (one by location, the other by subject) to more than 6,000 collections in American libraries, plus a vertical file of pamphlets and correspondence relating thereto. The *Index* is based on the Johnston-Mudge list of 1912, E. C. Richardson's essay in 1927, the *Special libraries directory*, 1935, and the *American library directory*.

The *Central catalog of Slavic translations and abstracts* was started in April, 1950, and now contains approximately 800 entries, 713 of which came from 9 libraries. This catalogue is being operated experimentally for a year. It resulted from requests by federal agencies for a record of Slavic language translations and abstracts available within these agencies.

Catalog cards from foreign sources, of which there are now approximately 1,200,000 in the custody of the Union Catalog Division, represent only a small proportion of the total produced since 1900 by libraries and bibliographical agencies abroad. Sixteen foreign countries have contributed. Cards printed before World War II are stored separately because it is "deemed possible to maintain them as separate catalogs or to interfile them into a single catalog" (10d). Cards from Russia or Japan are assigned to the Air Information and Orientalia divisions respectively, and those from the Vatican Library to the Catalog Maintenance Division which makes them available to the Descriptive Cataloging Division staff.

All of the foregoing catalogues record books or separates. An actual start with serial literature has been made, and if recent recommendations by Dr. Downs are followed (4), more union catalogue service in this area can be expected. The so-called *Checklist of certain periodicals* is a catalogue on loose-leaf sheets listing the holdings of more than 300 North American libraries of some 3,000 scientific and technical periodicals published in continental Europe and the warring countries of Asia from 1939 through 1945. Since the war, however, the value of the checklist has diminished to such an extent that the Division was authorized on 2nd May, 1951, to discontinue its development. Nevertheless, the need for a subject union catalogue of serials persists, and is emphasized by the uncertainty of the future of the Wilson title, *Union list* (5).

Non-book materials. At the time of writing union catalogs for non-book material are still very largely in the planning stages. But the appointment of an assistant director to develop "national registers of historical manuscripts and other special collections of maps, motion pictures, prints and photographs, sound recordings, etc., to be maintained as subsidiaries to the National Union Catalog" (10d), holds much promise. Meanwhile, one tangible step has already been taken by the establishment in the Union Catalog Division of a Microfilming Clearing House. Its purpose is to centralize information on extensive microfilming projects involving newspapers, serials and manuscript collections. During 1951 the Clearing House reported extensive microfilm runs of 897 newspaper titles, 379 serial publications, and 149 manuscript collections. Since March, 1951, the Clearing House has issued the *Bulletin* which appears at intervals as an appendix to the *Library of Congress Information Bulletin*.

Union Catalog operation. It goes without saying that the operation of this vast union catalog enterprise calls for careful organization. A staff of at least twenty is assigned to the Union Catalog Division, which is headed by a Chief with a "G 13" civil service classification. As at present charted there are three sections in addition to the administrative one. The Preliminary Filing Section, consisting of five library assistants, performs all of the sorting and arranging up to the filing in the National Union Catalog. This final filing, as well as editing, cancelling of duplicates, and other responsible duties, is performed by the Editorial, Filing and Searching Section, which is headed by an Editor of "GS 11" classification. The American Imprints Inventory Section is the third part of the Division. Broadly speaking, the operations of the Division deal with two major aspects, maintenance and service.

Maintenance. Maintenance of any union catalogue involves original and continuing solutions to at least four major problems. One of these is the problem of duplicate and conflicting entries. Because of the fact that the Union Catalog was started before the A.L.A. or L.C. practices had been codified, the varieties of entry form submitted by contributing libraries are legion. To reconcile these variations and to reduce inevitable duplication, the Division had to supplement accepted cataloguing practice with a Union Catalog code.

Part of this code includes some major decisions. For example, duplicates are weeded as far as possible without destroying information of bibliographic value. The best entry is always retained and any other entries with information not on the master card. All other cards are destroyed after library symbols have been noted on the master. In cases of entry form conflict, L.C. form is preferred. In the absence of an L.C. card the fullest entry and the printed card are favoured.

A second problem relates to the identification of libraries. Frank Peterson's symbol scheme (12) has been adopted. It is brief, geographic and mnemonic. Each symbol, in the case of most libraries, consists of three letters, one for each element, in this order: (a) state, (b) city, (c) library. For example, ICJ stands for Illinois, Chicago, John Crerar Library. The system, with some variation, is comparable to the one adopted by the Wilson *Union list of serials*.

A third problem deals with the filing rules to be followed. Because a union catalogue user, unlike the average catalogue consultant, is more concerned with location than with bibliographic information, the National Union Catalog has adopted certain deviations such as chronological arrangement for numerous editions of the same work and arrangement of certain groups by *British Museum Catalogue*, Jaggard's *Shakespeare* bibliography, etc.

A fourth problem relates to the acquisition and selection of cards from contributing libraries. At least six sources of acquisitions are identified by the Division: (a) routine ones from those libraries which duplicate mechanically; (b) treasure room items on shelf list cards; (c) borrowed catalogues of special collections for transcription; (d) gifts of discards resulting from recataloguing; (e) book catalogue clippings for mounting; (f) copies resulting from library visits. Each of these classes of acquisitions requires its own kind of procedure.

Service. Aside from the direct use made of the National Union Catalog, there are the numerous inquiries for location and search of individual titles. During fiscal year 1951 there were 5,270 requests for the location of 17,272 works of research interest. Over 12,000 of these titles were located immediately through the union catalogue. Another 1,088 titles were located through circularization, bringing the score for the year up to 76.8 per cent.

This circularization scheme is an interesting one. It is described in some detail in the *Manual* (10d). Each week some 64 large research libraries are asked to check a list of titles the Library of Congress was unable to locate through its union catalogues. In 1951 nearly 25 per cent of the titles sought were not located. How many of these were merely bad citations or fictitious works is not indicated. On the surface, however, it appears that our National Union Catalog falls somewhat short of that degree of completeness desired.

Reproduction. Despite its incompleteness, the N.U.C. represents one of the major achievements along the road to bibliographic organization. What concerns librarianship today is its vulnerability in case of war and its relative inaccessibility because of distance. For these reasons agitation for its reproduction has increased markedly in recent months. Dr. Downs (5) featured the question of reproduction in his monumental report on the National Union Catalog.

Fundamentally, librarians have been divided on the question whether to reproduce "as is" or edit first. The number of duplications and inconsistencies in the N.U.C. is not inconsiderable. What is more, the condition of some of the cards is not such as to make legible reproduction possible. As a result, numerous suggestions for editing or re-doing the form of the N.U.C. have appeared in library literature. Of the latter I should especially like to call your attention to the suggestion by my colleague, Harry Dewey (3), which proposes a plan of producing a union catalogue so cheaply that its reproduction should enable nearly every library to have a copy. Briefly, Dewey recommends the use of a universal call number system, such as the L.C. card numbers, in place of full bibliographic entries. An examination of either his master's thesis or his *Library Quarterly* article will convince you of the possibilities in his plan. Another stimulating proposal is that advanced by David and Hirsch for a "world thesaurus" (except for Asia, Africa and Australia) which would become a serial union catalogue issued in monthly, quarterly, annual, decennial and centennial parts (2). The important point is that librarianship has been aroused to the implication of bibliographic control as much by the National Union Catalog as perhaps by all other influences combined.

From the start the N.U.C. has had before it several concrete proposals for reproduction. The media considered have included micro-films, micro-card, and other micro-text forms. Also considered

is offset printing like that used for the *L.C. author catalog*. Mr. Ride
estimated tentatively that microcard reproduction for 60 subscriber
would make the union catalogue available to each at a cost of $3,60
over a six-year period. It was Mr. Rider's plan to have these sub
scriptions continued indefinitely. When the Catalog had been com
pletely reproduced at the end of six years, in his view the reproduc
tion of it should be undertaken anew at the same subscription pric
of $600 a year, to incorporate the additions made to the Catalog
since the beginning of the work of reproduction. Mr. Rider has no
yet made the Library of Congress a formal proposal to reproduc
the Catalog on microcards and the Library has more recently bee
investigating other media for publication of the Catalog (5). Tem
porarily, at least, this offer appears to have been shelved in favou
of another.

On two excerpted typed pages sent to me by Verner Clapp, it i
announced that "funds have recently become available for micro
filming the National Union Catalog. . . ." It has been decided t
copy "as is" on 16-mm. film, and the work is to be performed o
competitive bid by a commercial firm. The main catalog o
10,825,000 cards will be done first, and then the supplement o
1,500,000. It is estimated 2,500 rolls of film will be required, an
that the cost to other libraries will be about $10,000 per copy. Abou
six months will be required from the time the contract is awarded

It must be emphasized, however, that although the necessity o
copying the catalogue as a security measure has now been me
questions about the Catalog's bibliographic future have not. In th
very pages that carry the announcement of the microfilming venture
a series of seven basic questions are propounded. These concer
redefinition of purpose, scope, editing, reproduction form and cos
and are suggested for reference to a joint committee, which it i
hoped will represent the American Library Association, Specia
Libraries Association, and the Association of Research Libraries, t
work with the Library of Congress.

Conclusion. For a nation or region contemplating a union cata
logue, there are many lessons in the half century of the Library o
Congress' experience. Fundamental is the concept of listing all o
the records of civilization — not only books, or even print, bu

every type of medium through which man communicates his thoughts and experiences. But equally important is the effort to disseminate information so rapidly that the interval between discovery and application shall be shortened if not nearly eliminated. That is the end of bibliographic organization. And unquestionably the union catalogue of library holdings has a role in bibliographic organization that has yet to be developed.

REFERENCES

(1) Coffin, L. C. "National Union Catalog." *Special Libraries,* 1948. v. 39, p. 10-13.

(2) David, C. W., *and* Hirsch, R. "Cumulative world thesaurus." *Journal of Documentation,* 1947. v. 3, p. 43-45.

(3) Dewey, H. T. "Numerical union catalog." *Library Quarterly,* 1948. v. 18, p. 33-44.

(4) Downs, R. B. "Library of Congress; future of the National Union Catalog." *Library World,* 1949. v. 52, p. 55-56.

(5) ———. "Report and supplementary report on the National Union Catalog and related matters." *Lib. of Cong. Inf. Bulletin* Appendix, Aug. 9-15, 1949. p. 1-22.

(6) Evans, L. H. "Research libraries in the war period, 1939-45." *Library Quarterly,* 1947. v. 17, p. 241-62.

(7) "Libraries contributing to the National Union Catalog, 1927-49." *Lib. of Cong. Inf. Bull.,* Sept. 27-Oct. 3, 1949. p. 14-17.

(8) Schwegmann, G. A., Jr. "The National Union Catalog in the Library of Congress." (In *Union catalogs in the U.S.,* ed. by Robert B. Downs . . . Chicago, A.L.A. 1942. p. 229-63.)

(9) *Union catalogs in the United States;* ed. by Robert B. Downs . . . Chicago, A.L.A. 1942. 409 p.

(10) U.S. Library of Congress. *Report of the Librarian of Congress for the fiscal year ending June 30, 1901.*

(10a) ———. ——— *for the fiscal year ending June 30, 1909.*

(10b) ———. ——— *for the fiscal year ending June 30, 1950.*

(10c) ———. ——— *for the fiscal year ending June 30, 1951* (proofs).

(10d) ——— *Union Catalog Division Manual.* (Preliminary edition.) Washington, 1951. 39 p. and 3 appendixes.

(11) Vanderbilt, P. "Proposal for a national bibliography and bibliographical control." *College and Research Libraries,* 1948. v. 9, p. 156-64.

(12) Wyer, M. G. "Standardized abbreviations for the names of libraries." *Library Journal,* 1927. v. 52, p. 802-6.

On Library Education

The Education of an American Librarian

THE PROVERBIAL three score and ten years have now almost elapsed since Melvil Dewey presented his proposal to the American Library Association for the establishment of a school of library economy. In that time there has certainly been adequate opportunity for the members of our profession to describe what should go into the education of a professional librarian. Indeed, if one scrutinizes our library literature by topic, one will find none so readily discussed in recent years as the subject of library education in all of its various aspects. Yet the fact remains that there is still some fundamental disagreement among us as to what should go into the education of a librarian. There is, in fact, an even more fundamental disagreement among us as to just what this profession of librarianship is.

This disagreement is emphasized in the recent Unesco *Enquiry concerning the professional education of librarians and documentalists* (8: 10-13).* Despite a "tendency that has manifested itself in most countries to make librarianship into a distinct and exclusive profession . . . the kindred professions of librarian, archivist and museum curator are sometimes so intermingled that professional training involves troublesome and complex issues."

Nor are these three the only kin who complicate family unity. Contrary to the Unesco report's historical conclusion that the "teacher-librarian completely disappeared between 1870 and 1880 . ." (8: 4), teacher-librarianship flourishes in American schools and there are probably more agencies preparing students for these posts than there are library schools devoted to educating full-time librarians (4).

* Figures in parentheses before colon refer to numbered titles at end, and figures after colon to paging.

Reprinted from *The Library Association Record*, 55: 33-39, February, 1953, by permission of the publisher.

Furthermore, librarianship in the United States is now conceived, at least in some quarters, as embracing audio-visual service, communication and public administration, areas for which there have been developed recently separate new professions and either considerable professional programmes of education or full-fledged professional schools. When to all this is added the fact that modern librarianship has extended itself into a number of peripheral areas such as printing, photo-reproduction, architecture, business administration, statistics, book binding, publishing and therapeutics, to mention only a few, some reason for our disagreement on the scope of librarianship and education to librarianship is apparent.

Nevertheless, there is comfort in the thought that librarianship is not unique among professions in this characteristic of intermingling. The phenomenon of inter-relationships and inter-dependence should give the specialist cause for caution. And it should lend an aura of tolerance to the whole process of continually redefining our calling. For continual redefinition is not an evidence of no profession; it is more probably one manifestation of a young and growing body of knowledge. And as librarianship is redefined, professional education must not only readjust itself but contribute to the very process of professional redefinition.

If we accept the definition of the Institut Français de la Statistique: "No profession can be considered distinct unless it requires a special training" (8: 10), then we can conclude that at least since 1887 librarianship has been a distinct profession. For in that year Melvil Dewey's School of Library Economy was opened at Columbia University.

As Dr. Wilson has pointed out (12: 45), two significant decisions were made by American librarians in establishing what is probably the world's oldest library school: (1) to educate librarians in a professional school rather than through library apprenticeship; (2) to emphasize the practical almost to the neglect of the theoretical. Both of these decisions were extremely important because as the result of the first the foundation of the American library school system was established, and as a result of the second a body of knowledge, though severely practical, was systematically developed.

To the second decision "more than to any other one thing," in Dr. Wilson's opinion, "may be attributed America's acknowledged leadership in the field of modern library procedures."

From 1887, through the First World War, other library schools were established — Pratt in Brooklyn, Illinois at Urbana, Emory at Atlanta, and several others. All tended to emphasize the practical and public library service. In 1915 the Association of American Library Schools was organized, but that Association never assumed the accrediting function undertaken by comparable associations in other professions.

The next milestone in American library education was the Williamson report of 1923 (11). A study of fifteen library schools then in existence resulted in several significant recommendations. Among these the most important were (1) insistence that the library school identify itself with a university, (2) that a high percentage of the faculty be full-time instructors selected for their education and ability, (3) that the first year of study be general and basic, and that specialization be reserved for a second and for subsequent years of study, (4) that a distinction between clerical and professional studies be made and the former largely eliminated from the curriculum, and (5) that a national examining board be established for the certification of librarians and the standardization of library schools (11: 136-46). There were other recommendations affecting in-service training, specialized study, teaching staff and methods of instruction and, as a direct result of a textbook recommendation, the A.L.A. series was launched. In most ways the Williamson report was monumental. It, however, contributed to several subsequent complexities relating to levels, degrees, and the preparation of school librarians.

The Williamson recommendation of a national examining agency fortified the Board of Education for Librarianship for its significant work during the decade from 1923 to 1933. The B.E.L. prepared two sets of standards: the first, highly quantitative, was adopted by the A.L.A. in 1925 (1: 49-78); the second, more nearly qualitative, followed in 1933. The B.E.L. then visited and applied these standards accrediting fourteen library schools for the school year 1925-

1926 and adding to these a score more. It conferred with the Association of American Universities concerning appropriate professional degrees and as a result introduced the "B.S. in L.S." degree about which so much controversy subsequently developed. To those early days of the Board's existence, however, is due a mighty professional debt. It provided the profession for the first time with an objective measure of professional competence.

Without the financial support of the Carnegie Corporation much of the progress in library education would have been impossible. It was that Foundation which financed the Williamson report. A Carnegie annual grant of $25,000 for ten years stimulated the merging of the Albany and New York Public Library Schools at Columbia in 1925. Upon the recommendation of the B.E.L., the Carnegie Corporation contributed also to the support of other library schools and financed the establishment of a school for negroes at Hampton and one for whites at the University of North Carolina. But by far its most significant financial contribution to library education was a grant of one million dollars to the University of Chicago for the establishment of the Graduate Library School.

From the start it was apparent that G.L.S. was not to be just another library school. I can perhaps suggest its difference by describing the impact it had on me as a student there in 1929 and 1930, when Leon Carnovsky as classmate and Douglas Waples as teacher reshaped my whole professional outlook. After eight years of public and college library apprenticeship, followed by one year and one summer at Columbia library school and two years of administering a university library, I was completely committed to a life of technical processes. In the first three months at G.L.S. library techniques were placed in their proper relation to the high mission of librarianship. For the first time in my professional life I was able to look up from the catalogue cards and out on to the professional horizon. What G.L.S. did for me in those early years it did for a whole generation of librarians who are now everywhere advancing the frontiers of our professional knowledge. Evidence of this can be found in the 22 volumes of the *Library quarterly*, in the series of studies in library science and in the collected papers of the various institutes. From G.L.S. came our first, and up to this

ime probably still our only, doctor of philosophy in librarianship.
n the United States, and probably in the world, G.L.S. more than
ιny other force succeeded in establishing librarianship among the
›rofessions and the academic disciplines.

Although the Williamson report had urged both certification of
ndividuals and accreditation of institutions on a national, even
hough voluntary, basis, the B.E.L. had been able to undertake
esponsibility only for the latter. Certification, where it existed,
›ecame a function of state library boards for public and college
ibrarians, and of state departments of education for school librar-
ans. It was especially in connection with the preparation of the
atter that dissatisfaction with the B.E.L. standards developed. As a
esult several regional accrediting agencies and state departments
›f education undertook to establish their own criteria and accredited
ists of training agencies.

One of the most highly developed regional systems of library
tandards and accreditation was that sponsored by the Southern
Association of Colleges and Secondary Schools, beginning about
.928 and continuing until very recently. Its contribution to Amer-
can library education has significantly influenced the latest standards
ιpproved by the American Library Association in July, 1951. The
imilarity between the new A.L.A. Master's programme and the
Southern regional pattern is strikingly revealed in Dr. Wight's
eport of the pre-war Peabody conference on library education (10).

At the close of World War II, the Rockefeller General Education
3oard financed five regional conferences in the South, four devoted
›o the library education of school librarians and the fifth to the
ntegration of school library preparation with professional education
or other types of libraries. Comparable sessions on problems of
ibrary education were held in other sections of the country. Two
ιotable ones, for example, were held in 1948 at the University of
Chicago (3) and at Princeton University (5). The collected papers
rom these, plus a series of pre-war and post-war essays by Munn
(6), Wheeler (9), Danton (2), not to mention numerous papers,
ιddresses and articles, indicated clearly that the time had come for
ι re-evaluation of professional education for librarianship. New
›rogrammes launched in new schools like Florida State, Texas and

Indiana, and in old schools like Denver, Columbia, Illinois and Chicago, were rapidly adopted and have now almost universally replaced the old B.S. in L.S. plan with a new Master's curriculum. As a result, the B.E.L. in 1948 announced the suspension of accreditation under the 1933 standards and appointed four sub-committees to develop new standards for accreditation. I was privileged to serve as a member of the sub-committee on curriculum and degrees, and I am therefore in a position to report to you the latest developments.

The 1933 standards. To understand American library education it is necessary first of all to understand the standards which, although now superseded by the 1951 version, still form the basis for the list of accredited schools recently published by the A.L.A.

The 1933 standards divided library schools into three types:

Type III, *Undergraduate Library Schools,* in which a year of professional study was incorporated in the four years of college work normally required for the bachelor's degree in the United States. Usually this professional work constituted the fourth year after three years of academic non-professional work. The degree awarded was usually a B.A. or a B.S., supplemented by a certificate of competence in librarianship. Simmons College in Boston was such a school.

Type II, *Graduate Library Schools,* in which the year of professional study *followed* a bachelor's degree awarded for four years of academic, non-professional study. This fifth year had exactly the same content in most instances as the fourth year in Type III schools, and in a number of cases the same school offered both Type II and III programmes, graduates and undergraduates attending classes together. The degree awarded for this fifth year of work was the Bachelor of Science in Library Science (B.S. in L.S.). Most of us in American libraries today hold that degree or its equivalent. Columbia, Illinois, California, Emory were examples of this type school.

Type I, *Advanced Graduate Library School,* in which work beyond the first professional year was offered, leading to the M.A. in L.S. or the M.S. in L.S., and in only one school until recently (Chicago), the Ph.D.

Concentrating on the basic year for the moment, the curriculum presented usually, during the first half, a common core of librarianship, basic to practice in all types of libraries, and permitted some specialization in the second half. A typical Type II or III curriculum, pre-war, distributed the 30 semester hours which measure an academic year in American institutions of higher education as follows (a semester hour roughly represents 16 class sessions and 32 hours of outside preparation) :

First Semester (Oct.-Jan.)	Sem. hrs.	Sem. hrs.	*Second Semester* (Feb.-May)
Book Selection	3	3	Book Selection
Reference	3	3	Reference and Bibliography
Cataloguing and Classification	4	3	Cataloguing and Classification
Administration	3	6	Elections of type of library (college, public, school, special) and kind of work (cataloguing, children, government documents, etc.)
Principles	2		
	15	15	

Despite the recommendation of the Williamson report that the curriculum should be general, criticism by school, college and special librarians insisted that most library school courses were public library in their orientation. College and special librarians sought more subject research emphasis; school librarians wanted more attention to the educational aspects of librarianship. Because both school men and school librarians argued that a Type II or III graduate was not adequately prepared for school librarianship, a number of teachers colleges and schools of education introduced, under the direction of school librarians, professional library education programmes intended to meet the needs of schools.

To describe these programmes, the standards of the Southern Association of Colleges and Secondary Schools are taken as an example. In the South, a region of some fourteen states with a population of nearly a third the U.S. total, a strong regional education association had been in the habit of evaluating and accrediting its own secondary and higher educational institutions. It saw no reason for excepting libraries and library education and therefore in 1928 it constituted its own accrediting board which proceeded to develop its own standards and accredited list. Under these standards three classes of library education programmes were recognized:

Class A. Institutions offering 12 semester hours of library science, leading to preparation for teacher-librarianship in small secondary schools and elementary schools.

Class B. Institutions offering 18 semester hours, leading to advanced preparation for teacher-librarianship, desirable in most schools and ultimately to be required as a minimum.

Class C. Institutions offering 30 or more semester hours, leading to preparation for full-time school librarianship or supervisory positions in large secondary schools or school systems.

I was for 13 years director of one of the four library schools in the region that were accredited by both the A.L.A. and the Southern Association. The necessity of maintaining programmes acceptable to both accrediting agencies inevitably stimulated Peabody in the 1930's to anticipate the professional library education pattern that is represented by the new 1951 standards.

The 1951 standards. First in the concept of the 1951 standards is the fact that the basic education of a librarian is more than a single year of professional preparation; it is his total education before full-fledged admission to the profession, normally contained in the American system in about five years of collegiate education beyond the secondary school.

These five years are approximately divided into two years of general education, two of subject concentration, and one of professional library education. The sequence may be in that order or the last two may be taken concurrently. At the end of that period the library school has the responsibility of determining whether the student has attained the goals which the profession requires as a minimum for the practice of librarianship.

"Whether the library school assumes responsibility for the programme in the fifth year or at an earlier level, the programme shall be considered a unit with curriculum standards covering the entire period following secondary education and not as a programme consisting of four years of undergraduate study plus one year of study exclusively in library science" (1a).

Programme of general education. Among the sixteen educational objectives, "the five-year programme should show evidence of promoting" these seven which definitely fall within the scope of the general education area.

"(1) Acquaintance with the principal concepts and issues of the natural sciences, social sciences and humanities;

"(3) Understanding of government and free institutions in a democratic society with special reference to the educational process and the role of the library in education and free inquiry;

"(4) Comprehension of actions and motives of individuals, groups and agencies which libraries serve and with which they work;

"(6) Facility in oral and written communication;

"(7) Reading knowledge of one or more modern foreign languages" (1a).

Now these may sound like glittering generalities, but I can assure you that our sub-committee, committees and Association at large went through countless periods of the kind of soul-suffering which musicians insist is pre-requisite to creation. What is more, in the general colleges of American universities there is a sincere movement to realize these objectives more fully through a so-called integrated curriculum (7a). In such a curriculum the student no longer takes a separate course in chemistry or physics but instead enrolls in an integrated course in the Physical Sciences and in another in the Biological Sciences. Nor does he take separate courses in economics, political science, or sociology. He is offered an integrated course in the Social Sciences. Likewise, all of the fine arts and philosophy are treated together in an integrated course in the Humanities. An area called Communications includes written and oral language and number. And, finally, there is an area called Personal Development which features physical and ethical development and deals with such problems as those relating to marriage and the family. You may object to this last area as not within the province of higher education. In that case you will agree with Dr.

Faust rather than with me (3: 93-114). This general education programme is covered during the first two years in most of our colleges.

During the next two years, if the student is in a college that does not offer professional library education, he will major in, or concentrate on, an academic subject such as English literature, history, or one of the social or natural sciences, or foreign literatures, or fine arts, or indeed any subject offered by the institution. In that case he will earn a bachelor's degree and apply for admission to a library school. If, however, he is in an institution that does offer library science, he may take a part of his professional education concurrently with his academic subject specialization.

Largely through this part of the programme does the student aim to meet the A.L.A. educational objective.

"(2) Understanding of the accumulated knowledge, problems and methods of study of one or more subject areas typically represented by advanced collegiate courses" (1a).

Professional education. The basic professional education programme can be divided into three parts, with the entire programme, averaging today about 40 semester hours, leading to the Master's degree, as contrasted with the 30 semester hours of the previous standards leading to the B.S. in L.S.

What has been named by some of us as the *pre-core* consists of from 9 to 15 semester hours. It is generally available on, or acceptable from, the undergraduate level and is a pre-requisite to the *professional core.*

In the South it is tending to bridge the former gap between Southern Association and A.L.A. standards by enabling the teacher-librarian to count some or all of her preparation as the *pre-core.* The *pre-core* includes these courses or a selection of them:

(1) *Library Materials,* an introduction to the selection not only of books and other print, as in former courses, but to audio-visual materials as well, from pre-school to adult, and to the various general and elementary bibliographic aids.

(2) *Library Organization,* including the routine technical processes of order work, cataloguing, classifying, mending, processing, shelving, charging, inventory, etc.

(3) *Library Foundations*, an orientation in libraries, library organizations, ethics, history, literature, etc.

(4) *Library Observation and Practice*, for which no academic credit is generally given; and from the teacher-librarian programme these additional courses,

(5) *Library Materials for Children*, and

(6) *Library Materials for Young People*

are sometimes accepted by library schools in lieu of (1).

The *pre-core* aims to promote this educational objective:

"(15) Orientation in the ethics, organizations, publications, and activities of the library and related professions" (1a).

The professional core. The *professional core*, offered largely in the fifth or graduate year, compresses most of the technical information covered by the previous standards that are not included in the *pre-core*, and augments such information with content and approach that are more nearly of graduate calibre. For example, these courses are now nearly standard in the new Master's programme:

(1) *Library Research*, a course which introduces the student to the methods of research, to the research literature of librarianship and to current problems for investigation, and establishes a foundation for the student's own study, thesis, or bibliography.

(2) Bibliography or Literature of the Humanities.

(3) Bibliography or Literature of the Social Sciences.

(4) Bibliography or Literature of the Natural Sciences.

(5) Reference Sources and Services.

(6) Problems of Classification and Cataloguing, and, in addition, these are appearing in increasing frequency among the core courses:

(7) Audio-visual materials and services.

(8) Basic communications.

(9) Readers and reading.

Through the *professional core* and through what has gone before, the following educational objectives are promoted:

"(12) Understanding of the principles and methods of selecting, acquiring and organizing materials. . . .

"(13) Understanding of the principles and methods of distributing materials, supplying information, and guiding reading. . . .

"(14) Ability to identify library problems and to devise and carry out organizational, operational and service programmes" (1a).

Specialized electives. The third part of the professional programme offers the student an opportunity to lay a foundation for service in one or more specialized aspects of librarianship through course electives and through a Master essay which may take the form of a thesis, bibliography, or paper related to the specialization.

Among the specializations offered in American library schools, these are fairly common in the basic curriculum:

(1) Public libraries

(2) School libraries

(3) College libraries

(4) Special libraries. (There is a trend toward division of specialties among library schools. Pittsburgh has for long been associated with children's work. But it is too early yet to name schools and specialties.)

(5) Audio-visual service. (My own school at Florida State University was probably the first library school to establish a separate department in this field.)

(6) Cataloguing and classification.

(7) Government publications.

(8) Serials. (University of Michigan was the first library school to establish a separate course.)

In this part, also, the student completes his major project.

From the list of theses compiled by the Graduate Library School of the University of Chicago for all library schools, it is evident that, if no profound discoveries are emanating from these bits of orginal investigation, library school students today are certainly coming to grips with professional problems as they rarely did in my library school generation.

From this third period in the basic programme, the final A.L.A. educational objective gains promotion:

"(16) A basis for service in one or more specialized aspects of library activity . . ." (1a).

This, then, is the basic professional programme in library schools of the United States today. It leads to a Master's degree, usually in five years for the secondary school graduate, and a little over one year for the college graduate without previous library education or experience.

There are other aspects of professional education that should be considered but I omit them in deference to specific requests to touch on two subjects that relate only indirectly to library education — placement and pensions. Most American library schools assume placement responsibility for their own graduates. So universal is this that the A.L.A. itself has found it expedient largely to eliminate its own placement service. But library placement today is more a problem for the employer than for the employee. Demand still exceeds supply. Recently the Army, which has been unable to recruit enough librarians, has modified its requirement of graduation from an A.L.A. accredited school to graduation from a library school approved by a regional or state accrediting agency. The opportunities are especially plentiful in cataloguing, school libraries, government agencies and military establishments.

As for pensions, several plans are available to librarians. Those of us who serve in state-supported educational institutions are eligible for teacher retirement. The rates vary, but in our state approximately 5 per cent of our salary is matched by an equal amount from the state, and retirement after 30 years or at the age of 65 brings 50 per cent of the highest salary received. Privately-supported colleges and universities that participate in the Carnegie plan have a comparable arrangement. Finally, the A.L.A., through a commercial firm, offers librarians an annuity plan. Very recently, teachers have become eligible for national social security and many librarians have been included. Increasingly these plans are becoming interchangeable. Florida will grant credit for up to ten years of public service in another state. One may continue the Carnegie plan or the A.L.A. plan regardless of where or how often one moves. The tragedy of any pension plan is, of course, the continuous inflation that has beset society.

Conclusion. One of the urgent problems that must be considered by any nation planning a programme of training for librarians is the matter of national education. In the United States we have favoured accreditation of schools on a national basis rather than certification of individuals. This has not been the case in Britain, where the national examination administered by the Library Association is the gateway to professional status. At this point I am not convinced that our way has been better than that of Britain. Perhaps the answer is not either-or; perhaps it is best as in law and medicine, where they have both. I am convinced, however, that you would do well to study carefully both the history of the British national examination and the evolution of our American standards and their application in accrediting library schools, before you yourself decide on a national policy of standardization.

REFERENCES

(1)   A.L.A. Board of Education for Librarianship. *Second annual report*. Chicago, 1926. 85 p.

(1a)   ————. *Standards for accreditation of library schools, adopted by the A.L.A. Council, July 13, 1951*. (Mimeographed.)

(2)   Danton, J. P. *Education for librarianship*. Unesco, 1949. 97 p.

(3)   Faust, C. H., *and* Shores, Louis. "Preprofessional education of librarians." (In *Education for librarianship*; papers presented at the Library Conference, University of Chicago, 16th and 21st August, 1948. Chicago, A.L.A., 1949, pp. 93-114.)

(4)   *How shall we educate teachers and librarians for library service in the school? Findings and recommendations of the Joint Committee of the American Association of Teachers Colleges and the American Library Association* . . . N.Y., Columbia University Press, 1936. 74 p.

(5)   *Issues in library education: a report of the conference on library education, Princeton University, December 11-12, 1948*. Council of National Library Associations, 1949. 74 p.

(6)   Munn, Ralph. *Conditions and trends in education for librarianship*. N.Y., Carnegie Corp., 1936. 49 p.

(7)   Reece, E. J. *The task of training librarians*. N.Y., King's Crown Press, 1949. 91 p.

(7a)   Stickler, H., Stoakes, P., *and* Shores, L. *General education in action*. Des Moines, Ia., Brown, 1950.

(8)   Unesco. *Enquiry concerning the professional education of librarians and documentalists; final report presented by Mrs. Suzanne Briet to the Joint Committee of the International Federation of Library Associations and of the International Federation for Documentation*. Paris, 1951. 82 p. 4 annexes.

(9)   Wheeler, J. L. *Progress and problems in education for librar-
      ianship.* N.Y., Carnegie Corp., 1946. 107 p.
(10) Wight, E. A. *Evaluation and revision of the library school
      curriculum.* Nashville, Peabody Press, 1945.
(11) Williamson, C. C. *Training for library service; a report pre-
      pared for the Carnegie Corporation of New York.* N.Y., 1923.
      165 p.
(12) Wilson, L. R. "Historical development of education for librar-
      ianship in the United States." (In *Education for librarianship,*
      1949, pp. 44-59.)

Prologue to a National Plan: The Professional Association's Responsibility Toward Formal Education in Library Science.

ORGANIZATION LIBRARIAN IN AMERICA hovers over a potential as yet unrealized.

In considerably less than a century, library associations in the United States have accumulated at least 100,000 memberships.[1] The ALA, despite sharply increased dues, has today 30,000 members. With some duplication of individuals, SLA numbers another 15,000. There are 15,000 memberships in the other national independent organizations. If to these 60,000 librarian memberships are added those in the several regional, the fifty state, and numerous local associations as well as in peripheral bibliographic, documentation, audio-visual, archival, publishing and allied disciplines of the learned societies, to say nothing of professional organizations pledged to further libraries, the force of our professional effort should be considerable.

That it is not, troubles us. If we are honest with ourselves we must admit librarianship today is no decisive influence in the affairs

[1] For notes, see pages 243-244.

Reprinted from *The Southeastern Librarian,* 13: 88-96, Summer, 1963, by per-
mission of the publisher. The essay here reprinted is a paper read before the
Tenth Anniversary Meeting of the Georgia Chapter of the Special Libraries
Association, Emory University, Atlanta, Georgia, September 28, 1962.

of mankind. It sits at no treaty tables, exerts no influence on domestic policies, struggles for left-over financial consideration on the state and local levels. Numerically considerable as Organization Librarian is today it has not qualitatively attained the position in national life commensurate either with its own potential or with the critical challenge that now confronts the world. Reluctant as we may be, publicly, to admit it, we know in our professional privacy that world decisions hardly wait on us.

Yet, to some of us who made our decision years ago for a life with books, fundamental faith in the destiny of our profession persists. We believe fervently that we are the preservers and disseminators of man's noblest deeds and thoughts. Within our calling is the sum total of all man's knowledge. In our province is not only the substance of every separate discipline, but what is more important — the synthesis of all of them.

Why then have we not — 100,000 of us who compose Organization Librarian in America today — expressed what we represent more effectively than we have? Why have we not helped create a happier world? Why have we not so disseminated the great and good ideas from our libraries as to remove forever the trembling over a nuclear war? And why have we failed to show man how to replace poverty with plenty, illness with health, illiteracy with the ability to read? Indeed, why have we not at least made the literate more discriminating?

The answers to these questions will be furnished variously depending upon our commitment to librarianship, our concept of the mission of this profession, our philosophy of life and libraries. Some of us will insist indignantly that none of these responsibilities is basically ours. As librarians our role is essentially ancillary. Library literature abounds with self-subordinating declarations that libraries are subsidiary; that librarianship has no content of its own, and that in fact there is no library science.[2]

The professional associations' first responsibility, therefore, is *to identify the library science for which a formal education is desired*. If librarianship is a perpetual ancillary, as at least a considerable, if not the dominant, portion of the practicing profession believes, then formal education is indeed out of step with practice.

There is considerable evidence that librarians in all library types tend toward this ancillary belief with which library education does not readily concur.

School librarians, for example, have frequently exhorted their colleagues to study pedagogy and know the curriculum for the sole purpose of supporting it. As far as it goes this is a sound beginning. But it does not go far enough. It implies that a school curriculum is something too sacred to be questioned by anyone on the level of librarian. It does not allow that the librarian might participate in the development of this curriculum, or even lead in the creation of a new one. It bears out the experience I had with a principal of a college demonstration school who complained to me about his librarian. "She insists that book selection must follow the curriculum. She has repeated this shibboleth so often, that I never walk down the hall with the curriculum in my hand that I don't have the uncomfortable feeling that something sinister is following me."

But the tragedy is that while the school library is following the curriculum, the curriculum is not following the library. If we can judge by the repeated professional wailings "how can we get teachers to use the library more," our ancillary philosophy in the schools has not produced anything like the library-centered learning we had hoped for. Can it be that we school librarians have been too ancillary, too unwilling to lead rather than to follow the classroom teacher?

In the academic library, the ancillary complex is even more pronounced. Almost as if in dread that someone might really believe the Carlyle words that a true university is a library, most college and university libraries go about chanting as if to keep the devil away, "librarianship is ancillary to the disciplines. Find out what the faculty want and then hasten to meet their needs in the classroom and for research." Now please do not interpret what I say to mean this is wrong. I believe this is an important part of the academic librarian's mission. But I believe it is only a part, and probably not the better half of our marriage with higher education.

Twenty-eight years ago at the Chicago World's Fair Convention of the American Library Association I read a paper entitled "The Library Arts College,"[3] which the late J. McKeen Cattell, then editor of *School and Society*, requested for his journal. In that paper I suggested that we reverse our present practice of regular classroom attendance and irregular library reading. Instead of going to a history lecture every day at nine, and to a chemistry lecture Monday, Wednesday and Friday at eleven, the students go to the library during those periods and read intently on the topics in the syllabus. Only after considerable reading and thought should the students come together with the instructor for discussion and debate over differences and challenges. It was my contention that such a procedure would enhance learning.

Although college and university librarians have not generally accepted the role of leadership in American higher education, trends are inevitably thrusting us into a position of strategy. As honors reading, autonomous courses, and variations on the theme of independent study grow ever more fashionable on our campuses, the librarian finds himself inevitably teaching, not just how to use the library, but history, and English, and chemistry, and economics, and all of the other separate subjects that have characterized a college education in the past, but teaching them with a new dimension. In the librarian's hands, higher education is no longer a collection of segmented subjects each with more or less predatory rights in the college curriculum, but an integrated approach to reality. Through the rising undergraduate reading rooms, browsing corners, augmented exhibits and displays, reading and review forums, lecture series and library music recitals, and through the increasing use of ETV, classroom learning is rapidly withering on the vine. Last June at Kenyon in Ohio a small group of librarians met in a talk-shop to explore the possibility of a college that is entirely a library.[4] At long last the college and university librarian is approaching his real role in higher education, as the generalist who can bring some order and relationship to the separated subjects the faculty specialists offer their students.

In the public library there may have been cause for not more rapidly assuming our role of educator. Extension to all the people has been an uphill struggle. It has engaged most of our effort. There is no way to prove this now, but perhaps a more effective approach to extension could have been made through a less passive educational role. While we were proclaiming self-righteously that the school's business is to teach reading, the library's to supply books, we were also telling the taxpayer where the greater and prior support should go. That nowhere in our great public library movement a teach-reading program developed with the dramatic impact of the old Lancastrian method, or the modern Laubach "Each one teach one"[5] idea is a professional failure. I accuse myself, because I began my own career in public libraries to which I devoted my first eight professional years. How could we who insist our business is books stand off from teaching people the prerequisite to using them?

That this has troubled more than a minority of public librarians is patent in the recurring remorse about our adult education and our responsibility for school homework. Although we applauded professionally William S. Learned's monumental milestone[6] many years ago, our public libraries are still far from realizing quite so bold a community role. If modern advertising reflects the illiteracy of our literate consumers, the public library at least shares with our schools major blame.

Nor has the special librarian realized his potential. In some ways, his role has been easier because his assignment has been restricted to the specialty he serves. Because of this restriction the special librarian is in danger of being lulled into far greater passivity than his prospect deserves. Because of his ancillary approach a schism between documentalists and librarians threatens our profession.

Let me indicate this threat as I saw it again first-hand in recent visits to two different space-industry special libraries. In one place a well-organized special library served its constituency well but traditionally. Company administrators and researchers received and could always expect materials and information on subjects of interest to them. Employees generally found courteous and devoted attention to their informational and recreational requests. By our standards this library would rank in the upper quartile.

In the other place, the library was headed by a documentalist, a former chemical engineer with some library science courses but not an accredited library school degree. Of the dozen staff members only one held the accredited master's degree. The others were men and women with undergraduate majors in the sciences, for the most part, with perhaps a scattering of library science courses in their transcripts. I talked with all of them enough to be convinced that none of them felt it was "either-or." In fact I came away with the sensation that the librarian's association with physical science had rekindled her creative interest in library science.

Similarly I gathered the eerie feeling that the chemist had really not understood chemistry until he met library science. From his new library associations (such as he had never experienced as an undergraduate) he had gained a new perspective on his specialty. As never before he had come to realize that chemistry is not alone in this struggle with the riddle of the universe. Said this good chemist turned documentalist-librarian: "An important by-product is that library science restores some of the humility that made physical scientists so creative initially, a humility that has been difficult to retain under the pampering of lush government contracts."

In this second library the most striking fact was the *peer* relationship of physical and library scientist. Instead of passively waiting for requests, the library, as many times as not, initiated demand out of a full knowledge of research in progress. This knowledge stemmed from something beyond a so-called "Task Index," computer-keyed, which in itself was a monumental undertaking because it revealed not only generally every investigation under way in the plant, but facets of each investigation and their inter-relationship with facets of other investigations in and out of the company. This knowledge came from something the conservative reference librarian might oppose — active participation in the investigation itself. As one who might be called a radical reference librarian I was perfectly thrilled to hear a librarian tell a chemist informally and joshingly "Anyone who knows his colloid literature at all can see you don't have a clue on this problem. Here, try this. . . ."

If there really is a conflict between librarians and documentalists as Jesse Shera has indicated[7] then I venture the guess that part of the blame is in each camp. The documentalist in the argument is probably an old-fashioned subject specialist, one of the six blind men who described the elephant as being entirely the part he touched. And the librarian in the debate probably operates from a focus something like this: "Research — that's your problem; me — I'm organized to get you what you want."

I submit that the professional association's responsibility toward formal practice in librarianship antecedes its responsibility toward formal education in library science. Library practice, extremely critical of library education's conservatism continues too uncritically its own conservative way. In what has gone before I have contended that in all four major types of libraries — school, academic, public, special — library practice has not realized or even appreciated the potential of the only profession for which the late Jan Struther felt "she could have any respect."[8] In the two words of Emile Zola, "I accuse" library practice of incidentally or intentionally fostering the "ancillary" philosophy of librarianship, of contributing to the inferiority complex of our profession. To this "ancillary approach" by many of our colleagues I attribute the professional caricature Dr. Bryan says pictures librarians as "inhibited old maids, zealously guarding their precious books against mutilation, loss, and over-long use, while enforcing a tomb-like silence."[9]

I, therefore, challenge Organization Librarian to change the portrait of the practicing librarian. When Dr. Bryan writes that the current stereotype of us "in novels, plays, and on the screen is certainly not so glamorous as the popular conception of other professional groups, such as doctors and nurses, artists, poets and composers, scientists, explorers, and detectives" she accuses all of us. The way to change this picture is for the profession, collectively through our associations, to rid ourselves once and for all of the ancillary complex.

We have precedents. As late as 1883 in the United States, history as a discipline was generally considered to be ancillary to some other discipline.[10] The following year the American Historical Association was organized, and as a duly constituted group historians steadily have moved toward peerage in the family of disciplines. Higher educational history records that the sciences were not always considered elite in the curriculum, and disciplines like the classics no longer rank among the top subjects. I submit it is academic snobbery to declare my subject has content, yours not. It reminds me of George Orwell's *Animal Farm*: all are equal, but some are more equal than others. The true scholar will recognize that all subjects contribute content to the sum total of man's knowledge.

The first responsibility of the professional association, therefore, is to help library practice more nearly to realize its potential. Basic to realization is faith in our peerage with any profession. Demonstration of such peerage should be possible in virtually every type of library. In Shaker Heights, Ohio, I understand Ford Foundation money is supporting an experiment in elementary school that will just about demonstrate that the library *is* the school. The talkshop at Kenyon this past summer discloses that some higher educators are considering the possibility of a college which is totally a library. In some communities like Louisville, the public library is emerging as the adult education institute. And what is happening in industries like petroleum is that each research team has either a literature searching specialist, or every member rotates literature seaching responsibility. There are no perpetual ancillaries, only peers who give meaning to research teamwork in the quest for truth.

The second responsibility of the library association is to restrain specialism. The SLA by bringing together librarians who serve a variety of specialties exerts a profound generalistic influence. If it did not, there would be as many separate library associations in the United States as there are individual librarians. Some Europeans, indeed, accuse Americans of organizing every time as many as three librarians get together, the minimum number required to fill the three principal offices. This is not quite true; but minute special interests tend us that way.

I look for special associations to be formed shortly in these areas: Association of Central Processors; Association of Source Catalogers; Society for Perpetuating Word-by-Word Filing; and Organization for the Promotion of Pre-Binds. Certainly all of these interests deserve forum opportunities somewhere. But, all of them

contribute to a unified profession, I hope, and, therefore, belong to
the large association of librarians. The library association in its
second responsibility must help these passionate groups see the
importance to them of professional unity.

Unless such specialists are restrained by the library association,
even more schisms will develop. At the moment, school librarians
desiring to separate from the rest of the library profession face a
major separation within their own ranks by the audio-visualists.
Likewise, special librarians who felt the need for a separate association in 1909 now are confronted by separation from the documentalists. Recognition of special interests is desirable, don't mistake
me, but not at the cost of professional unity. Somewhere in this
nation, there is need for a single articulated and articulate voice to
speak for librarians and librarianship as a whole.

Let's look real hard at this clamoring by the subjects, and especially the sciences for a new brand of librarian to be called the
information specialist or documentalist, or literature searcher. Let's
hope the group won't decide on the title "Retriever." This would
certainly dramatize the librarian's ancillary position. Librarianship,
by insisting on being a technic primarily, has tended to stand off
from subject research. This has been particularly true in the sciences
since librarians are humanists in the majority. Consequently, the
scientists have felt the need for literature searchers with some
knowledge of the subject. Too often they have seen the housekeeping
"technic" librarian under her ancillary complex refrain from contributing a bit of what Count Keyserling once called "creative
understanding."

Inevitably this has led to the subject specialist without the technic
taking over. At the moment he is clamoring for a specialized education that he thinks will be completely different from that offered by
the ALA accredited schools. Perhaps to some extent this will prove
true. But all of us would feel better if the documentalist would first
examine the actual rather than the alleged content of library science.

Since 1947, at Florida State University, every doctoral dissertation and master's thesis, in all subjects, has passed through a
library school faculty member's hands to be approved for form and

documentation. Concurrently, a one-hour course "Library Use in Graduate Research" required of all graduate students not enrolled in the Library School was instituted. About 400 graduate students enroll in this course each year, grouped as far as possible, in sections accenting the natural sciences, the social sciences, or the humanities. The program has been described by Professor John Clemons who is the Library School faculty member primarily responsible.[11]

In 16 years of offering this course, some 5,000 graduate students majoring in all of the so-called "substantive" subjects have been exposed to this library course. It may come as a surprise to the "ancillaries" among us, but in writing and orally, scores of chemistry, math, physics, zoology, botany, meteorology, oceanography, as well as economics, history, English, foreign language majors have attested voluntarily and almost embarrassingly, "This course has more content than any we've taken. It should be given first." "Before I took it, *Chem Abstracts* was the only source I thought I needed to know." "From '500' I gained understanding of Math." "Literature searching is the beginning of all research. This course is basic."

If any evidence is needed that the subject specialist needs library science, we can submit several hundred case studies. The specialism of the chemist or the physicist needs the generalism of the librarian, not as a technic, but as a refreshed approach to knowledge. Only through the gestalt of library science can our deteriorating specializations be rescued. Marriage of the librarian and subject specialist can bring us a new, more creative research, one steeped in the perspective of unified content.

In this respect the pioneer efforts of Dorothy Crosland and Georgia Tech are salutary. From these two institutes have come valuable reconsiderations of library education. It is such efforts that the library association has a responsibility to support, encourage and even initiate.

If I have particularized on the current documentalist schism I have done so only to illustrate the library association's responsibilities of generalism. This responsibility is a critical one toward formal education in library science. From every professional corner the library educator is confronted by demands for specialized training. Even if resources were such that a 1:1 faculty-student ratio were possible it is doubtful that either subject specialists or librarians are best served by too much specialization. Only the library association can bring these specialists together to prevent professional isolation, and condition the climate for a creative generalism, librarianship's strategic contribution to a world frustrated by over-specialism.

And now for a third responsibility toward formal education in library science — evaluation. Accepting responsibility for peerage and generalism, what professional education is necessary? Library associations, and particularly the ALA of the United States and the LA of the United Kingdom, have taken this responsibility seriously, although differently. From the start, the ALA has favored accreditation of library schools; the LA certification or "chartering" of librarians. Either vehicle — accreditation or certification — enables the association to exercise its responsibility for evaluation, not only of the content but the method of library education.[12]

ALA through its COA and its predecessor the BEL has since 1924 provided evaluation standards for library schools, and personnel for applying these standards. These standards were the culmination of a responsibility the Association assumed toward formal library science in the first year of its life.[13] Led by Melvil Dewey who wrote in 1879, "We need a training school . . ." the ALA plan for a library school was accepted by Columbia College and as a result probably the first professional school for librarians was opened January 5, 1887. ALA followed this in 1890 by appointing a standing committee on training for librarianship which issued its first comprehensive report, under the chairmanship of Mary Wright Plummer, in 1903.[14] Then in 1909 ALA activated a professional training section to provide a forum on associational responsibilities. These were the steps that led to the Association's assuming the major responsibility for evaluation.

Much has been written about the famous Williamson Report of 1923. Basically, it summarized three associational responsibilities: (1) formulate a standard scheme of grading library positions; (2) determine minimum qualifications of training and experience for each job, and certificate those who qualify; (3) evaluate and approve schools and certify automatically its graduates.[15] That the ALA has taken seriously these responsibilities there can be no doubt. There can only be differences on how well that library association has exercised its responsibility toward formal library science.

As a member of the five-man ALA Committee responsible for the present library school curriculum, I am probably biased. The 1951 standards, in my opinion, were a bold step forward. Over considerable protest then and now they eliminated the old "type III" school and placed professional library education on the graduate level. In broad strokes the ALA Committee painted the desirable professional preparation as requiring five years of education beyond secondary school: (a) two collegiate years of general education; (b) two collegiate years of academic concentration; (c) one postgraduate year in library science. This still appears to me as sound preparation for librarianship in all of its special ramifications, including literature searching, or information retrieval or documentation.

But, in my opinion, a dozen years in these accelerated times is not too soon for the library associations to exercise their evaluation responsibility again. Activation of a commission on a national plan for library education is most timely.

As the senior among the heads of the accredited library schools, and one who now completes 33 years in library education in this region, these elements seem important to me in any consideration of a national plan:

1. *Concerted Associational Responsibility.* ALA leadership through its statesman-like COA should early enlist not only other library associations like SLA, but peripheral organizations, subject disciplines especially concerned with retrieval, educational and manufacturing groups and agencies concentrating on so-called educational media.

2. *Multiple Articulations.* Commendable studies toward correlating undergraduate and graduate programs in library science have been made both through the ALA-NCATE standards, and the series of regional meetings. But articulation within librarianship is not enough. Such restricted articulation is partially responsible for the training efforts of documentalists, audiovisualists and other peripheral library workers.

3. *Generalist Accent.* In a world of increasing specialization, some generalizing force is badly needed. Libraries as the composite record of civilization provide the origin for such a force. Librarians as the preservers and disseminators of these records have within them the potential for directing this force.

4. *Peerage Among the Disciplines.* A generalist is defined as one whose "studies, interests and information are extensive or widely distributed. . . ."[16] Among all the subjects we know there is not a single specialist as well qualified as the librarian. But the librarian must come to look upon his subject of library science without ancillary illusions. He must at least begin to respect the content of his own subject, to realize that while nearly all specialists deal with a portion of knowledge, library science encompasses the sum total.

To this librarian with over four decades of dedication to his profession, librarianship is a profession of destiny. I recognize in library science the subject of subjects that may yet help mankind to an understanding of the universe, not as segmented findings, but as a truthful whole. Then will our profession finally contribute to the welfare of the world.

---

[1] *The Bowker Annual of Library and Book Trade Information,* 1962, pp. 215-52.

[2] Edward Waters has expressed this conviction most recently in *Library Education Division Newsletter,* no. 42, p. 3, May, 1962.

[3] Louis Shores. "The Library Arts College," *School and Society,* XLI (1935), pp 1-11.

[4] Robert Jordan of the Council on Library Resources was the leader and mimeographed reports have been issued.

[5] Jamye Green. "Dr. Frank C. Laubach; A Bibliography" (Unpublished Master's Thesis, Library School, Florida State University, 1946), 119 pp.

[6] William S. Learned. *The American Public Library and the Diffusion of Knowledge* (New York: Harcourt, Brace and Company [1924]).

[7] Jesse Shera. "Without Reserve," *Wilson Library Bulletin.*

[8] Jan Struther [Joyce (Anstruther) Maxtone Graham], *A Pocketful of Pebbles* (New York: Harcourt, Brace and Company [1946], p. 397.

[9] Alice I. Bryan. *The Public Librarian;* A Report of the Public Library Inquiry, . . . (New York: Columbia University Press, 1952).

[10] Franklin Jameson. "The American Historical Association, 1884-1909," *American Historical Review,* XV (October, 1909), p. 2.

[11] John E. Clemons. "Teaching Bibliographic Sources and Styles to Graduate Students," *College and Research Libraries,* XVII (September, 1956), pp. 403-8.

[12] Louis Shores. "Qualifications of Personnel; Training and Certification," *Library Trends,* III (January, 1955), pp. 269-78.

13 Melvil Dewey. "Apprenticeship of Librarians," *Library Journal*, IV (May, 1879), p. 147.
14 American Library Association, *Papers and Proceedings*, 1903, pp. 83-101.
15 Carnegie Corporation of New York, *Training for Library Service*; A Report Prepared . . . by Charles C. Williamson (New York: The Merrymount Press, 1923).
16 *Funk and Wagnalls New Standard Dictionary of the English Language* . . . (New York: Funk & Wagnalls Company, 1958), p. 1018.

Education for Armed Forces Librarianship

SINCE WORLD WAR II the profession of librarianship has been augmented and stimulated by its members who practice in the Armed Forces, as by no other special group. The reasons for this phenomenon can be found both within the library world and without.

Although V-J day brought a close to actual physical combat with one set of adversaries it began a new struggle with an even more formidable combination of opponents. The difficulty of the new war stems not so much from the greater physical resources today's communist countries have over yesterday's fascist nations, but rather from the psychological method of their warfare. The regional military conflicts in Korea and Indo-China, despite their costliness in life and wealth, have been less significant in the struggle between east and west than the almost continuous world-wide war of ideas.

It is this war of ideologies that has thrust librarians to the fore as an occupation of destiny. For if a library is anything it is a collection of ideas. Regardless of the format in which these ideas are disseminated the modern library now has or can have them all. Librarianship all at once then becomes one of the vital professions in this world struggle and librarians are now the main component of our psychological forces.

Reprinted from *The Southeastern Librarian*, 5: 58-63, Summer, 1955, by permission of the publisher. The essay here reprinted is a paper given before the Armed Forces Librarians Group of the Southeastern Library Association, September 30, 1954.

In a total war such as we are now engaged in, there is total participation. Every librarian at home, whether he likes it or not, is actively concerned with the defense of our way of life. The public librarian's contribution to the bulwark of his home community is dramatized in the Heritage of America movement. On academic campuses everywhere, college and university librarians defend the western tradition of free inquiry by stocking and disseminating ideas on all sides of all issues. In the school rooms of the United States increasing quantities of instructional materials are being drawn from Materials Centers that librarians conscientiously develop with the child's full growth in mind. In industry and business, in government and research, librarians today are consciously at work as never before to aid the Search for Truth.

But if there is one segment of librarianship that is on the firing line, it is the Armed Forces librarians, serving in Army, Navy, Air Force and related agencies. To these Armed Forces librarians is assigned the critical task of disseminating the world's best ideas to those who must defend us in physical combat. And to these Armed Forces is also delegated the responsibility for aiding research in the discovery of even better ideas.

Because of their intimate relationship with the forces of World War III the Armed Forces librarians are in the vanguard of professional innovation. Only a few examples of this advance position can here be cited. Many more illustrations, possibly of a more significant character, could be pointed out in many individual bases of operations. But the purpose of this paper is not to review Armed Forces Library Service. That has already been done effectively elsewhere by Armed Forces librarians themselves. What is contemplated here is a design for education of Armed Forces librarians.

First among the library innovations for which Armed Forces librarians deserve considerable credit is the expansion of the concept of library materials to include audio-visual media. The Armed Forces in World War II took instructional advantage of 16 mm. films, of filmstrips, of graphics, as civilian educational agencies never had before. Armed Forces librarians were quick to stock and disseminate these non-book materials. Largely due to the librarians' foresight and vision, heterogeneous stockpiles of miscellaneous bits of equipment were brought together into a significant center in the base or research library. One of the most promising examples is the Audio-Visual Center in the Air University Library at Maxwell Air Force Base.

A second dramatic contribution to librarianship by the Armed Forces librarians is in the art and science of bibliotherapy. Although beginnings of this field existed in hospital libraries and even in public library readers' divisions before World War II, nothing like the concept or the potential that grew out of veterans' return to civilian life was ever considered before. It is significant that Armed Forces librarians' efforts in this field brought the endorsement of at least one outstanding medical school and of many hospitals and their staffs of physicians and nurses.

A third example of professional pioneering by Armed Forces librarians can be found in the area of documentation. In civilian reference, for years before the outbreak of World War II, we had meditated over and debated conservative versus liberal concepts of service. Dr. J. I. Wyer in his A.L.A. textbook on the subject had described the difference between the two theories of reference in this way: the conservative believes the librarian's function is merely to locate the sources for the investigator, the liberal believes the librarian should evaluate the sources, digest them, and in every way possible aid the investigator in his research.

The Armed Forces librarians have gone even beyond Dr. Wyer's liberal position. In military agencies concerned with research it can now be said that librarians are not only assisting the investigators to locate sources, but also actually actively participating in the research itself. This participation is occurring in a number of ways. Extensive, continuous abstracting by librarians doubly trained— professionally in librarianship and academically in one of the sciences—is speeding discovery on a number of critical fronts. Here is a new note to reference. Inquiries are anticipated. The librarian asks the question for the inquirer twenty-four hours before the investigator has himself reached that stage, and then answers it.

Closely related to this documentation development in research is a comparable bibliographic innovation in instruction. Peace time armed forces are continuously engaged in education. If I cite the Air University again it is only because my recent associations there as a member of the advisory board and as consultant to one of the schools has brought me into first-hand contact with specific projects. Since 1952 the Air University Library has had on its staff bibliographic assistants, each of whom has been assigned to an individual school or to a separate course. The duty of the bibliographic assistant has been to work with the instructors to develop courses of study, teaching methods, learning situations, all based on the library resources of Air University. Out of this innovation has come a library liaison with classroom instruction such as I have never seen at a civilian institution of higher education.

There are other innovations to cite, many more. But perhaps the technological contribution of the Armed Forces librarians should not be omitted. Spurred by the technological advance of the Armed Forces they serve librarians have been aroused to the possibilities of gadgets. It is impossible, for example, to be at APG in Eglin without wondering about the potential of jet propulsion for charging devices; or of radar for print transmission. Audio-Visual capitalization has already been cited. The use of aircraft for bookmobile service was practiced in my own C.B.I. theatre as early as 1942. Electronic devices for various technical processes from book charging to photo reproduction would reveal other innovations. But one Armed Forces invention that holds much promise for research librarianship is facsimile. This visual device was used during World War II for transmitting weather maps instantaneously around the world. Already our Armed Forces librarians have begun to ask: Why not the printed page? Do you see what a boon to research this might be? The investigator, in his laboratory 4,000 miles away from the library that owns the only copy in the world of that precious reference, radios his need. In seconds the page flashes on his screen.

The above innovations have been cited merely as frontiers that Armed Forces librarianship is pushing.

Obviously, librarians who hope to work in the Armed Forces need the basic education expected of all librarians. These are effectively stated in the 1953 Standards of the Board of Education for Librarianship. But the question here considered is what special education over and beyond that is needed by the Armed Forces librarian and what extra-ordinary opportunities for professional education can be developed to meet the overwhelming unfilled demand that now exists.

The time has now come for special attention by one or more library schools to the particular needs of personnel for the Armed Forces libraries. Such specialization should come toward the end of the basic master's program. It could come at first as part of the courses on special librarianship in those schools that offer such a course. Later, when enrollment and interest warranted, a whole separate course on Armed Forces librarianship might follow.

Such a course should examine mission and organization of the various major armed forces library services against the background of the Armed Forces. It should include orientation in regulations, channels, chains of command, military terminology. Understanding of what classification means and the handling of classified materials is essential. Detailed study of the agencies under which libraries serve in the Armed Forces should comprise another unit. Variations in methodology, materials, quarters, financing, acquisition, cataloging, circulation, and reference should be examined. Finally, some attention to the literature of military science should be given.

A laboratory for the training of Armed Forces librarians is possible on any campus with one or more R.O.T.C. units. A demonstration library to serve that unit might well resemble a base library and afford an opportunity for practice to library school students specializing.

From time to time, Armed Forces librarians might be invited to share with library school students their professional experiences. The Armed Forces librarians could help immeasurably in the difficult problem of recruiting by guiding both military and civilian personnel into library careers. Even more pertinent is guidance of veterans as they leave the service into this challenging profession.

Important as pre-service education is ultimately, the need for in-service training is more immediate. There are two aspects to this undertaking, affected by whether or not the staff member can leave his job for a period of study. If regulations are such that he cannot, then two avenues of study are open to which library schools can contribute.

One of these is on-the-job training. Together, Armed Forces librarians and library school faculties should be able to develop one or more manuals for library clerical workers that would be helpful to both civilian and military personnel assigned to library duty. Such a manual could include orientation in common library terminology, in order, preparation, technical processes, and circulation routines. It could certainly give the point-of-view of the library missions.

Through the United States Armed Forces Institute some library school or several library schools cooperatively should offer at least one basic library course. This course might be a survey of library materials, including selection aids, reference books, periodicals, recreation and information books, films, recordings, and other audiovisual classes. It would be desirable for this correspondence course, at least, to find a respectable acceptance in the library school curriculum.

In addition to manuals and correspondence courses, library institutes either on a miltary installation or on the university campus of a library school, or both, should prove highly profitable. These institutes should be planned and conducted jointly by Armed Forces librarians and a library school faculty. The content should be practical and pointed toward assisting both military and civilian personnel to perform semi-professional tasks more efficiently.

A different type of on-the-job education should be provided for professional librarians. Many of them have expressed a need for refresher courses that would bring them up-to-date on new library developments. Through U.S.A.F.I., it should be possible for a library school to offer a correspondence course in current trends.

In addition, a three to six weeks work conference at some library school devoted to the problems of Armed Forces libraries would prove mutually profitable to librarians and library school. Such a work conference might provide a valuable exchange, bringing civilian librarians up on military innovations in the library field and refreshing Armed Forces librarians on professional developments.

At this point it would be well to present the problem of the professional librarian in the military service. Each year the Armed Forces call library school graduates to active duty. In a great many instances these graduates' professional qualifications are not used. Often, as in my own case, this occurs because of the librarian's own choice. But in the majority of cases of recent library school graduates the preference is for duty assignment in their professional competence.

Last year I was able to arrange with the Army War College Library to be on the look out for a very promising young man who received his Master's degree from our Library School. He reported immediately upon graduation last February. After a period of basic training the Army War College Library requested him. I received a very happy letter from this capable young man reporting library assignment. In the words of the G.I., this is a "good deal" both for the draftee, who thus gains professional experience, and for the Army, which secures professional service for a fraction of the salary it would normally have to pay. The deterrent to this sort of cooperation is the lack of specified library courses and military occupational specialties covering professional librarianship. In view of the great shortage of professional librarians in the Armed Forces it would seem highly desirable for the Armed Forces Librarians' Section to explore through military channels several possible recruitment and education opportunities:

First, I should like to see a plan worked out with R.O.T.C. under which an additional year of library school study would be allowed those students with interest and potential in librarianship. Planning could be done on library school campuses with the R.O.T.C. and the student himself as early as the sophomore year. But cooperation in the Armed Forces itself would be necessary so that the library trained R.O.T.C. graduate would be assigned to library duty. In view of the great number of library installations, overseas as well as stateside, it should be possible to maintain the rotation policy of military personnel within the sphere of library duty. This R.O.T.C. plan might be extended to all potential draftees if the demand warrants.

Second, I should like to see an active recruitment program carried on with military personnel who will return to civilian life. Like other library schools we continue to have in each class some excellent students drawn from the ranks of discharged veterans. Last June one of these veterans returned to the Air Force as a librarian after completing the professional program.

Third, I suggest the possibility of a cooperative program under which two military staff members of an armed forces library could obtain a professional education by alternating between library school and library assignment. The plan, which I have already operated with civilian librarians, covers a two-year period. During the first of six terms, representing four academic semesters and two summer sessions, Student A is in library school and Student B is holding down a regular library job. At the end of that term the students exchange, Student B coming to Library School and Student A assuming the library duties. At the end of three alternations both students have completed the professional program. During this period the library has had continuously one position filled by increasingly professional personnel.

The plan should work especially well for armed forces libraries, since training is a basic part of military service and since the alternation between schooling and service is an established armed forces pattern.

The place of Armed Forces librarians in the profession of librarianship is a highly significant one. World War III is having a tremendous impact on professional thinking and innovation. And in the vanguard of some of the most startling library developments are those librarians who serve the military. The profession cannot escape its responsibility both to support military library service and to draw from it new vision. If it is true that every war compensates for its destruction with constructive discoveries, then it can be said that already World War III is pointing the way to not only a greater profession of librarianship but also to a more mature way of fighting war.

Portrait of a Library School:
Florida State University

FLORIDA'S NATIONALLY accredited Library School opened its doors as a school on the campus of Florida State University in the state's capital city of Tallahassee on July 1, 1947. It was one of the first three schools to be accredited by the Board of Education for Librarianship under the present standards. In June of this year [1956] it moved into its new quarters, some 15,000 square feet reserved for it on the ground floor of the just completed University Library Building.

In between these three milestones of the nine-year history of the Florida State Library School there are some library education innovations of note.

During the 1946-47 academic year the faculty drew its blue print for a Library School to fit the needs not alone of one of the fastest growing states in the nation, but of a region that has experienced a remarkable library renaissance during the past quarter of a century, and a nation that is engaged in an unprecedented cold war. In these three geographic challenges the faculty saw specific obligations and opportunities.

It saw first of all that there was a unity to our profession, despite the trend toward specialization. Anticipating the standards that followed, the faculty based its program on a solid foundation of general education, and a core of professional education that would permit its graduates first of all to serve as librarians and then as specialists by kinds of libraries or types of work.

It saw after, that this profession of ours was basically concerned with the dissemination of ideas, good ideas, through every medium man had thus far invented for communication. The faculty took

Reprinted from *Florida Libraries*, 7: 17, June, 1956, by permission of the publisher.

literally the message of the Rochester Public Library film, "Not By Books Alone," and set itself to provide opportunities for its students to know not only the best in books, magazines, and other print materials, but in films, filmstrips, recordings, and other media.

Out of this was born a strong Audio-Visual Department, and a field of specialization heretofore comparatively neglected by library schools. Today, the Florida State University Library School is the only accredited B. E. L. school which has also a nationally approved master's program in Audio-Visual Instruction.

The faculty saw also that opportunity for practice must be provided since no graduate credit could be allowed for acquiring skills. It therefore established from the start a demonstration library within the school in which students could serve and practice their profession much as interns do in a hospital. To this demonstration library the faculty added a demonstration audio-visual center, which soon developed into much more than a demonstration. Today this center operates a state-wide film library service, conducts weekly film previews, produces photographs and microphotographs, slides, films, and motion pictures, radio and television programs, and tape and disc transcriptions.

The faculty saw early the need for carrying professional education opportunities into the state. Through extension the FSU Library School has offered beginning courses in librarianship and audio-visual education in 29 Florida communities extending from Pensacola to Key West to some 3,000 students. Eastern Air Lines featured Florida State Library School's Flying Professor in its June 1955 magazine issue.

Faculty interest in the region and its unusual library history during the last quarter of a century led to the creation of a Southern Library History Center where library reports and publications of this region are being accumulated. These materials have and will furnish rich documentation for thesis work and advanced investigations.

Faculty awareness of the cold war has led to increasing attention to the librarian's role in psychological warfare and the preparation of a good proportion of its graduates for service in the armed forces and in certain government and private special libraries. In the

"Florida State University Studies" series of volumes, one sponsored by the Library School called *Challenges to Librarianship* and centered on the theme of the librarian as a professional of destiny in the struggle between east and west, gained such recognition that the first edition was sold out shortly after publication.

The Library School's growth in the last nine years has been due in no small measure to the support it has received from the state and from the University. During the past year, for example, the Florida Library Association adopted recruiting as its objective and established the Bohnenberger Scholarship Loan at the Library School. The University has been generous in its financial support and in its willingness to help a new school during its formative years.

The Faculty of Florida's School joins its colleagues in the Florida Library Association in welcoming the American Library Association to our state. It extends to all A.L.A. members an invitation to stop off in Tallahassee coming or going to Miami.

What is Right with Library Education

"ISN'T THAT a bit radical?" asked my friendly colleague as he looked at the title for this piece in the LIBRARY JOURNAL symposium.

His point is well taken. It is customary today to find things *wrong* with American education. From kindergarten to postgraduate, runs the national line, we are losing the race to the east. If you want to know why Sputnik reached outer space first you have only to look at the fourth graders in one of our Tallahassee elementary schools relaxing an hour a day on teeter ball instead of concentrating on calculus the way their Russian cousins do.

This sort of scapegoatism is, of course, epidemic in a climate of disappointment. Our patriotism is too strong to permit easy adjust-

Reprinted from *Library Journal*, 85: 1742-1744, May 1, 1960, by permission of the publisher.

ment to second place in anything. Education is an obvious beating boy and so we belabor the grade schools first, then secondary education, and after that colleges. By that time our national venom has risen sufficiently to overwhelm postgraduate and professional education together in one gulp.

Only a miracle could have protected library school from this mid-century educational inquisition. Tell an American in 1960 that something or other is to be investigated or surveyed and watch his eyeballs spark excitement. Treason, rape, payola and Perry Mason are the ingredients that apparently make life at all interesting. The heroes of the age are the witnesses against their fellow men, or the surveyors of education. And in librarianship, though the preparation of librarians has been found wanting nearly countless times in the brief period since Melvil Dewey opened the first professional school, any recent graduate knows the easiest way to break into print is to beat the belabored boy again.

Said one of our recent students to me: "You know I am on leave from Blank Public Library. I was told by several staff members I would simply have to suffer through a year of library school in order to get my union card. I'm disappointed. Although I majored in English literature at Ivy University I can truly say the most inspired course in literature I have ever had, undergraduate or as part of my English master's, is the children's literature course in this library school, and for which my grade is already in, I understand."

In our library school lounge where good professional philosophy is developed daily over coffee, I eavesdropped on this:

Miss Conservative: Library School is a bore. I haven't learned a thing in the six weeks I've been here. Now at Eastern Woman's College the professors knew their subject and every one of them was inspiring.

Miss Radical: But Miss C. Do you remember Professor Soporific in Psychology at Eastern and how you used to complain to us girls that even the worst teacher in Peoples High School in your home town was more interesting?

Nor is the "What's Wrong with Library Education" tune confined to the U.S. During my Fulbright year in U.K. I experienced some of the ASLIB-Library Association differences on what constitutes a proper professional education for librarians. To ASLIB, apparently, and possibly to a good many U.S. librarians, the L.A. examinations subordinated academic subjects to technical processes. The examination as a basis for professional qualification was itself educationally suspect. Asked some Americans and many Aslibers, "Is cramming for an exam to be the sole measure of professional competence?"

To which those in the L.A. camp strongly retorted, accreditation of a library school does not guarantee the qualification of all of its graduates. Furthermore, the mere tabulation of credit points on a typed transcript is a superficial evaluation of a librarian's equipment to perform on the job. In view of this difference in professional education between the two senior library associations of the world, it can readily be understood how our usually restrained British colleagues rose to echo "Hear! Hear!" when an American recently belittled U.S. library schools.

Normally, such differences between the two most advanced national library patterns of education would be all to the good. From debates across the sea and on such neutral battlegrounds as the forthcoming Montreal convention one might expect to develop guidelines for other nations in search of an adequate library education. Perhaps, the U.S. would add a national professional examination and the U.K. increased emphasis on subject specialization, academic degrees, and library school accreditation. Indeed, both nations might profit from a mutual pattern that incorporated the stronger points in each plan, as I suggested in my *Library Trends* article (Jan. '55, pp. 269-78) comparing the two.

There is strength in both of these fine patterns of library education, the inquisitors, witnesses and surveyors notwithstanding. And the time has come to set down what, in my opinion, is *right* with library education today.

At least, to begin with, the two great English speaking nations have a professional pattern of library education. Professional positions are filled on the basis of establishing competence in library processes and knowledge. A body of content is described in syllabi and textbooks on which applicants for permission to practice are examined by their peers. In this way librarianship moves steadily toward a position of distinction among the world's professions. This is more than can be said for our occupation in even some literate and enlightened nations.

Then, to concentrate on U.S. library education, to which I have devoted more than three decades of my professional life, I view with satisfaction the increasing campus recognition of library schools. This is not a celebration of status but a first-hand appreciation of the creative labor that has built solid, graduate professional schools on the three-score campuses in the U.S. and Canada where ALA accreditation has been earned. In all of these institutions of higher education, the deans of library schools and heads of departments share with administrators of other divisions responsibility for academic policy.

No small credit for this growing campus recognition is due to the growing stature of our library school faculties. Although degrees by themselves furnish neither a valid nor a reliable measure of faculty competence, against the background of American higher education the increasing number of doctorates on our library school faculties testify tangibly to an effort to comply with graduate school standards. More significant, however, is the fact that library school faculty are demonstrating in academic areas, as well as in library science, competence with the sacred scientific method and inspiration in the soul-searching arts. There can even be found in some places an academic awe for the library school professor who champions the generalist in a society of specialists.

Within the library school curriculum there is content now that needs no apology in any circle of knowledge. As an English major I think back hard to the brightest days of my absorption in Restoration Drama, Nicholas Rowe, the Parabases of Fielding, and the Poetry of Matthew Arnold (four passions of my graduate days) and the professors who inspired me. Were they really greater teachers then the book selection teachers I have known in library school? To check any aura that time and youth might add to my sentiments I have revisited classes in many academic areas. I am convinced the quality of instruction in library school book selection I know is on a par with graduate instruction in literature I have known. If there are mediocrities in library school education they can be more than matched by the mediocrities in American graduate education everywhere. If one has any doubt about the latter all he has to do today is read in newspaper and magazine at random. And if inspired teaching in library school is rare, study the history of education to discover how truly rare has been the great teacher.

Concern with the individual differences of students has always ranked high among the measures of education. It is my observation among graduate schools on university campuses that nowhere does the individual mean more than in library schools. This is true not only during student days but in the many alumni years that follow. Materially through placement, and spiritually through that bond the have-nots share in a work of dedication, library school teacher and student more often and more nearly develop the lifelong Guru-Disciple regard for each other than is found anywhere else in our education today.

All of this must mean something. To me it means what is wrong is considerably less than what is *right* with library education.

The College of Library Art, 1984

IF HISTORY DOES indeed repeat, library education will next be ready for another National Plan in 1984.[1] The design for our library schools must, therefore, be sketched to anticipate the next two decades.

Have we, the members of the American Library Association's Commission on a National Plan for Library Education, our colleagues in the profession of catholic librarianship, and protestant peripherals (like audio-visual, documentation, or information science) the courage, imagination, and good will to plan together for

[1]For notes, see page 271.

Reprinted from *Journal of Education for Librarianship*, 4: 125-136, Winter, 1964, by permission of the publisher.

the education of the next generation?[2] I believe we have faith in the destiny of our occupation.[3] The Commission and the concept behind it are evidence of a desire to plan.

During the dark early days of our entry into World War II, the columnist Henry McLemore pleaded for table cloths to be turned in to the Central Intelligence Agency before laundering. His contention was that somewhere in the United States over a dinner table, with knives, forks, and a salt shaker, some amateur military genius was indicating a master plan for victory over the seemingly invincible axis forces.

Perhaps somewhere today among practitioners and educators there are ideas for a national plan on library education. If the Commission's January, 1964, recommendation for a "Research and Experimentation Center" is adopted, its first assignment should be to examine, more carefully than the Commission's volunteers have been able to thus far, the "check lists of views" submitted by commissioners and others.

Commission assignments and meetings under the able chairmanship of Richard Logsdon, the intelligent direction of United States Office of Education Library Education Specialist Sarah R. Reed, and a thoughtful concern by the Steering Committee have stimulated many of the reflections in the following notes assembled into a preliminary design for the "College of Library Art, 1984."

Note 1. On the Role of Librarianship. We are an occupation of destiny. Among the academic disciplines we are, at least, peers; in the family of professions our mission is as lofty as any. We must begin by ridding ourselves of the professional diffidence that has created an "ancillary complex" in our ranks. To fortify our faith, let us reflect on these inevitable trends:

In the cold war between East and West we can and should be the main components of our psychological army in the struggle for men's minds.

On the campus we can, if we will overcome our inferiority complex, demonstrate the superiority of library learning over classroom teaching; introduce a more balanced generalist approach in both instruction and research that will relieve growing intellectual frustration over increasing specialization.

In the nation's schools we offer the only solution to the baffling problem of individual differences among children (as universal education extends the range) through matching individual differences of selected library media.

To industry, government, and other research efforts we give, on their present level of specialized thinking, computerized retrieval of separated facts. But we hold within our *gestalt* a synthesis which may yet save "the civilization western man has known (from) dying of facts. . . ."[4]

Among our American communities — urban, suburban, rural — we are extending a still embryonic force for toughening our intellectual fiber and giving us the national mind and spirit to overcome a materialist interpretation of history which is steadily shaping itself into the most formidable antichrist man's free spirit has yet had to contend with.

What we must become aware of, is that the substance of our calling is communicability, the philosophically essential evidence of life.[5]

Note 2. Role of Library Education. If library education has not been all that library practice has expected, it is possible that practice has been less sensitive than education to the high role of librarianship. It is not that the library school teacher has overlooked the library practitioner's long and frequently discouraging struggle for support and recognition. It is rather that the library educator has wanted the colleague in the field to celebrate his "grass roots" and extend more his branches ever upward; to dream some in the clouds even while pragmatically rallying for "feet on the ground."

To this point, the profession has favored practice, ("what is, is right") to a hazardous degree. If the profession is to prosper, evaluation must be reciprocal between practice and education. This defends the right of practice to be critical of education. But this also appeals for the right of education to be critical of practice.

The role of library education, therefore, is not solely to prepare for practice today. An equally important responsibility of library education is to help the next generation reflect on what library practice might better be.

I count one of my most exciting teaching assignments the one in the course "Literature of Librarianship" which asks the students to essay an "Ideal Library School." I charge them differently at different times. But one way: "You are a sophisticated staff member on leave to acquire an A.L.A. accredited master's. To retain your standing as an intellectual among your colleagues back home you should do three things: (1) be bored by library school; (2) console yourself that the 'union card' is necessary for survival; (3) break into print with the most scathing, 'what's wrong with library education.' I ask you to do a fourth, harder thing — describe library school as you would have it." Last year one of my most critical students wrote a paper entitled, "Utopia Library School." As soon as she had finished reading it to the class another critically intelligent student, in the fine informality of that group, exclaimed, "I wouldn't be caught dead in that kind of library school!"

Positively describing the role of library education is much more difficult than finding fault with it. After more than three decades in library education, I will risk this prime among the objectives of library education: a critical introduction to the evolution of today's best practice, and speculative meditation on tomorrow's potential.

Note 3. Pre-Professional Education. The emerging junior college, which is apparently changing our higher educational pattern into units of (a) two years general education, (b) three years academic concentration, (c) two years subject specialization, is the starting point.

Any general education that prides itself on a liberal arts foundation must of necessity include Library Art or admit to being less than liberal. Generalism in education manifested itself a few years ago when the scattered courses in mathematics, physics, and chemistry were drawn together into an integrated "Phy Sci" course; botany, biology, zoology, and physiology into "Bi Sci"; sociology, economics, and political science into Social Sciences; literature, art, philosophy, and religion into Humanities.

The junior college curriculum cries out for a capstone synthesis such as Library Art, and only Library Art, which conserves, describes, evaluates, and disseminates the records of all the separate disciplines, can effect. Our freshman library-use course is a meager beginning. Our capstone contribution to the general, pre-professional education of all junior college students could be a library-centered course which offers the student skill in the neglected half of knowledge — where to find facts, and an understanding of interdisciplinary relationships.

For the junior college terminal objective, a vocational library technician program is needed. It could be fitted into the 60 semester hours of the first two college years with not over one-sixth electives in two skills courses: (a) Library Technic, covering basic skills and routines in acquistion, preparation, circulation, and even fact-finding reference, as well as in housekeeping duties; (b) Typing, shorthand, and office skill.

Note 4. Professional Education. Recognizing the changing pattern in American higher education, basic professional education should occur in a three-year period following junior college, covering the present junior, senior, and master years. For convenience, the 90 semester hours of course credit that a student can normally be required to take in that time is used as a measure. It is proposed that equal thirds in (a) an academic concentration, (b) Library Art, (c) elective co-ordinates be taken concurrently. A bachelor's degree with approximately 20 semester hours of planned work in each third would qualify the graduate for first grade professional work in all types of libraries. An articulated master's degree would qualify for grade two, and above, positions. A post-master's year, either terminal or along the way to the doctorate, might lead to an advanced master's or a lower doctorate appropriately labelled. Finally, the doctorate itself, a Ph.D. only, bold and creative, might even stir the mediocrity of American doctoral effort in the other disciplines.

Note 5. Articulations. The time has come to recognize the pluralism in the problem. Since the pioneer Wight[6] editorship of the proceedings of the first conference on the subject in 1941, we have done little more than refine our efforts with undergraduate programs. But the articulation challenge is more than an internecine war in catholic library education. There is an urgent call for certification correlation, especially with the state variations for teachers, librarians, and audio-visualists. In an ivory tower one may attach some mystical significance to the magic number 18. But what does a library school do in a state where audio-visualists and librarians have, after years of study, suffering, and soul-searching, settled on a number like 21. Make the surplus post-bachelor, say the national accreditors. No, says the state agency. All other teacher areas come within the bachelor and specify up to 30 in the major.

Even more critical than certification is splinter articulation. Audio-visualists, archivists, documentalists or information scientists, and who knows what other protestants, find no salvation in present standards of accreditation. These and other splinters deserve representation in any commission on national planning.

There is at least one other major articulation to be added to undergraduate, certification, splinter. It involves the professions and disciplines we aim to support, or better yet, assume partnership with. Some of the principal ones are, of course, medicine, law, education, and engineering among the professions; chemistry, economics, art, and music among the disciplines.

Finally, higher education articulation must take into account recent trends in state planning.

Note 6. A State Plan for Library Education. There is an unmistakable trend toward state systems of higher education. The pattern follows the organization already indicated: (a) public, local junior colleges; (b) senior colleges and universities that begin at the junior year and end with the master's degree, or continue through the doctorate, and even post doctorate. Any national plan for library education that develops outside this pattern is likely to be antique long before 1984.

If I take Florida as an example, it is not because this pattern is farther along here than in California and New York. It is rather because I know Florida better and because in 1962 library science was selected as one of four liberally inclined disciplines for a state-wide exploration.

In August, 1962, the Florida State Board of Control, governing body for all public institutions of higher education, with the concurrence of the university presidents' council, invited heads of departments in biology and modern languages, business administration, and library science to organize into task forces to explore an advanced type of articulation in their respective areas, state wide. The opening charge was to think not of individual institutions, but of the state system of public higher education as one campus.

The Library Science Task Force after considerable deliberation, correspondence, and meeting drafted a preliminary report[7] proposing to articulate undergraduate programs in the state, both public and private, with the A.L.A. accredited program in Tallahassee so that students might complete half of the master's requirements on any one of the campuses before coming to Florida State University Library School for the final half.

The timing for this exploration was unfortunate. In the fall of that year, the University had its periodic visit from the Southern Association, and the Library School from the A.L.A. Committee on Accreditation. Because the draft was too preliminary for consideration, neither accrediting body had adequate background. It was the Task Force's hope that these explorations would not be a part of the visitation. But the accreditation agencies ruled otherwise and the conception aborted. Nevertheless, an idea was planted, and at a more favorable moment, both accrediting agencies will be challenged to make good on their concern with institutional experimentation.

The experiment points to a new horizon of articulation. State plans for library education comparable to the Florida effort might provide a solid foundation for a national plan by drawing some 300 undergraduate programs closer to the accredited graduate curriculums, and by intensifying the recruitment effort through a more orderly path of preparation for the profession.

Note 7. The Three-Year Professional Program. Based on either university preparatory or terminal junior college education, basic professional library education should be planned for the three years now represented by junior, senior, and master levels. In terms of present semester hour calculations, the minimum 90 total might be distributed: (1) Library Art concentration — 30; (2) Another concentration in one of the humanities, social or natural sciences — 30; (3) Collaterals, individually guided — 30. The degree awarded would be a master of arts, science, or library art, depending upon the total accent. With any of these degrees, the graduate will be admitted to general practice in librarianship. (Experimental three-year programs in other disciplines, subsidized by a special grant are now in process at Florida State University.)

Note 8. The Post-Master Program. Either terminal or doctoral preparatory, a year of advanced library education beyond the three-year professional master's is indicated by such state certifications as that of Georgia. A two-fold objective of this post-master's year would be (1) opportunity to investigate a problem of local concern, with possible wider implications, and (2) rehearsal for a doctoral effort, providing both the student and the faculty a basis for decision. Such a year would be characterized by a directed individual study supported by such advanced courses in Library Art and coordinate disciplines as would contribute to the student's professional development and solution of his problem.

Note 9. The Doctorate. It is now 30 years since I received my own doctorate. In these three decades I have sat on countless doctoral committees, counseling and examining students in a variety of disciplines; I have consulted with departments in fashioning their doctoral programs; I have contributed to shaping doctoral policy in a university. As one studies the doctoral requirements in American universities and especially of those graduate schools that have entered the arena since World War II there is an uncomfortable feeling of defense complexes on responsibility, conformity, and scholarship. Perhaps this determination to prove through catalog statement that doctoral standards are high has prevented any thing original or creative from occurring in the program for the highest degree in the academic world.

Here is a real challenge to library education. Though the road to graduate council approval may be rocky, the college of Library Art must resist climbing into the procrustean bed and prostituting its generalism to the currently favored specialisms. Beginning with the next doctoral program in library science, a graduate college of Library Art, somewhere, needs the courage to display an original proposal for a doctoral program.

To begin with, there should be no coyness about indicating a normal residence of two academic years beyond the master's, and course credits (as long as credits persist a measure of education) totaling 60 semester hours, more or less. Foreign languages as a requirement should be liberalized to break the unwarranted monopoly of French and German, and to include one or more selections from the whole range of classical and modern literatures.

The dissertation focus should be shifted to encourage humanistic creation as well as scientific research. A creative novel, play, epic poem, musical composition, painting, should be as acceptable to a doctoral committee, competent to evaluate, as a scientifically tested investigation.

As for concentration areas, these need loftier dimensions: (1) Library history, library philosophy, and comparative librarianship, the last with alliance for Latin American library progress accent; (2) Information science that is Library Art-based, and extended to the social sciences and humanities as well as to the natural sciences and their applications; (3) Classification or synthesis of knowledge, steeped in philosophy's epistemology, and not apologetic about comparing Dewey with Linnaeus; (4) Paleography, with less attention to serifs and more to man's earliest incentives to record and communicate; (5) Media formats and content analyses; (6) Bibliography, enumerative, descriptive, eclectic, trade, national, with the universal objective to complete the record of man's records; (7) Library education, as the art of communicating from generation to generation, the achievements, responsibilities and challenges of a discipline of thought synthesis and a profession of idea dissemination.

Note 10. Curricula. Comparable to what we have previously labelled non-professional, sub-professional, and professional library courses, there is need, pre-school through post-graduate education, for instruction in (a) Library Use, (b) Library Technic, (c) Library Art.

(a) *Library Use* is concerned basically with that neglected half of knowledge — knowing where to find facts. At a higher level, instruction in library use should also develop inter-disciplinary perspective for a more balanced approach to both realism and reality than any one of the disciplines or applications can provide alone, or through partial integrations. *Library Use* units for all of the grades and subjects through junior college require a new accent on the two objectives of *knowing where* and *perspective*. *Library Use* units beyond junior college should stress literature searching keyed to increasing subject concentration, and critical evaluation of sources, as well as bibliographic method. Content is illustrated by the Florida State University "500" course required of all graduate students in all subject fields.[8]

(b) *Library Technic* is concerned with instructing clerical and sub-professional library workers in the skills and routines of library processes. Such instruction begins with school library assistants, informally on the job and formally in classes and workshops. At the junior college at least one course aims to prepare library technicians to serve in sub-professional positions in libraries of all types. The content of a basic course will include skills in the routines of acquistion, preparation, circulation and reference, care and operation of equipment.

Note 11. Library Art — The Three-Year Professional Curriculum. Library Art is essentially concerned with identification, evaluation, and dissemination of man's significant deeds and ideas. One academic concentration in the humanities, social or natural sciences, an individually patterned selection of coordinates, and Library Art comprise the approximately equal thirds of the basic professional curriculum for what are now the junior, senior, and master's years.

Note 12. Library Art Core. A possible Library Art curriculum organization is suggested by these re-oriented required courses:

Course (a) KNOWLEDGE: An interdisciplinary approach to man's noblest deeds and ideas through library classifications.

Course (b) LIBRARY AND SOCIETY: History, philosophy, and contemporary place of books, libraries, and librarians.

Course (c) MEDIA: Identification, evaluation, and dissemination of the best examples in content for the humanities, social and natural sciences in the whole range of formats from textbook through television, suggested by format classification in *Instructional Materials*.[9]

Course (d) INFORMATION: Sources and methods for fact location, consolidating traditional reference and bibliography with peripheral documentation and information science, and introducing a synthesis prospect for the current analytic-retrieval approach.

Course (e) LIBRARIANSHIP: Comparative overview of organization, personnel, finance, housing, technical processes, reader service, as found in major library types.

Course (f) INTERNSHIP (no academic credit): Practice in technic in the skills laboratory, the College of Library Art Media Center, the university library; observation in local libraries; a field trip to representative libraries; a three-months assignment one summer during three-year period, preferably at end of core, between second and third year.

Note 13. Library Art Specialisms. The second half of the three-year master's program in the Library Art concentration might include:

Course (g) LITERATURE SEARCHING and research method in Library Art.

Course (h) SUBJECT LITERATURES for the student's choice of academic concentration and library community level.

Course (i) LIBRARIANSHIP for a special community level: (a) Young people, for elementary, secondary school, junior college, and public children's and young adult libraries; (b) Academic communities serving specialized need — senior college, graduate school, faculty research; (c) Government, industrial, institutional.

Note 14. Special Programs. Experimentally the College of Library Art should undertake special programs of library education illustrated by these, planned or already fairly well established.

(a) *Extension.* Since 1947, the Florida State faculty have carried library education to centers in 37 counties, extending geographically from Pensacola in the extreme northwest to Key West 850 miles to the Southeast. Over 5,000 students have been enrolled in these classes, mostly teachers who have carried the gospel of library learning to their pupils and colleagues. But many good students have been recruited for librarianship, and some have completed their accredited master's requirements through a combined summer residence-local extension program. The 1984 College of Library Art will do well to consider extension of library education to off-campus centers.

(b) *Service Instruction.* At the junior college level, the traditional Library Use course can assume its essential role in general education only as a synthesis of area courses. Without detailing content here, the key is an interdisciplinary approach to basic reference sources. Practically, how can the diverse assignments of the students' several courses re-enforce each other through mutual reference tools? What searching skills can improve subject mastery, reduce preparation time and effort? There is a strong argument for the library education agency rather than for library administration to assume this teaching function. Even if the recruitment result is low, the layman appreciation and support of libraries can be high. This despite the recent inconclusive Association of American Library Schools anti-service-course poll of library schools.

At the senior college-graduate level a literature searching instruction program can open new doors for students in other disciplines, if the library school is willing. Florida State has pioneered a "500" course offered by Library School faculty which is required of graduate students in all areas, unless exempted by test or inclusion of a departmental course that covers the same content.[10] Sources and techniques for searching, plus some attention to comparative bibliographic form, shape the scope of the course. In addition, Library School faculty passes on form for theses and dissertations in all departments. Again, even if professional recruitment is low, library orientation among those who, as our colleagues, will instruct and do research on the campus and in industry and government, is high.

(c) *Cooperatives.* The work-study program originated at the University of Cincinnati by Engineering Education was first tried at Peabody before World War II. Since then Florida State has had cooperative agreements with several libraries, notably the Miami and Jacksonville Public Libraries. Under the co-op plan, two students team for a work-study schedule. While one student is in library school, the other is on the job. Alternations occur every semester for two years. The library pays the student only for the time on the job; the library school provides aid during the study terms. Advantages to the library, the student, and recruitment are obvious.

(d) *Honors.* Contemplated at Florida State, subject to C.O.A.

approval, is an honors reading program in library education for superior staff members in accredited libraries. It is planned to provide honors students with syllabi, to plan periodic seminars in the Library School, and a reduced residence (the last trimester). Comprehensive written and oral examinations, a master's essay, and skills tests would provide tangible measures of the student's achievement.

Note 15. Faculty. By 1984 Library School faculty should include a considerable number of College of Library Art graduates. Their professional and general education will have been described by what has gone before. Perhaps their research production will be greater than now; I hope not. In my crystal ball I see a decline in what we call "research in depth," a growing rejection of the scientific method as an approach to reality. Consequently, the intangibles of the great teacher, marked by compassion and self subordination to the maturation of the student, will be ever more sought for in faculty. Exchanges with practitioners in libraries will be more frequent than now.

Note 16. Students. Tests and testing, whether of aptitude, information, personality, or other qualifications, will grow in disfavor. The interview, school records, and references will dominate admissions considerations, until, at least, telepathy, clairvoyance, precognition, and other phenomena of parapsychology are better understood. But after 1984, extrasensory perception may play a part in student selection. Material reward and new challenges of psychological warfare, science information, and bibliotherapy are attracting different students. Men may soon outnumber women in librarianship in the United States, even as now in the United Kingdom.

Note 17. Facilities. The separate library education building, possibly in a quadrangle that includes the library, is already predicted in the plans at Illinois. A demonstration library, skills laboratory, individual study desks for all students, and close access to university facilities like the computer center are already in evidence. Special laboratories for documentation, technical processes, reader services, and media evaluation are on the drafting board.

In addition, and with considerable opposition, each College of Library Art will assume responsibility through its faculty and students for the demonstration, organization, and operation of a neighboring school, community, junior college and/or special library.

Note 18. After 1984. There will be other worlds, literally, and the next commission will wonder at our lack of omniscience. Young graduates will write, with equal indignation, for library journals, about the inadequacies of library education. Practitioners will blame educators, and *vice versa.* By that time, however, librarians may take less comfort in "identifying problems" and "recommending research in depth." But in all other respects, history probably will repeat.

[1] The last two sets of American Library Association Standards are dated 1933, 1953.
[2] Shores, Louis: The Next Generation. *Education,* 75: 167-172, Nov. 1954.
[3] Shores, Louis: A Profession of Faith. *In:* Marshall, J. D.: *Of, By, and For Librarians.* Hamden, Conn., Shoe String Press, 1960, pp. 196-207.
[4] Weismiller, Edward: Fact and Fancy. *Atlantic,* 212: 93-95, Oct. 1963.
[5] Shores, Louis: Books — Continuous Communicability. *Saturday Review,* 41: 26, March 22, 1958.
[6] Wight, E. A.: *Evaluation and Revision of the Library School Curriculum.* (Peabody Contributions to Library Education, No. 1) 1945.
[7] Florida State Board of Control. Report of Library Science Task Force. May, 1963. (Unpublished typescript.)
[8] Clemons, J. E.: Teaching Bibliographical Sources and Styles to Graduate Students. *College and Research Libraries,* 17: 403-408, Summer 1956.
[9] Shores, Louis: *Instructional Materials.* New York, Ronald, 1960. 408pp.
[10] Clemons, *op. cit.*

On the Unity of Library Media

Audio-Visual Dimensions for an Academic Library

WHEN A UNIVERSITY LIBRARIAN and a library school dean pause between meetings at a conference what do they talk about? Usually, of course, about filling that staff vacancy. But almost as frequently these days about audio-visual (A-V) media.

It is no secret that quite a few librarians of institutions of higher education wish these new-fangled non-book gadgets were somewhere near the bottom of the more unfathomable ocean depths. In the last six months alone I have talked with at least one administrator for every type of academic library represented by our ACRL sections who wished the question of A-V media in libraries had never come up. Frankly, they say, in agreement with Joseph Wood Krutch, and many other defenders of books, these newer mass media are enemies of reading, and we wonder if our professional responsibility does not call for all-out war. Certainly, the scholarly university library has little reason to cut into its precious research funds for back volumes of the *Berichte der Deutsche Chemische Gessellschaft* in order to buy a half dozen questionable motion pictures.

Although this position hardly represents even a considerable minority of academic librarians' thinking it is worth considering as a starting point for an A-V decision on any campus. For there is considerable fear today that the printed word as a medium of communication may be on the decline. This concern is found not only in the publishing industry, and among writers, but in the profession of librarianship itself. It has already been most fatally predicted by that Frenchman of letters, Georges Duhamel, who wrote as early as 1939:

Reprinted from *College and Research Libraries*, 15: 393-397, October, 1954, by permission of the publisher.

The decadence of the book, the greatest instrument for the
diffusion of knowledge, may be delayed a little longer. . . . As
far as France is concerned the evidence seems to point in one
direction. . . . For the man in the street, the book, defenseless,
is henceforward to be supplanted by less laborious methods of
information and recreation.[1]

Strangely enough the answer to this sort of pessimism comes
from an audio-visualist, possibly the foremost audio-visualist in
America, and most certainly from the audio-visualist who is authoritatively quoted in research literature in both the A-V and reading
fields. In a memorable lecture sponsored by the Library School on
the Florida State University campus, Edgar Dale called librarians'
attention to the fact that printed books were not always respectably
accepted in college libraries. During the 15th century the Duke of
Urbino "had a mind to do what no one had done for a thousand
years or more; that is to create the finest library since ancient
times." But, adds Vespasiano Da Bisticci, the bookseller,

In this library all the books are superlatively good, and
written with the pen, and had there been one printed volume
it would have been ashamed in such company.[2]

Now, after all, Dr. Dale points out, are not these fearful, 20th
century librarians in danger of evaluating A-V media in the same
terms as their 15th century forerunner reflected on the products of
the printing press? What is more serious, asks Dr. Dale — are
librarians not turning their backs on the real mission of libraries?
The librarian, as Dr. Dale sees the problem, must not look upon
himself

. . . merely as an agent for the custody and distribution of
printed materials but also as an agency for the custody and
distribution of illuminating ideas no matter whether they
appear on tape, wax, film, paper, or a television screen.[3]

It is well thus to be recalled to our professional mission. If we are
dedicated to the dissemination of good ideas, first, the format of these
ideas must be of second importance. Our obligation then becomes
clear. As administrators of academic libraries we are responsible for
the acquisition and dissemination of these ideas whether they appear
in book, map, picture, recording, film, or any one of a dozen or

[1]For notes, see pag 282.

more forms. As a matter of fact, it would be difficult indeed to discover a single academic library in these United States without some non-print materials.

For example, one chapter in any one of the standard A-V textbooks deals with maps and globes.[4] The fact that a cartographic unit is part of any respectable A-V service argues nothing for removal of all geographic representations from the academic library. Maps have always been an integral part of college and university collections and even the most conservative university librarian would probably concede that he is already partly in the A-V business.

In addition to cartographic and graphic media, however, A-V concerns itself with what audio-visualists call museum objects and with local resources. Do not be misled. Both classes of A-V are now and have long been an integral part of library collections and services. Our exhibit cases are full of both art and science specimens, some owned outright by the library and others borrowed from instructional departments on the campus for the purpose of cooperative display. And as for local resources which provide the media of communication for field trips and school journeys, libraries have been a far more important accessory in the past than generally has been recognized. Consider for example the variety of local indexes developed, not only by public libraries, but by academic libraries, to various cultural, social, educational, and other agencies, to industrial and commercial activities in the town and county, to the faculty researches and interests and specialities, and hobbies, and yes, even to the natural resources of the campus environment. Without these library operations the field trips of A-V would be less meaningful if not more difficult.

And so we come to the more frightening categories of A-V materials. To the audio-visualist the "flat picture" is a must among media. Do not let the word "flat" frighten you. Library vertical files are full of pictures. Among library reference books there are even a few indexes to these same pictures. Even the conservative librarian who does not keep a picture file must admit he is not representative and that a great number of his colleagues have been A-V for a long time.

But what about phono-records, as the *Saturday Review* now calls them. It does not take a very old librarian to recall the Carnegie collections of fine recordings presented to scores of colleges in the United States. Many of the college browsing rooms still maintain record libraries of good music, drama, elocution, and language. Other libraries have cooperated with foreign language departments to promote speaking as well as reading and writing in a foreign tongue. And in a few instances research on the campus has been assisted by the library's recording and preserving men's dialects and animals' sounds. Perhaps here the conservative university librarian would agree the academic librarian has been and of right should be A-V.

This brings us to the film and projected materials. Certainly there is no argument about the microfilm now. To us the machine we use with it is a reader; to the audio-visualist it is possibly just another projector. At the very least it puts both librarian and audio-visualist in the same camp as far as using another format — a film format for the dissemination of ideas. Probably the one medium on which the librarian might balk is the 16mm motion picture. But an increasing number of all kinds of libraries are renting these films for classroom use and for library study, and in some instances purchasing them.

It can be seen, therefore, class by class, that A-V media are no strangers to libraries. They are potentially other formats for ideas. Basically, they lend themselves to the library processes of acquisition, preparation, interpretation, and dissemination. Physically and financially they confront librarianship with certain peculiar problems, but with problems no more peculiar than the various classes of media already professionalized in our library literature.

Let's examine some of these problems. In the first place the academic library should look toward the centralization of responsibility for A-V media on campus. This need not mean centralization of housing, but it certainly should mean centralized inventory. Along with central inventory at least coordinated acquisition should be sought. The argument is the same as that for centralization of print material acquired by the institution of higher education through its library.

In the second place, as soon as possible, the academic library should provide personnel qualified to serve the campus in as many of the A-V media as possible. To begin with, the smaller library may assign part time to the best qualified staff member. As soon as possible however, the library should plan to employ a librarian trained in the A-V field. Increasingly our library schools are incorporating A-V courses and units in the basic professional curriculum, equipping a new generation of librarians for A-V service.

In the third place the agencies and departments of instruction most audio-visually inclined should be enlisted in developing a plan for the campus. On most campuses the school or department of education and the extension agency will be in the A-V vanguard. But let not the traditional scholar take comfort in that. The colleges of arts and sciences are by far the heaviest users of these A-V media: 1) 16mm film, 2) glass slides, 3) maps, 4) opaque objects. Departments in the general college, in the sciences, in the fine arts, among others, should therefore be approachd early in any plan to coordinate A-V services for the campus. A very good beginning is the appointment of a representative faculty committee on A-V services to plan with the librarian. This committee may be either a sub-committee of the library committee or a separate committee.

In the very beginning about eight basic aspects of A-V services as aids to campus instruction and research should come under the survey by the library and its A-V committee. The *cartographic unit* in embryo will already be functioning in most academic libraries. In cooperation with the history and geography departments and with other heavy users the available maps, globes, atlases and geographic services on the campus will be canvassed. Augmented indexing and cataloging will be undertaken where necessary and additional accessions recommended to support the campus' total holdings, now inventoried in the library. If production of special or local maps is called for it will probably be decided to do the work in the geography department or in the library.

Next the *graphics unit* will come up for consideration. Civilian institutions are still lagging behind in instructional use of various charts, graphs, demonstrations and other graphics used in military instruction. The average library, however, produces considerable

bulletin board material and reproduces through mimeograph, litho-
graph or photostat both research and instructional materials that
might be filed for future reference. This the library frequently does
for its own graphics. But on the campus various other graphics are
being produced, that are either dead, stored in some department
office or destroyed, though their value is not necessarily limited to
a single use. If the library could at least start a campus pool of
instructional graphics organized for subject use another valuable
contribution to the dissemination of ideas might well be made.
Whether the library should undertake production of graphics
material for various departments of the campus will need particular
study in cooperation with the fine and industrial arts departments.

The third inventory will involve *museum objects*. Many of these
are already in the library. Others are in various art and science
departments. If the campus has a museum a huge collection will be
there. It is important to emphasize that the campus library does not
have to become a museum, even though the British Museum is one
of the greatest libraries in the world. But the library has an obligation in keeping with its mission to disseminate ideas in whatever
format they may be found in and on the campus. And in keeping
with that mission the library should endeavor without duplication to
organize for bibliographic dissemination the museum objects that
will contribute to more effective instruction and research carried
on by the institution. In this connection and in relation to other
classes of library materials the library should have available opaque
projectors for departmental and library use.

A fourth inventory of local resources will consist basically of a
review of the *indexing, abstracting, and other bibliographic services*
now part of the library. Whatever human and environmental
resources, available within a convenient radius, are not readily
known should be cataloged and disseminated to the part of the
campus concerned. Certainly, faculty planning field trips and expe-
ditions should be expected to utilize what the library can contribute.

A fifth canvass will involve *pictorial illustrations* of all kinds —
separate, in books and periodicals, in the art department, and elsewhere on campus. There is nothing new here for libraries. Many
remarkable collections can be found in libraries now. Libraries

without such collections will find untapped sources among citizens, alumni, friends.

A sixth investigation will involve *recordings*, both disc and tape. Increasingly the library must build its collections to serve the many departments that now use sound in instruction and research. The creation of listening posts in the reading rooms as well as listening rooms acoustically treated deserve campus librarians' consideration. The listening post in the reading room may have as many as six sets of earphones, thus providing the language, or music, or speech student with an auditory accompaniment to his reading effort. Tapes of significant radio programs may be the most valuable of all books for particular instructional situations. This means that the library must include tape recorders in its equipment as well as playbacks for discs.

The seventh consideration is *film*, and this is the one the worried librarian looks upon as the A-V problem. Microtexts and the readers needed with them are already an integral part of the academic library. But the 16mm motion picture is not. What is more the investment required for even a small collection of films to say nothing of the projector is disproportionate to the budget of the average small college library. There are two solutions to this budget problem. Film renting from the state library of films or from out-of-state film libraries is within the range of most libraries. Cooperative buying with other college libraries and the organization of film circuits provide an opportunity for each participating library to disseminate many highly effective instructional films to the departments using them. It must also be remembered that many of the best films are free. The steadily rising quality of the sponsored film is making it an ever more effective medium for college instruction.

Finally, the place of *radio and television* in the library must be thoroughly considered. Libraries are already indexing and disseminating information about good programs. Some libraries tape them. But the real library opportunity is in shaping television programs yet to come. In this connection I cannot resist quoting Edgar Dale's remarks to librarians:

I should like to propose a slogan for libraries that may

suggest what they can do: "Your library has the best ideas in the world." Through television you will have an opportunity to show . . . just what your resources are . . . books, reference materials, encyclopedias . . . in short television gives you a showcase in every television home in your community. You can display your wares in their living room.[5]

These are some of the audio-visual dimensions of an academic library. Despite the general terms in which they have been presented these dimensions are not only academic but applied. In at least one case when the library school dean advises the university librarian to go A-V there is a tangible basis for the advice. On the campus of Florida State University there is a centralized A-V service, administered by the Library School in cooperation with the University Library and the various schools and colleges on the campus. All eight of the aspects are represented. Various degrees of centralization have been accomplished. But the growing concept of unity of library media is an unquestioned asset to both instruction and research. By means of all of the formats the world's best ideas are increasingly permeating the process of higher education.

1 Duhamel, Georges. *In Defense of Letters.* New York, Greystone Press, 1939, p. ix.
2 *The Vespasiano Memoirs* (Lives of Illustrious Men of the XVth Century) trans. by William George and Emily Waters. New York, Lincoln MacVeagh, 1926, pp. 102, 104.
3 Dale, Edgar. "The Challenge of Audio-Visual Media," *In* Shores, Louis, ed., *Challenges to Librarianship,* Tallahassee, Florida State University, 1953, p. 101.
4 See for example, Wittich, W. A., and Schuler, C. F., *Audio-Visual Materials: Their Nature and Use.* New York, Harper, 1953, 564 p.
5 Dale, *op. cit.*, p. 104.

Library and AV Center —
Combined or Separate?

SOME SCHOOLS have a school library and a separate audio-visual center. Other schools place all instructional materials and equipment in one place, which is called either a school library or a materials center.

Advocates of dual centers contend that there is a difference between library materials and audio-visual materials, that librarians and audio-visualists differ in their educational concept and technical procedures. For these reasons, separatists argue that every school should have separate audio-visual and library centers, or at least different people in charge of administering them.

Among both librarians and audio-visualists, there are separatists. Some librarians say they already have their hands full caring for printed materials and cannot take on the additional responsibility of films, filmstrips, and the equipment necessary to project them. Some audio-visualists support this position and say that librarians and audio-visualists should cooperate but should not integrate their services.

Advocates of the single center, however, who include many librarians, audio-visualists, and a new generation of instructional-materials specialists, believe that teachers and pupils are best served by a single resource center in the school and by a unified, integrated instructional-materials program in the school system.

The integrationist sees any separation of audio-visual and library materials and services as artificial, costly, confusing to teachers and pupils. He believes that dual materials centers in the long run reduce the effective use of school materials.

From the professional literature of both librarianship and audio-visual instruction, it is almost impossible to determine where library

Reprinted from *NEA Journal*, 47: 342-343, May, 1958, by permission of the publisher.

materials leave off and audio-visual materials begin. The following classes of school materials are claimed by both librarians and audio-visualists: maps, globes, charts, pictures, bulletin boards, exhibits, discs, and tape recordings.

Consequently, in a school with dual centers, there must be a division of spoils between the audio-visual center and the school library to determine which of these items should be housed where. In one school, for example, maps and globes are housed in the library and charged to the audio-visual center's budget. This confronts both teachers and pupils with the necessity of having to decide which center to go to for the specific materials they need.

Nor is the line clear-cut on books and films. Some school libraries house, catalog, and classify filmstrips. Some even rent films. Because of the interrelationships among all school materials, the integrationist advocates housing the full range of instructional materials in a single resource center.

Part of the separatist's argument is that the combined job is too much for one person. The integrationist sees this argument as illogical.

In some small schools with separate audio-visual and library centers, there are part-time teacher-librarians who devote half-time to teaching and half to administering the library. Another teacher is relieved part-time to administer the audio-visual service. The integrationist believes the school program would be better served by a full-time librarian who would administer a unified materials center which would procure, house, classify, catalog, disseminate, and guide the use of the whole range of instructional materials.

In the larger schools with dual centers, there is usually at least one full-time librarian and one audio-visual coordinator operating separate centers.

The integrationist advocates combining the two centers by providing:

1. A single catalog of all of the school's instructional materials, so that at a glance teachers and pupils can discover what resources are available on a topic — books, films, periodicals, filmstrips, discs, pictures, tapes, objects, an index of community resources

2. A single charging and booking system for all of these classes of materials

3. A unified guidance and reference service for pupils and teachers — organized judiciously by levels or subjects if necessary.

The integrationist believes that when two people are assigned to guide the use of instructional materials in the school, they would be most effective in a single center, dividing the work between them — if such division is desirable — not by type of materials, but by level or subject specialization.

In a high school, for example, the integrationist feels that one materials specialist might perhaps serve the sciences and industrial arts; the other, the language arts and social studies. He believes these people would serve learning more effectively by becoming specialists in levels or subjects rather than in a particular area of materials.

On the other hand, the separatist argues that education is best served by having one specialist handle audio-visual materials and equipment and the other handle library materials — usually in two different places in the building.

Here is an issue that is clear-cut. In the years ahead, universal education will increase the range of individual differences. This will make it necessary to have more and varied instructional materials, expertly adapted to pupil learning requirements. How to organize the school's instructional-materials program must be decided now. It seems to me that a unified materials center in the school is clearly supported by trends and logic.

Enter the Materials Center

LIBRARIANS NOT IN THE SCHOOL FIELD have recently begun to hear that the historic term LIBRARY is about to give way to another agency in our elementary and secondary education. To some academic and public librarians the appearance of the MATERIALS CENTER is added evidence that school librarians are a different specie, perhaps only distantly related to the profession of which they are a recognized division. But to a great many other librarians the metamorphosis of the school library occurring contemporaneously with other startling educational developments suggests absorbing study for possible counterparts in community and on campus.

What is this new agency the Materials Center? As yet, both the literatures of education and of librarianship are exceedingly unrevealing. The sparsity of writings can be attributed in part to the recency of the subject. But to an even greater extent much of the hesitancy about written expression is due to uncertainty over the real nature of the Materials Center movement.

As a starting definition, the Materials Center is the agency in our American schools responsible for the acquisition, organization and dissemination of all instructional materials used in the learning process. This says at once "not by books alone" but by every medium useful to teacher and pupil in furthering education does the Materials Center perform its role. The range of materials, encompassing all those we now call "audio-visual", is one of the basic differences between a Materials Center and a School Library.

But that is not the only difference. The relative position of the various kinds of instructional materials also distinguishes the Materials Center. For example, in considerable library literature, reference to "non-book" materials is still accepted terminology. Likewise in audio-visual writings, such as the very fine brochure number 3 of

Reprinted from *A.L.A. Bulletin*, 49: 285-288, June, 1955, by permission of the publisher.

the Department of Audio-Visual Instruction, the impression is left that print or so-called "verbal" materials are an appendage. Neither one of these approaches quite describes the concept of the content of a true Materials Center.

A preliminary inventory of school materials in Florida, for example, reveals some two score classes of media used by teachers and pupils in the learning process. Without identifying all of them here, it is possible through partial enumeration to indicate something of the potential range of content in the Materials Center of tomorrow.

To begin with, the textbook is a fundamental instructional medium. It, with its supplementary workbooks, study guides and assorted teaching aids, constitutes an important class of Materials Center accessions. Despite acquisition, organization, and circulation procedures greatly different from those followed for conventional library materials, textbooks must be considered an integral part of the Materials Center content.

It goes without saying that the traditional core of a school library — books and magazines — constitutes a major element of the Materials Center collection. So also do pamphlets, newspapers, clippings, pictures, charts, and other items librarians have long considered essentials of their vertical file. Bulletin boards have always accented the library's exhibit and display services. And from time to time various collections of art and science objects have been absorbed in the school library collection. Maps and globes have certainly been almost standard library equipment. But it is interesting to note that recently some school libraries have begun to charge these to their "audio-visual budget."

Which brings us to the third great division of the Materials Center collection. In the previous paragraph no fewer than six classes of instructional materials have been mentioned that are claimed as stock in trade by both school librarians and by audio-visualists. This underlines the thin gray line that may be said to exist (or not) between audio-visual and non-audio-visual materials, depending upon how much of a separatist the school librarian or the audio-visualist may be.

To the separatist in both conventional camps the sixteen-millimeter motion picture is the audio-visual symbol. Almost as symbolic is the filmstrip. Other audio-visual media, probably in descending degrees of anti-verbalism and anti-abstraction, are disc and tape recordings, radio, television, the field trip.

These are by no means all of the forty classes of instructional materials used in our schools. But they give an idea of the expanded scope of the Materials Center collection. And they emphasize the content difference between a school library and a Materials Center. For in the former, "books and other materials" is still the vogue; in the latter all are instructional materials, and each class of media has its particular best contribution to make to an individual learning situation in which teacher and pupil create conditions as individual as fingerprints.

Which brings us to a second important difference between the Materials Center and the school library. Although historically the school library can be said to have begun as a way of learning, a multi-material teaching method, in the years of struggle for funds and recognition, the educational ends have often been subordinated to the means. It is an irrefutable tenet that better learning occurs in an orderly house. The devotion to organization of the school library by generations of school librarians has been no inconsiderable contribution. Inevitably, such consecration has sometimes resulted in placing second things first.

The point is illustrated by the school librarian who says today one of two things that represent the difference between the school library concept on the one hand and the emerging Materials Center idea. One common quotation is this: "I am so overworked now with just books and magazines that I cannot take on the additional responsibilities of audio-visual." This is a school library point of view.

The Materials Center point of view does not see that choice. To one who works in a Materials Center the either-or might just as logically be "I am so overworked now with books that I haven't time for magazines." Or to put it another way and positively, the Materials Center person believes all classes of instructional materials are his responsibility in the proportions required by the school program. Fundamentally, he does not believe his profession is a mission of formats as much as it is of ideas. The Materials Center has as its high aim the dissemination of good ideas in the form best understood by the individual child.

The other quote which distinguishes the school librarian's thinking from that of the Materials Center person is this one: "I am so far behind in my cataloging that I shall have to neglect nearly everything else until I am caught up." Now the Materials Center person has a high regard for the accessibility that comes from good organization. But the Materials Center librarian is thinking these days most enthusiastically about cooperative cataloging, acquisition, and other organizational activities.

Which brings us to a third difference. The Materials Center is tending toward greater dispersion than is found in the school library. As viewed today there are three echelons of Materials Centers service. The top echelon is the system center-city or county school system. This is the control for all of the centers. It performs the organizational tasks — acquisitions, classification, cataloging, and other technical processes for all of the centers in the system. In this system center is the vast reservoir of materials on which any of the subordinate centers can call to supplement its own resources. In the System Center is the central inventory, a kind of union catalog for all varieties of materials found anywhere in the school system.

The next echelon consists of the school Materials Centers. This middle echelon is the control for all the centers in classrooms in the building, as well as in other places. It houses in quarters differently planned from the quarters previously recommended for school libraries the whole range of instructional materials required by the school it serves. Its materials come from the system center fully classified, cataloged, and largely processed for immediate use. The school center's concern is largely with the problem of dissemination to the classrooms and other points of learning.

The third echelon is the classroom. It too is a Materials Center. For the classroom today has almost no resemblance to the classroom of yesterday. Such a "3-D" classroom was heralded in the N.E.A. exhibit of a few months back. Such a classroom is a tribute to the multi-materials concept of teaching and learning. Indeed such a classroom is a tangible acknowledgment of the educational theory that inspired the leaders of both the school library and the audio-visual movements before the techniques of book charging and film booking became major professional absorptions.

The first part of this century produced the distinguished psychologist J. McKeen Cattell, father of "individual differences." The psychological principle was made to order for librarianship since it proved that no two individuals in the world brought exactly the same preparation to a learning situation. In view of that fact even the best group teaching methods would fall short of meeting adequately the needs of the individual learner. What was needed was a method or a device so flexible that learning could be custom tailored to the unique figure that distinguishes each human.

Such American educators as Horace Mann, W. T. Harris and William Russell, among others, saw immediately the method in the multi-materials concept and the device in the increasing quantity and variety of instructional media. From these educators and others like them came the first impetus to the earlier school library movement and the later audio-visual operation. From librarians who sensed the power of their calling and from audio-visualists who came later and share this concept came the embryo of the present Materials Center idea.

At the moment the school librarians are doing most with this teaching aspect of librarianship. They are in the vanguard of a movement within our profession to recall us to our educational responsibility. In the history of American library service, academic, public, and special librarians have each as groups made significant contributions to the body of professional principle and practice shared by all librarianship. And now it appears as though school librarians are about to make one of the most significant of all contributions to our profession with the Materials Center. By means of this multi-material concept alone librarianship may provide the key to mass education. Led by the school librarians on the elementary and secondary levels, and followed by the academic librarians on the college level and the public librarians on the adult level, librarianship may yet assume its rightful educational role and provide the answer to the doubts about the possibility of universal education.

Looked at in that way the Materials Center is not a replacement but an augmentation of the mission of the library.

Portrait of a Materials Center

EVERYWHERE IN OUR AMERICAN SCHOOLS today we hear the term "Materials Center." It is a term that is rapidly replacing such terms as school library and audio-visual center. In the minds of many, the Materials Center is merely the union of the library and the audio-visual center. But actually, the Materials Center is much more than that.

Essentially the Materials Center is the culmination of an educational concept — a concept so basic that it may well save the day for America's courageous attempt to accomplish what no other nation in the world's history has undertaken before: complete and continuing education for all of the people from cradle to grave.

In two words this concept may be called multi-materials. In a few more words it may be simply stated that good teaching is good communication between teacher and pupil; and the key to good communication is acquaintance with and accessibility to a wide range of instructional materials. Providing such acquaintance and accessibility for teachers and pupils is the mission of the Materials Center.

How the Materials Center does this today varies from separate and conventional school libraries or audio-visual centers, in some schools, to integrated resource centers in entire school systems. In between these two extremes are various degrees of evolution toward the ultimate Materials Center. What that ultimate Materials Center will be is still open to experiment and discussion. What it will probably not be seems more certain.

It does not appear likely the American school will "go for" separate audio-visual and library centers in each building. Economically, the small school cannot afford such separation, and most American schools are still small. Educationally, it is almost impossible to divide Instructional Materials into "audio-visual" and "non-

Reprinted from *Peabody Journal of Education*, 33: 66-74, September, 1955, by permission of the publisher.

audio-visual." Even if one accepts symbolically the 16mm. motion picture as "audio-visual," and the book as symbolically "library," there are still some two score additional classes of materials that are claimed by both librarians and audio-visualists.

For example, the audio-visualist speaks of "flat pictures" and the librarian of "picture files," yet both terms describe approximately the same instructional materials. There is a considerable *audio-visual* professional literature about "recordings" and an equally voluminous *library* professional literature about "records." Nor should the teacher be expected to ask the child whether he has an *audio-visual* globe or a *library* globe when they are one and the same globe.

Basically the school library movement and the audio-visual movement are successive waves of the same educational concept; individual differences in children can best be met by individually tailored media of communications. Only a well-stocked, carefully selected, well-organized, carefully directed instructional materials service can strengthen the bond that ties pupil to teacher in a good learning situation.

So we begin our portrait of a Materials Center with a soul. Directing this operation in the school is a good teacher—one so good that she could not only return to the classroom and demonstrate good teaching, but innovate exciting new ways to arouse, stimulate, and inspire children. Call him librarian, audio-visualist, building coordinator of Materials, Materials Specialist or Materials Teacher. The label is of secondary importance. The important thing is that the job is assigned to a superior teacher, teacher educated and certificated, who has seen the vision of multi-materials and who can lead the school in developing a real multi-materials education.

Then give this teacher the specialized education in Instructional Materials he will need. Let him have this specialty on a teacher education base, preferably on the graduate level, but acceptably, too, on the undergraduate level as part of his specialization area. The specialization should include as thorough a knowledge of all kinds of materials, as he has of children from his educational psychology, and of teaching method from his education courses. He should learn the content of children's and young people's books, magazines, films, filmstrips, tape and disc recordings, graphics, radio, television, and some two score other categories of school materials including the local resources for field journeys. He should gain skill in the operation of projectors and playbacks and other necessary equipment. He should learn sources for acquiring these media, criteria for evaluation and selection, techniques for classifying and cataloging, charging and booking, and above all the ways and means of utilizing these materials in the interest of better learning.

Now let us proceed with our portrait to consideration of housing. Give the Materials Center generous space, much more generous space than is accorded it in most schools. And let it not be an afterthought. No architect has a right to put "school" in front of his specialty who has ever been party to designing a building without provision for library or materials center. Nor can an administrator who has shared in such an omission ever be considered an educator. The full Materials Center is a suite of rooms that recognizes at least seven distinct functions.

One of these functions is ACTIVITY. It requires a room by itself. Because here both the "pin-drop" principal and the "tip-toe" librarian will be unhappy. But the Materials Specialist, the Materials Teacher, and above all the pupil, will be exceedingly happy, because here part of the multi-materials way of learning, a very important part will be carried on.

Let me describe the ACTIVITY room in the Materials Center suite as I see it in my mind's eye. It will be very *unlike* a library reading room. It will be very *like* a Super-Market. Instead of upright shelves with books arranged six feet, ten inches high, there will be many counters and tables. Each counter or table, instead of featuring a particular kind of vegetable or meat or staple grocery, will feature a teaching unit. Over here will be a table entirely devoted to a fourth grade weather unit; over there another table devoted to a third grade North American Indian unit; and on a third counter an entire unit on the home. Other tables and counters will each feature some one unit currently the concern of one classroom learning situation.

On each of these unit tables will be a selection of every type of instructional materials: books, magazines, pamphlets, documents, of course. But also recordings, tapes, filmstrips, slides, films, posters, pictures, cartoons, realia, stereographs, puppets, and to avoid further listings of categories, *et cetera*. There will also be *Target Folders*.

"Target Folders" describe a medium that Air Force Intelligence devised for its pilots who were about to visit enemy territory for the purpose of bombing objectives. These Target Folders describe by word and picture all of the local resources of the area to be visited — both natural and artificial resources. Although these Folders were devised in time of war with a destructive purpose, they suggest a most constructive idea in time of peace for our schools.

The Target Folder in the School Materials Center can do much to make the Field Journey a meaningful teaching medium. Each Target Folder should describe a local resource so as to be helpful to the teacher and class about to embark on a field trip. There will be a Target Folder for the local water works, airport, paper mill, phosphate mine, shoe factory, department store, newspaper, or whatever else has a potential contribution to learning. In this folder will be the name of the person to contact, the route or transportation to and from, the diary of the last class visit, with suggestions and cautions for improving the next trip, and such pictures, diagrams, questions, regulations and other information as will be helpful.

There will also be a Listening Post on each or every other table so that recordings may be listened to through several sets of earphones without disturbing others. And there will be convenient viewers for slides and stereos.

The ACTIVITY room, however, is primarily an exploration room; not a reading, or viewing or studying room. Here a very important part of the multi-material way of learning is carried on. Together teacher and pupil come to the Materials Center to SHOP for teaching and learning materials. As they enter the door they pick up a basket on wheels just as they would in a super market. They proceed to their unit table and begin to examine and rummage among the varieties of materials. Each pupil attempts to discover, evaluate and select for himself some materials that arouse his individual background. It may be that a picture or a slide or a book or a magazine article tells him best what he wants to know about the unit they are studying. Then he puts it in his basket with the intention of studying, exhibiting, expounding, and defending its content and form to his classmates. At the end of the hour, pupils and teacher will have gathered together in their baskets enough different materials on the unit for their classroom to make possible the creation of a classroom materials center on that unit which will provide real learning opportunities for the period of time agreed on.

This then is the ACTIVITY room. It serves pupil and teacher in the important exploratory stage of learning. It provides essentially a learning situation as important as any the teacher and child can create back in their home room. If nowhere else the ACTIVITY room alone gives the lie to the artificial distinction some school systems make between so-called "teaching" and "non-teaching" personnel. Because in the ACTIVITY room, as elsewhere in the Materials Center, classroom teacher and Materials Center Teacher are teaching together as creatively and industriously as anywhere in the school. And it is quite evident that pupil activity in a classroom becomes good as it approaches the quality of pupil activity in the Materials Center.

A second distinct function of the Materials Center is ORIENTATION. Here pupils learn the skills essential to efficient materials use. The Tachyscope, ophthalmograph and other reading devices provide analysis and practice opportunities for pupil and teacher. Projectors of all kinds — motion picture, slide, opaque — are available for instruction in equipment use and for viewing projected materials selected in the ACTIVITY room. Playbacks and recorders for both tape and disc, and graphics tables and equipment and supplies for creating school-made materials present additional learning opportunities.

A third function is study, and a STUDY room properly insulated and isolated needs to be provided. Let it never be forgotten that much learning still goes on without physical movement. Some place in the Materials Center Suite there is need for a quiet, study and reading room. Here a little corner for the teacher and her professional collection might well be preserved.

A fourth function is conference and group discussion. There will need to be a place in the Materials Center where students and teachers can meet and confer and talk. The CONFERENCE room need not be large.

The other three functions of the Materials Center are largely organizational and administrative. A good Materials Center must be well organized for use.

The first of these functions is storage. A STACK room which might be better understood if it were called a STOCK room would shelve as economically as possible the collection of materials. This Stock Room should have a variety of shelving, cabinets, files and other receptacles to accommodate books, magazines, newspapers, films, filmstrips, recordings, tapes, slides, and again the *et cetera*. This is the part of the Materials Center that would most resemble the conventional library and audio-visual centers. From this organized stock would be taken the selections for the unit counters in the AC-TIVITY room.

The next of these organizational functions is BOOKING and CHARGING. This would constitute the control desk, the point of reception and disbursement for all materials. Here pupils and teachers would come with baskets of materials to be charged and returned. Here also could come pupils and teachers from the STUDY and ORI-ENTATION rooms to charge books and book films. It is a function that should be performed almost wholly by pupil assistants or by clerical workers; and the professional librarian, materials teacher, or coordinator should never permit herself to be burdened with these routines to the detriment of her teaching function. In this Charging and Booking Area will be the card catalog and the various periodical indexes, also.

The final organizational function is technical processes. These usually are accomplished in a WORKROOM, which must have running water in it. Here many of the behind-the-scenes routines are performed. It is hoped that at the school level no classification and cataloging will be necessary, since the trend is for this job to be done in the School System Materials Center for all schools. It is hoped, too, that a decreasing amount of processing that has tied down so much of the school librarian's time will be done at the building level. Nevertheless, some processing will have to be done, and here again it is hoped that help in the form of pupil assistants or clerical workers will relieve the professional teacher or librarian or coordinator.

These then are the seven functions and the seven units of a School Materials Center at the building level. This level represents the middle echelon in a Materials Center System. Each of these middle echelons, that is the building Materials Centers, is a key link between the overall Materials Center in the county or city headquarters of the school system and the classroom Materials Centers in the building. Recognition of these other two echelons of Materials Centers service completes the concept of the new School Materials program.

Essentially the so-called "3-D Classroom" exhibited recently by the NEA is a Materials Center. It is designed and equipped to utilize every one of the two score classes of school materials. It can be darkened for projection. It is wired for sound. It comes equipped with TV and radio. It is in all essence a small materials center and goes further to prove there is no essential difference between the so-called classroom teacher and the Materials Center teacher, librarian or audio-visualist. Look at a good socialized recitation or at any other group activity in a classroom and you are immediately struck with its comparability to a Materials Center.

The Classroom Center should be equipped physically and pedagogically to receive materials from the Building Materials Center. These materials should be selected periodically by teachers and pupils from their shopping trips as needed for the current unit. Materials and equipment should not remain permanently in the classroom but should be changed to meet the needs of the unit under study. The classroom that has had the same pictures on the wall and the same books on the shelves for as long as the teacher has occupied that room is losing an environmental advantage for learning. The change of pace occasioned by frequent swapping of materials through the building center is an unquestioned cause for classroom stimulation.

The System Center in the county or city headquarters has a quite different function from either the building or classroom center. The System Center is the wholesaler, just as the building center is the retailer, and the classroom center the ultimate consumer. To the System Center come classroom teacher and Materials Center teacher together to find supplements for particular units on which the building center needs help. In the System Center all teachers find professional help in a good pedagogical library and in curriculum guides. The System Center classifies and catalogs all materials for all schools, maintains a central system inventory so that materials may be located in any school in the system. The System Center buys for all schools, thus gaining the benefit of the better discounts. It offers a cooperative reference service to all teachers and in general performs many of the inter-library functions that are part of good regional cooperation on a research level.

This then is the concept of the Materials Center for our schools. It has not yet fully arrived. But here and there, in Florida and Texas, in Oregon and New York, in countless counties and cities, the new concept is tangibly revealing itself through numerous signs. Steadily we see separate audio-visual and library centers in some schools merging into integrated Materials Centers. Increasingly we hear of librarians and audio-visualists becoming directors and supervisors of instructional materials. Certification trends point to the recognition of a cross between the librarian and audio-visualist in the person of a materials teacher. And this is all to the good for better learning and teaching.

For the school administrator, today, there is no one development that offers more educational promise than the MATERIALS CENTER. To take advantage of its full potential the school principal must first understand that audio-visual and library are two aspects of a school materials program that must be planned, organized and administered together. Second, he must secure the services of a teacher with broad training in the whole range of materials — audio-visual as well as print. Third, he must provide adequate housing for this important function of materials service. Finally, adequate financing is an inevitable requirement.

From this investment of thought, personnel, space, and funds, the return to good teaching and learning is limitless.

On the Library's Role in Education

Mark Hopkins' Log

THE TWENTIETH PRESIDENT of the United States, James A. Garfield, once said his idea of a college would be met by

"a log with a student on one end and Mark Hopkins on the other."

In that symbolical idea of a college are the three elements of higher education — the Teacher, the Learner, and the Medium.

English literature abounds with tributes to the teacher. From Roger Ascham's *The Schoolmaster* to Jaques Barzun's *The Teacher*, he has been portrayed in fiction and in fact as everything from a saint to a sinner. The great teachers have been blessed with many of the attributes of the Great Master. Others have been somewhat less, all the way down to the disillusioned and bitter example portrayed in one of the recent novels, *The Hickory Stick*. Frustrated and disillusioned at secondary school teaching in a small Ohio town, the hero of that novel at one point appears to subscribe to the definition conveniently ascribed to "Anon" when that unidentified author wrote "classical education in the English public schools consists of casting sham pearls before real swine."

As an antidote to *The Hickory Stick*, the young teacher is urged to go back to an earlier best seller — James Hilton's *Goodbye, Mr. Chips*. That essential self-subordination to the interests of one's pupils that above all makes a good teacher made Mr. Chips the hero that booklovers and movie-goers applauded so avidly. That kind of a teacher, Mark Hopkins undoubtedly was. From all accounts by alumni, the experience of log sitting with the president who served Williams College for over a generation profoundly influenced the graduates during the middle third of the last century.

Reprinted from *The Peabody Reflector*, 24: 68-70, March, 1951, by permission of the publisher. "Mark Hopkins' Log" was delivered as the Founders' Day Address at George Peabody College for Teachers in Nashville, Tennessee, on February 19, 1951.

Nor has the learner been neglected, either in humanistic or in professional literature. There are full libraries that describe imaginatively, realistically and scientifically, three general classes: namely, the brilliant, the stupid and the average.

Every teacher has had experience with the near genius in his class. Sometimes that experience has been pleasant and stimulating, at other times it has been exasperating.

There is a young lady who sits on the front row of one of my classes right now. I am sure her I.Q. is so high that no standardized test can contain it. I am further certain that she has accumulated so much information that very little is new to her. Often I know what I say must be a little bit, if not a whole lot, old to her. She always seems to have such a bored and indifferent look on her face. I could take time and say to her, "there are others in this class less favored by heredity and environment whom you should consider if the pace is a little slower than you would like it to be." But instead there is something within me that still likes a little competition, and so occasionally I sacrifice most of the rest of the class and go off on an abstract discussion of Existentialism and the look in my eye intends to say to this bright young lady "now try that on for size."

Then of course there is the dull student, not endowed so well as the young lady. I mean to make no comparison between the sexes. It just so happens that the student with the lower I.Q. has been especially well portrayed by James Thurber in recounting his experiences at Ohio State. You may recall the story about the big Tackle, needed badly for the all-important Michigan game. It was mid-term, however, and if this big Tackle flunked the examination he would be ineligible.

Contrary to some student opinion, many of the faculty are much more interested in football victories than is generally believed. The professor of Economics wanted, as much as anyone, for Ohio State to beat Michigan. Consequently, knowing the big Tackle's difficulties with Economics, he announced in advance that he would not give a written examination but would instead ask one question orally of each member of the class, and if that question were answered correctly the student would have passed the mid-term examination.

Came the day of the mid-term. Came the turn for the big Tackle's question. It was evident that the professor had devised this question with great care. It was, "Name one form of transportation."

The professor and all the students moved to the edge of their seats in anticipation. Nothing happened. The great big Tackle sat in his chair solidly, and not one word did he utter. He was a tremendous man with tremendous hands that could handle a football capably. But there was nothing above that powerful neck that could cope with even the simplest question in Economics.

The discouraged professor pleaded, "Name any form of transportation. It doesn't matter what it is, but any kind of transportation you can think of."

The room's quiet was perfect. Beads of perspiration began to break out all over the giant Tackle's face and neck. It was evident the question was too difficult.

The professor had a supplementary question. "Tell the class how you got to Ohio State."

"That's easy," said the Tackle. "The alumni are paying me."

"No, no, no," said the professor. "That isn't what I mean. I want you to tell how you got here, what form of transportation did you use to get here?"

"I hitch-hiked."

By this time the class had entered into the question. Way back in the room could be heard very faintly an imitation of an engine's chug-chug. In another corner there was a slight engine whistle. Even the professor began moving his arms at the elbow in imitation of a piston. Suddenly, the electric light bulb lit up in the big Tackle's eye. "Oh, a train."

Well, between the brilliant young lady and the great big Tackle, literature recognizes a mass called the average. No one knows exactly what this average is. Pedagogical literature is increasingly taking a dim view of that part of the bell-shaped curve that comprises the most area. Enough dissenting voices are being raised to defy anyone to produce that average student.

More than ever education is everywhere returning to the pedagogical phrase "individual differences."

There are many elements in common among all human beings, but fundamentally the human being is an individual and that education seems most effective that is tailored to the individual.

In any classroom of twenty to forty students it is virtually impossible to plan a lesson for the very bright young lady alone or for the great big Tackle, though it hasn't seemed possible to teach forty different lessons during a single class period. Consequently the average student comes into his own there, at least mythically. The teacher plans a lesson which will fit the natural and acquired equipment of most of the students in that class. The obvious weakness is of course that even if this lesson does interest and instruct the majority of the class, it has nothing, or very little for the bright young lady, and too much for the great big Tackle. Tragically enough, we see increasing evidence that this average lesson apparently finds fewer average students than was anticipated.

Which brings us to the log, the third essential element in President Garfield's definition of a college. Perhaps President Garfield meant only a log of wood. But I doubt that. The fact that Mark Hopkins was at one end and the student at the other indicates to me that symbolically, the log was the link between the teacher and the learner. And therefore, I should like you to pay some attention to this third element in the concept of a college.

There are many material resources that go into a college in addition to the teacher and the learner. Among these resources are, of course, buildings and equipment and laboratories and stadia and light and heat, and food, and of course money. And too often as an afterthought, there is also a library — the library which Carlyle considered the only thing necessary to have a university. Many speeches refer to the library as the heart of a college. Unfortunately, as it has been observed, when a depression comes along, too often institutions of higher education amputate first of all the heart.

When I speak of the log, however, I do not have in mind the conventional concept of a library. At least President Garfield had more nearly in mind the media of communication used by teacher and learner in this process we call education.

In higher education today, many media of communication are

used. Besides the lecture and the recitation there are the textbooks and many kinds of library books and periodicals. There are also what we call Audio-Visual aids, including film and film-strip, recordings and transcriptions, maps and globes, flat pictures and charts, museum objects, and field trips to some man-made or natural resource, slides and stereoscopes, mock-ups and models, and so on and on. It is safe to say that in the universe of print and audio-visual materials, there is all the knowledge known to mankind. But more than that, there are so many different presentations of all that knowledge that it is very likely that somewhere among those millions of books and hundreds of millions of magazine articles, thousands of films and recordings and the other media there is one particular medium that is suited for the bright girl and another equally well adapted to the big Tackle and thousands of others, graded almost with micrometer precision to the exact background and equipment of every man, woman and child in this world. Altogether, I believe this world of print and audio-visual materials constituted what President Garfield had in mind when he talked about a "log" between the teacher and the learner.

If you will indulge a personal experience, I should like to illustrate the point. Every child probably has one or more big moments in his grammar school days. I had two. One occurred in the fourth grade when I stood in front of the class and named all the presidents of the United States. My teacher then sent me up to the eighth grade to do the same thing for the big boys and girls.

The other moment came during my junior year in high school, in a physics class. We had been studying physics out of a single textbook. There were thirty of us in that class. Being a public school, we all brought different backgrounds to the room. The teacher was undertaking to present one lesson right down the middle of the classroom for the average student. The textbook was probably doing the same. I believe as far as physics was concerned I was more nearly in the class of the big Tackle. The harder I read that textbook the less I seemed to understand it. Apparently, most of the rest of the class was having the same trouble. Each period we would sit with our fingers in the textbook, reading one paragraph ahead of the one being recited on by a classmate. As soon as a child was called on to recite on a topic, we all opened our books and began reading the next paragraph so we would be prepared. Physics meant absolutely nothing to us except a check on the teacher's card for having recited correctly.

My soul revolted, and one day I went to the little school library we had. We were studying magnetism, and I could not make anything out of the discussion the textbook had on the subject. So I pulled down six books on science and spread them out before me. I turned to the index under "M" and listed the page references for magnetism. I read each of the books in succession. There were just a few pages on magnetism. But somewhere, probably around the fourth or fifth reading, light came. Suddenly, I understood the principle of magnetism. All at once I could see the little molecules arranging themselves. I read on. I noticed that one author differed from another. I saw a direct contradiction in one book to something said in my textbook. I became aroused. I began arguing with the authors and with my teacher in my own mind.

All I recall is that I walked into that next recitation period a free man. I believe I held my head a little higher. I pushed the textbook away from me. I might even have been a little bit defiant. In my heart and in my mind I challenged the teacher to ask me a question on magnetism that I could not answer, in or out of sequence. My turn came. I arose and talked for five minutes on the question asked me, going into considerably more detail than the textbook included, and quoting my sources. I took direct issue with the textbook author and asked my teacher to settle between us.

I can recall the gasp that went around the classroom, and the silent admiration that was shown in my teacher's eyes. Needless to say, my grade was made in that class for the rest of the term. I believe that was one of the incidents that contributed to my entering the library profession. I have believed continuously ever since that one of the elements in good teaching was the ability to select the right medium for the right child on the right subject at the right time.

More than half of my life has been devoted to education. It is inconceivable to me that a teacher can be good without knowing the learner and without thinking less of "how am I doing" and more of "how is he progressing." It is almost equally inconceivable to me to think of a teacher who is good and who does not know the universe of print and audio-visual materials well enough to meet individual differences precisely and finally.

That is what I believe was meant by Mark Hopkins' log. There are three elements that go into the making of a college, one is the Teacher, another is the Learner, and the third is the link between the Teacher and the Learner — the Log, the universe of the materials of learning.

Today is Founders' Day for Alma Mater — your alma mater and mine. George Peabody, whom you and I and Peabodians all over the world have come together to honor, was born on February 18, 1795. He died in 1869. He was therefore a contemporary of Mark Hopkins.

President Hill has written in his article for *Collier's Encyclopedia* that George Peabody became the first person to give one million dollars to education. He gave many millions of dollars after that. He established two institutes before that, one in Baltimore and one in Peabody, Massachusetts. He also established two museums, one of natural history and natural sciences at Yale, and one of archeology and ethnology at Harvard. He endowed also the Academy of Science at Yale. But by all odds his greatest educational contribution was the Peabody Education Fund, which he established on February 7, 1867. That fund was to be used "for the promotion and encouragement of intellectual, moral or industrial education among the young of the more destitute portions of the Southern and Southwestern states of our union." Four United States presidents, Grant, Cleveland, Hayes and Theodore Roosevelt were among the distinguished members who served on the Board of this foundation. Our Alma Mater resulted from these many benefactions.

I cannot help feeling that since they were contemporaries, George Peabody must have been thinking of Mark Hopkins when he so ably explained on so many occasions what he conceived education's function to be. Here was George Peabody, a financier, a leader in merchandising, a philanthropist, not a professional educator at all, who yet understood and conceived the meaning of education as fully

as his great contemporary, the teacher, Mark Hopkins. I feel sure
that George Peabody would have wanted a college named for him
to consist of those three elements, good teachers, good students and
good books.

This is homecoming for me. As I return to my Alma Mater,
memories troop through the halls of the building, in the classrooms
and in the offices I have visited. I walk across the campus and look
at the stately pillars, and out on the lawns and under the trees, and
many summers of school administrators' conferences, stunt nights
and watermelon cuttings, and picnics at Knapp Farm, crowd everything else out of my mind and heart. I try to summarize in my own
words what it is that has made Peabody good. I ask myself why
alumni everywhere all over the world crowd to Peabody gatherings
or in reminiscing groups of twos and threes. And I find the best
summary can be made under those three elements, the Teacher, the
Learner and the Log.

Peabody's greatness, first of all, has been in its faculty. Even
within my two decades of experience there have been many Mark
Hopkinses here. I hesitate to name any for fear that I may, due
to time, omit more deserving ones. But of those who have passed
on I recall Dr. Roehm and Dr. Demiashekevich, Dr. Phelps, Dr.
Peterson, Dr. Garrison, Dr. Knudsen, Dr. Little and Dr. Payne. Dr.
Bachman, Dr. Didcoct and Dr. MacMurry were just before my time.
I wish I had time to tell you the many influences they had on my life.
Of those still here who were my teachers, there are Dr. Crabb and
Dr. Wirth. I owe them all very much. They and many others on
the staff and faculty are this first and most important element in
Peabody.

And then there are all my fellow students, fellow alumni now,
who have gone out and made names all over the world. There are
college presidents, state superintendents of schools, there are deans
and teachers and high school principals, superintendents and librarians, and officers in various educational and other professional associations. Every one of them is a Peabody man or a Peabody woman.
if you can forgive me for believing so, even more distinctly, than
what is known as a Harvard man.

Finally there is the library, the whole noble concept of the Joint University Library, with its steadily growing universe of man's records, and that part of Peabody nearest and dearest to me, the Library School. In that school the mission which is the heart of my Founders' Day address is being carried on more effectively than ever under the guidance and direction of Dr. FitzGerald. In that school the teachers are being prepared especially to help other teachers utilize the log that extends between teacher and learner.

There are no words to tell you how deeply honored I am to be able to talk with you on this occasion so dear to all of us to whom Peabody belongs.

The School and the Book

IF THERE ARE TWO adjectives in the educationists' vocabulary which have been overworked they are "new" and "changing." Nearly every professional paper or speech these days sooner or later reminds us that our education is new and that our social order is changing. It is therefore with considerable diffidence and professional humility that the present essay suggests that there may be something newer than new on the educational horizon and that we are again to witness one of those pedagogical metamorphoses which periodically rock us to our professional foundations and overnight render antiquated even those nationally prominent demonstrations we generously label experimental.

Not that there is any great cause for alarm. Like every other wave of "new" education the incoming one is as old as the sea itself. It has been anticipated for centuries, predicted within the last gen-

Reprinted from *Texas Outlook*, 22: 45-48, June, 1938, by permission of the publisher.

eration and crudely experimented with now for nigh on the second decade. But as yet its consummation awaits the near future. The various signs accumulate, bequeath fame to an obscure educator here or to a successful school there, perplex the conventional if progressive school administrator, threaten the conscientious but aging teacher, and make all curriculum investigators review and revise their latest revisions. Yet the essence of this new reform has been inherent in all educational progress since the fifteenth century.

In 1464, one Johann Gutenberg invented printing. The effects were far-reaching in every human activity and promised major change in pedagogical method. At one fell swoop manuscript copying, an integral part of medieval education, gave way to the mechanical and economical method of reproduction made possible by the press, and the scholar's time was released from the drudgery of writing exercises. But the classroom continued the ancient procedures, the teacher as before dictating and the pupil copying. There was sufficient reason for this: in spite of the printing press, printed books were still too expensive to provide every pupil with a copy.

Gradually books and reading took on increased significance in our educational processes. A century after Gutenberg's epochal invention, Comenius gave us the series of reforms which marks the beginning of modern education. These reforms were characterized by greater reliance on the printed rather than the spoken word, and he himself authored the first illustrated schoolbook, "Orbis Pictus."

In the middle of the eighteenth century there appeared an English printer whose whole concern was to provide good and reasonably priced books for children. From the press of John Newbery came innumerable little "pocket books" containing entertainment and information — an early edition of "Mother Goose," and probably the earliest school encyclopedia we have any record of. It was called The Circle of the Sciences, "a compendious library, whereby each branch of polite learning is rendered extremely easy and instructive," and was issued in seven volumes by Newbery and his successors from 1745 to 1770.

American textbook independence from England came sometime between 1687 and 1690 when there appeared one of the first and most important elementary texts. Its publisher was one Benjamin

Harris located at the London Coffee House in Boston and the publication the famous New England primer. For nearly a century it was the textbook of the American school, appearing in edition after edition, one of which, that from 1749 to 1766, ran into 37,100 copies.

In 1785 Noah Webster's American Spelling Book called by Historian Dexter perhaps "the greatest inanimate force in American education" was published. Its sale at first was small, but by 1815 the annual number of copies sold was estimated at 286,000 and by 1838 something over 350,000. By 1847 the annual sale was averaging 1,000,000 copies and the total output had passed the 24 million mark. Down almost to the last generation over 60 million copies of the famous "Speller" had been used in our American schools.

Texts like the "New England Primer" and "Webster's Speller" became the goal of every American textbook publisher, and although no one ever again succeeded in cornering the school market as these two had done, several like McGuffey's readers made huge sectional conquests.

The essential of textbook education was restriction to one book in each subject. A specific number of pages was assigned by the teacher and on the following day the pupils were asked to recite on these pages. At this stage education had evolved from dictation and copy to reading and reciting. Under such methods of instruction no other printed materials were needed. The pupil might be reciting words; the particular author may have failed entirely to touch the child's background of interest, but at least there was a definite assignment which the pupil could be held responsible for and by the mastery of which the teacher could determine the progress of the learner.

By the twentieth century the spread of printed material, the rise of the penny newspaper, the increase in book production and the growth of libraries challenged the single textbook standard. Colleges first threw off the yoke by adopting a reserve book system under which professors referred students to sources and to many commentaries, encouraged comparison of treatment on the part of students and sought as far as possible to suit reading to the background of the individual student.

The growing importance of books and libraries occasioned considerable speculation on the future of higher education. President Eliot of Harvard with his famous Five Foot Shelf implied that a better college education could be obtained through careful reading than by attending four years of college classes. President Harper of the University of Chicago, strangely prophetic, predicted that the library would soon become the center of college education and might finally be the only educational building on the campus.

Then came a series of educational experiments on the college level, the last of which have not yet been undertaken. First Harvard and Princeton with their tutorial and preceptorial system, and later Swarthmore with its "reading for honors," Antioch with its autonomous courses, Chicago with its new plan, and dozens of other colleges with their supervised reading and independent study schemes. And now one college announces its intention of replacing all classroom instruction with supervised reading. A Michigan professor discovers experimentally that students who do supervised reading learn better and more rapidly than students of equal ability who attend conventional classes.

Gradually these discoveries and innovations begin to filter down to the secondary and then to the elementary school level. First, the college adviser begins to realize that many high school graduates are unable to carry on successfully their college freshman work because they can not read properly. Doctor Pressey at Ohio State conducts a series of experiments with controlled groups of college freshmen and discovers that many failing students' difficulties are due not to science, languages, history, mathematics and the other studies but simply to inability to read rapidly and comprehendingly. Astoundingly enough, Doctor Pressey learns that even grades in mathematics can be raised by increasing a student's reading proficiency.

Back to the schools go these findings. Early in 1936 appears a volume by a personnel director in Chicago junior college dealing with remedial reading on the secondary school level. In the meantime school library standards which had experienced an aborted revival in the early twenties take on new importance. In the vanguard is the Southern Association which in 1928 sets to work on school library standards that draw the admiration and citation of educational leaders everywhere. By the fall of 1935 these standards are fully enforced and the school library in the South is on the upgrade as nowhere else in America. A North Central representative at a Southern meeting publicly admits that the mid-west lags behind the South in school library standards.

But the South influences the rest of the nation and there is shortly appointed an interregional standards committee representing each of the accrediting agencies. Its purpose is to draw up a national set of standards for the secondary schools and when the first draft of these new cooperative standards appears, lo and behold, the library standards lead all the rest.

Nor does the library renaissance stop with the high school. Soon it becomes evident that reading diagnosis and remedying should begin much sooner. Silenced are the more rapid Rousseauists among the progressives who would delay reading instruction even later. Forgotten are those who shout learning by doing to the exclusion of learning by all other methods. It becomes increasingly apparent that life is far too short to learn all things by doing or even a major portion of all things that way. Impressed on the minds of those struggling with the problem is the fact that most things must be learned vicariously and that of all vicarious experiences reading is perhaps the most effective, most economical and least harmful.

So to work go the elementary school people. A half dozen books on preventing and correcting reading difficulties, on primary reading, on reading readiness and pre-reading appear. Great laboratories go to work on the health aspect of reading and we have produced instruments of diagnosis and correction such as the Opthalmograph, Metronoscope, etc. Elementary school libraries begin to be talked, installed, and used. An era of elementary school library development rivalling the secondary school library renaissance seems to be upon us.

And educationists and librarians look around and see what is happening to the schools from kindergarten to graduate school. And

those in the vanguard begin to meditate, experiment, discuss the
education of the future. First they look back to U. S. Commissioner
W. T. Harris' famous declaration — "The school is set at the task
of teaching the pupil how to use the library in the best manner —
that, I take it is the central object toward which our American
schools have been unconsciously tending."

Then to the late Sir John Adams who in 1931 proposed the
library-integrated school — a school program built around the
school library and the basic skill of reading.

> "The integralists and totalitarians are now on the look-
> out for some more wholesome method of attaining unity,
> and they might do a great deal worse than turn to the school
> library. Here we have the seat of the school soul, the nature
> center of school unity, the meeting place of all the more or
> less conflicting claims of all the school subjects. Here, all the
> faculty, specialists included, meet on common ground."

The whole movement seems to have been best summarized and
perhaps forecast by Dean Russell of Teachers College, Columbia
University, who declared:

> ". . . Something new is in the process of creation. For
> the education of children we have schools. Into these we have
> introduced libraries. For the education of adults we have
> libraries. Into these we have introduced schools. This paper
> suggests that the time may come when there will be neither
> libraries in schools nor schools in libraries, but a new edu-
> cational institution will emerge which combines the best fea-
> tures of both."

It is, of course, presumptuous for anyone to detail what was in
the minds of the authors when these paragraphs were written. One
can only develop the idea along futuristic lines — an extremely
hazardous undertaking in an educational world where the proof
of the pudding is generally found in a statistical formula. But fortunately, along with the inspiration from Dean Russell and Sir John
has come encouragement from the book of Dr. B. B. Bogoslowski
bravely entitled "The Ideal School." Now that the Pestalozzian and

Rousseaun semi-fictional form has been re-introduced into our professional literature with the promise that there may be hereafter some art as well as a great deal of science in our educational meetings, the following description of the library-centered school may be permitted even though visionary.

The chief points at which the library-centered school is likely to differ radically from the conventionally progressive school are in personnel, teaching methods and teaching materials.

Of these, unquestionably the change in teaching personnel is likely to be most far-reaching. Perhaps the major obstacle to the fullest development of the library in the school has been the inadequate preparation of teachers and school administrators. Until now the school library has been too largely the product on the one hand of the librarian who unfortunately was too often either untrained in, or out of sympathy with, the problems of education, and on the other the school administrator and teacher whose preparation from the standpoint of modern education has been inadequate.

Both groups are benefiting from increasing contacts with each other on the common ground of the school library. For example, most library schools which undertake to train librarians for schools insist that the candidate bring for admission a minimum number of credits in education and often give preference to entering students who already have a teaching certificate in their native state and perhaps several years of actual teaching experience. Through the joint committee of the N.E.A.-A.L.A. and through teachers meetings like this which librarians attend, members of our profession are enabled to develop a more balanced view of the library's place in the educational program.

On the other side, an increasing number of teacher training institutions are including compulsory library instruction, not only of the freshman variety on library use but also elementary courses in bibliography, school book selection and children's literature.

The report of the joint committee of the A.L.A. and the A.A.T.C. recommending a minimum library instruction program for all teachers, as well as such actual library instruction programs as are offered to all teachers and administrators at Peabody and Teachers College, Columbia, are exceedingly hopeful signs.

What this will mean ultimately can only be surmised. As far as the teacher is concerned, increased library knowledge is certain to mean increased library use in teaching and research. Unquestionably many a textbook teacher today retains her antiquated teaching methods solely as a defense complex. She knows little about the library, is ashamed to have any part of it explained to her by the librarian or by a library trained teacher and therefore will have nothing of these new fangled things. Likewise the study hall principal today looks upon the library as a luxury and delegates it to some dark closet or hallway where discipline cases can be sent. At best he tolerates the librarian in a corner of the inviolable study hall and the still less violable study desks. Often only lack of information prevents him from replacing the desks with tables and chairs because he believes he will be sacrificing seating capacity. Frequently, too, he will assign all sorts of miscellaneous duties to the librarian because he does not know what she has to do.

I have heard recently that a certain high school inspector has a sure-fire remedy for both the study hall principal and textbook teacher. Upon visiting a school he always calls on the librarian for a list of the teachers who use the library in their class work. With the principal's consent this list is posted on the teachers' bulletin board. The result is always the same: there is a tremendous wave of library use almost immediately, artificial to be sure, but no doubt an occasional textbook teacher is converted in this way by forced library contact.

Increased knowledge of educational problems on the part of the librarian is also beginning to mean that the librarian sees her department as a part of the school whole. No longer do the technical processes, of increasing importance as the size and specialization of a library increases, receive undue emphasis. Rather the librarian more and more assumes her place with the other teachers and not infrequently is herself the best equipped teacher on the school faculty.

This is being increasingly recognized by school administrators despite discouraging individual cases. Only three years ago the following request from school administrators came in nearly every mail during placement season:

I want a librarian to teach one class in English, one class in history, one in Latin, one in French, to coach basketball, play the piano at assembly, type my letters and catalog the library. Salary $75 a month.

Now bad as this sounds, the principal was unconsciously paying the library profession a great compliment. His difficulty was that after having assigned each teacher a full load there remained four unassigned classes as well as some other curricular and extracurricular duties. Only a superteacher could hold down that kind of a superjob and in his mind the librarian knew everything and could probably teach everything. Unfortunately, this high opinion did not translate itself into higher salary, but even there noticeable improvement is occurring. Most city school systems now recognize the B.S. in L.S. as equivalent to the master's and worthy of extra salary. In some states, notably New York and California, librarians' salaries are comparable to those of department heads and supervisors rather than to those of teachers. Personally, I believe librarians are making a mistake by asking for as much salary as teachers get; I believe they should ask for and get more.

Ultimately, I believe every teacher will have enough library training to carry on library teaching effectively. I believe every librarian will be first and foremost a teacher and that gradually the two positions will merge and we will have library trained teachers of English, library trained teachers of the social studies, library trained teachers of the sciences, and of course always library trained teachers of boys and girls. This will be made possible by a reduction of the number of organizational duties now assumed by each school librarian. For example, the Wilson project of publishing school library catalogs cumulatively will largely eliminate the necessity for each school librarian doing her own cataloging and classification. Likewise centralized acquisitions for several school libraries either in one county, city or region, as well as centralization of all preparation routines should also do much to relieve the librarian from clerical duties and enable her to concentrate on the important bibliographic and reference functions accessory to good teaching.

A second major obstacle to the development of library education has been the old-fashioned textbooks. In a significant editorial, Fredric W. Melcher, Editor of *Publishers' Weekly*, asks is the textbook passing from the picture, and if so what is to be the fate of the textbook publisher?

If the question applies to the old-fashioned textbook, the answer unquestionably is "yes," the textbook is passing from the picture. In another few years it will be completely out. No one realizes that more practically than the publishers themselves. Time was when a textbook could be spotted almost a mile away — the stereotype cover, the drab page, the dull style. But not now. Walk out to the exhibit tables at any conference and you will have difficulty distinguishing between the wares of the general and the textbook publishers — at least from the standpoint of format.

Time was when we taught and talked children's literature as something entirely apart from school texts. But not now. If I may mention one and by no means the only set of readers, The Alice and Jerry books of Row, Peterson and Company, except for the covers which retain a "readerish" appearance, are comparable in type, illustrations, style, page make-up to any other attractive children's book. The famous Fascist readers of Italy and the modernistic Soviet readers of Russia point the way unmistakeably to a new era of schoolbooks.

Most striking of all is the work of the leading school encyclopedias. To most adults the pictures in *Life* and the style of *Time* are still something of an innovation. But the school encyclopedias years ago developed the picture and style technique to a point far beyond even what it is in those magazines today. In addition, through scientific selection of materials and proportionate allocation of space the school encyclopedia has succeeded in relating itself to the school program so vitally that it is virtually impossible to teach any school study effectively without them.

Ultimately, I believe the shift in teaching methods from the single text to many materials is bound to result in a greatly increased volume of books. This must be apparent to all progressive publishers. The rise of school libraries, the use of many books, pamphlets and periodicals where only one book was used before, the resulting increased attention to reading can not but enlarge the book business as never before. Competition, however, is certain to become keener as schools and state departments of education are staffed with librarians and library trained teachers and administrators qualified to select books for state lists with a discrimination not always exercised in the past.

This brings me to the last and perhaps most challenging change which may be accomplished by this library-centered education. We boast of one of the world's lowest illiteracy rates. We can also claim a quantity of printed material surpassed by few if any nations on the globe. Gradually the areas without library facilities are disappearing and in their place are coming attractive opportunities to read. Yet with these material advantages there is the tragic situation so ably expressed in the title of a recent book: The Illiteracy of Literates.

Yes, our people with very few exceptions can now combine the various letters into words and the words into ideas. But can they read? If they can, how account for the fact that an advertisement will stampede millions into buying a particular brand of cigarette because Mrs. Van Ritz Astorbilt says they are good for her complexion? Why will countless others purchase a mineral water whose properties have been proved harmful in less blatant but more reliable publications. What causes us, 100 million strong, to submit to guinea pig experiments? And more seriously still, why does so large a portion of our electorate fail to register an intelligent opinion or indeed any opinion at all?

Those of us who remember the World War recall how ability to read was exploited to whip us into a war frenzy. We know that one advertising agency has boasted that with control of certain organs of information they could make the American public think any way it wanted them to think.

The dangers and the possibilities of reading mastery must be apparent. An unscrupulous and selfish demagogue might by means of the press and other means of communication sway an entire nation to Fascism, Communism, or any other ism contrary to those American principles we hold dear. But a nation of discriminating readers would not be so easily persuaded.

The major duty of the school library like that of the school should be to carry reading instruction beyond the present elementary stages of mere technical proficiency into the field of reading discrimination. Critical and intelligent reading can come not from reading one textbook and reciting the opinion of one authority, but from reading many authorities and weighing one against the other, by selecting critically the good from the bad and thus developing a literacy in our young Americans that will never permit any individual, agency, or movement by means of the printed word to snatch from us those liberties and institutions we hold sacred.

Library Logistics in Ideological Warfare

I DON'T KNOW who your favorite radio announcer is. Regularly, I listen to Martin Agronsky at 8:00 every week-day morning.

In one of his recent broadcasts he described the pattern for Communist conquest.

If we may judge from the reports of the Korean war and of the Communist successes in China and elsewhere, the Russians are using three tangible weapons to support their military might. One of these, apparently, in Asia, consists of a sack of rice, the staple of Oriental food. The second tangible weapon is the land of the community, which is divided up among the people. The potency of these two weapons in making conquest permanent cannot be discounted.

But, to my way of thinking, the third weapon has the most lasting possibilities of all. This third weapon appears to be a library, composed of materials suited to the reading, listening and viewing capabilities of the people. If the people cannot read at all, the library consists of pictures or motion pictures. If they can read a little, there are simple books and pamphlets which tell the story. If the people are intellectually equipped, there are documents and journals to challenge their equipment.

Reprinted from *Peabody Journal of Education*, 29: 18-23, July, 1951, by permission of the publisher.

For a long time we have suspected that the Russians have taken the American idea of libraries and carried it possibly one step further, just as they have done in a good many scientific fields and technological development, for which up until recently we have been unwilling to give them credit.

We long have suspected that the Russians have extended our idea of library extension beyond the concepts of our most successful state programs.

But Russian library strength has been not only in the quantity of libraries and in coverage, but in the dynamics, which apparently has gone into the whole concept of library dissemination and research.

We can only piece a few facts together, exposed to us occasionally through the Iron Curtain, but from the few facts we have, we gather that Russian libraries are actively and categorically undertaking to indoctrinate the people wherever they can. This indoctrination is going on cunningly and with a great deal more scientific attention to communications than is generally found in this country. In short, I am inclined to believe that they have refined the techniques of reader guidance to a point where Communist propaganda can be made delectable to anyone, regardless of his educational background.

Now we in this country believe fundamentally that the strength of democracy lies in the belief that the people should know all the facts. Our libraries have gone on record as wishing to present to the people the best information that is available. In this sense, American libraries, if there were enough of them, and if they could devote themselves, could be a powerful weapon in the ideological war now being fought between the two ways of life.

To make of this library weapon a more potent force it would be necessary to do two things: first, increase the techniques of dissemination, and second, restudy and reorganize the system of research.

From the standpoint of dissemination, more attention has to be devoted both to quantity and to quality.

Quantitatively, we are confronted by the statistical fact that nearly a third of the population in the United States has no access to free public library service. If I were addressing the Public

Library Section now, I would say, "In the interest of national defense, it is immediately and urgently important that public library service be extended to all the people." This extension should be even more dispersed than at present, should go into the most remote rural areas as well as into every urban neighborhood. In regard to quality, libraries should take an even more active part in the creation of media of communication. Libraries, through first-hand studies of what their patrons read and look at and listen to, should contribute to the production by publishers, film producers, and radio and television companies more actively than is now done.

But this is primarily a college and university library group, and therefore I should like to concentrate upon the mobilization of research support.

There is no question that at the moment the U.S.A. and the U.S.S.R. are engaged in a research race. Contrary to belief, this race is not only in the area of the natural sciences and in technology, but in the social sciences and the humanities as well. Victory will go not only to the nation with the best specialists, but to the country which can organize its research resources in libraries most effectively.

That places a new challenge on the research libraries of this nation. It confronts the college and university libraries with an important problem in co-operation.

Last month in Atlanta, on the call of the Southern Board of Control on Regional Education, college and university presidents of the southern region met with representatives of Federal defense agencies and of other agencies concerned with research, to study methods in which the institutions of higher education in the South might contribute more effectively to defense research. It was pointed out that during the last war institutions of higher education in this region contributed only five percent of the total research carried out for Federal agencies. Part of the reason for the other ninety-five percent going to other regions was undoubtedly due to the greater library resources and the greater number of specialists available in those regions. But that was only part of the reason. I am sure that the rest of the reason was due to the fact that the institutions in the North had a better public relations program for contacting Federal agencies with contracts to offer and were, on the whole, better organized for research than we are in this region.

Aside from the selfish fact that we want to carry a larger burden of the research in this region, there is a very important national defense reason why the South should have a larger share of the research responsibility.

We hear much talk these days about dispersal — dispersal of government agencies, dispersal of business, dispersal of resources. There is a very sound reason for dispersal. Ever-present in our mind, of course, is the atomic bomb and the dangers from air attack. It is a well-known principle of air warfare that a concentrated target is more vulnerable. This question of dispersal versus concentration was fought and settled in the Second World War. We learned our lesson bitterly, for example, in the Philippines, where the ground forces insisted upon concentration of our airplanes as protection against sabotage, and the Air Force insisted upon dispersal for protection against air attack. Unfortunately, our planes were concentrated when the Japanese came over the Philippine Islands and destroyed most of the air force we then had.

For some time our philosophy of research has favored concentrated centers. We ourselves, in the 1930's, developed the notion that there should be a concentrated research center in Atlanta, another one in Nashville, a third in the Durham-Chapel Hill area, a fourth in New Orleans, and possibly a fifth in Texas. These concentrated research areas were compared with similar research areas in the big centers in the North.

There is nothing in warfare that can protect libraries and cultural institutions from destruction. In spite of desires of certain military men and statesmen to the contrary, libraries will be destroyed, and so will all the rare and precious materials that are housed in them. In view of that, the idea of concentrated research areas is not entirely in the interest of national defense.

Over and against that, certain technological trends are mitigating *against* the concept of concentrated research areas and *for* dispersal. Principally, we must consider the effect that the increasing quality and economy of reproduction will have against concentration and for dispersal. If the microcard and microfilm develop at the rate in which they have developed in the last few months and years, and if we continue to make progress with offset printing and other devices for reproduction, there will soon be no reason in the world why, for example, a full set of the *Justus Liebig Annalen* should be found in only one place in the Southeastern region. Microfilm and microcard may indeed provide a set of that very expensive journal, not only for every university library, but for every four-year college library in the Southeast.

For these two reasons, namely, the need for dispersal, accented by our world at war, and technological developments in duplication, the library philosophy of concentrated areas of research is likely to become antiquated. There is, indeed, a very good possibility that the scholar specialist, no matter where he is, may be in as good a position from the standpoint of library resources, to carry on his research as he would be anywhere else.

If this be true, then all at once every college, as well as every university library, finds a new and important role in the overall program of research for defense. All at once, every scholar, no matter where he may be located, every college, regardless of its proximity to a large library, may have an important part in the total program of research.

In recognition of this fact your Southeastern Library Association, which represents the 5,000 college and university, school, public, and special libraries in these nine states, has taken some important steps during the past few months.

One of these steps has already led to tangible results. Under a contract with the Tennessee Valley Authority several important scientific journal sets are in the process of being reproduced on microfilm. This project is under the direction of Dr. Lawrence Thompson of the University of Kentucky, who is Chairman of the SELA Committee on the reproduction of scientific journals. The grant of $7,000 from the Tennessee Valley Authority plus the hours of work by Dr. Thompson's committee, composed of members from each of the nine states, will soon result in a real boon to scholarship not alone in the Southeast but all over the United States. When the first phase of the project is completed July 1, there will be available at modest cost to all libraries microfilm reproductions of the most needed and scarce scientific journals.

A second important step is about to be taken, we hope in co-operation with the Board of Control on Southern Regional Education. It seems very important if the South is to undertake to carry its share of research in this Third World War that we know where and how much library support for research is available in the Southeast.

With that in mind the Southeastern, in co-operation with the Southern Board and, we hope, with the Southwestern Library Association, is about to embark upon an inventory of library resources in the South. This inventory would look forward to indicating just where library materials to support research in certain subject fields can be found. This inventory would bring the Downs list up-to-date and would provide a means for keeping all the libraries continuously informed of sources available to research in various subject areas.

It has been said many times that this is an ideological war. In any ideological war it is inescapable that *research* which produces ideas and *dissemination* which spreads them are important weapons. The arsenal for these weapons is, as has often been pointed out, the libraries of our country. In the interest of national defense let's mobilize our libraries. Let's accelerate extension for dissemination, and let's disperse our scholarly acquisitions. So reorganized, the libraries of America can supply our forces more effectively in the current world struggle. So conceived, libraries can contribute a new dimension to military logistics.

The Essence of Learning

OF COURSE all librarians are educators also. But school librarians are educators in a unique sense. In some ways, the school librarian is nearer to the educators' firing lines than his colleague in the college or university library. For one thing, the school librarian must be evaluated and certificated by the state agency first as a teacher. For another thing school librarians are virtually required to identify themselves with teacher organizations. Consequently, it is no surprise that school librarians as individuals have membership in the National Education Association as well as the American Library Association. But it is a real tribute to the American Association of School Librarians that it is the first division of ALA to gain divisional status in NEA as well. If any official recognition of the fact that librarians are also educators is necessary, we at long last have it, thanks to the school librarians.

Somehow, this achievement, the first all-librarian division in the colossal NEA, is a triumph for the whole library profession. It signals a long delayed recognition of the role of librarianship in education. Here is a symbolization of the fact that libraries not only support classrooms and librarians aid teachers, but that libraries, and librarianship in its own right, may present an educational philosophy espoused by no other segment of the pedagogical profession.

For many years my library soul has protested against the subordinated position assigned by professional education to librarianship. Tragically, too many librarians have acquiesced and even penlashed in the journals certain colleagues who did not appear to be up on the latest researches in child psychology and pedagogical method.

Reprinted from *Library Journal*, 86: 313-316, January 15, 1961, and *Junior Libraries*, 7: 1-4, January, 1961, by permission of the publisher. The essay here reprinted is from a speech delivered before the 1960 Conference of the New England Library Association.

I recall a certain university librarian colleague of mine who was forever repeating the shibboleth, "Books must follow the curriculum." One day the principal of the demonstration school, mimicking him, said to me, "Often as I walk down the hall thinking of our curriculum I am conscious of the fact that something is tiptoeing behind me."

The time has come to challenge this educational dogma. I recall how many times I have worked with curriculum developers who always ended by saying, "Now that we have a curriculum constructed will you develop a list of books to go with it?" In the article I wrote for the *Saturday Review* (March 22, 1958) which they made the editorial for the first National Library Week I said, "The book is the composite of man's communicability, his evidence of life."

I repeat this here and add *the book is the composite of the school curriculum*. Rather than the book following the curriculum, I believe a better course of study would result if the curriculum followed the book.

Nor is the curriculum the only pedagogical area in which we should assert ourselves. I believe libraries have within them the very essence of learning. With due respect to the scientific studies of child psychology, I hope that neither the psychologist nor the librarian will ever conclude that now at last we understand precisely how children learn. Indeed, the more I read in psychological literature the more I doubt some of the principles of learning espoused there.

Of course I can be put in my place summarily by pointing out that none of my theories has been scientifically demonstrated. But I am afraid I will persist stubbornly that the scientific method has as often as not led to mistaken conclusions. Study the history of education for evidences of reversals in theories about learning. Or compare debates among contemporary Watsonians, Freudians, Koffkans, Deweyites, and others. In my book there is still one to be heard from: J. B. Rhine. I agree with him that psychology has been too busy with physiology. It is parapsychology alone that considers the body less and the psyche more.

I have just experienced on Broadway that moving miracle of Helen Keller. On one occasion her teacher exclaims "Obedience is the basis of understanding." And we have been through that in education. A little later as she struggles with the blind, deaf, mute child she cries out in despair, "But obedience is not enough for understanding." With the pedagogical book before her at night after the child has at last fallen asleep, she masters all the psychology that science has been able to muster. Conscientiously she teaches touch spelling by the best scientific method. But yet there is no understanding in the child, nor real comprehension. "O, God," she prays. She herself had just conquered her own blindness. "O, God, you owe me a resurrection. Or do I owe you one? How do I teach understanding to a child short three of her senses?"

I shall not spoil the play or the book for you. The miracle transcends the scientific method. It has nothing to do with child psychology. It is out of this world, not in the trite sense of the colloquialism, but because in Hamlet's words, "There are more things in heaven and earth, Horatio,/Than are dreamt of in your philosophy." And these things come from meditation, and introspection, and inspiration. They belong to those eons that make our three score ten on earth sink into insignificance. And a scientific method bounded by the five senses of one of the tiniest planets in the universe simply doesn't have a chance of understanding. It behooves education to observe diligently the chief school unit that nourishes imagination and provides the atmosphere for meditation. *No scientific study will ever discover how many miracles of understanding are created in the school library.*

As a librarian, too, the whole professional literature of reading readiness has irritated me. It is probably scientifically sound. The accent seems to me to be in the wrong places. "Delay reading," conclude some investigators, "until the child is ready." This strikes me as a negative approach. With a librarian's bias I would advocate, "Expose babies to books as early as possible, even pre-natally. Let the infant be born in the presence of books, and do not let a single day pass that the baby and the book are not contiguous at least for a few minutes. The physiology will adjust to the psyche, I believe, without injury to the eye."

Nor can I refrain from resisting the pragmatic foundation of much of our educational philosophy. "Learning by doing" is a phrase popularized from the writings of John Dewey. It has been translated into the activity school. As an example, the child learns Latin by constructing a model of the Roman forum. Said the Latin teacher in my school cafeteria as she jumped up from lunch, "Since we've gone activity, I can't stay away from my room too long for fear the children will annihilate each other with hammer and saw." Taking a cue from *Orbis Pictus* we now illustrate everything, making sure that abstract ideas become concrete images. I am sure that my friend Edgar Dale who has done so much for reading had no intention of placing the book in an unfavorable position among instructional media. Yet many an audio-visual teacher so presents his "cone of experience" that students conclude the printed word is the lowest form of educational communication. Dr. Dale has himself said otherwise in his *Challenges to Librarianship* [essay].

I have long been an advocate of audio-visual media in libraries. In 1935 I introduced the first audio-visual course ever offered in an accredited library school. Florida and Florida State University Library School have for years championed the union of school libraries and audio-visual centers. In *Instructional Materials* (Ronald 1960), my latest book, I attempted to introduce the teacher to the whole range of learning resources at her disposal in a well-stocked school library or materials center. I cannot say better than I have said in that book (p. 100) that we must never underestimate the importance of abstract learning through the medium of the printed word: "What we must never forget is that there are still some children who learn better and more through reading than through almost any other kind of activity."

For a final contribution librarians have to offer to education, I turn to my reference specialty. Over the door of our former library building at Florida State University are the often quoted words, "The half of knowledge is knowing where to find it." I assume, therefore, if the nation's schools will make it possible for the librarian to perform her reference function, half of the job can be done right in the library.

Of course I believe that. And much more, too. Reference is the very essence of learning. I think I chose the profession of librarianship at the ripe age of 15 as much because of a reference discovery as for any other reason. We were studying magnetism in physics. As in preceding chapters of the textbook, I was suffering from lack of understanding. In despair I went to the library where I accidentally developed an approach that was novel for me. I consulted two encyclopedias and the indexes of four science books. Somewhere in those six references I found one that kindled my individual pile of dry fuel. A fire leaped up and in a flash I began to understand how the molecules arranged themselves. I read on and on for contrast and comparison, and even for contradictions. This was the element of learning. For me, understanding was born in that school library. I went to class with the first confidence I had ever had in physics. My recitation, especially when I pointed to a contradiction in the text, brought gasps from my classmates. My *A* was assured.

From this reference experience I gradually built a learning approach that helped me in college as well as in high school. Stimulated by my experience in magnetism, I made it an unfailing rule to begin each term with a reference overview of all the subjects in which I was enrolled. Because the encyclopedia is the composite of almost all of the other reference book types, I began by overviewing the subject of each course in one or more of the good sets. Unknown to me then, I had discovered the perfect preface to learning. The overview enabled me to anticipate what the teacher would teach in that course. If she developed the subject as I had been led to believe it should be developed by my reference book reading, I was properly gratified. If she did not, I would compare her treatment with the one I expected, and differ or accept. In any event, I was learning, forcing myself to try to understand.

Comparison and overview are only two of the aspects of the reference approach to learning. Who will gainsay the elements of documentation and bibliography, of spot checking and verifying, of the many habits of scholarship that are by-products of reference-book handling. You can see why the fourth R for me has always been *reference*.

I must restrain myself from developing further this reference devotion. My thesis is larger than the mere half of knowledge. When Carlyle wrote that the true university is a library, he was not merely providing a commencement quotation for an orator. He believed as I wrote for my address "The Library Arts College" (*School and Society* 1935) at the American Library Association meeting in

Chicago during the world's fair, the potential for learning in the library is greater than the potential for learning in the classroom.

This I believe today more than ever, after nearly four decades of library and education work. This I reassert to you my colleagues. And to the school librarians among you, especially, I add, we have an unparalleled opportunity. Our Sputnik-frustrated nation is casting desperately for a panacea to our real and imagined educational deficiencies. Through the National Defense Education Act they voted partial confidence in instructional media. Our schools are now ready, even if out of the desperation of national dissatisfaction, to turn to us as never before.

I pray God that we librarians will have the courage and the wisdom during these critical years ahead to harness the tremendous potential of libraries in the interest of better learning.

The Library in General Education

INADEQUATE LIBRARY USE has long been considered one of the major deficiencies of undergraduate instruction.

From the data in his study for the Association of American Colleges, Harvie Branscomb concluded "Undergraduates do not make very much use of the college or university book collection."[1] Comparable statements have been made by teachers, librarians, and even by the students themselves. In Kenneth Roberts' *Saturday Evening Post* article on one of our great midwestern universities[2] a student was quoted directly as saying if his teacher would turn him loose in the library he could learn more about his subjects than he possibly could in an equal number of classroom hours.

[1]For notes, see page 341.

Reprinted from *The Peabody Reflector*, 23: 131-132 ff., May, 1950, by permission of the publisher.

This dissatisfaction with library use in undergraduate instruction can be said to result not alone from the quantity of library use but from the quality of the materials assigned and from the nature of the assignments. Across the nation in college after college the most characteristic library assignments are still inclusive pages in text or reserve book. This pattern of undergraduate home work carries with it too often an undue emphasis on pages that parallels overemphasis on credits, with the resulting loss, in both cases, of an essential appreciation for knowledge. It is this rut of text and reserve over-dependence and the almost wholesale neglect of a vast and varied collection of library materials that have been largely responsible for inadequate library use in undergraduate instruction.

The rise of the general education concept in the undergraduate program has brought many revaluations, not the least of which has been a new look at library materials. Out of this new look has come (1) new emphasis on a wider range of instructional media and (2) new ways to employ the resources of changing libraries.

To the traditional text and supplementary reserve readings general education has added not only every variety of format for the printed word yet devised, but has besides enlisted the whole range of audio-visual materials. It has introduced quantity and variety not alone in the humanities and social sciences where library use has always been heaviest, but in the sciences and mathematics, as well.

For the purposes of classification, library materials may be grouped as follows:

1. The Printed Word.
   a. Books: text, reference and "great."
   b. Serials: periodicals, newspapers, government publications.
   c. Ephemera: pamphlets, broadsides, brochures.

2. Graphics.
   a. Flat pictures and stereographs.
   b. Charts, diagrams, tables.
   c. Maps and globes.
   d. Mock-ups, demonstrations.

3. Museum Objects.

4. Projections.
    a. Slides and film strips.
    b. Silent films.
    c. Sound films.
5. Sound.
    a. Radio and transcriptions.
    b. Recordings: disc, tape, wire.
    c. Television.

It is difficult to draw a line between traditional library materials and so-called audio-visual aids. All of the five classes of media can be found in most of our better American libraries. Besides the printed word libraries have long collected, organized and diffused pictures, charts, maps, globes. In the American public library, mock-ups, demonstrations, and museum objects have long been a prized part of exhibits. Up and down the land, in city after city, and on campuses uncounted, film forums have sprung up in library rooms where 16mm film showings are daily occurrences. The collection of slides, filmstrips and Kodachromes has always been an integral part of the library and today their demand is on the increase.

There remains only sound. Fifteen years ago, at least, there were libraries with individual earphones for readers in the reading room to listen to foreign language records or to an opera without disturbance to others in the room. And today, sound-proofed rooms provide access by library patrons to radio, recordings, and even television.

As the American library changes to encompass the newer media, general education surveys the entire range of library resources and seeks to employ each class of instructional materials with maximum effect.

In spite of recent phenomenal advances by other media there is no immediate danger of replacing the printed word.[3] Books, periodicals, newspapers and other printed sources still retain certain advantages of accessibility, timelessness, and convenience. These advantages have not always been apparent in undergraduate instruction because of an over-reliance on one or two types of books.

Textbooks. For example, textbooks, the most hallowed media of communication in college classes (next to the lecture, perhaps), have maintained an instructional importance, despite recent improvement in content and format, beyond their intrinsic worth. It is generally recognized that the textbook's primary function is not to contribute to knowledge but merely to summarize existing information. Often the information is sixth-hand, the digests and redigests of textbook writers before. Removed by that many hands from the original contribution no wonder the undergraduate so frequently fails to thrill at a discovery that comes to him in the form of so many pages for tomorrow.

To insure this separation from the source some college instructors insist on library duplication of texts in some cases to as many as forty copies. The philosophy behind that type of duplication guarantees that not only will all students study the same content at the same time, but in exactly the same form, and from the same point-of-view. It is a lock-step learning against which the whole soul of general education must cry out.

Why write and speak of individual differences. The single text denies the existence of any variations in background. It insists that one presentation, and only one, can fit all learning needs of the undergraduate.

Yet the textbook, intelligently used, has a place in undergraduate learning. As a syllabus, as an outline of course scope, as an organizational guide, the textbook can serve a useful function in the general education area. The textbook's usefulness steadily declines, however, as it tends to become the only printed word in undergraduate instruction.

Reserve Readings. In the past a major portion of most college circulation has been reserve reading. Specific pages in certain books assigned to whole classes at a time have meant necessity for some library machinery to insure equal access. That machinery is the reserve book system with its regulations of use within the room or overnight charge.

Now, while the reserve book system has certain advantages over the single-text, such as varieties of presentation, frequent reference to the original sources, and different points of view, there remains the undesirable emphasis on page references rather than on subject. There is the further fact of complexity of circulation and consequent waste of time in securing books. And there is the general turbulence of the reserve book room, frequently anything but a quiet place for study.

For these reasons of disadvantage and for the reason that faculty reserves fail to stimulate student use to the degree expected, from 25% to 50% of the reserve books are almost never circulated. In certain college libraries careful checks of reserves have revealed that some titles hopefully placed on shelves by faculty have failed to tempt a single student even once. As a result the reserve book like the textbook has tended to play an even less significant role in general education.

Great Books. More recently the classics in all fields have returned to prominence. Throughout the nation the so-called "Great Books" have become the content of both undergraduate residence instruction and adult extension courses. Once again the *Harvard 5-foot Shelf*, the St. John's list, the *Good Reading* collection sponsored by the National Council of Teachers of English Committee on College Reading[4] have become popular indoor sports. General education has been quick to harness this interest in the integrated areas to good advantage. The "Great Books" movement has the advantage of returning the student to original sources.

Reference Books. Some 5,000 titles in the world not meant to be read through from cover to cover but intended to be referred to for specific information are known as reference books. Dictionaries, encyclopedias, annuals, handbooks, biographical directories, atlases, indexes and bibliographies are some of the classes of reference books. Their potentialities in general education are only beginning to be recognized.

Reference books have these advantages for undergraduate instruction: they are authoritative, they are compact, they are organized for quick use. Reference books have this disadvantage: they are comparatively unknown to faculty and students.

The shelves of the main reading room of every college library are lined with so-called "R" books. Except for dictionaries, encyclopedias, atlases, and possibly almanacs, reference books are unused.

Even these four types of reference books are often improperly used. Take the case of the English teacher who assigned her class to

look up the meaning of a word in the "big" dictionary. The indolent
pupils looked up the first meaning and stopped. Half of them were
rewarded with a "right" and half reprimanded with a "wrong,"
simply because two different "big" dictionaries had been used.
Webster's *New International* gives the oldest meaning of a word
first; Funk and Wagnall's *New Standard* gives the commonest first.
Surely if assignment to these two dictionaries is to be made in terms
of "big," then nothing less than "colossal" can distinguish reference
to the *O. E. D.*

Or take the case of the freshman who looked in the *Britannica*
for something on "phalanx" and finding no article silently thanked
God and satisfied himself he had fulfilled his assignment. No one
had told him about the difference between long-article and short-
article arrangements. In the *Britannica* some 500,000 subjects are
treated in only 40,000 articles. Unless the 24th volume index is consulted the chances of finding a subject in that encyclopedia are no
better than two in twenty-five.

Aside from dictionaries and encyclopedias, however, there are
many other types of reference books with general education potentials. Like dictionaries and encyclopedias these other reference tools
have the advantage of high authority combined with superior treatment and arrangement. Only a multi-million dollar work such as
these great reference sets often are can afford to enlist the pre-
eminent subject specialists and the experienced editors to present
information with accuracy and freshness.

For example, there are these representative reference sets with
still untapped resources for general education: the *Dictionary of
National Biography* and the *Dictionary of American Biography*,
rich in readable and scholarly accounts of the work of notables in
all of the integrated areas; the *Encyclopedia of the Social Sciences*,
unlimited in quality and quantity of information for the humanities,
health and personal adjustment, communication, and even the biological sciences, as well as the area included in its title; Thorp's
Dictionary of Applied Chemistry with its applications for both the
biological and physical sciences.

And then at random, let us consider some single reference volumes from the standpoint of general education assignments. What

does the *Statesman's Yearbook* mean to the undergraduate who waits in line for a social science reserve book? Does he know that in *S. Y.* there are maps of current and recent boundary disputes, brief descriptions, up-to-date, of all the governments of the world, economic and other statistics, identification of heads of nations? Or consider the *American Yearbook*. Without exception the undergraduate can find there a summary of the last year's developments in any subject area or human activity prepared by the learned society or trade or professional association most concerned. Van Nostrand's *Scientific Encyclopedia*, Hourtiq's *Encyclopedia of Art*, Grove's *Dictionary of Religion and Ethics*, the *Dictionary of American History* and Larned's *History for Ready Reference*, I daresay are only a few reference sources that many undergraduates have failed to experience so that they might concentrate on texts and reserves less challenging and inviting.

Serials and Ephemera. What librarians call serials are publications issued in parts at regular intervals and comprise periodicals, newspapers, pamphlets or ephemera, and government publications. The use of these classes of printed-word media ranges in most undergraduate instruction from generous in some courses for periodicals and newspapers to restrained for pamphlets and government documents.

It is a tenet of good college library selection that there shall be at least one subscription to a national newspaper like the *New York Times* and another subscription to a good regional daily like the *Louisville Courier-Journal*. These shall be in addition to local and state newspapers.

Further, since the *Readers' Guide* indexes over 100 carefully selected American and Canadian popular periodicals, and the *International Index* analyses the content currently of more than 200 scholarly journals there is usually a fair representation of these nearly 400 periodicals subscribed to by the library.

Now, the question is how many of these 400 periodicals and newspapers are a part of daily undergraduate assignments? With some concern the faculty must take notice of the teacher testimonials on what the *Reader's Digest* has meant to class instruction. That concern relates not to the controversy over the value of that one periodical but rather to the tendency in the periodical field that is the counterpart for the single textbook device.

Comparison of points-of-view, differences of organization, variations in presentation of fact contribute to the learning process. The single-text, the one-magazine, the only-newspaper pattern of communication carries with it the menace, intentional or not, of a "line" — of a "line" as fraught with danger as any "line" forced on the people of a totalitarian state. If for no other reason than to insure democratic communication, variety and multiplicity of media in general education are essential.

Today, the largest publisher of the printed word in the world is the United States Government. From its great Printing Office and from the processing equipment of its many bureaus pour an endless stream of timely, authoritative, and increasingly readable information. There are guides to these materials that have tremendous potentials for general education. Generous use of these government documents and of pamphlets issued by many private agencies will greatly relieve the pressure on text and reserve books.

Book use in the general education areas at Florida State University shows a growing emphasis on the "Great Books" and "Reference Books" and a declining interest in texts and reserve assignments. This is especially noteworthy in the communications and in the humanities areas.

In the syllabus for Freshman English, for example, study is made of 29 basic reference tools whose value throughout the four college years should be constant. These tools include the following careful selection:

DICTIONARIES (3) *Webster's New International; Funk and Wagnall's New Standard;* the *O. E. D.*

ENCYCLOPEDIAS (4) *Americana, Britannica, Columbia, New International*

BIOGRAPHICAL DIRECTORIES (5) *D. A. B., D. N. B., Who's Who in America, Who's Who, Webster's Biographical Dictionary*

ATLASES (3) *Rand McNally Commercial, Hammond New World, Goode School*

SERIAL INDEXES (3) *Readers' Guide, International Index, N. Y. Times Index*

YEARBOOKS (5) *World Almanac, Britannica Book of the Year, Statesman's Yearbook, American Yearbook, Statistical Abstract*

QUOTATIONS AND CONCORDANCES (4) *Bartlett, Stevenson, Strong, Bartlett's Concordance to Shakespeare*

PAMPHLETS (1) *Vertical File Service Catalog*

GOVERNMENT PUBLICATIONS (1) *Monthly Catalog*

With these basic reference tools the student is armed for many academic problems in his college career. Because of the outstanding authorities who edit and contribute to these sources, the undergraduate is in a position to meet first-hand rather than sixth-hand the results of investigation and research.

An examination of the syllabi for the integrated humanities work reveals seven books in the first, six in the second, and five in the third quarter of the course. Although these titles are listed under the heading "Textbooks" only one of the eighteen, McKinney and Anderson, *Music in History*, published by the American Book Company, can be said to resemble the traditional textbook. Sixteen are "Great Books"— *Iliad, Oedipus Tyrannus, Aeneid; Bible, Republic, Divine Comedy, Hamlet, Don Quixote, Moliere's Plays, Discourse on Method, Utilitarianism, Destiny, Faust* and *War and Peace*. One, Helen Gardner's *Art Through the Ages*, is a basic reference book.

Other printed-word media increasingly effective especially in the social sciences area are so-called serials and ephemera. The syllabus for Introduction to Contemporary Civilization, while not free from reserve and textbook readings, shows a generous dependence on such significant periodicals as the *Annals of the Academy of Political and Social Science*, that distinguished bimonthly which features one socially significant topic in each issue, as well as frequent reference to articles in *Harper's, Atlantic, Foreign Affairs, American Sociological Review*, and *American Journal of Sociology*.

An Audio-Visual Service in the School of Library Training and Service undertakes to provide for the general education program the classes of library materials known as graphics, museum objects, projections and sound.

Graphics. This category includes flat pictures. In the University Library a well-organized picture collection is at the disposal of the general education classes. The University Photographic Service, part of the Audio-Visual Laboratory, takes and develops additional photographs. Charts, maps, globes and posters, too, are made available for class use.

Museum Objects. These are included in various campus collections, notably the Inca Museum and the scientific collections housed in various departments on the campus. It is increasingly considered a library function to index and act as a clearing house for all such resources.

Projections. Glass slides, film strips, silent and sound movies are the most common projected materials. But there are other projections, too. For example, a special microprojector enables biology micro-slides to be projected on a screen for class use. Microfilm and microcard readers reproduce whole rare books and manuscripts. The opaque projector enables large classes to view small museum objects.

Sound. Radio and recordings — disc, tape and wire — have been enlisted by general education in many new and ingenious ways. Humanities, for example, lists the following audio-visual aids for the course:

Illustrated lectures on art, dance, and music units.

Recordings of parts of literary works (in the original).

Recordings of extant music.

Exhibits in libraries.

Art exhibits brought to the campus.

University artist series.

Trips to Ringling Art Museum.

Motion pictures of Greek plays and dances.

In the health and personal adjustment and in the biological science area, showing of the McGraw-Hill film "Human Reproduction" to nearly 2,000 students in groups of twenty have provided some of the most stimulating class periods.

During the tense, dramatic twelve hours between twilight of the

1948 presidential election night and dawn of the following day the Audio-Visual Service recorded the radio broadcasts of returns. As soon as Mr. Dewey conceded defeat the staff which had sat up all night to do the tape recording edited the tape for a 50-minute class period. For the general education students the day after election there was provided one of the most effective media for understanding our phenomenon of a presidential election. That tape-recording is a significant part of the library for general education.

Post-war General Education has brought a new emphasis to library materials. With all due respect to Mark Hopkins something more than the "log" is needed. Nor is the textbook or the reserve book or the lecture alone an adequate supplement.

General education has been more willing to use the whole range of expanding library media from textbook to television. The integrated areas have shown a willingness to turn to a variety of printed-word and audio-visual sources. As never before, undergraduate instruction through General Education has employed film, radio, graphic, reference book and serial for day-by-day assignments. The result has been a broader subject understanding to keep pace with the intent of the integrated areas.

As General Education advances on all fronts it will claim as one of its greatest achievements the first adequate instructional use of library resources on the undergraduate level.

---

1 Branscomb, Harvie. *Teaching with Books* (Chicago: American Library Association, 1940), p. 37.
2 Roberts, K. L. "Murmuring Michigan," *Saturday Evening Post*, vol. 206 (1934), p. 10.
3 Duhamel, Georges. *In Defense of Letters* (New York: Graystone Press, 1939).
4 Penguin Books, first edition, November, 1947, in its first 11 printings distributed 340,000 copies of this 35-cent paper book.

The Library Arts College: A Possibility in 1954?

THE SPONSOR of any untried plan, no matter how worth while, faces at the outset two discouraging types of criticism. There are first of all those reactionary critics who defend the *status quo* by hurling charges of charlatanism or radicalism at any proponent of change, without pretending to examine the proposal itself. And then, there are those, of course, who will listen kindly and tolerantly to the presentation of a reform, and at the conclusion dismiss it as Utopian and fanciful.

To the first group of critics the sponsor of the present plan can merely say solemnly and with all the sincerity at his command that he honestly believes the changes he proposes are vital to the education of our young men and women, and therefore important to society. It is somewhat easier to tell the second group of critics that the library arts college idea is not new, that it has been predicted for over a half century, and that trends in current college reform point inevitably to the consummation of the plan, possibly before the assigned 1954 date.

Every librarian has used the Carlyle quotation, "The true university is a collection of books." That pioneer historian of pedagogy, Gabriel Compayré, commenting on Abelard's ability as a lecturer, prophesied the downfall of classroom methods over a half century ago, when he wrote in his epochal work:

> Human speech, the living word of the teacher, had then an authority, an importance, which it has lost in part *since books, everywhere distributed, have, to a certain extent, superseded oral instruction*. At a time when printing did not exist, when manuscript copies were rare, a teacher who combined knowledge with the gift of speech was a phenomenon of incomparable interest. . . .

Reprinted from *School and Society*, 41: 100-114, January 26, 1935, by permission of the publisher.

How much more strongly Monsieur Compayré would have stated this thought had he lived to witness the replacement of the single-textbook method by our modern reserve book system can only be surmised.

If time permitted, a series of statements by educators and librarians culled from writings and speeches of the last half century and arranged chronologically could be presented here to support the contention that the education of the future will inevitably be a library education, that is, an education which will be centered in the library. A few such quotations may suffice. For example, in the National Education Association proceedings of 1889, the U. S. Commissioner of Education, W. T. Harris, is quoted as declaring, "The school is set at the task of teaching the pupil how to use the library in the best manner — that, I take it, *is the central object toward which our American schools have been unconsciously tending.*"

The present president-elect of the American Library Association, writing in the *Library Journal* for November, 1910, quoted President Harper, of the University of Chicago, as follows:

> That factor of our college and university work, the library, fifty years ago almost unknown, today already the center of the institutional intellectual activity, half a century hence, with its sister, the laboratory, . . . *will by absorbing all else have become the institution itself.*

Nor have these remarks come from educationists alone. In 1916, Librarian Richardson made a startling substitution for Mark Hopkins on his end of the log when he declared,

> It is conceivable that a university should be a university, and a student get a university education if the university consisted only of a library and a student, without a lecturer, tutor, or preceptor, or research professor, or librarian — absolutely only a student and a library on a desert island.

We pass by the hosts of criticisms directed against the American college during the two decades following Librarian Richardson's observation, omitting such readable if not absolutely accurate books as Upton Sinclair's "Goose-Step" and Abraham Flexner's "Universities," for the words of a college professor and a college student.

The professor is Carter Davidson, writing on the "University of the Future" in the *North American Review* for March, 1931:

The faculty and the better students find the lecture and classroom recitation repetitious, boring, and a waste of time; the inferior students feel that lectures are hard to understand, and that the classroom recitations are too rapid, failing to make clear the more difficult problems.

The student is Kenneth Roberts' University of Michigan composite (referred to by the chairman), who when asked if he could suggest a remedy for the lack of scholarship in the "lit" school shot back:

I certainly can! I came here to study and if somebody'd tell me what to study, I could do more by myself, in my own room and in a library, than I could by tramping around to a lot of lectures. . . . I don't get much of anything out of classes. . . .

If these few quotations appear to deal harshly with the conventional college and the sacred faculty we college librarians so humbly serve, look at what current reform has done to American higher education. The 31st yearbook of the National Society for the Study of Education lists 128 reforms which differ only in the degree of instructional responsibility placed on the library. Whether the innovation is styled honors reading, as at Swarthmore, or autonomous courses, as at Antioch, whether the teacher appointed to instruct is called tutor, as at Harvard, or preceptor, as at Princeton, or even professor of books, as at Rollins, whether courses are abolished, as at Chicago or Olivet, and comprehensive examinations instituted, the educational department fundamentally affected is the college library. Current college reformers have at last begun to realize that the material unit of cultural education is the book, and that actually, as well as oratorically, the library is the liberal arts' laboratory. Only the conception of the library as the college and the college as the library remains prerequisite to the birth of the library arts college.

Just how do these trends affect us as college librarians? In the first place, I should like to make a distinction between educational librarianship on the one hand and research librarianship on the other. This is fundamental because I believe the two (education and research) are as incompatible in the library as they are in education on the secondary school and college levels.

The notion is rapidly gaining ground in college circles that a good researcher is not necessarily a good teacher. Indeed, there are those courageous enough to declare positively that the instructor engaged in research is invariably a poor teacher. No small part of the blame for the inferiority of undergraduate instruction can be traced to the fact that every American college is anxious to become a university engaged in research. The college president is forever exhorting his faculty to produce, because he knows he can interest foundations in studies much more easily than he can in that intangible something called "good teaching." As a result, the college neglects its real job — the training of young men and women. If the truth were told, a high positive correlation would be found to exist between the amount of time and energy expended by the college faculty on research and the amount of time and energy devoted by the students to extra-curricular activities. Mutually bored by the learning process as carried on in the classroom, the teacher seeks for fame and advancement through research, and the pupil, left to his own resources, endeavors to while away the four years' time as pleasurably as possible in the fraternity houses and stadia.

It is not the purpose of this paper to disparage the recent movement to create research librarianships. So long as American universities continue to produce tons of studies, useful and otherwise, each year, there will be need for research libraries and their staffs, whose duties will include the acquisition and organization of printed material *ad infinitum*, and the provision of even larger quarters for their accommodation.

Far different is the function of the educational library, such as the average undergraduate college should have. Its collection should be highly selective and definitely limited in size and scope. Whereas the research library's book selection problem may be solely one of acquisition, the educational library will be equally concerned with elimination. As protection against the nuisance of research ambitions, the college collection should have a maximum, say 35,000 volumes, imposed upon it, beyond which its collection may *never* expand. Each year the college may undertake to purchase 500 new titles, on condition it weed out 500 old works from its collection for discard or for presentation to some ambitious research university endeavoring each year to report a bigger and better library. In this way only the number will remain static; the educational library's contents will always include the basic books, plus an ever-changing collection of ephemeral material. The result will be a highy serviceable educational library with abundant material to furnish a true culture to young people who want it. Another result of this selectivity will be to eliminate the necessity for providing expansion in college library buildings. Contrary to the Carnegie standard, I see no reason for planning future expansion in a college library building, if those responsible for book selection do a full job.

With the collection definitely limited in size and the actual titles standardized by some such basic list as that prepared under Mr. Shaw's direction, the acquisition and organizational duties in the college library will be reduced considerably and rendered largely routine. For example, it is entirely likely that college titles will be purchasable completely classified and catalogued, or that perhaps the H. W. Wilson Company will issue book catalogs cumulatively in which each college will be able to indicate its own holdings. In any event, it is very unlikely that the services of a highly trained cataloger and classifier will ever be needed in an educational library.

The question then arises what, if any, will be the librarian's duties? Primarily, the professional librarian will be a teacher. The positions of librarian and professor will merge. Every college instructor will be library trained; every college librarian will be either a professional teacher in some such field or a semi-professional housekeeper performing the necessary routines accessory to library education.

With this preliminary interpretation of higher educational trends, it is now possible to look at the library arts college of 1954. A somewhat more detailed description of the plan has been placed in Professor Austin's hands, and no doubt his comments will elaborate the bare outline given here. The plan resulted from the writer's undergraduate experiences, which, like those of many other college students, convinced him he could learn much more in the library reading than he could by attending most classes. Since then, the plan has gradually developed an ambition to undertake undergraduate instruction to a small group of college men with a selected book collection of not over 1,000 titles, three library-trained instructors, and a small amount of equipment.

At the outset it should be realized that the library arts college is merely the logical culmination of such current trends in American higher education as are exemplified by honors courses, comprehensive examinations and other reforms of the last decade. Unencumbered by outworn appendages, the library arts college benefits from advantages minimized by the transitory experiments of today. It differs from the conventional college in at least five essentials.

In the first place, the library arts college reverses the conventional college's practise of compulsory, regular class attendance supplemented by voluntary and irregular library reading. The library arts college student is definitely scheduled for supervised reading periods and permitted to ask for a class meeting whenever he feels his readings have failed to answer questions in his own mind. The supervisor of the reading period is a library-trained subject-matter teacher. When the student reports to the history reading room for his history reading period, he finds there a history teacher thoroughly trained in library methods, who, among other things, combines the duties of the history instructor and the reference librarian.

In the second place, all instructional quarters, like classrooms, reading rooms and laboratories, are concentrated in the campus' one educational building — the library. A plan for such a building drawn to scale is available among my notes for anyone who cares to examine it. In general, the drawing calls for four units, one for each of the three subject divisions — humanities, natural sciences, social sciences — and a fourth for administrative and general reading quarters.

In the third place, the instructional scheme employs a principle of the Lancastrian schools which influenced American educational development in the early years of the nineteenth century, and which disappeared only because of improper conditions. Briefly, the principle calls for upper-class students to tutor lower-class students. This practise is mutually beneficial since it insures individual instruction for each lower classman and excellent training for each upper classman. Beginning teachers frequently attest they learned more about their major subject the first year they taught it than they learned in all their undergraduate study. Obviously, when a student has to know his lesson well enough to make it clear to an underclassman, that student not only masters his material, but what is more important, he is able to express himself clearly on the subject. This type of tutoring, reinforced by faculty supervision, supplemented by occasional inspirational lectures, and checked by the requirement of frequent papers, tests and a final comprehensive examination, will do much to restore scholarship to its rightful place on the college campus.

As for the faculty members themselves, they will be library-trained, subject-matter experts, but not specialists in the restricted sense which describes our present research professors who teach only incidentally. The chemistry man, for example, will not be so thoroughly consumed by his interest in colloids that he will be unable to supervise a general reading course in science. It is very likely that he will be able to express an intelligent opinion on James Joyce or the Herbartian influence in American education. But above all, he will be vitally interested in the young people he teaches, study their development as zealously as the average researcher does his experiment, and be as proud of the young man or woman he graduates into society as the average scientist is about a notable discovery.

Finally, the curriculum, instead of including a great number of frequently unrelated courses, will represent a carefully planned reading program intended to acquaint the student with man's accomplishments of the past and problems of the present. There is no more direct method of achieving this end than through the reading of the right books. To the library-trained teacher of the future is assigned the task of selecting intelligently the right book for the right student at the right time. That American Library Association motto might well be adopted as the major aim of our library arts college education.

The Undergraduate and His Library

WITH SOME of the mystery and much of the sense of destiny that has heralded each nuclear and space advance in recent years, I am tempted to open this eleventh lecture with the breathless announcement that we are on the verge of a breakthrough in undergraduate education. All the signs point to an early stilling of the cacophony that has dinned "what's wrong with the American college?" The evidence is in the three letters "UGL."

The Undergraduate Library, although a recent phenomenon in higher education, has been in the making for a great many years. We are told, indeed, that the Harvard College Records as early as 1765[1] cited the need for separate library facilities for undergraduates. Certainly by the end of the last century when German research specialization had all but overwhelmed the remaining campus vestiges of generalists, it was apparent the undergraduate would soon become the forgotten little man of American higher education.

Undergraduates who choose to attend large universities for their college education are confronted by one of two kinds of library situations. If they attend institutions like Princeton or Chicago, they will find no separate library selected to meet their class and recreational reading needs from freshman through senior year. Instead they will be expected to use from the several million volumes primarily related to research whatever they choose for their instructional needs. "In principle," the Princeton librarian contends, "the undergraduate should be constantly confronted by books a little beyond his grasp. . . ."[2]

[1]For notes, see page 360.

Reprinted from *University of Tennessee Library Lectures: Numbers 10-11-12, 1958-1960*, edited by LaNelle Vandiver (Knoxville, Tennessee: University of Tennessee, 1961. Copyright © 1961, the University of Tennessee) by permission of the publisher. The essay here reprinted is Number Eleven in the University of Tennessee Library Lecture Series; this lecture was delivered in Knoxville on April 15, 1959.

Chicago, which tried a separate undergraduate library in 1931 in connection with the so-called Chicago plan abandoned it in 1942. Although the library was established for the dual purpose of supplying books to prepare students for the comprehensive examinations and to encourage undergraduates to read beyond the assignments, in the words of the Chicago librarian ". . . students under the Chicago Plan . . . borrowed from their library only the books they were required to read."[3]

Despite these two negative experiences, an increasing number of universities, since World War II, have moved to provide separate library facilities for undergraduates. Without in any way curtailing the college students' access to the great university research collections, state universities like Colorado, Florida State, Michigan, Nebraska, New Mexico, Oklahoma and the municipal University of Cincinnati have proved that carefully selected and attractively housed separate undergraduate libraries have not only increased support for classroom instruction but have stimulated considerable voluntary reading. In connection with the latter a revival of "lists of books every college graduate should have read" before receiving his degree is taking the campus.

Symbolic of this surge to the undergraduate library is the picture many of you saw in the March 9 issue of *Life* over the legend:

"In scholarly confinement math major John Kasdan props up his shoeless feet for comfort as he studies his Roman history in a Lamont alcove walled entirely by books."[4]

Harvard's commitment to the separate undergraduate library is so emphatic that when the Lamont gift made it possible not only a separate room but a separate building was created. It has three main floors and two mezzanines constituting eight levels in all. Two of these levels are underground and one of them has a tunnel leading to the Widener Research and the Houghton Rare Book and manuscript collections. Stacks are in the center of five levels, each with three wide aisles through them making book accessibility virtually inescapable. Although the Lamont catalogue[5] contains about 39,000 entries there are approximately 100,000 volumes in the Library itself. In addition to the printed books there are also audio-visual formats, such as disc recordings for the Poetry Room, FM receivers for good radio broadcasts, a Printing and Graphics collection, and a viewing room for documentary films.

On a more limited scale separate undergraduate reading rooms have been created in a number of large universities. Basically the UGL contains from about 12,000 to 100,000 carefully selected books and other materials housed in a room separate from the university collection. The separated library materials are intended to provide (1) support for undergraduate courses, including reserve and other classroom assigned readings, and (2) opportunities for enrichment, discovery and entertainment.

It is the second provision, as often as not, that has brought question and opposition to the whole idea of a separate collection. The contention is that the library has no business competing with the professor and the classroom for the undergraduate's attention. Whatever learning goes on in the college is a matter between the professor and the student. The library's business is to provide the books that the professor prescribes for the student.

With this position this paper takes direct issue. There is no question that professor and student are essential elements in undergraduate learning. But so are the library and the librarian. What is more, by the very nature of learning, the library is in a position to provide the breakthrough for which all of the critics of higher education today are yearning. In short, the argument of this paper is that the present relationship between classroom and library is undergoing a complete reversal and that inevitably class meetings now scheduled regularly will become as voluntary and irregular as today's reading in the library is, and that reading room periods will be scheduled regularly. Furthermore, the librarian who has fought for and defended his faculty status largely on a qualification basis will increasingly be able to convince doubters by his sharply augmented teaching responsibilities.

As we look at the American undergraduate today there is no one fact that stands out more than the range of his ability and interests. Never before in the history of the world has a nation undertaken to provide higher education for all of its young people. Even in England today where the "Red Brick" university has begun to appear, higher education is directed toward the top ten per cent, the intellectual upper crust. This is quite different from our U.S. campus climate, from the Joe and Jane College we know with their "togetherness" in sorority and stadium, their affinity for large classes with actor-like instructors where they can see and be seen. According to one so-called wit, American undergraduates seek help from only two books: mother's cook book and father's checkbook. Recently, when a professor was asked how many students there are at the University of Michigan, he replied, "About 10%."

James Thurber has stereotyped part of the 90% with his story of the much maligned football player, in a reminiscence of his economics class at Ohio State. As I recall the story, the big Michigan game was approaching. What stood between the Buckeyes and victory over their arch Wolverine rival was the mid-term examination of their great tackle, a wonderful physical specimen with a jaw-breaker of a name something like Malinowski. Contrary to popular opinion his economics professor was a football fan who was determined to help win that Michigan game. Conscientiously, therefore, he announced in advance that the mid-term would be an oral, and that each student would be asked one question.

One can well imagine how much time the professor spent formulating the football hero's question. It must be pertinent to the subject of the course, capable of being answered incorrectly as well as correctly, yet so free of hazard that success for even so doubtful an economist as Malinowski would be certain. This was the question when it came the turn of Malinowski to answer:

"Name one form of transportation."

Thurber describes eloquently the breathless hush that enveloped the classroom as ed and coed outprayed the conscientious professor for gridiron victory. But alas, the body of the big tackle sat silent and frozen in his seat, except for the back of his neck, which Thurber described from his vantage point directly behind, as suddenly breaking out into a hundred beads of dew.

"Think Malinowski, think. How did you manage to get to Ohio State?" the professor prompted him.

"Oh," said Malinowski, much relieved, "that's easy. The alumni are paying me!"

"No, no," the professor hastily added. "Take your time. You didn't obviously understand the question, and so of course we won't count your answer." By this time the students had begun to support the professor. Arms were moving piston fashion all over the room. From the back came a faint "choo choo" and even a simulated locomotive whistle, and at last Malinowski said the one word "train." A completely exhausted class was immediately dismissed by a coronary-case professor.

If the Thurber stereotype really represents one extreme of the undergraduate range in American colleges it is only fair to cite the problem at the other end. That the upper ten percent will more than hold their own in any academic weather is abundantly demonstrated by our Phi Beta Kappas and Phi Kappa Phis. Unfortunately, these gifted undergraduates are chained to the learning pace of that mythical average that bulges the middle of the professional pedagogue's bell-shaped curve.

An illustration can be taken from one of my own recent classes. A senior girl who had nearly knocked the top out of every intelligence test that had ever been given her sat through a period obviously bored by elementary bibliographic instruction most of the rest of the class needed desperately and labored over with endless questions. Throughout the deliberations she looked at her watch frequently, put it to her ear to assure herself, but graciously refrained from shaking her wrist in an effort to hasten time. Challenged by this and the opportunity at the end of the hour to analyze Rollo May's recent book on Existentialism, and her apparently aroused attention, I could not help tossing a look in her direction that said, "Now try that on for size."

The contrast of Thurber's tackle and my Miss IQ places in relief the difficulties of our American college learning. As long as higher education belonged only to the top ten percent — the students who can cope with the abstract as well as the applied — the professor could present a single lecture and make one assignment with reasonable expectation of universal appeal and fulfillment. But once the bars were let down and a college education became the right of every young man and woman in the land, the range of individual differences stretched beyond the compass of the most carefully prepared single lesson plan.

Let this be clearly understood. I believe in higher education for all. What the critics of American higher education have almost universally failed to understand is the magnitude of the task that now confronts our colleges and universities. Popular higher education is a necessity for national survival. Against the perspective of history, at least one contributing cause of the decline of nations has been the widening gulf in understandings between leaders and followers. The top ten percent have tended in the past to move so far away from the people that almost two different languages have developed. As a result revolution, peaceful or violent, has inevitably followed.

The question today is not whether we shall provide higher education for all the people, but rather what and how. Opinions on what differ most often on the subjects proper in a college course of study. There is some justification for alarm over the inroads of applications, or as liberal arts partisans call them, "trade subjects." These subjects are concerned with making a living, with things rather than with ideas. They have disturbed the austerity of academic introspection with restless activity and efficiency gadgets. Courses in cooking and baking science, driver education and first aid, preparation for marriage and infant care and countless other skills and techniques have accented a material here and now. At the same time reduced concern with ideas and abstract thought has made something less of today's campus than we have come to expect of higher education.

That is not to say with the extreme liberal arts advocates that only certain subjects have predatory rights in a college curriculum. Important as languages and philosophy, history and economics, biological and physical sciences are to the education of man and the culture of society, they are by no means the only subjects worthy of liberal education. Much as purists look down on courses in pedagogy, it is my firm belief that no traditional course in philosophy or literature I ever had on the way to my bachelor of arts degree was as rich in ideas as a philosophy of education course I had with the late Michael Demiashkevich at Peabody College in this state. I have also the temerity to believe that the reference course I have taught these many years has many of the elements of liberal arts I tried to absorb in my own English literature undergraduate major. The truth to me is that the quality of liberal education is not so much a characteristic of any subject as it is of the approach to that subject.

And that brings me to the main thesis of this paper. The primary reason for the failure of much of our college education today can be found in the current approach. Confronted by a greater number and range of individual differences in our students than ever before in the history of higher education, we continue to teach with one lesson plan, directed either traditionally at the top ten percent, with the result that we lose the other 90% to less desirable devotions; or superficially at the lowest common denominator, in which case we bore and frustrate the intellectually superior. As long as we continue the present classroom emphasis, and minimize or make incidental the library's role in learning, undergraduate education must continue something less than society has a right to expect of its investment in the next generation.

Viewed in the perspective of American college history the current Undergraduate Library trend is but another milestone along the road to educational revolution. So that there may be no doubt of the argument in this lecture, the Undergraduate Library is simply another evidence that reading room and classroom are about to exchange relationships. College education has been inexorably leading to a reversal of the present regimen which calls for regularly scheduled lectures followed by irregular periods of library reading.

When Thomas Carlyle made his much quoted declaration that "The true university is a collection of books" I am sure he had no intention of eliminating the professor. He was merely saying then what many have said since, if the library is really the heart of higher education then it is about time to let this important organ perform as it should.

In the same mood the noted French pedagogue Jules Gabriel

Compayré commenting on Abelard's competence as lecturer predicted the inevitable replacement of the classroom by the reading room in these words:

> Human speech, the living word of the teacher, had then an authority, an importance, which it has lost in part since books, everywhere distributed, have, to a certain extent, superseded oral instruction.

About the same time the then U.S. Commissioner of Education, William Torrey Harris made this startling declaration:

> The school is set at the task of teaching the pupil how to use the library in the best manner — that, I take it, is the central object toward which our American schools have been unconsciously tending.

Somewhat later President Harper of the University of Chicago prophesied:

> That factor of our college and university work, the library, fifty years ago almost unknown, today already the center of the institutional intellectual activity, half a century hence, with its sister, the laboratory . . . will by absorbing all else have become the institution itself.

Encouraged, no doubt by this and other equally far seeing statements by educators, Ernest Cushing Richardson, the librarian, made this startling substitution for Mark Hopkins on his end of the log:

> It is conceivable that a university should be a university, and a student get a university education if the university consisted only of a library and student, without a lecturer, tutor, or preceptor, or research professor, or librarian — absolutely only a student and a library on a desert island.

Writing on the "University of the Future" in the *North American Review* for March 1931, Carter Davidson dared this opinion:

> The faculty and the better students find the lecture and classroom recitation repetitious, boring, and a waste of time; the inferior students feel that lectures are hard to understand, and that the classroom recitations are too rapid, failing to make clear the more difficult problems.

About the same time Kenneth Roberts interviewing one of the superior undergraduates at the University of Michigan received this suggestion:

> I came here to study, and if somebody'd tell me what to study, I could do more by myself, in my own room and in a library, than I could by tramping around to a lot of lectures . . . I don't get much of anything out of classes. . . .

Ernest Renan wrote to Romain Rolland, "Despite the respect I feel for higher education I think that reading is more important than anything your instructors can teach you." (Quoted by T. W. Koch, *Reading: A Vice or a Virtue*, 1929, p. 1.)

If these few quotations appear to deal harshly with the conventional classroom we librarians so humbly serve, look at what independent study and the growing emphasis on honors reading have done. In one undergraduate program after another provision is being made for the superior student to be excused from classes to study at his own pace. Whether the innovation is called honors reading as at Swarthmore or autonomous courses as at Antioch, whether the instructor is called tutor as at Harvard or preceptor as at Princeton, whether courses are abolished as at Olivet or compehensive examinations instituted as at Chicago, the part of the university most affected is the library. Inevitably, the librarian must assume a different and greater responsibility for the student's instruction.

The first tangible evidence of this educational breakthrough in our universities is the separate undergraduate library. Its potential is far beyond the present simple purposes of providing course assigned readings and optional enrichment materials. Its real strength is in its provision for individual differences, its balance of overspecialization and its creation of a true learning climate.

There is only one way to match the varied individual differences now found in our undergraduate population. That way is with the individual differences in the universe of instructional media. If education is really communication between the teacher and learner then the medium is truly critical. It is impossible for the professor alone to convey his message equally to all of his students through the single lecture or text. He must rely on assistance not only from the assigned reserve readings but from the multitude of formats which comprise the total record of mankind. For in that vast collection of hard and soft covers, of serials and ephemera, of opaques and transparencies, of still and motion pictures, of discs and tapes, yes even of transcriptions and kinescopes, there may be found the individual medium that will communicate with the individual difference that distinguishes one undergraduate from all of the others. This is the essence of education anywhere, anytime. This is the particularly critical element in learning for a nation dedicated to universal higher education.

To the specialist nothing is more important than his specialty. There is nothing disparaging implied for extreme specialization as advocated by our research universities today. The undergraduate today falls only too readily into the belief that becoming an expert in one field is all that counts. There is only a plea here for some balance for the college student, some gestalt approach to the significant knowledge of mankind. This the library is in the best position to undertake. Although many of us have tended to decry the librarian as a generalist, in the undergraduate setting on our college campuses the librarian is the faculty member in the best strategic position to stand guard over the undergraduate's true liberal education. Unlike the professor of philosophy or physics, French or political science, Greek or botany, or any other academic discipline the librarian-generalist has no subject axe to grind. He is in a position to promote them all, and many subjects not in the college course of study, and to fill in the interstices with recreation and adventure, discovery and exploration, speculation and fantasy in a way that no single specialty can. Here then is a second unique responsibility for the librarian as faculty member.

Finally, I am old fashioned enough to believe that education is individual and introspective. Without some suffering I feel there is no real learning. If I have any concern over the present race between the East and West it is not that we shall be outdistanced by Russia in atomic and space machinery, but rather that our restless accent on group activity will in the measure of eternal verities be no match for the individual meditations of the Chinese. Our national mind is in grave danger. Its component mentalities are losing the inclination to think alone, and independently of committees. By the very nature of its atmosphere and the purpose of its materials the library encourages introspection and individual thinking.

Next fall, the University of Tennessee, will through its new separate library for undergraduates begin a profound contribution to college education. I beseech all who participate in it — lecturers, students, librarians — to recall hourly the destiny of this undertaking. Within this new library are the means for an undergraduate educational revolution. Among these separated library materials are the possibilities of arousing individual members of the next generation to new heights in science, society, and humanity. But above all there is in this new Undergraduate Library of the University of Tennessee the chance that men and women will come away equipped to meet a peril so great that the chances for survival are less than even. May this new library concept flourish and prosper and show us the way.

I congratulate you on your opportunity and pray for your success.

A BRIEF BIBLIOGRAPHY ON THE UNDERGRADUATE LIBRARY

Dix, W. S. Library service to undergraduates; undergraduate libraries. College and Research Libraries. 14: 271-2, July, 1953.

Dix, W. S. Library service to undergraduate college students; undergraduates do not necessarily require a special facility. College & Research Lib. 17: 148-50, March, 1956.

Gwynn, S. E. Library service to undergraduates; College library at the University of Chicago. College & Research Lib. 14: 267-8, July, 1953.

Hamlin, A. T. Special library for undergraduates. Library Journal. 82: 50, January 1, 1957.

Kuhn, W. B. New Mexico's undergraduate library; three years later. College & Research Lib. 16: 148-58, April, 1955.

Lundy, F. A. Library service to undergraduate college students; the divisional plan library. College & Research Lib. 17: 143-8, March, 1956.

McAnally, A. M. Library service to undergraduates; introductory remarks. College & Research Lib. 14: 266, July, 1953.

McNiff, P. J. Library service to undergraduates; Lamont Library, Harvard College. College & Research Lib. 14: 269-70, July, 1953.

Parker, W. S. Library in the liberal arts college. College & Research Lib. 16: 177-82, April, 1955.

Parker, W. S. Library service to undergraduates; the vital core. College & Research Lib. 14: 272-5, July, 1953.

Rohlf, R. H. Freshman-sophomore library at Minnesota. College & Research Lib. 14: 164-6, April, 1953.

Shores, Louis. The library arts college. School and Society, 41: 1-12, Jan. 26, 1935.

Taylor, C. M. Meeting the needs of undergraduates in large university libraries; problems and attempted solutions. 1956. 172p. Thesis (MLS) University of Texas.

Wagman, F. H. Library service to undergraduate college students; case for the separate undergraduate library. College & Research Lib. 17: 150-5, March, 1956.

Williamson, W. L. Relating the library to the classroom. College & Research Lib. 14: 167-71, April, 1953.

[1] P. J. McNiff. "Library Service to Undergraduates," *College and Research Libraries,* XIV (July, 1953), pp. 269-70.

[2] W. S. Dix. "Library Service to Undergraduates," *C & RL,* XIV (July, 1953), pp. 271-72.

[3] S. E. Gwynn. The College Library at the University of Chicago, *C & RL,* XIV (July, 1953), pp. 267-68.

[4] *Life,* (March 9, 1959), pp. 83-84.

[5] Catalogue of the Lamont Library, Harvard College. Prepared by Philip J. McNiff and staff. Cambridge: Harvard University Press, 1953.

Library-Trained Teachers

THE PRESENT GENERATION of teachers is overtrained in methods and undertrained in materials. In support of this bald statement nothing will be said about methods since it has already been said so eloquently, if sometimes unfairly, by those critics, academic or otherwise, who believe that if a man knows his subject he can teach it. But a great deal will be said about materials, since these involve the library.

It is no secret that teachers colleges generally have lagged far behind liberal arts colleges in library development. Taken from the standpoint of per-student expenditure or per cent of total college budget the teacher training institution thus far has not approached the standards for library expenditures set up for other institutions of higher education. In general, book collections, personnel, quarters and equipment, and administration have been maintained on a level so low, that until recently the teachers college librarians were classed more with school library workers than with professionals in the college field.

The result of this deficiency has been a generation of teachers who have had few of the library advantages necessary for an adequate understanding of the library's part in the teaching process. These teachers are now in charge of our public schools. From among them, have come many of our school administrators who have never felt the need for a school library and who have looked upon the rising library standards with considerable alarm if not with outright antagonism. In spite of all of our progressive tendencies, the fundamentals of the learning process, to these school people, revolve about the assigned lesson in the text, and the study hall. Even where the teacher or school administrator has permitted or even encouraged

Reprinted from *Phi Delta Kappan*, 22: 303-306, February, 1940, by permission of the publisher.

the introduction of a library in the school, he has frequently clung tenaciously to the study-hall idea and the textbook lesson. As a result the advance of the school library has been immeasurably retarded.

Such advances as have been made, have been due largely to the efforts of librarians and progressive educators. Shortly after the First World War, library training agencies began to direct an increasing portion of their attention to the training of school librarians. The assumption on which this effort was made was the belief that trained personnel would bring libraries into the school as they had brought public libraries into communities without free reading facilities. To support this influx of trained librarians into our public schools, the American Library Association directed a barrage of publicity toward accrediting agencies and educational organizations intended to influence the introduction of standards. In spite of discouraging experiences, especially in their efforts to sponsor library programs at National Education Association meetings, the idea of the library in the school found its way into regional standards and then into educational literature. The culmination of these efforts was found in the Co-operative Study of Secondary School Standards reports which gave major recognition to the school library.

At no time was it true that educators opposed libraries. On the contrary, most school administrators had learned well the sentence, "The library is the heart of the school," and had not other needs appeared more pressing, the library would undoubtedly have had its share of the educational income. But the fact was, that the educator knew very little about the library. In his own school and college days there had been meager library facilities. He had earned his diplomas and degrees by "boning" with a text in a study hall, and much as he might have learned to dislike study halls they meant school to him.

Whatever progress the library idea made, was due to the co-operation of the progressive educators who saw at once the importance of many materials for the implementation of the theory of individual differences. To them, the library took on the aspect of a reading laboratory where materials graded to the interests and abilities of the child were useful as they never were in the classroom.

Unfortunately, the librarian too frequently was not aware of the educational philosophy involved, or was unwilling to go that far. To her, school-library work meant largely a matter of organizing materials in public-library fashion for school use. She did not care about the new school philosophies, nor their implications; or if she did, she frequently considered that these were matters for school administrators and teachers. It was her duty to see to it that the library was classified and cataloged, that the books were properly charged and discharged, and that reference questions were answered as they arose.

That all was not well in the preparation of personnel for school libraries soon became evident. As a result of persistent criticism, the Board of Education for Librarianship developed a curriculum especially for the training of school librarians. There were several unfortunate aspects to this program. In spite of the best intentions there rapidly developed in library circles the notion that the school-library worker was an inferior grade of librarian. This became apparent when the Board prepared its list of accredited library schools in such a form as to suggest that although school librarians were not qualified to hold positions in other types of libraries, librarians trained for work in other kinds of libraries could hold positions in school libraries. At least one state library certification board developed a certification law on this unjust assumption. Progress toward the desired goal was consequently retarded in that state.

But the major problem was in the preparation of teacher personnel. It was too much to expect the librarian by herself to effect a revolution in teaching methods or administrative philosophy. As long as the teacher continued to teach from a single book, the library would have to play second fiddle to the study hall, and the principal would have to insist either that the librarian supervise the study hall, or that she take the overflow and disciplinary cases. It was apparent that neither teacher nor principal was seeing the library's possibility in the educational program and that this oversight was due largely to inadequate teacher training.

In 1934, Mabel Harris, then a graduate student in the Peabody Library School, undertook to study just what library instruction teacher training institutions were providing. She found[1] in more than half of the American teachers colleges not only elementary courses on how to use the library but also some advanced courses in children's literature, reading guidance, and bibliography. There was not any evidence of a planned program, however, for all student teachers, and Miss Harris proceeded to develop a suggested course of study which has subsequently been the basis for plans adopted in several institutions.

The following year, the American Library Association and the American Association of Teachers Colleges appointed a joint committee to study this problem[2] further. Under the direction of Lucile Fargo, another program of library instruction was developed for teachers as well as for teacher-librarians.

In 1936, a special conference of librarians and educators of the South was held in Atlanta[3] and a series of recommendations to the Southern Association were drawn up. Among these was the following:

> "Inasmuch as a knowledge of the place, function, and use of the library in the school, a wide acquaintance with books and reading for boys and girls at elementary and secondary levels, and an understanding of the services available through varied library agencies should be a part of the professional equipment of every teacher, it is recommended to the Southern Association of Colleges and Secondary Schools that instruction in these fields be designated under the teacher's professional requirements."

Long before any of these studies and recommendations appeared, however, individual institutions were developing library instruction programs. The freshman course in the use of the library had found its way into the teachers college curriculum either as a separate course or as a unit in the English course. Children's literature, too, became an integral part of the teacher training curriculum when several of the institutions began to experiment further. This experimentation had for its objective one or both of two aims: (1) to enable the student of education to use library materials effectively

[1]For notes, see pages 367-368.

in research, and (2) to acquaint the teacher and administrator with the library's share in the learning process.

The first aim has probably been most effectively realized in Teachers College, Columbia University, under the direction of Carter Alexander, whose official title is "Library Professor of Education." Out of this program has developed the first library education text[4] as well as patterns for similar courses found in Peabody College, Rutgers University, University of Texas, and an increasing number of other institutions.

In general, these courses on library use in educational research provide the graduate student at work on a master's thesis, or doctor's dissertation with a bibliographic approach to his problem. Among the topics included are: the use of the library catalog, educational classifications of the Dewey Decimal and Library of Congress systems, educational bibliographies and indices, reference tools especially useful in education, bibliographic form, manuscript style, government and society publications, and a general work methodology. At some institutions, these materials constitute a separate course; at others they are units in a general research course required of all graduate students. At Peabody, for example, a graduate course called "Techniques of educational research" is offered by four faculty members and includes instruction in statistical, experimental, historical, and library methods of research.

The second aim has probably been developed most at Peabody.[5] Beginning with the freshman year and extending to the doctoral examination provision is made for library instruction. On the junior college level the usual lessons on the use of the library have been incorporated in the freshman rhetoric class. These lessons are given by the English instructors who have previously gone over the materials to be included in conferences with a faculty member of the library school. A standardized library information test is administered to all junior college students.[6]

On the so-called three-year professional level, which comprises the junior, senior, and first-graduate years, units in various basic education courses as well as complete courses are offered. The three units that aim to assist all teachers and administrators in training are those offered in elementary education, secondary education, and the core administration course. School principals and superintendents in actual service attend the latter course. This is especially true during the summer session.

The separate courses include three in children's literature and one called "Library use in research and teaching." There is also the advanced course previously mentioned called "Techniques of educational research." In general, these courses or units on library use in teaching cover the following topics: American libraries, including types, organization, services especially useful to the teacher; books, including format, history, classes, and national bibliography; periodicals; general reference materials useful in teaching; teaching materials for elementary school, language arts, social studies, science, and the arts; aids in selecting materials; non-book materials (audio-visual aids); and reading interest.

What has been said of the library education program is true only in a very few institutions. For the most part, those state teachers colleges that have become interested in the library problem have ignored the responsibility to the teacher in training and concentrated on the preparation of librarians. This has been unfortunate in many instances, because the assumption of a library-science program has not meant a comparable increase in library personnel or budget. In some cases, the teaching load has been added to the duties of the already overworked librarian, and the additional expenditures required for instructional materials and equipment have been taken out of the inadequate library budget.

Other aspects which indicate an incomplete consideration by the teachers college of its responsibility in the library education, center in the curriculum. As at present constituted, the four-year teacher training program includes professional educational courses up to one-fourth of the total number of credits required for graduation. When to this amount there is added, on the undergraduate level, a whole year of library science, it is apparent that only one half of the program remains for so-called "content" or non-professional studies.

The other, more serious, aspect involves the law of supply and demand. Should every teachers college undertake to offer courses in library management for even a short period of time there would soon be far more school librarians than can ever find positions. It is true that there are at present more school library positions in proportion to available qualified librarians than there are English positions in proportion to the number of English teachers available, but it would take the teachers colleges a comparatively short while to reverse the situation.

There are at present, an adequate number of agencies for the preparation of librarians, but there are at present entirely inadequate provisions for library instruction of teachers. In order to remedy this situation, it is necessary to distinguish clearly between library education and library science. In the latter program, library management is taught to librarians who will have major responsibility for the organization and administration of a library. In the former program, library use is taught to teachers and administrators so that they may integrate the library and the rest of the school in carrying out the learning process. If the teachers college would truly further the development of school libraries it should concentrate on a program of library education for its students.

This article began with the bald statement that teachers are over-trained in methods and undertrained in materials. A program of library education would remedy this condition for it would have as its aim concentrated attention on the most effective teaching materials. It would undertake to help the teacher discover in the library a practical method of catering to individual differences through graded materials. It would, in short, give the school library the opportunity to serve the entire educational program in a way that can be only imperfectly pictured as long as our teachers and school administrators remain library uninstructed.

[1] Harris, Mabel. "Non-professional Library Instruction in Teachers Colleges," *Peabody Journal of Education*, 1934, vol. 12, pp. 86-95.
[2] The Joint Committee of the American Association of Teachers Colleges and the American Library Association. *How Shall We Educate Teachers and Librarians; Findings and Recommendations*. New York: Columbia University Press, 1936.

3 *A.L.A. Bulletin*, 1936. p. 29-32.
4 Alexander, Carter, *How to Locate Educational Information and Data.* Teachers College, Columbia, 1935, 272 p.
5 Shores, Louis. "Library Instruction for Teachers," *Peabody Journal of Education*, 1936, v. 14, pp. 128-133.
6 Shores, Louis, and Moore, Joseph E. *Peabody Library Information Test.* Minneapolis: Educational Test Bureau.

Library Logistics in Teacher Education

WORLD WAR III may well be decided in the libraries of the world. It has been said again and again that the struggle between the U.S.S.R. and the U.S.A. is fundamentally one over ideology. In this struggle it has been repeatedly pointed out in popular articles that psychological warfare will be of ever-increasing importance. In that case, the logistics of this third holocaust may well center in the library. The details of discovering and disseminating ideas to our psychological armies may confront librarianship with the most startling assignment of its centuries-old professional life.

The Moscow blueprint for ideological conflict shows clear red lines. In the Korean conflict, for example, the Communist armies moved into the native villages with three potent weapons: A bag of rice, a piece of land, and a library. That library showed evidence of keen application of American library principles to war. The collection of print and Audio-Visual materials, propaganda packed, indicated an astute awareness of the Koreans' reading or lack of reading ability.

Back of that blueprint is undoubtedly a high degree of library mobilization. With Slavic intensity, the Russians have apparently succeeded in harnessing that library power of which we Americans

Reprinted from *Vital Speeches of the Day*, 17: 701-703, September 1, 1951, by permission of the publisher. The essay here reprinted is a paper read at the Seventy-Fifth Anniversary Conference of the Association of College and Research Libraries, Chicago, Illinois, July 11, 1951.

talk at commencements. This power is apparently being used in the Soviet Union to propel ideologic bombs into the spaces before the Iron Curtain.

A stern self-evaluation of our American librarianship on all fronts, from school through graduate school, reveals a mechanical precision in organization and techniques beyond what we know the enemy now has. We have crossed our t's and dotted our i's neatly, and with daily regularity the routines of acquisitions, preparations and circulation are proceeding satisfactorily. We have made great strides in the areas of research and dissemination, but we are not yet at the point where either of these ends of librarianship is effective enough to tip the balance of world conflict in our favor.

It is said that at the opening of World War II the aircraft we had was concentrated for protection against possible sabotage. In vain did the Air Force plead for dispersal of our few Flying Fortresses against possible air attack. When the Japanese Air Force came over the Philippines they found an ideal target, and with a few well-directed bombs destroyed most of our available Philippine air power.

Analogies are always dangerous. In librarianship we have in the past committed ourselves to the concentration of research resources in great centers. In the South, for example, we have our great regional research centers — in Nashville, in Atlanta, in Chapel Hill-Durham, in New Orleans and in Texas. The planning and philanthropic funds that went into these library centers during the 1930's represented a high type of library leadership. In terms of the world we knew before Munich, that type of research concentration represented a significant step in the Library's cooperation with scholarship.

Today, with the experience of Hiroshima behind us, and technological terrors ahead, we must heed the lessons. There is at least an argument for the dispersal, rather than the concentration of research resources in these United States. Research contract monopolies by our most respected universities, deserving though they may be, dare not be risked by a nation engaged in an unprecedented war.

That those who are responsible for the research now being carried on for and by our Armed Forces and by industry and other agencies of the government are favoring dispersal is encouraging.

In the recent Atlanta and Memphis meetings sponsored by the Board of Control for Southern Regional Education and participated in by representatives of all the Armed Forces, war agencies, industry, and Southern colleges and universities, the keynote was dispersal of research contracts to even the smallest colleges of the region. Equally important was the indication that parts of one whole research project might be scattered over various parts of the nation.

Previously, such dispersal was probably not desirable. In any case, it was much less possible. The technological advance in microphotographic reproduction undoubtedly lends a hand to the overall strategy of dispersing our research efforts. Very recently, for example, the Southeastern Library Association, under a contract with the Tennessee Valley Authority, has succeeded in microphotographing some significant scientific journals, which will now be available to libraries everywhere at very low cost. Committee S of the Southeastern Library Association, under the chairmanship of Dr. Lawrence Thompson of the University of Kentucky, is continuing its efforts to make available to an increasing number of libraries sets of journals which, heretofore, have been a luxury only the largest libraries could afford.

There is an important morale factor also to be considered. The dispersal of research contracts and of research resources gives every part of our vast American system of education a feeling of belonging to the great war effort. Since teacher education institutions, for the most part, are colleges that have been too often overlooked in the research picture, the trend toward dispersal offers these important institutions an opportunity they have never had before.

Discovery of ideas is of course an important part of the whole war effort. In the technological race between their side and ours, inevitably success will go to the armies that are supported by the best talent, the most resources and the least vulnerable research organization. In that competition, it seems quite evident we have thus far been able to hold our own.

We do not appear, however, to be showing up as well in the other phase of psychological warfare — namely, dissemination. To date, the Communists have appeared to be advancing their cause in the ranks a little bit more effectively than we. They have, of course, the advantage of the "outs" over the "ins." To the peoples outside of the Iron Curtain they can promise much. Ours is the more difficult task of fulfilling. But even so, we may not have utilized all of the strength we have.

Certainly the concepts of reader guidance, of audio-visual aids, of advertising, have been pioneered by our side. But, being a peaceful nation at heart, we have thus far used these techniques for nothing more dangerous than cigarette indoctrination. Now, the time has come for us to apply our talents wherever we clash with the other way of life.

For example, one of the basic weaknesses in any totalitarian system, where the ideas from above are imposed upon those below, is the development of a "line." Dependence upon this line by the people destroys the flexibility and adaptability required under the stress of battle. This was proved again and again during World War II, when the American soldier's broader acquaintance with many lines provided him with greater adaptability.

Now we have no one "line" in the United States such as is found in the Iron Curtain countries. We believe in informing the people on both sides of issues, or on several sides if there are more than two. This is the keystone of our library philosophy.

Unfortunately, however, we are in danger of developing a "line." This line, unlike the one in the U.S.S.R., is not deliberate. It is, in many cases, purely accidental.

The accident is caused by the fact that as Americans, we tend toward the stereotype. It is probably a manifestation of mass production, which we have perfected here. As a result, we tend to be "one newspaper" readers. We tend also to go to about the same type of movie regularly and to hear about the same type of radio program. Let me make it clear. We in the United States provide all kinds of newspapers, with all shades of opinion. We provide all kinds of radio programs, with a variety of points of view. Diversified problems and diversified solutions are presented in our movies. However, we, as Americans, tend to read what we want to read, tend to hear what we like to hear, tend to go to the movies we like to see. The result is an unintentional line for many Americans.

Let me cite the MacArthur controversy. I believe the American press tended to favor the General. As one American, I believe the President was right. Unintentionally perhaps, the Press built up the notion that the General's plan was clear, that the President had no plan. To me, one American, and without political bias, President Truman's plan for conducting the Korean war was stated several times on the air, and printed in the press. As I read it, it seemed to me crystal clear, and the events of the Korean war prove it was the best strategy we could have followed.

Yet, day after day the General was favored over the President, in space, in position, and in editorial comments in the press of the United States. I read as much as I could, because I was interested. It seemed to me here was an opportunity for us, as Americans, to consider the facts critically and exert our judgment. Because of the intense emotionalism, especially on the General's side, it seemed to me at times that we were in danger of condemning anyone who favored our Commander-in-Chief's position as subversive. For just a brief day during the height of the General's New York reception I had the sinking feeling that "it could happen here." And then the American way asserted itself. Steadily, we, as citizens, began to weigh the evidence, to read the testimony, and to decide deliberately and unemotionally to support our Commander-in-Chief functioning under the Constitution of the United States. We asserted again that the military could not and should not make final decisions for a nation of civilians.

That illustration will suffice for the point now to be made. Librarianship has a deep responsibility for dissemination. In the library we can destroy that one line toward which we tend and which is so contrary to our American way of life. We can and should provide all kinds of newspapers, every type of magazine, all the audio-visual aids, that our limited budgets will permit.

I believe a more active effort on the part of all libraries in this nation to see to it that the people get all the facts and from all points of view is the great defense against Communism. Let me specify.

You are librarians in the teacher education agencies of the United States. Your institutions prepare the teachers who go to all the elementary and high schools of our land. These teachers are a first line of defense. They must begin early, in the first grades of school, to teach the strength of truth. They must build up in these youngsters an armor against untruth that is impenetrable. That kind of an armor is made only when an opportunity is provided for the people to know all of the facts, all sides of all issues. That is the sacred responsibility of libraries. That is why every school in these United States must have a well-stocked library. That is why every teacher who comes out of a teacher education agency must know how to use library materials to promote the great truth.

In your teacher education agencies the teachers are being taught many things. They are being taught the subjects that make up the curricula of our schools. They are being taught how to teach and how to understand youngsters. But they must be taught by you how to use materials with the children and young people so that when the great controversies come along these children will be armed to exert a critical judgment and be able to select the truth from the untruth.

School Library 21

THE YEAR is 2001 A.D. The place is Turkey Run. Four decades have passed since the Indiana School Librarians last met here. More than half of the delegates present are men. A few of them are old enough to remember the 1961 meeting. None of the women is, of course. If my commentary on the 20th Century is too subjective, I hope the few who still remember will forgive me.

Those of us today, who are over 50 years of age recall that 1961 marked the real beginning of the space age. In April of that year Russia shot the first man out of this world. Although to our young generation today, 180 miles from earth is considered no space distance at all, the feat was considerable then. The notion that anything as crude as a rocket had to be exploded to get out of

Reprinted from *School Libraries*, 12: 11-17 ff., May, 1963, by permission of the publisher.

our atmosphere seems ludicrous to us now. But remember that although our parents worshipped science, they got their ideas from science fiction. They could not resist the imagination of Jules Verne. And when we see the horizontal torture to which the astronauts were subjected at take off, our laughter soon gives way to admiration.

In those days we took the Russian triumph not too graciously. That nation was then emerging as our only real rival in a world that still had international rather than interplanetary vision. After the Second World War, America persisted in underestimating Russian science, attributing Soviet successes to captured German scientists. But as historians increasingly gained access to documents relating to the war on the eastern front, it became abundantly evident that only the prospect of having to fight the western powers afterward delayed Russian conquest of Germany. When the Russians succeeded in orbiting the first satellite, space superiority was reluctantly conceded.

We now know that both the U.S.A. and the U.S.S.R. had more to fear than each other. Apparently the Soviets recognized first the great potential of China. Living right next door, the Russians knew only too well how many more Chinese there were than of any other kind of earth human, and how much more rapidly they reproduced their population. There was a story then about the Chinese general captured by the Japanese in World War II. When told by his captors that China's cause was hopeless because there were ten Chinese killed for every one Japanese, and that he might as well surrender, the Chinese general hesitated for a moment and then repeated soberly: "You say ten Chinese being killed for every one Japanese? Hah. Soon no Japanese!"

Our history tells how near the brink we were. With the same underestimation for human life, China for all the maturity of its oriental civilization attempted to punish its two rivals at the traditional ten to one cost without fully realizing the boomerang quality of the nuclear weapons it possessed. Then the first Flying Saucer finally landed. What the Chinese sages had surmised, the Martians confirmed. The planets without life had been unable to restrain their Chinas with nuclear power.

As we look back now, it is difficult to understand science's reluctance to study more carefully the sightings of unidentified objects. Unquestionably there were many hallucinations and hoaxes. But the U.S. Air Force offered again and again to submit its so-called "Blue Drawer of UFO Sightings" unexplainable by hallucination, hoax, or meteorological phenomena. Almost like the medicine men of Indian tribes, scientists responded in defense of their folklore which they described as the scientific method.

As you know, this so-called scientific method of the last century has been the subject of many volumes. In perspective we will be less critical of the scientists than we have been during the past decade. They did not really hold back progress. Science, the scientific method, and the mass worship of the gadgets that resulted was as inevitable a concomitant of the 20th Century as Scholasticism was of the middle ages. Without the scientific age, the incentive for extra-sensory exploration would have been retarded.

Of importance to us as school librarians is the fact that this scientific method shaped the educational foundations of our 20th Century schools. In the name of objectivity our children were measured statistically. If enough tallies were registered on controlled groups of youngsters, this became incontrovertible evidence that that was the way children learned.

A whole cult of measurers developed who worshipped something called a bell-shaped curve. This became a symbol not unlike the swastika and other signs accepted by primitive tribes as omens of fertility and fortune. When children did not fall within the big part of the tent curve, they were called atypical.

One of the superstitions believed vehemently by most teachers then was that children learned best through physical activity. There was indeed a respectable segment of the national professional association which identified itself as sponsors of the activity school. In order to learn anything, these cultists contended, it was necessary for the child to do it. Indeed, the phrase "learning by doing" was used so many times at conventions and in articles that our statistical computers today record it second, among 20th Century pedagogical cliches, only to the line, "But the children come first."

With this last bit of pedagogical demagoguery it was always

possible to annihilate any advocacy no matter how profound. Only it was important to get the line in first, at the right critical point, and in a way comparable to the effect produced on a dinner table story by requesting audibly just before the punch line, "Please pass the sugar." While we are discussing 20th Century educational vocabulary, a few other pet phrases of our professional parents should be noted. They loved the term "meaningful experience," but there was less than unanimity on *what* experience had meaning to *whom*. If you could use "frame of reference" somewhere in your deliberations, you belonged. Similarly, an amateur *planned* a meeting, but if you "*structured*" it you were a "pro."

In addition to "learning by doing" it was considered most important to convert everything abstract to concrete. Beginning with the third decade of the last century, a movement, first called visual education and later audio-visual education, caused librarians considerable growing pains. Although libraries had for years stocked pictures in their vertical files, once the term "*flat picture*" was applied it became audio-visual. There had never been a library without maps and globes and although school libraries continued to include them in their collections, in some instances they were charged to the audio-visual budget. As early as 1928 the Carnegie Corporation strengthened library phonograph recordings with grants totalling a million dollars. But in the decade that followed, these became audio-visual media known as discs.

The audio-visual movement, which gathered force in the 1930's and grew to stature by mid-century, contributed significantly to schools and libraries. It furthered educational use of other formats such as 16 mm motion pictures, filmstrips, radio, television, and electronic media. It accented the multi-material approach toward which libraries strove but never could devote themselves to sufficiently because of a frequently greater devotion to housekeeping than to education.

But the audio-visual movement at times also lost sight of its ends in favor of the means. Matching some librarians' dedication to technical processes was the absorption of their AV counterparts in electronics gadgeteering. Camera bugs, radio hams, do-it-yourself mechanics all tolerated the educational objective as a means to their gadgeteering ends.

There were others, too, both among librarians and audio-visualists who never understood or lost sight of the real mission of Instructional Materials. Librarians in this group could be identified by their frequent reference to "non-book" materials. To them, audio-visual responsibility consisted of a foreign, electronic substance brutally thrust upon the serenity of the library scene. If it had to be part of the library it was fiercely admitted only on condition that an extra staff member was given the audio-visual assignment.

As sometimes happens in differences, the anti-audio-visual librarians and the anti-library audio-visualists supported each other in keeping school libraries and AV centers separate. Their campaign slogan was "Let each do what comes naturally." The fact that pupil and teacher preferred to find all their resources in one place was considered secondary.

It was inevitable that the latent learning power in Instructional Materials should be harnessed. All that was needed was the unification of the segmented efforts of the sponsors of individual formats. Shortly after World War II, Florida took a long step by educating all librarians first, in the whole range of instructional media, and then elementary, and, finally, secondary classroom teachers. It introduced the first unified librarian, audio-visual certification under the cumbersome heading of Instructional Materials (Librarian, Audio-visual). Florida librarians and audio-visualists working together tried desperately to invent a term for this augmented profession that would describe it more adequately. At one seminar in Florida State University, it was proposed that since materials were a major professional concern, that school librarians be redesignated "Materialists." However, as neither the compensation nor the outlook was represented by the meaning of that word, it was then counterproposed that the synonym representing the other extreme be adopted and that librarians be called Mediums. Because of the disrepute then of spiritualism, this too was rejected and the age-honored designation *librarian* regained its position.

Systematically, each of the 67 Florida counties was encouraged to appoint an Instructional Materials Supervisor, a new generation librarian educated in the whole range of materials. Joint efforts by school librarians, audio-visualists and the new IM specialists resulted in increasing support for school libraries. After a series of annual clinics for teachers on the use of IM in teaching (clinics attended by about 1,500 classroom teachers each year in seven regional centers), the State Legislature appropriated a million dollars earmarked for IM. In 1960 appeared the first professional textbook for teachers presenting the whole range of school materials rather than separate books on library, audio-visual, television and other media. At least a half dozen teacher education institutions began combining their separate library science, audio-visual, and children's literature courses into unified IM offerings.

By 1961, Florida was attempting to provide unified library services in 99.3% of its secondary schools, 82.5% of its elementary schools, and 82.6% of its combined elementary-secondary schools.

But the financial support was still meagre. Although the librarians recommended a modest $4 to $6 per pupil for library materials, supplies and rebindings, the average in 1961 was only $1.72. The highest per capita went to the combined elementary-secondary schools — $2.21. Secondary schools averaged $1.85 and elementary schools $1.54.

As we look back at the records four decades ago in the state that pioneered the Instructional Materials concept, we find that although a modest 10 books per pupil was recommended, less than 5 were actually provided. The average was 4.6 books per pupil, with secondary school pupils averaging 6 and elementary 3.5.

In 1961, the Southern Association accrediting agency recommended one full time professional librarian for each 15-teacher school of 450 pupils. The library-conscious State of Florida had one librarian for every 1,074 pupils. But it had come a long way from much worse conditions. For example, in 1961 among the secondary schools, 82% had a full-time librarian and another 6% had a part-time librarian. Elementary schools which had long been almost without any professional library personnel had full- or part-time librarians in more than half the schools. Indeed, 35% of all elementary schools in Florida had full-time librarians. What was happening in Florida soon caught fire in the northwest states of Washington and Oregon and by 1961 nearly half of the 50 states were supporting the unified Instructional Materials concept. The national standards which appeared in 1960 went very far in that direction but not far enough for states like Florida, Washington, Oregon and Pennsylvania which found the separate identification of library and audio-visual materials artificial and impossible of definition for the ultimate consumers, the teachers and pupils. With the professional literatures of both librarianship and audio-visual education claiming maps, globes, pictures, bulletin boards, museum objects, slides, tape and disc recordings, and numerous sub-classes of media, teachers and pupils were frequently perplexed in schools with dual centers, as to which center had responsibility for which format?

Florida solved this dilemma in some of its schools by avoiding a division of labor by formats. When additional librarians were added to a school library staff, their special responsibility was frequently a curriculum area or a grade level. For example, one librarian might serve the social studies with the whole range of materials from textbook to television, and another the science area. In a school system, instead of a supervisor of libraries and a supervisor of audio-visual education, a county would frequently have one supervisor for elementary and one for secondary Instructional Materials. This was the beginning of School Library 21 organization which we know so well today.

As we look at our school libraries today we know four decades have revolutionized our concepts and our execution. Our professional parents would probably appreciate the finances most. Poor things, while they would have considered themselves fortunate to have had as much as 3% of the educational dollar spent for libraries, in this year 2001, we spend nearly 30%.

The expenditure is of course justified by our different method of education. Back in 1961 their classrooms were still fundamentally recitation and lecture centers. True they disguised this with such terms as activity, socialized recitation, children-centered learning, and democratic procedures. But basically they still operated on a lesson plan with accent on everything but instructional materials. It couldn't be otherwise. Teacher education, by and large, made much of incidental learning of library materials. You studied materials not *per se* but quote "in relation to something else — children, subjects, the weather outside." This way, the pedagogue argued, it was more meaningful. But strangely no one ever seemed to advocate that you study the other things in relation to materials. When you constructed a curriculum you developed a course of study of democracy, or in keeping with learning by doing. It rarely occurred to anyone to begin with library materials, the composite of which represents all that man had ever done or thought — the basic curriculum.

Today, as you know, we begin with the library. Instead of as then when the library followed the curriculum, the curriculum now follows the library. This is so because today we have not only librarians but library-trained teachers. As a result teachers teach with materials. Every classroom is basically a library. In each room from kindergarten up we take for granted the core collection for that grade supplemented by the rotating unit selections from the building center. Teaching and learning are intrinsically exploring and searching under the guidance of the library-trained teacher, who in turn consults the building librarian as he plans his unit. Both classroom teacher and building librarian have still additional resources at their disposal in the school system center. The pattern for this organization was already in embryo in 1961 in Florida counties and elsewhere.

What handicapped this organizational pattern then was the extreme autonomy of each school building and classroom. Meticulously, some librarians fought for the right to classify and catalog their collections individually. By 1961, however, central processing and even cataloging at source were gaining recognition. Unfortunately, the first was still largely manual, although crude photoduplicating equipment was beginning to appear in progressive systems. A pilot cataloging-at-source project received a cruel rejection at the hands of our national Library of Congress, but not for long. At the world's fair in Seattle in 1962, a few of our leading library scientists stimulated by such data processing corporations as IBM and RCA anticipated much of the library electronics we have today and which freed us to devote ourselves to creative librarianship. For example, at Seattle the American Library Association converted some raw form periodical index entries from the H. W. Wilson Company (which at that time was indexing cumulatively more serial publications than any other agency) to machine processing. This pilot venture laid the foundation for the present worldwide electronic bibliographic control with its thousands of satellite controls, ranging from complex research centers to comparatively simple school systems controls. You are well aware of how instantly a picture, or glass slide, or pamphlet, or filmstrip can be located in any one of the thousands of classrooms in the Indianapolis school system.

But they anticipated much more electronically. The tailored bibliographies we now produce in seconds to match the individual differences of each of our millions of public school children were first conceived for Seattle. In my hands I have a copy of Joe Becker's January 9, 1961, typescript, now yellow with age, titled "Library-21: Preliminary Analysis of IBM Data Processing Requirements for Element 3 (Information Service)," (and please note how early they developed the mechanistic vocabulary that dominated pedagogical literature in the 7th and 8th decades of the last century). I quote:

"This section will feature an automated Reader's Advisory Service. Based on the criteria of age, education, fiction or non-fiction, and language, an exhibit visitor will be able to request a list of book titles from a predetermined list of subjects."

With very little augmentation this could be used to describe the electronic service our school libraries offer teachers and pupils on any curriculum unit in all of the nation's schools.

But even more prophetic is the description of the "Remote Inquiry" section. To quote again, "This phase deals with answering stereotyped questions from remote stations. . . . Pre-punched IBM cards containing the stereotyped printed questions . . . serve as the key for making a remote inquiry. . . . The print response . . . contain the correct answer . . . cite the library's . . . source . . . in English, German, transliterated Russian or romanized Japanese." Replace the word "stereotyped" with our "recurring questions" and you have almost a perfect description of our electronic keying to periodic curriculum unit queries, and this more than 40 years ago!

It was perhaps too much to have expected our professional predecessors of 1961 to have anticipated as fully the extra-sensory wonders unfolding before us now. We must not be too hard on them lest we be judged even more critically 40 years hence. Instead, we must try to understand our national absorption in the 1960's in the sensory sciences. It paid off, in the language of the man in the street, with such comforts and wonders to them as laundry and dish washing machines, air conditioning, that museum piece the automobile, which in those days transported most Americans to and from work, and of course the rocket, which first took them out of this world, albeit in a most ludicrous manner. (I sometimes think we are most thoughtless laughing at our parents' generation. It was certainly natural for them to think they had first to imitate the planets and go around the earth in circles before setting off for the moon. Remember, magnetism was a complete mystery to them, and the degravitater was something reserved for their comics just as their orbits are for ours.)

The 20th Century American was an extremely physically active being. He was always on the go. He loved excitement, movement, glamor. He worshipped celebrities, or should I say she. It was not uncommon in TV shows for a sexy singer who snapped her fingers and moved other parts of her anatomy to be paid $15,000 for 15 minutes performance, while teachers who reared the nation's children for most of the waking hours of the day were fortunate to earn half of that amount for a whole year's hard work. The 20th Century American was restless, frustrated, mentally ill in greater numbers than ever before. He went to psychiatrists with enthusiasm and one of the cartoons handed down to us is the sign outside of one of these mental doctor's offices: "No Waiting. Two Couches." To an age like this only the physical and sensory counted. Anything else was for Sunday School or science fiction.

Nevertheless, parapsychology had its beginnings even before the last century. By 1961 it was becoming respectable to read the books of J. B. Rhine and Gardner Murphy, but not about another Murphy named Bridie. Puzzling as many human inconsistencies are, none is more incredible than pedagogy's reliance in the 20th Century upon something called the psychology of learning. The truth is that 20th Century psychologists ignored the psyche and concerned themselves almost exclusively with physiology and neurology, probably because they wanted so desperately to be accepted as scientists. Endlessly they absorbed themselves in constructing mazes with which to confound rats, but the rats seemed always too smart for them. There had, of course, been a school of psychologists known as introspectionists, but they were discredited. The Watsonian Behaviorists seemed to dominate, although popular interest was in the Freudian Psychoanalists, largely because of their sex appeal. Beginnings of 21st Century parapsychology can be found in Kaffka's *Gestalt* and in MacDougall, the professional godfather of Rhine.

You of course know what happened in 1988 with the landing of the first flying saucer from outer space. But for that, Orwell's prediction first and Nevil Shute's afterward would most certainly have occurred. The saving of this planet from becoming another dead world in the universe was the most important result of this visit. But almost equally important was the confirmation of extrasensory phenomena. Although this revelation reduced the physical sciences to a minor study, it opened new vistas for a truer approach to reality.

For us in education, and particularly in school libraries, it offers an exciting prospect. Now that we know for certain that learning is extrasensory and not senory we can free ourselves from the 20th Century fetters of pragmatism. We need no longer concern ourselves with posturing physical activity, the natural inclination of the physical body on this planet, and devote ourselves to developing that universal consciousness that must struggle against the earth's environment. Since it thrives in quiet and with meditation, it develops best in cathedrals and libraries. Now that all study proves that reading is a prelude to meditation, libraries have their greatest challenge of all times. The mystery of the universe will undoubtedly be revealed at some not too distant time, possibly in one of God's littlest libraries. My guess is it will be in a rural elementary school library in Indiana somewhere near Turkey Run when the Indiana School Library Association meets there again some 40 years hence.